GRASS

ITS PRODUCTION AND UTILIZATION

EDITED BY

W. HOLMES

SECOND EDITION

PUBLISHED FOR

THE BRITISH GRASSLAND SOCIETY BY
BLACKWELL SCIENTIFIC PUBLICATIONS

OXFORD LONDON EDINBURGH

BOSTON MELBOURNE

© 1980, 1989 by
Blackwell Scientific Publications
Editorial offices:
Osney Mead, Oxford OX2 0EL
(*Orders*: Tel. 0865 240201)
8 John Street, London WC1N 2ES
23 Ainslie Place, Edinburgh EH3 6AJ
3 Cambridge Center, Suite 208
  Cambridge, Massachusetts 02142, USA
107 Barry Street, Carlton
  Victoria 3053, Australia

First published 1980
Reprinted 1982
Second edition 1989

Set by Setrite Typesetters,
Hong Kong
Printed and bound in Great Britain
by Billings and Sons Ltd, Worcester

DISTRIBUTORS

USA
Publishers' Business Services
PO Box 447
Brookline Village
Massachusetts 02147
(*Orders*: Tel. 617-524-7678)

Canada
Oxford University Press
70 Wynford Drive
Don Mills
Ontario M3C 1J9
(*Orders*: Tel. 416-441-2941)

Australia
Blackwell Scientific Publications
(Australia) Pty Ltd
107 Barry Street
Carlton, Victoria 3053
(*Orders*: Tel. 03-347-0300)

British Library
Cataloguing in Publication Data
Grass. — 2nd ed.
  1. Great Britain. Crops: Grasses.
  Production & use
  I. Holmes, W. (William)
  633'.2'02'0941

  ISBN 0–632–02461–5

Library of Congress
Cataloging-in-Publication Data
Grass: its production and utilization/edited
by W. Holmes.
  Includes bibliographies and index.
  1. Grasses. 2. Range management.
  3. Rangelands. 4. Grasses — Economic
  aspects. I. Holmes, W. II. British
  Grassland Society. SB197.G76 1989
  633.2 — dc19

  ISBN 0–632–02461–5

Contents

List of contributors

DAVID E. BEEVER BSc (Hons) (Dunelm), PhD (Newcastle upon Tyne)
Head of Ruminant Nutrition and Metabolism, AFRC Research Institute of Grassland and Animal Production, Hurley, from 1985. Previously, Grassland Research Institute (1970–1985). Stapledon Memorial Fellow (1976–1977), CSIRO Division of Animal Production, Sydney, Australia. Nato Senior Scientist Fellow (1984), Texas A & M University, College Station, Texas, USA.

MARGARET GILL BSc (Edinburgh), PhD (Massey)
Member of staff of Ruminant Nutrition and Metabolism Department, Institute for Grassland and Animal Production, Hurley. Previously member of staff of the Grassland Research Institute from 1976, with one year's secondment to the Overseas Development Administration working in the Dominican Republic (1980–1981).

BRYNMOR HUGH GREEN BSc, PhD (Nottingham)
Sir Cyril Kleinwort Professor of Countryside Management at Wye College, University of London. Formerly Senior Lecturer in Ecology and Conservation in the Department of Environmental Studies and Countryside Planning at Wye College. Regional Officer (SE) and deputy for the Nature Conservancy Council (1968–1975). Lecturer in Plant Ecology in the Department of Botany, University of Manchester (1965–1968). Member of the England Committee of the Nature Conservancy Council. Countryside Commissioner.

WILLIAM HOLMES BSc, PhD (Glasgow), DSc (London), NDA (Hons), NDD
Emeritus Professor of Agriculture. Head of Department of Agriculture, Wye College, University of London (1955–1987). Member of staff and then in charge of the Grass and Dairy Husbandry Department, the Hannah Dairy Research Institute, Ayr, Scotland (1944–1955). President of the British Grassland Society (1969–1970). President of the British Society of Animal Production (1970). First recipient of the British Grassland Society Award (1979). Correspondent étranger de l'Academie d'Agriculture de France from 1986.

JOHN C. MURDOCH OBE, BSc (Glasgow), PhD (Edinburgh)
Professor of Crop and Animal Production, Queen's University, Belfast and Director of the Agriculture Research Institute for Northern Ireland, Hillsborough, County Down (1966–1986). Previously in the Department of Dairy Husbandry, National Institute for Research in Dairying, Shinfield, Reading (1951–1965). President of the British Grassland Society (1978–1979). Chairman of the United Kingdom Seeds Executive from 1986.

JOHN S. NIX BSc (Econ), MA (Cantab), CBIM FRSA, FR Ag S

National Westminster Professor of Farm Business Management from 1982 and Head of Farm Business Unit, Wye College, University of London from 1974. Previously Agricultural Economist and Senior Agricultural Economist/Senior Research Officer in Farm Economics Branch, School of Agriculture, University of Cambridge (1951–1961); Farm Management Liaison Officer and Senior Lecturer/Reader in Farm Management, Wye College, University of London (1961–1981). Chairman, Centre for Farm Management (BIM) (1979–1981).

DENNIS F. OSBOURN BSc (Hons), Dip Agric (Cantab), Dip Trop Agric (Trinidad), PhD (Reading), FIBiol

Pro Vice Chancellor and Professor of Agriculture, University of the South Pacific, Western Samoa from 1986. Previously Agricultural Officer, Her Majesty's Overseas Civil Service (Tanganyika) (1959–1961). Lecturer in Animal Production, University of West Indies (1961–1964). Member of staff of Grassland Research Institute (1964–1985). Head of the Division of Animal Nutrition and Production, Grassland Research Institute, Hurley, and Assistant Director (1978–1985).

ANTHONY J. PARSONS BSc (London), PhD (Reading)

Principal Scientific Officer, Department of Plant Nutrition and Growth, AFRC Institute for Grassland and Animal Production, Hurley.

MICHAEL J. ROBSON BSc, PhD (Reading)

Principal Scientific Officer, Department of Plant Nutrition and Growth, AFRC Institute for Grassland and Animal Production, Hurley.

The Late T.E. WILLIAMS BSc (Hons) Wales

Research Assistant Welsh Plant Breeding Station (1938–1940). Agronomist, Ministry of Agriculture and Fisheries, Drayton, Stratford-on-Avon (Grassland Improvement Station) (1940–1949). Agronomist and Head of Agronomy Department, Grassland Research Institute (1949–1976); Deputy Director (1955–1968).

Foreword

by W.I.C. DAVIES

President of the
British Grassland Society
1987–1988

The first edition of *Grass: its Production and Utilization* was published in 1980. The British Grassland Society (BGS) had commissioned Professor W. Holmes to edit the book and he had wisely called on several outstanding grassland specialists to contribute. The result soon became recognized as an authoritative textbook on grassland science and husbandry and has been widely read by students, researchers, advisors and forward looking farmers.

The food production scene has changed considerably in the last 8 years with many commodities produced, now surplus to requirements within the EEC. This has led to the introduction of milk quotas and other moves to restrict over-production. With output limited, reducing the unit cost of production has become a key factor in profitable livestock farming and has placed increasing emphasis on the role of efficient production and utilization of grass.

Many developments from research in recent years have considerably enhanced our knowledge of efficient grassland use; the BGS has therefore asked Professor Holmes to prepare a second edition to incorporate these latest developments. He agreed to do this, and, again with the help of leading specialists, has produced a book which will provide essential reading for all those interested in getting the best out of grassland.

Preface to the second edition

In 1979 the Council of the British Grassland Society invited me to organize the preparation of a book on the production and utilization of grass. The first edition was published in 1980 and a reprint with minor revisions appeared in 1982.

There has been considerable development in grassland research and development in the 1980s and the time was ripe for a substantial revision. Accordingly I have invited authors, or in some instances their successors, to reconsider the contents and to provide a completely revised version of this book.

Much more has been learned about the growth of grass, its response to fertilizer and to grazing, and improved techniques of grass conservation have been developed. But in addition the rapid technical advances in agriculture within the EEC have resulted in embarrassing agricultural surpluses and there is a search for methods of reducing production and ameliorating the harmful environmental effects sometimes associated with intensive agricultural production.

While concentrating primarily as before on technical aspects of production and utilization, this edition includes an additional chapter concerned with conservation and amenity and within other chapters gives some consideration to matters relating to lower input systems.

The work is the responsibility of the contributors and editor but we also acknowledge our debt to the large band of research and development workers who, whether referred to or not, have advanced the subject. In particular we are grateful to those who revised sections 2.4–2.10 which were originally written by the late T.E. Williams: Dr S.C. Jarvis (2.4); Lewis Jones (2.5); Professor W. Holmes and R. J. Haggar (2.6–2.9); Dr R.O. Clements and G.C. Lewis (2.10). We also wish to thank Colin Dibb for his helpful comments on Chapter 8 and the Appendix (p. 272). Finally we thank the publishers for their encouragement, tolerance and assistance in providing the final copy.

W.H.

Preface to the first edition

The preparation of this book was initiated by the Council of the British Grassland Society. The editor was invited to organize its preparation and enlisted several authors, each expert in his field to contribute chapters within a general plan. Although the original intention was to prepare a concise book, such is the breadth of the subject that despite editing and condensation, the present volume is fairly substantial. Nevertheless no book can be fully comprehensive in such a wide-ranging and developing scientific subject. We have therefore listed other publications of particular interest under the heading of 'further reading' and give a full list of references at the end of the book. To the many workers whose efforts whether referred to or not, have increased our knowledge of the subject, we offer our thanks.

The book has adhered to metric units but we have at times preferred percentages where the insistence on $g\,kg^{-1}$ would have appeared pedantic and we have retained weight (W) and liveweight gain in preference to mass when dealing with animals.

The work is the responsibility of the authors and editor but we are grateful to many colleagues and assistants who have willingly given of their time and advice, in particular to Dr R.C. Campling of Wye College who read the whole text in draft and made many helpful suggestions. We also thank the publishers for their work in producing the final copy.

Finally we express our gratitude to our wives for their assistance, or at least their tolerance, even if they did not always share our enthusiasm for grass.

W.H.

Abbreviations and conversion table

ADF	acid detergent fibre	kf	efficiency for growth
ADL	acid detergent lignin	kg^{-1}	per kilogram
ATP	adenosine triphosphate	kl	efficiency for lactation
CC	cell contents	km	efficiency for maintenance
CF	crude fibre	L	degree of lignification
CP	crude protein	LAI	leaf area index
CW	cell walls	LW	live weight
CWD	cell wall digestibility	MADF	modified acid detergent fibre
d^{-1}	per day	ME	metabolizable energy
DCC	digested cell contents	MJ	megajoules
DCW	digestible cell wall	MLC	Meat and Livestock Commission
DE	digestible energy	MMB	Milk Marketing Board
Dg	degradability	MP	microbial protein
DM	dry matter	MPa	megapascals
DMD	dry matter digestibility	N	nitrogen
DOMD	digestible organic matter in dry matter	NAN	non ammonia nitrogen
		NFE	nitrogen-free extractives
DOMI	digestible organic matter intake	NPN	non-protein nitrogen
D-value	DOMD	OMD	organic matter digestibility
EE	ether extract	PN	protein nitrogen
EV	energy value	RDP	ruminally degraded protein
FCM	fat corrected milk	RO	retention time of organic matter in the rumen
GE	gross energy		
GM	gross margin	RSD	residual standard deviation
HI	heat increment	t	tonne
ha^{-1}	per hectare	UDP	undegraded dietary protein
IP	protein entering the small intestine	VFA	volatile fatty acids
		W	liveweight
		WSC	water-soluble carbohydrates

1 litre = 0.22 gal
1 kg   = 2.205 lb
1 tonne = 2205 lb
1 metre = 3.28 ft

1 hectare = 2.471 acres
$1\,kg\,ha^{-1}$ = 0.89 lb $acre^{-1}$
             = 0.8 'units' of fertilizer $acre^{-1}$
$0.1\,kg\,l^{-1}$ = 1 lb gal^{-1}

Chapter 1

Introduction

1.1 Objectives

The term grassland refers to a plant community in which grasses (*Gramineae*) are dominant, and shrubs and trees are rare. Grassland is a major agricultural resource of the UK and is of considerable importance in many other temperate and tropical regions. Its study can be traced over 200 years but only in the last 60 years has grass received sustained scientific attention. Indeed the major advances in our knowledge of grassland and in their application to practical farming have been made in the last 40 years. It is the aim of this book to provide a concise outline of the current state of knowledge on the production, feeding value and utilization of grassland in a temperate climate. The authors have endeavoured to assemble and outline current knowledge on the main factors affecting the production and utilization of grass and forage crops with full reference to other important sources of information. The book is intended to give guidance to students and farmers and to give a broad outline of the subject for more specialist scientists.

1.2 The development of grasslands

There are few natural grasslands in Britain. The major grasslands of the country are not areas of natural climax vegetation but are the result of man's past activities. The clearing of forest, its cultivation for arable crops, the subsequent development of grassland, and the discouragement of the regeneration of forest by herding cattle or sheep on the pastures, or by cutting or burning: these practices, or less frequently the deliberate sowing of grass seeds, have formed the majority of our pastures. But the sequence of regeneration to the woodland climax can still be seen wherever land is enclosed and protected from fire, and from grazing by domestic or wild animals.

These influences have resulted in large areas of the UK being under grassland. Table 1.1 shows the areas in Great Britain designated as temporary grass, permanent grass and rough grazing between 1875 and 1985. Changes in the total agricultural areas because of urbanization, and changes in the definition of the categories, prevent precise comparisons, but throughout the period, temporary and permanent grassland on the lowlands have considerably exceeded the total arable area while rough grazings, generally areas more than 300 m above sea level have exceeded that of permanent pasture. Grassland has therefore accounted for the major portion of the effective agricultural area of Great Britain during the past 100 years.

Grass is not uniformly distributed over Britain. In the drier east and south on land over sedimentary rocks, which is suitable for arable cultivation, grassland occupies a small proportion, while in the west and north where rainfall is higher and topography less suited to arable crop production, it is the dominant crop. An indication of the proportions of grass and arable crops in different regions in the UK is given in Fig. 1.1. The suitability of soils for grassland is treated in detail by Harrod (1979).

Table 1.1. Changes in land use in Great Britain from 1875 to 1985, measured in Mha.

Land use	1875	1938*	1944*	1975	1985
Total crops	5.57	3.36	5.55	4.74	4.94
Temporary grass	1.76	1.44	1.71	1.84	1.55
Permanent grass	5.39	7.01	4.37	4.60	4.50
Rough grazing	—	6.50	6.69	6.32	5.89

*1938 and 1944 were the years of minimal and maximal tillage in the last 50 years.

1.3   Leys and permanent pastures

Much of the impetus for improved grassland farming in Britain followed the publication of *Ley Farming* by Stapledon and Davies (1942) which coincided with the ploughing up campaign of the 1939−45 war, when increased home food production was vital.

The essentials of ley farming were the alternation of crops with grass in a regular sequence, with temporary grass, sometimes referred to as a ley, normally lasting from 2 to 5 years. This provided a 'balanced' system of farming with many technical and managerial advantages. The particular rotation was chosen to fit the conditions of the farm, while retaining the principles of balanced exploitation of soil fertility, with control of weeds, pests and diseases. However, agro-chemicals have reduced the need for

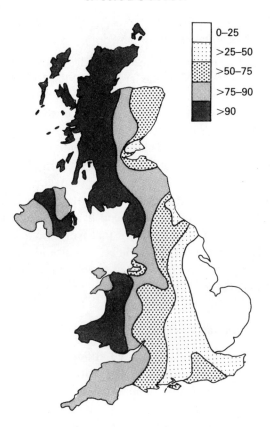

☐	0–25
⬚	>25–50
▨	>50–75
▩	>75–90
■	>90

Fig. 1.1 Percentage of agricultural land under grass and rough grazing in the UK. (From agricultural census data.)

crop rotations and the disadvantages of ley farming have become more evident. For example, the financial returns from all but the most intensive use of grass are less than from many cash crops; fencing and water supplies are costly and the capital investment for livestock is high; establishment of grass leys is costly and failures can occur. Moreover, short grass leys do not suppress all weeds, e.g. couch grass (*Agropyron repens*) thrives under conditions of high fertility and infrequent utilization, and wild oat and black grass seeds can persist for many years.

These factors and a growing realization that leys could never occupy a major proportion of the land of Britain led to a resurgence of interest since 1970 in the permanent pastures of the country. The merits and attributes of the various pasture types are referred to later.

1.4   Grassland potential

Grass as a crop receiving and transforming the sun's radiant energy into the products of photosynthesis has great potential for the production of biomass. It covers the ground almost completely, so that the leaf area index (LAI) (the total area of leaf in relation to the area of ground covered), is typically from 2 to 6, and light energy is fully received throughout the year. In these conditions provided temperatures are not below 5°C and soil moisture is not limiting, grass can grow throughout the year. In Britain growing days range from about 200 on hills and arid areas to over 300 days in favoured lowland areas. Maximal yields of some 25 t dry matter (DM) ha^{-1} could be produced in the normal British growing season of 5−7 months (Cooper 1970). Moreover, unlike the arable crops, such as cereals, potatoes or sugar beet, the useful economic yield at 60−90% of the whole crop exceeds that from the total DM from a cereal crop (about 52%) (Monteith 1977).

1.5   Grass utilization

The grass crop requires to be harvested either by an animal or machine and utilized by an animal, directly or after storage, before it is converted into useful products. Losses occur in harvesting and in conservation and the animal then converts a relatively small proportion of its feed into edible nutrients (and conversion efficiency to wool is also low). As a result, even the maximal yield of 25 t DM ha^{-1} which would provide 360 GJ* of gross energy and about 215 GJ of metabolizable energy (ME) ha^{-1} would yield, in animal products, about 41 GJ edible energy and 486 kg of protein if converted through dairy cattle, and only 10 GJ and 110 kg protein if converted by a beef suckler herd or sheep flock (Holmes 1980). It is in this area, the definition and quantification of the many steps in the process of efficient grass utilization, that much new information has been accumulated in recent years.

1.6   Grass as a source of feed

Wright (1940) estimated that in the late 1930s grass contributed about 67% of the total animal feed supply for farm animals in the UK. The most recent figures indicate that about 71% of ME and 67% of the crude

---

* GJ (gigajoules) = 1 000 000 000 joules or 1000 megajoules.

protein consumed by British ruminant livestock are derived from grazing and conserved grass. On average in Britain, dairy cows derive 60%, beef cattle 79%, and sheep 97% of their daily feed energy from grass (Jollans 1981).

1.7 Changes in grassland productivity

The measurement of grassland productivity is difficult, but comparison of the data of Wright (1940) with NEDO (1974) suggests that the average utilized ME from grassland almost doubled from 1938 to about $40\,GJ\,ha^{-1}$ in 1972–73, and dairy farms now commonly exceed $80\,GJ\,ha^{-1}$ (MMB 1987). This increase is probably related to a greater realization of the potential of grassland, an increase in fertilizer use and an increase in the proportion of silage which conserves grass more efficiently than hay making and now accounts for about 67% in terms of DM of all grass conserved in the UK. But there is still a vast gap between potential and performance. Many factors contribute to this discrepancy. Production may be impaired by unsuitable soil conditions such as an excess or deficiency of moisture, by soil acidity, mineral deficiencies, and by the presence of unproductive grass species and of weeds. The crop is usually harvested incompletely by machine or animal and losses always occur in conservation and in utilization by the animal. These factors have been the subject of much research and development in recent years and are considered in some detail in later chapters.

1.8 Grassland, conservation and amenity

The agriculturalist has come to regard a uniform, dense green leafy sward as the acme of perfection in grassland but the growing interest in, and popularity of, nature conservation now emphasizes the merits of the greater ecology diversity associated with lower input, less productive systems of grassland management.

While the objectives of the British Grassland Society remain 'to encourage research on grassland which will lead to improvements in the efficiency of its use' and the dominant theme of this book is the production and utilization for agricultural purposes of grassland, it was considered appropriate to include a new chapter which deals with grassland from the points of view of amenity and conservation since both in Britain and in western Europe the development of systems of management appropriate for environmentally sensitive areas is now a matter of concern.

Further reading

Heath M.E., Barnes R.F. & Metcalfe D.S. (1985) *Forages*. Ames, Iowa State University Press.

Jollans J.L. (ed) (1981) *Grassland in the British Economy*. CAS Paper No. 10. Centre for Agricultural Strategy, Reading.

Lazenby A. (1981) British grasslands, past, present and future. *Grass and Forage Science* **36**, 243–66.

Stapledon R.G. & Davies W. (1942) *Ley Farming*. Penguin Books, Harmondsworth.

Wilkinson J.M. (1984) *Milk and Meat from Grass*. Granada, London.

Chapter 2

Herbage production: grasses and legumes

Future emphasis in grassland farming must be on increased cost-effectiveness and whole farm profitability, rather than on higher productivity. One way of achieving this is to put greater reliance on home grown forages and less on costly concentrates. If farmers are to move towards all forage diets, they will need sound management guidelines, based on a clear understanding of how forage crops grow and respond to management, to ensure that they get the best out of their crops. This chapter aims to provide that understanding.

Grass is likely to remain the pre-eminent forage, although legumes, principally white clover in a mixture with grass, have an important role. Legumes not only fix their own nitrogen, and thereby have the potential to save expense on fertilizer nitrogen, but they also have a generally higher nutritive value than grass. However, only 20% of UK grassland currently contains more than 5% of white clover. Because of this, and because the physiology of leguminous forages has been less well explored than has that of the grass crop, this chapter concentrates on grass. Perennial ryegrass (*Lolium perenne* L.)*, is the most widely sown north temperate forage grass, and is taken as the standard.

2.1   The grass plant

Forage grasses have evolved to withstand periodic defoliation. Throughout most of the year the vegetative growing points, from which new leaves are produced, remain at or near ground level, where they escape removal by cutting or grazing. The turnover of leaves, however, is rapid. At the height of the growing season, a typical grass shoot may bear three live leaves per tiller and produce a new leaf every 7–10 days (Alberda & Sibma 1968). Leaves that are not harvested senesce and die. Thus, the whole leaf canopy can be replaced within 3–4 weeks. Grass tillers are also relatively short-lived. Most die within 12 months of being produced

* Latin and English names of the common grasses are listed in the Appendix (p. 272).

but the crop persists through the continuous production of new tillers from axillary buds on the surviving shoots.

In spring, the shoot apex of most of the tillers that have survived the winter, switches from the production of new leaves to that of floral parts, and the true stem begins to elongate. This transition from vegetative to reproductive growth plays a major role in bringing about the high and sustained rates of dry matter production characteristic of the spring crop (Parsons & Robson 1982). Flowering also profoundly influences the pattern of tiller production and death. Flowering tillers not only lose the ability to produce leaves but, having flowered, they ultimately die. Moreover, the shade created at the base of a dense reproductive sward leads to the death of many small vegetative tillers. Thus, flowering can lead to a high tiller mortality in spring, and the survival of the crop depends on the production of replacement vegetative tillers in early summer (Langer 1956, Robson 1968).

In a newly sown grass sward, the way the individual plant responds to environment, management and the increasingly influential presence of neighbours, is crucial to its success and that of the crop. As the sward ages, some plants die while those that remain grow larger, invading and colonizing gaps that appear in the sward and even on these survivors, old tillers die causing the plant to fragment. Thus, the identity of the original plant, the product of a single seed, is lost. This study of the grass plant, begins with the seed.

2.1.1 *The seed*

Each grass seed develops from a single fertilized ovule within the ovary of a flower (floret). As well as the ovary, with its twin stigmas, each floret contains three stamens and two very small scales (lodicules), all enclosed within two large bracts (lemma and palea) (Fig. 2.1a). A number of florets make up a spikelet and a number of spikelets the inflorescence (Fig. 2.1c). The great bulk of the seed is starchy endosperm used to sustain the embryo during germination and early seedling growth. The embryo consists of a primary shoot (plumule) within a protective sheath (coleoptile) and a primary root (radicle) also within a sheath (coleorhiza). These are attached by a short mesocotyl to a flat shield-like structure (scutellum) abutting the endosperm (Fig. 2.2a). As the seed matures, its coat fuses with the ovary wall to form a dry, one-seeded, indehiscent fruit known in the *Gramineae* as a grain. When sown, the grain may be naked, as in timothy, or enclosed by a persistent lemma and palea as in ryegrass; in some agriculturally less important grasses, the 'seed' may be the entire spikelet (Fig. 2.1d).

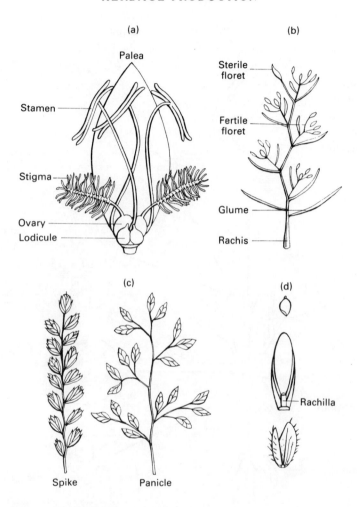

Fig. 2.1 (a) Floret with lemma removed to expose reproductive organs. (b) Diagrammatic spikelet showing two basal glumes, five fertile florets and one sterile (terminal) floret. (c) Types of inflorescence: spike and panicle. (d) Types of 'seed'; from the top: naked grain of *Phleum pratense*, enclosed grain of *Lolium perenne* and an entire spikelet of *Holcus lanatus* (after Robson *et al*. 1988).

2.1.2 *Germination and seedling emergence*

The germination of a viable seed is dependent largely on an adequate supply of water and oxygen, and a favourable temperature. The first stage in germination involves the passive uptake of water and takes about 12–24 hours. Following this, cells in the aleurone layer surrounding the endosperm begin secreting enzymes which break the starch down into

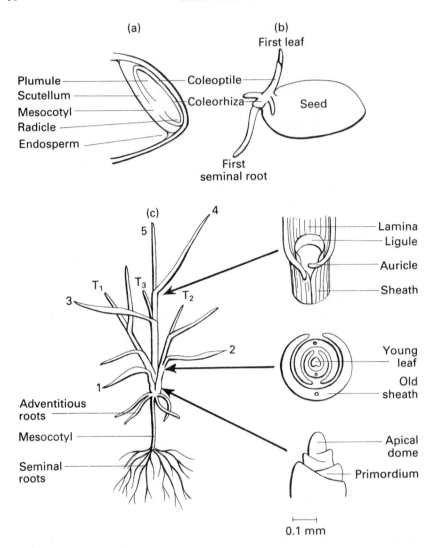

Fig. 2.2 (a) Diagrammatic cross-section of the embryo region of a seed. (b) Germinating seed. (c) Young plant with five leaves on the main stem, four of them fully expanded and three subtending daughter tillers (T_1, T_2 and T_3). Also, from the top: the junction of lamina and sheath, a cross-section of the pseudo stem (sometimes sheaths are folded rather than rolled) and the vegetative main stem apex (after Robson *et al.* 1988).

sugars. These the scutellum absorbs and passes on through the mesocotyl to the embryo. There they supply the energy and the raw materials necessary for the growth of the plumule and radicle; when these break through the seed coat, germination is complete (Fig. 2.2b).

The radicle grows downwards through the coleorhiza with one or more secondary roots arising at its base. These develop, through branching, into a highly efficient seminal root system on which the young seedling initially relies for its supply of water and inorganic nutrients. Later its functions are taken over by adventitious roots which arise from basal nodes on the main shoot and daughter tillers. As the radicle grows downwards, the young shoot or plumule is carried towards the soil surface by the elongation of the mesocotyl (Arber 1934, Brown 1960). This elongation is a response to darkness which ceases when the tip of the coleoptile emerges into light thereby positioning the shoot apex just below the soil surface (Fig. 2.2c).

The growth of the unemerged seedling is totally dependent on reserves in the endosperm. If sowing is too deep, particularly with small-seeded grasses such as timothy, the seedling may never emerge. From a depth of about 1 cm, emergence normally takes 6–8 days (Jones 1971). During this period, respiration associated with mobilizing reserves and transforming them into new plant tissue, can account for over one-third of the initial weight of the seed (Anslow 1962). Usually, endosperm reserves are exhausted within about 5 days of the coleoptile breaking the soil surface. The young plant must by then have expanded sufficient leaf surface for photosynthesis to meet the demands of respiration and new growth.

2.1.3   *Leaf morphology and development*

In the seedling, the only site of leaf production is the meristematic apex of the main shoot; at a later stage, leaves also develop from the apices of daughter tillers. The first leaf produced on the main shoot is very small, especially in small-seeded grasses. Subsequent leaves increase progressively in length, width and hence in area, until a maximum size is reached.

Each grass leaf consists of a blade or lamina connected at an angle to a generally shorter sheath, the junction being marked by a membraneous ligule and, in some species, two claw-like auricles. What appears to be a 'stem' is in reality a collection of sheaths rolled or folded one inside the other with the oldest sheath on the outside (Fig. 2.2c). Young leaves are extruded in succession through the centre of this pseudo-stem, disposing their laminae alternately left and right. The 'true stem', located at the base of the shoot, is concealed entirely by encircling sheaths and remains short (< 1 cm) as long as the shoot remains vegetative.

Leaves originate from primordia which are laid down in alternating order along the opposing flanks of the apical dome (Fig. 2.2c). As a leaf primordium grows, cell division and expansion become restricted to a basal meristem, divided in two by a band of parenchyma cells from which the ligule ultimately develops. The upper portion of the meristem is associated with lamina growth, the lower with that of the sheath. This restriction of growth to a basal meristem means that extension is already complete in that part of the leaf emerging from within the encircling sheaths of its predecessors. Moreover, the tip of a leaf is always older than the base, totally unlike white clover, where the leaf is of uniform age. Not surprisingly, when a grass leaf dies the most mature portion, the tip, dies first.

2.1.4 *Factors affecting leaf growth*

The rate of leaf extension is a sensitive indicator of the well being of the grass plant, and falls off rapidly when stress is experienced. For example, nitrogen deficiency slows leaf expansion more than it does photosynthesis, the products of which (simple carbon-based compounds) accumulate until such time as the application of nitrogen fertilizer restores the balance between these essential elements. In a similar manner, a shortage of water limits leaf expansion even before stomata (pores in the leaf through which gaseous exchange can take place) can close to reduce water loss, and, coincidentally, CO_2 uptake and photosynthesis. Water stress results from an imbalance between the evaporative demand on the plant and the ability of the plant to meet that demand from the soil. During a dry period, as soil water deficit builds up, leaf expansion is restricted first during daylight hours when demand is highest, and only later at night. Cell expansion is more sensitive to water stress than is cell division. Thus, unexpanded cells may accumulate during a dry period and then expand rapidly when rain comes, offsetting, in part, some of the effects of drought.

Light and temperature are perhaps the most important variables affecting leaf growth. Although during periods of low light intensity, photosynthesis and hence the supply of raw materials for growth are reduced, leaf growth is less affected than might be supposed. The temporary storage of sugars in sheath bases, and other intermediate metabolites in the growing leaves themselves, provides a buffer against short-term fluctuations in the current supply of photosynthetic products (Gordon *et al.* 1977). Thus, leaf growth reflects underlying trends in the light environment rather than its instantaneous state. Moreover, more of the products of photosynthesis are retained by the shoot at the expense of root, and the new leaves produced are thinner ('shade' leaves) than those produced in bright light ('sun' leaves). As a result, leaf area (the plant's light intercepting surface) is maximized, per unit weight of plant tissue, offsetting to some extent the effects of reduced carbon assimilation per unit of that leaf area. These compensatory effects only apply to spaced plants. Within an already closed crop community, a greater allocation of resources to the production of thinner leaves may increase the harvestable fraction of the crop at the expense of roots, but it cannot increase light interception and so offset the effects of a depressed rate of photosynthesis on total DM production. Thus, when a sward is open, and acts essentially as a collection of spaced plants, periods of cloudy weather may depress crop growth less than when the leaf canopy is closed.

Temperature affects the rate of appearance, as well as the expansion of new leaves. In mid summer, ryegrass tillers expand new leaves every 5−7 days but at only a tenth of that rate during mid winter. Leaf senescence also slows so that the mean number of live leaves remains relatively constant at about three per tiller. Temperature also affects the final size and shape of a leaf, and its rate and duration of extension. In general 'high temperature' leaves extend more rapidly, for a shorter period, to a greater final length than 'low temperature' leaves; they tend to be longer in relation to their width, thinner, and have proportionately more lamina relative to sheath. The optimum temperature for leaf growth is in the region of 20−25°C for most north temperate grasses, with the night temperature equal to or slightly lower than that of the day (Evans et al. 1964, Robson 1972, 1973c).

The rate of extension of the growing leaf is very sensitive to current temperature, responding to a change within minutes. The width of a leaf reflects the basal circumference of the shoot apex at the time when the leaf was still at a primordial stage (Abbe et al. 1941), and so is much less sensitive to the current temperature. As a result, the rate of extension of the youngest growing leaf has been used as an index of the rate of leaf area expansion of the whole shoot and even, if the tiller population is relatively constant, of the crop itself (Roy & Peacock 1972). In using leaf extension in this way, it is important to realize that different plant parts can experience temperatures that differ by as much as 30°C, and that the key temperature for the control of leaf growth is that of the shoot apex (Peacock 1975a, b).

In spring, many north temperate grasses are able to expand leaves faster, at a given temperature, than in summer and autumn (Peacock 1975c, 1976). The transition from an 'autumn' to a 'spring' mode of growth coincides with the earliest stages of reproductive development and with a major change in the carbohydrate strategy of the plant. These changes can have a major impact on the seasonal pattern of production of north temperate grasses (see section 2.2.2).

2.1.5 *Reproductive development*

The first sign of reproductive development is an acceleration of leaf primordia production and a lengthening of the shoot apex. Soon afterwards, bud primordia develop both at the tip of the apex and in the axils of the older leaf primordia, giving the apex its characteristic 'double ridge' appearance. These developments at the shoot apex, together representing 'ear initiation', occur at any time between January and May, in the northern hemisphere, depending on species and variety (Fig. 2.3). They are accompanied by a wave of cell division and expansion in the younger stem internodes which lifts the developing inflorescence above the surrounding foliage. This culminates in the emergence of the ear from the sheath of the flag leaf, the last leaf produced. The ear may be a spike, as in ryegrass, with each bud primordium developing into a spikelet bearing 3–10 closely packed florets. Or it may be a panicle, as in tall fescue, with each bud developing into a primary branch, or branches, terminated by a spikelet (Fig. 2.1c).

Most north temperate perennial grasses must pass through winter conditions of low temperatures and/or short daylengths, if they are to flower subsequently, although such a requirement may be less marked or entirely absent in biennials and annuals, respectively. Among the perennials, timothy is the only one in which no winter requirement has been identified (Cooper 1958). Satisfaction of a winter requirement causes no visible change in the shoot apex. Confirmation that it has occurred can be gained only retrospectively by observing the subsequent behaviour of the shoot. With plants in which the 'winter requirement' has been met, the onset of reproductive growth is triggered by exposure to lengthening days during spring. The critical daylength varies with species and cultivar, ranging from 8 to 13 h in the ryegrasses and from 15 to 16 h in timothy (Cooper 1951, Ryle & Langer 1963). Even after the shoot apex has made the transition to reproductive growth, long days are still necessary for normal inflorescence development (Langer & Ryle 1958) with the timing of ear emergence again depending on genotype and environment. Early flowering ryegrasses, for example, are particularly sensitive to temperatures in March and April; late flowering types to those in April and May. Small, young or poorly positioned tillers may fail to flower, even if they experience the required sequence of environmental conditions. Conversely,

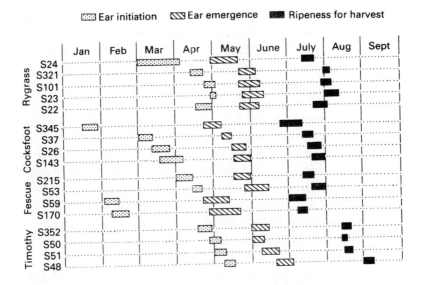

Fig. 2.3 Inflorescence development in some grass species and varieties (after Spedding & Dickmahns 1972).

young vigorously growing tillers that did not themselves experience winter conditions may still flower if they retain functional organic connections with older tillers that did.

2.1.6   *Tiller production*

The production of daughter tillers is most important to the rapid establishment and perenniality of the grass crop. Tillers arise from buds in the axils of leaves, and the coleoptile. In tussock-forming grasses, such as the north temperate forages, they generally grow upward within the encircling sheaths of the subtending leaves to emerge at the ligule, whereas in stoloniferous or rhizomatous grasses, such as rough-stalked meadow grass or couch, the tiller more often breaks through the base of the encircling sheath to give rise to a creeping stem with elongated internodes.

In perennial ryegrass, the first tiller usually emerges from the axil of the first leaf on the main shoot, but only when this leaf and its successor are fully expanded. Subsequent tillers on this axis generally arise in acropetal succession keeping pace with leaf production. In small-seeded grasses, such as timothy, the early leaves are particularly small and the first two or three sites may remain unfilled, the first tiller appearing in the axil of the third or fourth leaf (Ryle 1964). In all grasses, these 'primary' tillers may in turn subtend 'secondary' tillers, and so on.

In favourable conditions, the early pattern of tillering in perennial ryegrass tends towards that shown in Fig. 2.4. The pattern in other north temperate species is broadly similar. High temperatures accelerate tiller production, mainly through an increased rate of production of leaves, and hence axillary sites (Robson 1974). High light intensities also enhance tillering. Here the effect is not on the rate of site production, but rather on the extent to which sites are filled (Mitchell 1953a, b). As a plant grows larger and denser, it becomes increasingly self-shaded. Inevitably, this leads to a reduction in tillering, the rate of tillering diverges from the exponential and many sites remain unfilled. Even so, a single plant can produce 300 tillers in a single season if competition from neighbours is prevented (Robson 1968).

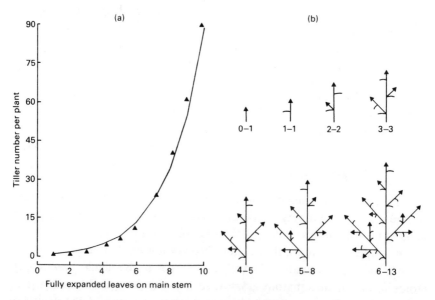

Fig. 2.4 Tiller production in young, spaced plants of *Lolium perenne* growing in favourable conditions (Robson 1982b). (a) Increase in tiller number per leaf interval on the main stem (▲), approximates to the Fibonacci series (——): each number is the sum of its two predecessors (1, 1, 2, 3, 5, 8, 13, 21, etc.). (b) Generally a tiller (▲) appears in a leaf axil once that leaf's successor is fully expanded. The numbers under each diagrammatic plant (e.g. 6–13) refer to fully expanded leaves on the main stem (6) and the total tiller number per plant (13) (after Robson *et al.* 1988).

When plants grow in communities, tillering is even more restricted, with a severity proportional to the plant population. Indeed, under a given management, a common tiller density is usually achieved independent of the plant density (Kays & Harper 1974). In well established grass communities, tiller populations fluctuate around a common baseline as old tillers die and new ones are produced. On average, each tiller produces many leaves but only one daughter tiller (i.e. it replaces itself). Thus, in practice, the great majority of potential sites remain unfilled.

2.1.7 Leaf and tiller production in the community

So far, we have dealt almost exclusively with the single plant or tiller. In bulk, these make up the dynamic community of the crop whose response to environment and management, including the presence of the grazing animal, determines its seasonal pattern of growth and development, and its total annual yield (see section 2.2). This section illustrates the patterns of leaf growth and tillering of grass plants growing with neighbours from a collection of spaced seedlings to a closed canopy at ceiling yield. Data are presented from a model community: a uniform population of regularly spaced, vegetative plants of S24 perennial ryegrass, growing without interruption in constant and favourable environmental conditions, abundantly supplied with water and nutrients, and free from pests and diseases (Robson 1973a).

From seedling emergence, main stem leaves appear, one every 5−6 days, slowing to half that rate 12 weeks later (Fig. 2.5), a decline common in communities but less evident in spaced plants. Concurrently, the time taken for successive leaves to reach full size doubles, so that the number growing at any one time remains constant at just under two. The rate of leaf extension peaks at about 50 mm day^{-1} for leaf 5 and the final leaf length (lamina and sheath) at about 70 cm for leaf 8. Leaves accumulate on the main stem until there are five or six before the oldest dies. The number of live leaves then falls rapidly to level off at just under three; typical of field swards. Meanwhile, tiller number rises, at first exponentially but then more slowly as the crop canopy closes, until it too levels off at about 26 per plant, or just over 1 cm^{-2} of ground area. Taking leaf length as an index of leaf size, it is clear that, by the end of the 12-week period, the amount of live leaf on the main stem has reached a ceiling. As fast as a new leaf is produced, an old leaf of the same size dies. With tiller number also constant by now, the community as a whole reaches a ceiling in terms of the amount of live leaf tissue (see section 2.2.1).

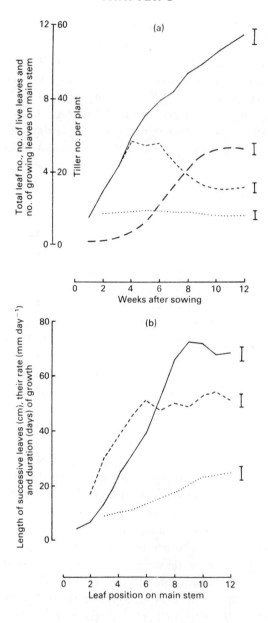

Fig. 2.5 Leaf and tiller growth, and death, in seedling swards of *Lolium perenne*. (a) Tiller number per plant (– – – –) together with the total number of main stem leaves (——), the number alive (----) and the number growing at any one time (....). (b) Total length (lamina + sheath) of successive (1–12) main stem leaves (——), their rate of elongation from appearance to the appearance of their successor (– – – –), and their duration of elongation (....). Vertical bars ± s.e (after Robson 1973a).

2.1.8 *Leaf photosynthesis*

Tissue production and ultimately crop yield depend on photosynthesis, the process by which solar radiation, intercepted by green leaves, provides the energy to convert CO_2 and water into simple sugars. Over 90% of the plant dry weight consists of complex carbohydrates and the carbon-based fractions of other organic compounds such as proteins, all derived from those simple sugars and, thus, stemming directly from the photosynthetic assimilation of carbon. This section considers that assimilation and the factors that affect it.

All living tissues, including green leaves, respire; they oxidize substrates to produce energy necessary for metabolism with the release of CO_2 and water, essentially the reverse of photosynthesis. In young, well illuminated grass leaves, the photosynthetic uptake of CO_2 vastly exceeds the respiratory efflux, but at progressively lower light intensities the gap narrows until, at the 'compensation point', net photosynthesis (the excess of photosynthesis over respiration) is zero. At even lower intensities, respiration exceeds photosynthesis and the leaf is in negative carbon balance.

The relationship between net photosynthesis and light intensity accords with the 'law of diminishing returns' in that each successive increment in light intensity brings a progressively smaller return in terms of carbon fixed until the leaf is 'light saturated', and net photosynthesis plateaus at a value representing the maximum capacity of which that particular leaf is capable (e.g. Prioul 1971). It follows that a given amount of solar radiation will cause more carbon fixation if it is spread over a large leaf area (at low intensity) rather than limited to a small leaf area (at high intensity), just as a given amount of fertilizer will better enhance yield if spread evenly over the whole of a nutrient deficient crop rather than concentrated on a small corner of it.

Temperature also directly affects carbon assimilation. The net rate of light-saturated photosynthesis of ryegrass leaves increases almost three-fold between 5 and 25°C (Woledge & Dennis 1982), although water stress, which often accompanies high temperatures, can completely counter that effect in the field.

As leaves age, their photosynthetic capacity declines, starting soon after full expansion and well before any visible sign of senescence, with the older tip declining before the younger base. The decline is slowed by low temperatures and shade, and the leaves live longer, unless that shade is extreme (Woledge & Jewiss 1969, Woledge 1971). The rate of photosynthesis which a leaf exhibits in low light intensities declines more slowly with age than its light-saturated rate (Woledge 1972). Since many leaves in a dense grass crop, especially the older ones, are poorly illuminated, the adverse effect on photosynthesis is less than might otherwise be expected.

The environmental conditions that a leaf experiences during its development affect its subsequent photosynthetic capacity when it reaches maturity. Of these, the effect of light intensity is the best understood and the most important. Leaves developed in low rather than high light have a much lower photosynthetic capacity at light saturation. Within a vegetative sward, growing for some weeks without interruption and becoming increasingly dense, developing leaves are more and more shaded as the light environment at the base of the sward worsens. As a result, each tiller in the sward produces a succession of leaves with progressively lower photosynthetic capacities (Woledge 1973) (Fig. 2.6a). When these leaves emerge into bright light, they are unable to make full use of it, leading to a substantial short-fall in carbon fixation by the crop (Robson 1973b).

By contrast, in flowering swards there is no reduction in the photosynthetic capacity of successive newly expanded leaves, even when the crop is very dense. Stem extension keeps the developing leaves in high light near the top of the canopy. Thus, each tiller produces a succession of leaves of high photosynthetic capacity (Fig. 2.6b), ensuring a high rate of photosynthesis by the crop (Woledge & Leafe 1976). This difference in the photosynthetic capacity of vegetative and reproductive swards is a major reason for the greater DM production exhibited by the reproductive crop compared to its vegetative counterpart (see section 2.2.2).

There appears to be substantial genetic variation in the extent to which the photosynthetic apparatus of grass leaves is impaired by shade during development (Wilson 1981), variation which breeders may be able to exploit. Some genotypes are relatively unaffected, and hence might prove valuable under infrequent cutting or rotational grazing where a high leaf area is sustained for an appreciable time. Others are very sensitive to shade, but when well illuminated produce leaves of high photosynthetic capacity and so might be particularly useful under frequent cutting or continuous grazing where a build up of leaf area is prevented (Robson 1981).

Although nitrogen deficiency reduces grass yields by restricting leaf expansion, and thus light interception, it also impairs photosynthetic capacity when the organic nitrogen content of the leaves falls below about 3%. Since this happens quite frequently in the field, even in heavily fertilized crops, photosynthesis will often be limited to some extent. In

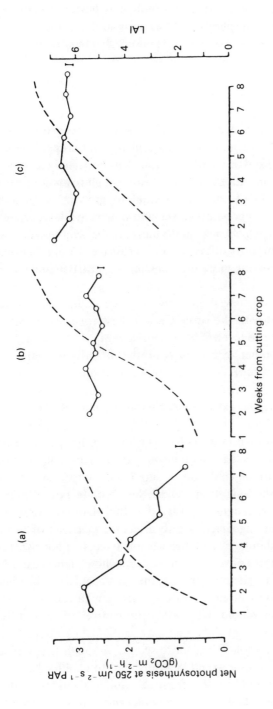

Fig. 2.6 Photosynthetic capacity of successive leaves in a sward, measured when newly expanded (——), and canopy LAI (– – –). (a) Vegetative ryegrass. (b) Reproductive ryegrass. (c) White clover. Vertical bars ± s.e (after Woledge & Parsons 1986).

infrequently harvested crops, nitrogen supply may have conflicting effects in that it may increase leaf photosynthesis early in the growth period but, by stimulating leaf expansion and so mutual shading, depress it later (Woledge & Pearse 1985).

2.1.9 *Tissue respiration*

In the last two decades, it has become possible to construct accurate carbon balance sheets for individual grass plants and crops. These show that of the carbon fixed in photosynthesis, at best, only a quarter is ultimately harvested; no less than half is lost through respiration (Robson 1973b). Respiration is, of course, essential to growth; it releases the energy required for metabolic processes and makes available the carbon building blocks from which new molecules can be synthesized. Nevertheless, is all this respiratory efflux of CO_2 necessary? Could it perhaps be reduced thereby conserving more of the assimilated carbon and increasing yields?

Respiration can be viewed in terms of two components (McCree 1970), one associated with the production of new tissue ('synthetic' respiration) and, hence, concentrated in meristematic regions such as the shoot apex, and the other with preserving the integrity of mature tissue ('maintenance' respiration). The concept is very similar to that of the dairy farmer who gives each cow so much feed to meet its own requirements (maintenance) plus extra for each litre of milk expected from it (production).

Most aspects of growth (e.g. leaf expansion) are temperature dependent. So too, therefore, is the *instantaneous rate* of 'synthetic' respiration. Equally, since growth depends on a supply of substrates, 'synthetic' respiration must, in the long-term, reflect the absolute rate of photosynthesis, and therefore the light intensity that the plant experiences. But neither temperature nor light significantly affect the *efficiency* of 'synthetic' respiration; always about 25% of the carbon fixed in photosynthesis is respired in the cause of converting the rest into new plant tissue. Moreover, that conversion already follows the most efficient biochemical pathways (Penning de Vries 1972), so that any attempt to reduce 'synthetic' respiration would be counterproductive. It would reduce growth itself.

Maintenance respiration offers more scope, although it is difficult to characterize. A 'typical' rate would be equivalent to about a 1.5% loss of dry weight day^{-1}, but could differ from this quite widely depending on the type and age of the tissue and on previous and current environmental conditions. Maintenance respiration also varies with genotype, and so may be amenable to breeding (Wilson 1975). In S23 perennial ryegrass, for example, lines selected to have a 'slow' rate of 'maintenance' respiration outyield 'high' respiration lines (Wilson 1975, Robson 1982a, Wilson & Jones 1982) and, more importantly, their common parent by between 5 and 12% depending on management (Wilson & Robson 1981). The outlook is promising. Slow respiration may bring penalties with it, although none have been detected so far, and any tendency to genetic drift will have to be overcome. It is essential that the character is stable, and that the advantages it conveys survive both the generations of seed multiplication necessary to get new varieties onto the farm, as well as the management procedures experienced there.

2.1.10   *Adaptation to defoliation*

In the grass crop, as distinct from many others, the leaves are not only the photosynthetic 'factory' but the harvestable fraction also. This would not matter if the crop were annual and harvested only once, but it is perennial and harvested repeatedly within a single year. It must regrow rapidly, even though the prime source of raw materials to enable it to do so, the leaves, may have been largely or entirely removed.

A previously uncut grass plant will lose the bulk of its photosynthetic surface when harvested and so find itself in negative carbon balance; current photosynthesis cannot match the respiratory efflux of CO_2, and the plant loses weight. It must re-establish that photosynthetic surface or it will go into terminal decline. While vegetative, it continually pushes out new leaf tissue from each shoot meristem, and continues to do so after a harvest, as long as substrates to support that leaf growth can be found. In many north temperate grasses these come almost entirely from the stubble, and far less than had been supposed from the root. The root suffers, however, in that its supply of current assimilates dries up leading to a drastic reduction in many of its functions, such as nutrient uptake, cell division and expansion and cytokinin production.

The shoot bases of many grass species store significant amounts of simple sugars. These are the first substances to be drawn on during regrowth, followed a day or two later, by hemicelluloses and proteins. Stubble weight declines rapidly at first, but then more slowly as each new section of leaf to emerge begins to fix carbon. Within a very few days the plant as a whole may cease to be in negative carbon balance, although substrates continue to flow from stubble to shoot. Ultimately, the flow is reversed and the weight loss made good, but this may take 2 or 3 weeks.

If, before then, the plant is cut again, it will have few reserves to draw on and regrowth will be severely impaired.

Even so, grass plants can adapt to repeated cutting, by reducing leaf and tiller size, while often increasing tiller number (Jones et al. 1982) and adopting a prostrate habit, so that a substantial fraction of the photosynthetic surface avoids removal and the assimilation of carbon continues without major interruption (Parsons et al. 1984).

It is the availability of substrates, whether from reserves or from current assimilation, that determines the vigour of regrowth rather than a shortage of sites (vegetative shoot meristems) from which the leaf can be expanded. The vegetative meristems of grass avoid removal by cutting or grazing almost entirely, and are unlikely in an established crop to be in short supply. When plants growing in a dense community flower, however, few vegetative tillers remain at the base of the sward. Moreover, most of the young nodes from which replacement tillers might arise are carried up, away from the soil surface, by stem elongation. If (aerial) tillers do develop at these nodes, they may be removed or they fail to root and often die. Even here, it is not certain that regrowth is limited by a lack of sites rather than of substrates, for the stubble of flowering plants is also virtually devoid of leaf area and low in reserves.

2.2   The grass sward

Section 2.1 dealt with the morphology of the plant and the effects of environmental factors such as temperature and light on the development and function of individual leaves and tillers. This section considers the grass crop as a whole, and how its growth and development are affected by seasonal changes in the environment and by defoliation management.

2.2.1   *Growth to a ceiling yield*

In all green plants the basis of growth is photosynthesis. The quantity of light energy intercepted by the sward is thus a vital determinant of DM production. However, the accumulation of DM is not the result of a single process but represents the net balance between a number of processes, some (principally canopy gross photosynthesis) adding weight to the crop, others (such as respiration, and leaf and tiller death) losing weight from it. The balance between these processes changes markedly as the crop grows.

Initially, the small leaf area of the crop permits only a low rate of gross canopy photosynthesis per unit ground area (Fig. 2.7a). Consequently, the crop expands new leaves at only a modest rate. However, even a small increase in leaf area leads to greater light interception. This increases canopy gross photosynthesis and so, in turn, leads to an even greater rate of leaf area expansion. Eventually the leaf canopy intercepts virtually all of the available light and the rate of canopy gross photosynthesis levels off at a high value (or may even decline a little as successive leaves, developed now in low light at the base of the dense sward, exhibit an impaired photosynthetic capacity: see section 2.1.8). Thus, canopy gross photosynthesis supplies carbon to the crop at a rate that changes as the crop develops (Fig. 2.7a). But there are also changes in the rate of loss of carbon from the crop in respiration and leaf death. Respiratory losses are associated both with the *synthesis* of new tissue, and with its subsequent *maintenance* (see section 2.1.9). As the crop grows from a low LAI, there is a marked increase in 'synthetic' respiration reflecting the increasing rate of canopy gross photosynthesis and, hence, of the conversion of assimilate into new tissue. That conversion is not 100% efficient. The efficiency depends on the biochemical composition of the tissue created, but on average, for every 75 units of carbon in the new tissue produced, a further 25 units are respired (Penning de Vries 1972).

Once tissue has been produced, energy is needed to maintain its integrity. In the grass crop, a third of the carbon entering new tissue is

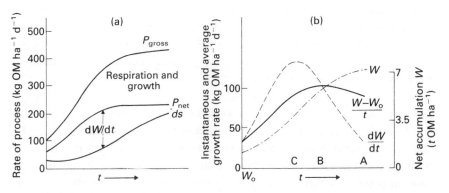

Fig. 2.7 (a) Changes in the rates of gross canopy photosynthesis (*P*gross), gross shoot tissue production (*P*net) and tissue death (*ds*) with time, during the growth of a grass sward from a low to a ceiling LAI. (b) Corresponding changes in the weight of the crop (*W*), the instantaneous growth rate (d*W*/d*t*) and the average growth rate (($W - W_o/t$)). See text for explanation of the effects of harvesting the sward at times A, B and C (after Parsons & Penning 1988).

essentially unchanged assimilate that is gradually consumed in 'maintenance' respiration. Thus, of every 100 units of carbon fixed in photo
synthesis, 25 are lost immediately (synthetic respiration), and a further 25
are lost as tissues age (maintenance respiration) leaving only 50 in the
tissue from its production to its death. In the crop as a whole, during the
early stages of growth when much of the tissue is still young, total
respiratory losses account for not much more than 25% of gross photosynthesis on a 24 hour basis. Later, when the crop has a full complement
of tissue of all ages, respiratory losses account for at least 50% of the
carbon fixed (Robson 1982b).

At any point in time, the difference between the rate of gross photosynthesis and the rate of respiration represents the *gross* rate at which
carbon is added to the crop (i.e. the rate of net photosynthesis or gross
tissue production). This declines in *percentage terms*, from 75% of the
carbon fixed to 50%, as the crop develops and respiratory costs rise.
Nevertheless, because the rate of canopy gross photosynthesis increases
many-fold over the same period, the *absolute rate* of gross tissue production also rises, so that even in a dense crop of high LAI, the rate of
gross tissue production, like that of gross photosynthesis, is sustained at
close to its maximum.

As growth proceeds, old tissues die, and at a changing rate. The
change in the rate of leaf death has a profound effect on the rate of *net*
tissue production (gross tissue production minus tissue death) and hence,
in temperate climates where the dying herbage is removed by soil fauna,
on the net accumulation of herbage seen in the field. As described
previously (section 2.1.7), grass leaves turn over rapidly. Typically, an
individual tiller bears three live leaves. Each time a new leaf appears the
oldest leaf dies. Since, during the main growing season, new leaves may
be produced about one every 7 days, the time interval between the
appearance of a leaf and its death can be about 3 weeks. Hence leaf tissue
produced at any one time, dies and is lost about 3 weeks (or three leaf
intervals) later. In other words, the current rate of leaf death equals the
rate of leaf production 3 weeks previously; death mirrors production, but
with a 3 week time lag. Thus, early in the development of the crop, when
rates of gross photosynthesis and hence gross tissue production are rising,
leaf production (reflecting the current rate of gross photosynthesis) exceeds
leaf death (reflecting an earlier and lower rate of gross photosynthesis)
and the crop makes a net gain in live dry weight. Even when light
interception first becomes complete and the rate of gross photosynthesis
levels off, leaf production continues to exceed death for about 3 weeks.
During this period, the rate of leaf production remains high, while the

rate of leaf death climbs to meet it (Fig. 2.7a). When death matches production, the crop no longer makes a net gain in live weight and a ceiling yield of live tissue is achieved (Fig. 2.7b).

It is important to stress that the mechanism by which the temperate grass crop achieves a ceiling yield is not that which has sometimes been proposed (e.g. Donald 1961). Mature tissue does *not* build up inexorably until its respiratory demands equal gross photosynthesis, leaving no carbon from which new tissue can be synthesized. Rather, leaf death intervenes, preventing an extreme build up of tissue, and ensuring that there is always sufficient carbon to sustain leaf production at a high rate. The crop is not static therefore, but dynamic, replacing its entire leaf mass at frequent intervals.

When accumulated over the growth period, the changing rates of net accumulation of live tissue illustrated in Fig. 2.7a describe the characteristic sigmoid pattern of net accumulation of herbage (W) seen in numerous agronomic studies for crops growing from seed or after a harvest (Fig. 2.7b).

2.2.2 *Seasonal changes in the physiology of the crop*

Superimposed on this basic description of grass growth are seasonal changes in the physiology of the crop which affect the pattern and duration of growth and the ceiling yield achieved, (Parsons & Robson 1980, 1981a, b, 1982). Many temperate perennial grasses show a marked seasonal pattern of accumulation of 'reserve' carbohydrates, typically fructans (Pollock & Jones 1979). These accumulate throughout summer, autumn and winter but are 'mobilized' in early spring when they may alleviate some of the restrictions to growth imposed by the low leaf area and light energy receipt at this time. They also play a role in frost tolerance, and their consumption in growth too early in spring could prejudice survival (Cooper 1964). Coincident with the mobilization of 'reserve' carbohydrates, there is an important increase in the ability of leaves to extend at a given temperature. This makes it possible for the plants to achieve an effective rate of leaf area expansion in early spring when, in southern England for example, soil surface temperatures are 8°C lower than at a time of equivalent light energy receipt in autumn.

Moreover, during spring, leaves sustain a high photosynthetic capacity. This, combined with a pattern of increasing daily light energy receipt (as both light intensity and daylength increase) leads to a rise in the rate of gross canopy photosynthesis which continues beyond the time when the sward intercepts virtually all the available light. Thus, the period during which gross tissue production exceeds the rate of tissue death is also extended, and the sward displays a longer 'linear' phase of DM accumulation, and achieves a higher ceiling yield than at other times of the year (Leafe *et al.* 1974, Parsons & Robson 1982).

In autumn, on the other hand, the photosynthetic capacity of successive new leaves declines as the LAI of the sward rises. This, combined with a pattern of decreasing daily light energy receipt, leads to a maximum rate of canopy gross photosynthesis which is lower and achieved sooner. The rate of leaf death equals the rate of gross tissue production at an earlier stage, and a lower ceiling yield is achieved. The significance of the seasonal *pattern* of light energy is often overlooked. Mathematical models show that this alone can account for much of the observed seasonal differences in herbage production (Johnson & Thornley 1983).

Perhaps the most important seasonal difference in the crop, is the change from vegetative to reproductive growth shown by many tillers in the spring. Elongation of the flowering stems ensures that the crop has a high photosynthetic capacity by elevating young leaves to the top of the leaf canopy where they both develop and photosynthesize in high light. Moreover, stems and flag leaves do not show the same rapid turnover as do leaves on vegetative tillers, and so their formation leads to an accumulation of tissues that would otherwise have been lost by death. Finally, more of the above-ground tissue is elevated above a typical height of defoliation so that, when the sward is harvested, a greater proportion is removed (i.e. the harvest index is increased). In swards of Italian ryegrass, for example, harvested for the first time late in spring, elongated stems plus ears can make up some 80% of the crop, perhaps $6\,t\,OM\,ha^{-1}$ (Fig. 2.8) out of a total annual net accumulation of about $12\,t\,OM\,ha^{-1}$. Of course, flowering also affects the digestibility of the crop by decreasing the proportion of digestible leaf relative to indigestible stem.

2.2.3   *Physiology of growth under continuous grazing*

The relative merits of harvesting the crop through continuous grazing, or by intermittent defoliation, have been the subject of much controversy which the development of theoretical models has only recently begun to resolve (Johnson & Parsons 1985a, b, Parsons *et al.* 1988). The next few sections compare these two contrasting approaches to harvesting the crop, and analyse the physiological basis for optimizing production and utilization in each case. Two characteristics of the crop are central to our understanding: firstly, because of the rapid turnover of leaves and tillers in the sward, the crop must be harvested repeatedly or (as at a ceiling

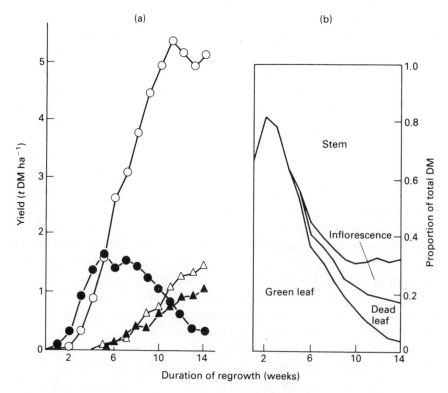

Fig. 2.8 The morphological development of a crop of S22 Italian ryegrass over 14 weeks after a cut in late April (after Wilman *et al.*, 1976). DM yields from: stem (○), green leaf (●), dead leaf (▲), and inflorescence (△); (a) in absolute terms, and (b) as a proportion of the total.

yield) virtually all the tissue produced dies unharvested and is lost; secondly, since the major photosynthetic organs of the crop (the leaves) are removed, the act of harvesting has a profound effect on the amount of grass subsequently grown.

Continuous grazing is the most common means of harvesting the grass crop but until recently it had received little attention. This largely reflects the difficulty in measuring grass production where for long periods, there may be little or no net change in weight. Under this management, the principles of production can be understood only by considering the *flow* of matter through the crop rather than its state at any one time. Grass leaves turn over rapidly, and if not harvested, they die and are lost. In a continually grazed sward, the animals harvest a proportion of the leaf tissue flowing through the system, and so the loss by death is reduced. Increasing the proportion harvested, by grazing more intensively, further reduces losses, but the continual removal of a large proportion of the leaves reduces the overall leaf area of the sward and so reduces photosynthesis and the amount of leaf produced. To optimize production, it is necessary to strike a balance between the amount of leaf removed by grazing and the amount that remains in the sward to photosynthesize. The effect of the intensity of continuous grazing on the balance between these processes is shown in Fig. 2.9 (Bircham & Hodgson 1983, Grant *et al.* 1983, Parsons *et al.* 1983a, b).

In swards maintained at a high LAI, canopy gross photosynthesis is close to a maximum, and the maximum amount of new tissue is produced. However, the only way to maintain the sward at a high LAI is to harvest a small proportion of the leaves produced. As a result, most of the leaf tissue dies unharvested and is lost. At a sustained high LAI (A in Fig. 2.9), gross shoot production may be close to $30\,t\,OM\,ha^{-1}$, yet of this only $4\,t\,OM\,ha^{-1}$ are harvested and $26\,t\,OM$ are lost. Such a situation is not uncommon, with some UK farms recording a grass utilizable metabolizable energy (UME) of just $40\,GJ\,ha^{-1}$ (approximately $4\,t\,OM\,ha^{-1}$) on high quality soils receiving large inputs of fertilizer nitrogen. Clearly, the intensity of grazing under these circumstances should be increased.

In swards maintained at a lower LAI (B in Fig. 2.9), a far greater proportion of the leaf is harvested and a smaller proportion lost. However, not all light is intercepted and canopy photosynthesis and shoot growth are reduced. Fortunately, the increase in the overall efficiency of utilization (the proportion of gross tissue production harvested) more than outweighs the decrease in the amount of grass grown, and the amount harvested is actually increased. Indeed, at B the maximum yield $(10\,t\,ha^{-1})$ is achieved, not because this management leads to maximum light interception and photosynthesis, but because it achieves the best balance between photosynthesis, gross tissue production, intake and death. At very high intensities of continuous grazing, where only a very small leaf area is sustained (C in Fig. 2.9), all components of production and utilization are reduced, and the sward is clearly overgrazed.

2.2.4 *Physiology of growth under intermittent defoliation*

Under continuous grazing, fluctuations in the LAI and the productivity of the crop are characteristically gradual. By contrast, under intermittent defoliation, the leaf area of the crop fluctuates markedly as the sward alternates between periods of regrowth and harvest. Each harvest may be more or less instantaneous, as when the sward is cut; or it may take a considerable period, as under rotational grazing when the number of

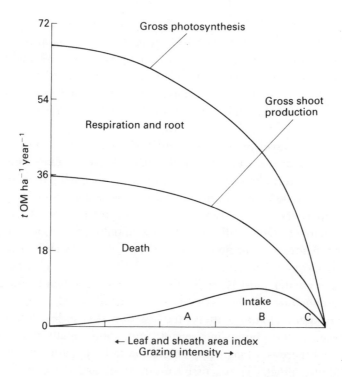

Fig. 2.9 The effects of the intensity of continuous grazing on the balance between photosynthesis, gross tissue production, herbage intake and death (after Parsons *et al.* 1983b).

paddocks is small. Moreover, both the frequency and the severity of defoliation can be varied. Only recently have we come to understand the physiological principles that govern the performance of the crop under the many possible combinations of defoliation frequency and severity.

A severely defoliated crop, allowed to regrow without interruption, will follow the characteristic sigmoid pattern of net DM accumulation (W_o to W) shown in Fig. 2.7b. If such a crop were repeatedly defoliated with the same severity, the frequency of defoliation would determine when the regrowth curve was interrupted. Frequent defoliation repeatedly interrupts the curve at an early stage, perhaps even before the canopy is closed so that light constantly falls on bare ground. Infrequent defoliation extends each regrowth period so that the crop may be close to ceiling yield before it is harvested. At what stage of growth should the crop be harvested repeatedly if long term yield, bulked over several harvests is to be maximized? Several workers (Maeda & Yonetani 1978, Watanabe & Takahashi 1979) have shown that the growth curve must be interrupted when the *average growth rate* $((W - W_o)/t)$ is at a peak, that is at time B in Fig. 2.7b. This is after the time C, of maximum instantaneous growth rate (dW/dt), but before the time A, of ceiling yield (W). This peak is not a sharp one. Following severe defoliation, the average growth rate rises fairly rapidly at first, but then changes much more slowly and becomes less sensitive to the duration of regrowth above a lower limit — in practice, about 14–21 days (see section 2.2.10).

The effect of severity of the defoliation on yield is now considered. It is important to appreciate that a crop defoliated more leniently than in Fig. 2.7b would not retrace the same growth curve, or even a part of it, shown by the severely defoliated crop. Following severe defoliation (e.g. line 1 in Fig. 2.10a) the rate of canopy net photosynthesis (gross tissue production) is low initially, reflecting the low initial leaf area, and it takes a long time before the maximum rate of net photosynthesis is regained. Following more lenient defoliation (lines 2 and 3) the rate of net photosynthesis is greater initially, reflecting the greater residual leaf area, and the maximum rate of photosynthesis is regained sooner. However, the severity of defoliation also affects the loss of matter in leaf turnover and death (Fig. 2.10b). Following severe defoliation, death rates are low initially and there is a long delay before the rate of death equals the rate of net photosynthesis (gross tissue production) and there is no further net gain in weight. Following more lenient defoliation, not only is the rate of photosynthesis higher initially but so too is the rate of tissue death, and maximum death rates are achieved sooner. The effect of the severity of defoliation on the instantaneous growth rate, and on the average growth rate, is shown in Fig. 2.10c and d respectively. Following lenient defoliation, not only is the maximum average growth rate achieved sooner, after a shorter duration of regrowth (e.g. line 2 compared with 1, or 3 with 2), but, after the most lenient defoliation (lines 4 and 5), average growth rates are lower overall and may actually decline throughout regrowth.

From this analysis it is apparent why, to maximize production under intermittent defoliation, severe defoliation is best associated with a long duration of regrowth, whereas more lenient defoliation requires a shorter duration of regrowth, as has long been recognized in practice (Reid 1966).

2.2.5   *Continuous and intermittent defoliation compared*

Continuous and intermittent defoliation may be regarded as two seemingly contrasting means of pursuing a desirable balance between photosyn-

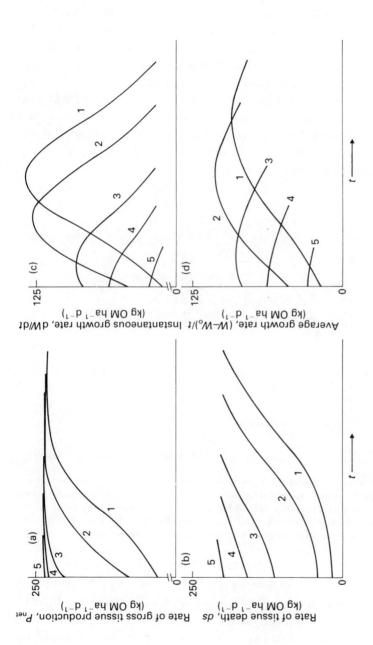

Fig. 2.10 The effects of the severity of intermittent defoliation on: (a) the rate of gross tissue production ($Pnet$); (b) the rate of tissue death (ds); (c) the instantaneous growth rate (dW/dt); and (d) the average growth rate (($W - W_0)/t$), as the duration of regrowth is extended over time, t. The LAIs to which the swards had been cut, and from which they are regrowing, were 0.5, 1.1, 3.4, 5.3 and 6.8 for lines 1 to 5 respectively (after Parsons *et al.* 1988).

thesis, gross tissue production, the amount harvested and death. Under continuous grazing a yield is achieved because a proportion of leaves is intercepted continually by grazing animals, whereas under intermittent defoliation a yield is achieved because, during regrowth, there is a lag between the increasing rates of photosynthesis and gross tissue production and those of respiration and death. This leads to a net accumulation of herbage which is harvested when the sward is cut or grazed. However, both systems give rise to similar average levels of net herbage production when compared on the same basis, namely in terms of the *average* amount of leaf area sustained (Fig. 2.11). Moreover, in both cases, maximum yield ha^{-1} is achieved when the swards are sustained, on average, at the same optimum sward state.

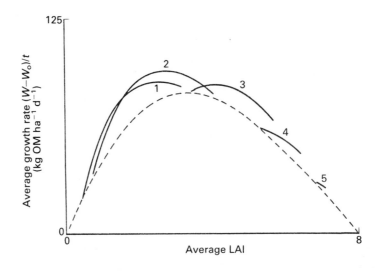

Fig. 2.11 The relationship between the average growth rate achieved and the average LAI sustained when the sward is harvested following each of the five severities of defoliation and after every duration of regrowth, t, seen in Fig. 2.10 (a–d). The dashed line is the average growth rate (i.e. the rate at which herbage is consumed ha^{-1}) in swards maintained at the same average LAI by continuous grazing (after Parsons *et al.* 1988).

Even within systems of intermittent defoliation, there has been controversy over the merits of 'frequent–lenient' versus 'infrequent–severe' defoliation. However, as the analysis in Fig. 2.11 shows, even widely contrasting combinations of frequency and severity of defoliation can give rise to similar levels of production, provided they can achieve a similar average LAI.

2.2.6 'Sward state' as a basis for grassland management

Because the average LAI of the grass crop has proved such a powerful indicator of performance, there has been increasing interest in using it, or other attributes of 'sward state' linked to it (sward height or mass), both to characterize grazing managements in research, and as a practical guideline for monitoring and controlling the supply of grass on the farm (Parsons 1984, Hodgson *et al.* 1985b, ADAS 1987). The approach has particular value in that 'sward state' is also more closely linked to the behaviour (bite size, bite rate, time spent grazing) and intake of grazing animals (Hodgson 1986, Penning 1986) than are measures of 'stocking rate' or 'herbage allowance' (Hodgson 1985, Parsons & Johnson 1986). Through this common basis for describing the performance of plants and animals, progress has also been made in understanding the complex plant−animal interactions that occur during grazing. (See also Chapter 4)

2.2.7 The stability of grazing

Changes in the intensity of continuous grazing (traditionally defined in terms of 'stocking rate') affect not only the balance between growth and utilization, but may also affect the *stability* of grazing. A mathematical model of grazing (Johnson & Parsons 1985a, b) allows examination of the effect of stocking rate, separate from the effects of seasonal changes in the environment which confound experiments in the field. The effects of stocking rate on intake ha^{-1}, and intake $animal^{-1}$, illustrated in Fig. 2.12 are consistent with the classic accounts of Mott (1960) and Owen & Ridgman (1968). However, in addition the model shows *how* these relationships arise through the effects of stocking rate on sward state.

At low stocking rates, the total amount of herbage removed is limited by the number of grazing animals. To satisfy the demand for intake, only a small proportion of the leaf tissue produced each day needs to be eaten, and so plant growth and animal intake come to a stable equilibrium at a high LAI (Fig. 2.12c). As stocking rate is increased, intake ha^{-1} rises almost linearly (Fig 2.12a) while each additional animal sustains close to its maximum intake (Fig. 2.12b). To satisfy the increased demand of the flock, or herd, a greater proportion of the leaf grown is continuously removed and photosynthesis and gross production are reduced. Nonetheless, plant growth and animal intake may again come to a stable equilibrium, albeit at a lower LAI. However, the capacity of the sward to continue to respond in this way is not unlimited.

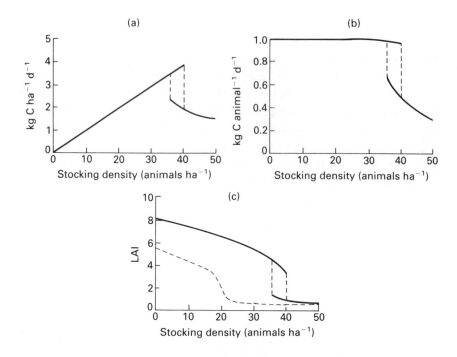

Fig. 2.12 The effect of stocking rate on: (a) intake ha^{-1}; (b) intake per animal; and (c) sward state (LAI), under continuous grazing as predicted by a model of plant/animal interaction (Johnson & Parsons 1985a), assuming a constant daily light energy receipt of 8 MJ m^{-2} d^{-1} PAR and 15°C. The dotted line in (c) is re-calculated for environmental conditions typical of September at Hurley.

As stocking rate is increased further, the situation must arise where the demand for intake cannot be satisfied by a further increase in the proportion of leaf that is removed as this is now associated with too great a decrease in photosynthesis and gross tissue production, for an adequate flow of matter to be sustained, so that the interaction between plants and animals becomes unstable (Morley 1966, Noy-Meir 1975). Under these circumstances (as when stocking rate is increased to 40 sheep ha^{-1}) the sward fails day by day to meet the demands of the flock or herd and despite little further increase in stocking rate, leaf area and productivity both decline markedly. It is only because the decline in sward state also restricts animal intake, in perennial ryegrass (Hodgson 1986, Penning 1986) that the sward is not grazed to extinction and an equilibrium is re-established at a much lower LAI at which plant growth, intake ha^{-1} and intake per animal are all markedly depressed.

This analysis shows that the relationship between stocking rate and sward state is far from simple and may differ as a result of seasonal changes in environmental conditions (Fig. 2.12c) as well as depending on whether stocking rate is increasing or decreasing (Johnson & Parsons 1985a). In Fig. 2.12c for instance, the LAI of the sward and consequently productivity, declines markedly when stocking rate is increased beyond 40 sheep ha^{-1} but is not restored until stocking rate is decreased below 36 animals. Under less favourable environmental conditions, marked changes in sward state occur at just 20 sheep ha^{-1} regardless of the direction of change in stocking rate.

The apparent simplicity of observing the effects of stocking rate on production (and so attempting to identify an optimum stocking rate) in practical trials is deceptive. The results will be a complex mixture of these features and will be difficult to interpret. Most important, the stability of the system will not have been considered.

2.2.8 Effect of management on sward morphology and development

Grassland managements have a marked effect on the structure of the grass sward. After several successive seasons of continuous grazing by sheep to maintain a low LAI, a dense sward develops with a large number of small tillers each growing at a relatively low rate. Numbers fluctuate during the course of the season but may rise to a maximum of some 30–50 000 tillers m^{-2} in mid summer (Grant et al. 1983, Parsons et al. 1983a). By contrast, swards maintained at a high average LAI, by whatever management, develop a far more open structure with a smaller number (5–10 000 m^{-2}) of larger tillers (Jones et al. 1982) each growing at a relatively high rate. As yet there is little evidence to demonstrate any benefit to grass production (ha^{-1}) from the greater number of tillers (ha^{-1}) seen under hard continuous grazing.

However, these contrasting swards undoubtedly differ in their distribution of leaf area with height and, as described earlier (section 2.1.10) this may have important consequences for plant survival. In a dense sward of small tillers, defoliation to within 3 cm of the ground leaves behind an appreciable leaf area and hence ensures the continuity of growth from current assimilation rather than from reserves. By contrast, cutting or grazing a sward of few, larger tillers to the same height leaves little leaf area and would prejudice survival if no adaptation occurred. Moreover, although the sward may develop a structure appropriate to continuous grazing only gradually, this structure can be lost very easily. When such dense swards are allowed to grow to a high LAI, (for example prior to a single heavy conservation cut) there may be a rapid and

substantial loss of tiller numbers (Parsons *et al.* 1984). This phenomenon
of self-thinning (Kays & Harper 1974) is widely recognized as beneficial
to the growth of the remaining tillers, but it can have serious consequences
for production if the same sward is returned, with a now inappropriate
structure, to continuous grazing.

Management also affects the expression of reproductive development
(Table 2.1). Under lenient management a large proportion of the over-
wintered tillers flower the following spring, leading to a marked accumulation of elongated stems in the crop. Contrasting management, such as
severe continuous grazing, have little effect on the *number* of tillers that
become reproductive. However, maintaining a low LAI in spring greatly
increases the number of new vegetative tillers produced at this time, and
so reduces the *proportion* of reproductive tillers in the sward. Moreover,
as the apices of the reproductive tillers are elevated into the grazed
horizon, they are immediately removed, leading to a marked reduction in
the amount of elongated stem tissue present (Table 2.1.).

Table 2.1. The effect of some cutting and grazing managements on sward structure and the
expression of reproductive development in a perennial ryegrass sward in June (Johnson &
Parsons 1985b).

	No. of tillers m^{-2}	% of reproductive tillers	Weight of elongated stem (g DM m^{-2})	Stem length (cm)	LAI during spring
Cutting					
Uncut until 7 June	8330	74	548.0	—	—
4−weekly cuts until 7 June	12097	69	388.2	—	—
Continuous grazing Sward surface height (cm)					
3	43464	14	44.2	1.3	1.6
6	33765	31	105.5	3.6	2.3
9	20132	47	201.7	7.1	3.8
12	14311	59	333.0	9.2	4.6

2.2.9   *Seasonal patterns of grass production and utilization*

The preceding sections show that management has a profound effect on
the amount of grass grown, and on its structure and development, as well
as on the degree to which the amount grown is harvested. As a result, it
is not possible to describe a single, seasonal pattern of production, and

then ask, how best should we utilize this production? The way in which the crop is harvested is a major determinant of the annual production achieved, and its seasonal pattern.

Nevertheless, this is exactly what has been done many times. Typically, the seasonal pattern of production of herbage harvested by a complex over-lapping sequence of 4-weekly cuts (Fig. 2.13) and supplied with abundant water and nutrients, has been taken to be the *potential* production of a particular species or variety. The effectiveness with which different managements (usually consisting of, or including, grazing) might realize this potential, that is, harvest it rather than allow it to go to waste, has then been debated. There are two serious weaknesses in this approach: (i) the performance of the sward under whatever management is proposed, will not be the same as that under the 'standard' system of over-lapping 4-weekly cuts; at its crudest, production under cutting can never accurately predict production under grazing, and (ii) the amount harvested under the 'standard' cutting system is no more a measure of the 'potential', that is of the *gross* production, of the sward than it is under any other system of management; in all cases the amount harvested represents production *net* of tissue death.

Recent developments have made it possible to determine seasonal patterns of production (herbage harvested) under grazing, and understand why they differ from the pattern established under a system of over-lapping cuts. Under this 'standard' management, the amount of grass harvested per unit time is far greater in spring than in mid summer or in

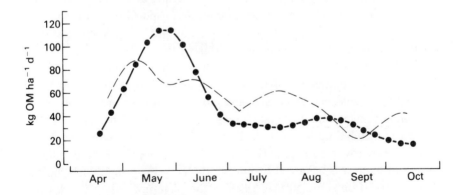

Fig. 2.13 Seasonal patterns of grass production: the amount harvested ha^{-1} under a standard 4-weekly overlapping sequence of cuts (——) (from Corrall & Fenlon 1978), and the amount harvested ha^{-1} (intake by ewes) under continuous grazing in swards maintained at close to the optimum sward surface height (– – –) (after Orr *et al*. 1988).

autumn. The production of herbage in spring benefits considerably from reproductive development, particularly the accumulation and subsequent harvest of elongated stems on reproductive tillers. However, it is the removal of the apices of these same tillers during harvest in late spring that is the cause of the poor regrowth and the 'depression' of net production in mid summer.

By contrast, the seasonal pattern of production (the amount harvested ha^{-1}) of swards maintained by a system of continuous grazing is far more uniform than under cutting (Lantinga 1986, Orr *et al.* 1988), largely because reproductive development is suppressed (Fig. 2.13). Production in spring is lower. The large numbers of vegetative tillers present at this time show few of the physiological advantages of reproductive tillers (Parsons & Robson 1980, 1981a, b, 1982). But because there are vegetative tillers to maintain the continuity of the crop through the summer, there is less evidence of 'mid summer depression'. In such a sward, maintained at a constant low LAI the seasonal pattern of net production largely reflects the seasonal pattern of light energy and temperature.

2.2.10 *Optimizing grass production and utilization, theory into practice*

Having established the theoretical basis of grass growth and utilization, we can now consider how to apply this understanding on the farm.

It is well established that the greatest amount of DM is harvested by a system of infrequent severe cutting, although the digestibility of the cut herbage may be depressed. Studies of the effect of the height of cutting suggest that maximum yield is achieved by cutting at 5 cm (Harrington & Binnie 1971), which harvests a substantial proportion of the herbage accumulated during the *previous* regrowth, and provides a suitable starting point for continued net accumulation during the *subsequent* regrowth.

Studies using fixed harvest intervals have shown that cutting every 6 weeks leads to greater yields than cutting every 3 weeks (Anslow 1967). Nevertheless, seasonal changes in the physiology of the grass crop and its environment dictate that the maximum annual yield will be achieved from a single, extended period of growth in spring, followed by several shorter periods of regrowth thereafter (Leafe *et al.* 1974). In practice, the optimum timing of harvest is achieved by cutting the crop in spring, when the ears have emerged on some 50% of tillers. This stage not only coincides with the maximum average growth rate of the crop, but avoids the marked decrease in digestibility that accompanies the later stages of reproductive development (Green *et al.* 1971). In the purely vegetative crop, the maximum average growth rate is achieved by harvesting at, or soon after, the time when some 95% of light interception is achieved (Tainton 1974).

However, maximizing DM production is unlikely to be the sole objective of the grass farmer and it is unlikely that grass swards will be harvested throughout the season by cutting. In practice, more consideration must be given to maintaining the sward for production under grazing.

In swards harvested by rotational grazing, a high proportion of reproductive stem is undesirable since animals are reluctant to graze stem tissue (Rattray 1978, Barthram & Grant 1984) and the amount harvested by grazing characteristically falls short of that which could be cut (Brougham 1970). Rotational grazing, even when grazing is severe, is ineffective in controlling the accumulation of reproductive stems if a long duration of regrowth is used. However, the average growth rate is relatively insensitive to the duration of regrowth, beyond a minimum duration of about 14–21 days, and this frequency of defoliation severely limits stem elongation. Thus, under rotational grazing, a greater number of relatively short periods of regrowth (compared to cutting) are effective in achieving close to the maximum yield of highly digestible forage and in sustaining a dense, leafy sward which animals can reliably be expected to graze (Parsons & Penning 1988).

If the grazing fails to remove a substantial proportion of the material accumulated at a given harvest, and defoliation is only lenient, then the principles described earlier (section 2.2.4) dictate that the duration of the subsequent regrowth should be reduced. Failing this, productivity is wasted, as the average growth rate will decline, and the structure of the sward deteriorate. Although once widely advocated in New Zealand (Brougham 1956, Harris 1978), frequent lenient defoliation has rarely been practised in the UK as this can lead to a long-term deterioration in sward structure (Hunt & Brougham 1967, Smetham 1975). In New Zealand, severe 'clean-up' defoliations are necessary in early spring, and again in autumn, to restore sward structure (Korte et al. 1982).

Guidelines for management are essential for effective continuous grazing, as with little net change in the weight of the grass crop, there is little indication either of the supply of grass to grazing animals, or of their performance, until it is too late. The most accurate indicator of the performance of the grass sward, as well as of the intake behaviour and the performance of grazing animals is the state of the sward; specifically its average LAI. Guidelines for management based on sward state, albeit translated into an optimum grazing height rather than an LAI, have recently been advocated for both grass and grass/clover swards (Grant et al. 1983, Parsons 1984, 1987).

Under continuous grazing by sheep, maximum production has been achieved from swards maintained at 4–6 cm, with the optimum height of grazing increased within this range as the season progresses. Similar guidelines are given for dairy and beef cattle with the optimum height increased slightly to 5—8 cm, (Hodgson *et al.* 1985b). The advantage of this approach is that in order to maintain the grazed areas of grass at the desired sward state, it is necessary to exclude the animals from a proportion of the total area in spring. This effectively increases the stocking rate and the enclosed areas may then be cut for conservation. In summer and autumn, these same areas are returned to grazing as grass growth rates decline. In this way, the system ensures the most effective use of grass on both the grazed areas and the cut areas and so the optimum integration of cutting and grazing (see MAFF dairy management calendar, and Chap. 4). As grass surplus to requirements is conserved, rather than lost by death, the balance of conserved and grazed grass production provides the best indication of over or under-stocking on the farm. This approach effectively matches the supply of grass to changes in the demand for intake by the livestock, and, because of the more uniform seasonal pattern of production on the grazed areas, the movement of animals to control grazing is kept to a minimum.

2.3   White clover

White clover is by far the most important legume of grassland in the UK (see section 2.4.2) Two key features separate white clover from the other major forage legumes (red clover, lucerne, sainfoin): (i) white clover is nearly always grown in mixtures with grass, whereas the others are typically grown in monocultures. Thus, it must coexist with a plant that is morphologically and physiologically very different from itself. (ii) White clover is stoloniferous (it spreads by means of creeping elongated stems) whereas the other forage legumes, and many of the improved grasses with which it is normally grown, are not. Thus, its habit enables it to explore the sward, invading and colonising gaps wherever and whenever they appear. To be of value to the grass farmer, white clover must be present in sufficient quantities to enable it to contribute effectively as a provider of fixed nitrogen to the community, while also significantly enhancing the digestibility of the harvested herbage (Thomson 1984).

2.3.1   *Growth of the single plant*

Following emergence from seed, white clover develops a short primary stem, carrying a rosette of trifoliate leaves and a tap root. Stolons soon arise in the axils of leaves on the primary stem and grow out close to the soil surface. The meristematic apex (growing point) of each stolon cuts off leaves in regular succession, each one attached by a petiole to its node. Each node has the potential to produce roots if it makes contact with moist soil, and to develop a daughter stolon (branch) from its axillary bud. The primary stem and tap root normally survive less than 18 months. When they die, the daughter stolons, which may themselves have branched by then, become independent with no organic connections between them (Fig. 2.14b). As each daughter stolon grows forward at the apex, so the oldest portion dies back from one rooted node to the next. In this way, the original plant fragments as it spreads through the sward.

2.3.2 *Stolon branching*

Stolon branching is essential for the initial establishment of clover in the sward, and to ensure its survival by replacing stolons that are lost. The apical portion of the stolon may be damaged or severed by the grazing animal through treading or pulling. The apex itself may succumb to pests which attack young developing leaves, disease or extreme environmental conditions such as low temperatures. Branching enables the plant rapidly to colonize bare patches that appear in the sward. Moreover, it enables the plant to respond to changes in the environment or management. For example, a sward adapted to continuous hard grazing tends to have a high population of small, compact stolons bearing small, short-petioled leaves. In a tall dense sward, there will be fewer, more elongated, stolons bearing larger leaves on longer petioles. This response to management parallels that described earlier for grass (section 2.2.8). A change in management may lead to a decline in clover growing point numbers when, for instance, a previously hard grazed sward is allowed to grow unchecked, many small young stolons die and few replace them. Or there may be a build up of growing point numbers as a previously dense crop adapts to continuous hard grazing, with many axillary buds growing out into new stolons.

Within any particular management system, there will be seasonal (and shorter-term) fluctuations in growing point numbers, generally, a rise in spring and a fall in late autumn. But, if the management is sustained over a number of years so that the mixed community becomes adapted to it, those fluctuations will be around a stable base line population. This means that each clover stolon (just as each grass tiller) will produce *on average*, only one daughter before it dies. This principle applies as much to managements (or varieties) that sustain a high stolon population, as to those that support few stolons.

Casual observation in the sward would appear to conflict with this conclusion, in that many mature stolons can be seen bearing several daughters. However (unless we are observing a transitional increase in stolon numbers) this can mean only than an even larger number of immature stolons die without themselves having produced *any* daughters. This is very likely; a newly initiated stolon is totally dependent on its parent, and very vulnerable. Many unbranched nodes bear scars indicating where young stolons or buds have aborted at an early stage of development (Dutta 1988). Those few new stolons that survive and go on to produce their own daughter, however, must have a greatly enhanced life expectancy and will, very likely, branch again several times. Thus, the population may well consist of two classes of stolons, a large class of short-lived unbranched stolons, and a much smaller class of long-lived stolons that bear several daughters. Very few stolons may actually produce one daughter, and one daughter only, but the *average* will still be one.

2.3.3 *Axillary bud development*

There is evidence that an axillary bud does not develop into a stolon until the leaf at that node, and the next youngest leaf, are both fully expanded. Moreover, the development of an axillary bud may depend on the bud itself, or the leaf that subtends it, being exposed to light (Davies, personal communication).

On an unshaded and undefoliated stolon, growing in otherwise favourable conditions, some ten or more live leaves are maintained and virtually all axillary buds develop into daughter stolons (Fig. 2.14b) but this situation rarely obtains in the field. In dense swards, little light reaches the stolons which then (like grass tillers) bear only two or three fully expanded leaves each. Thus, there is only a short period when a node is sufficiently mature for its axillary bud to develop, and during which the leaf at that node remains alive to intercept light. Not surprisingly, only a small proportion of axillary buds grow into stolon branches.

In a continuously hard-grazed sward, although leaves are removed at an early stage in their development, the stolons are well illuminated. Thus, virtually all sufficiently mature nodes might be expected to develop daughter stolons. The fact that they do not implies that other factors restrict branching. Perhaps the supply of assimilates from the severely reduced leaf area is insufficient to support many daughters; perhaps buds initiate but then abort unobserved. An inadequate supply of inorganic nutrients, particularly phosphorus (P) and potassium (K) can also restrict branching, as can a shortage of nitrogen (N) in grass.

Rooting at stolon nodes is important to the success of stolon branches. Although, if root growth at a particular node is suppressed, the ability of the associated bud to develop into a daughter stolon is not impaired, the subsequent growth of the stolon branch may be. The relationship between a stolon branch and the roots at its subtending node appears particularly close. A high proportion of the carbon fixed by the young stolon goes to those particular roots (Chapman, personal communication) which, in turn, may supply the stolon with water and nutrients, particularly N.

In the spring, some axillary buds develop into flowers (Fig. 2.14b). White clover is a long-day plant, and requires a critical daylength of greater than 13.5−15.0 hours, depending on variety, before it will flower. Persistent clover varieties (e.g. Kent, S100 and S184) also have a winter (low temperature and/or short day) requirement; less persistent varieties do not. About half the buds that experience the appropriate sequence of environmental conditions subsequently flower. In grasses, the inflorescence is terminal and prevents further production of leaves by that particular shoot. In clover, the flowers are axillary. Thus, the shoot apex continues to produce leaves.

2.3.4 *Leaf production*

Clover stolons produce leaves at a rate of one every 3−4 days in favourable conditions, about double that of most grasses. The rate of appearance of leaves is relatively unaffected by cutting, slowed by water stress, and brought almost to a halt by low winter temperatures — leaf appearance in white clover is more sensitive to low temperature than in grass.

Clover leaves develop from primordia, with the distinction between petiole and leaflets evident at a very early stage. Unlike grass leaves, which extend in a linear fashion from the basal meristem, clover leaflets expand in two dimensions, with cell division and expansion taking place uniformly over the surface of the leaflets which remain folded until expansion is almost complete. Carlson (1966) has defined ten stages (scored 0.1−1.0) in the externally visible development of clover leaves (Fig. 2.14a)

As with leaf appearance, leaf expansion is dramatically reduced over winter, with small leaves of low specific area (area per unit weight) produced on short petioles. With high temperatures or low light intensities, large, thin typically 'shade' leaves are produced on elongated petioles.

Petiole extension comes from a meristem positioned just below the leaflets which moves up with them; it starts early in the development of

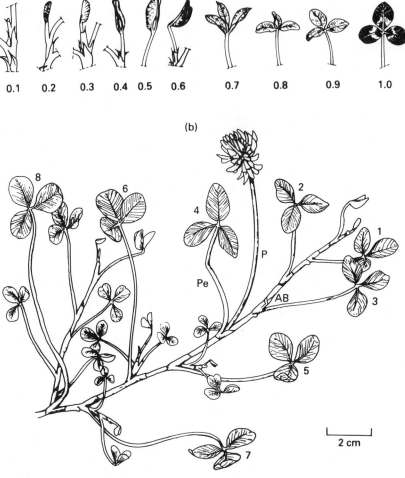

Fig. 2.14 (a) Ten stages in the development of a leaf of *Ladino* clover (from Carlson 1966, redrawn by Thomas 1987a). (b) An unshaded and undefoliated parent stolon of white clover bearing eight fully expanded leaves (numbered 1−8, youngest to oldest). Note, the axillary bud (AB) in the axil of leaf 3; the flower on its peduncle (P) in the axil of leaf 4, itself on its petiole (Pe); young daughter stolons in the axils of leaves 5−7, and an older daughter in the axil of leaf 8 (after Thomas 1987b).

the leaf, and is rapid. Final petiole length depends greatly on the light environment within the sward, with a high degree of overlap between supposedly short *versus* long-petioled varieties. When a sward grows without interruption (whether from seed or after a harvest), and the light conditions worsen at the base of the increasingly dense canopy, successive leaves are borne on progressively longer petioles. Thus, each leaf in turn is positioned in high light close to the top of the canopy by the time its leaflets are unfolded (Dennis & Woledge 1985).

2.3.5 *The performance of clover, relative to grass, in mixed swards*

Although in some parts of the world, e.g. New Zealand, mixed grass/ clover swards are the norm, they have not been so widely used in the UK. Clover has been seen as unpredictable, and the mixtures as difficult to manage. Although there have been numerous agronomic studies of mixed swards, these have not sought to establish the physiological mechanisms that underlie and control the balance of grass and clover in mixtures, and so have limited application. Current work seeks to correct this deficiency.

It used to be thought that the main reason why clover often disappears from infrequently defoliated swards (leaving aside effects of disease and drought) is that it is 'shaded out' by the grass, particularly if high levels of N fertilizer are given. However, this is *not* the case under UK conditions, with UK forage species. Here the clover almost invariably disposes a greater proportion of its leaf area in the upper layers of the canopy than does the grass, and so is not shaded out by it.

As with grass, the photosynthetic potential of a clover leaf depends on the environmental conditions it experiences while its photosynthetic apparatus is being laid down. In particular, development in low light impairs photosynthetic efficiency. Fortunately, even clover leaves whose development begins in low light at the base of a dense sward, reach high light at a sufficiently early stage (Carlson, 0.7−0.8) for their photosynthetic capacity to be unimpaired (Fig. 2.6c). In this respect, petiole elongation in clover acts in the same way as elongation of the flowering stem in grasses (Fig. 2.6b). There is no sign of the progressive decline in the ability to fix carbon shown by successive grass leaves produced on unelongated stems in an increasingly dense *vegetative* sward (Fig. 2.6a).

Once the photosynthetic potential of the clover leaf has been established, its realization depends very largely (as it does in the grass plant) on light and temperature; high light, and temperatures of up to about 25°C, enhance photosynthesis. Since young fully expanded clover leaves are both photosynthetically efficient, and tend to begin their active lives in high light at the top of the canopy, they also tend to have high initial rates of photosynthesis (Dennis & Woledge 1985). As a result, clover holds its own with grass during the regrowth of high N swards, and does very much better than its N deficient companion in low N swards (Davidson &

Robson 1985, Davidson *et al.* 1986, Woledge 1988). Indeed, in terms of its ability to intercept light, and to make efficient use of it, clover would seem more likely to 'shade out' grass than the other way round.

Of course, having a higher proportion of its leaves in the upper layers of the canopy makes the clover more liable to defoliation. Proportionately more of its leaf surface is removed at harvest, than of the grass, and proportionately less is left behind. This applies whether the crop is cut or grazed. While some grazing animals might actively select clover in preference to grass, a greater clover content in the diet than in the sward is not proof of this, it may simply mean, that proportionately more of the clover leaf is above the height to which the sward is grazed.

Although, when a dense sward is harvested, clover loses more leaf area than does grass, it recovers quickly. The leaves that are harvested are those with long petioles. Those left behind are a mixture of young leaves whose petioles have not yet elongated sufficiently to carry them into the harvested horizon, and perhaps some old leaves which were produced when the sward was open and petioles were short. Recent work has shown that if all other expanded leaves are removed, the photosynthetic capacity of the youngest is enhanced by about 5–10%. Similarly, if the leaf left behind is old, with a photosynthetic capacity that has declined to 50% of its peak value, that decline can be reversed, at least temporarily (Chapman, personal communication). No parallel effect is observed in grasses. Thus, the clover recovers rapidly from defoliation and restores its parity with the grass (high N swards), or its advantage over it (low N swards), by the next harvest.

In *low N* swards, under a wide variety of managements from infrequent cutting to close continuous grazing by sheep, the proportion of clover tends to increase, quite consistently, over the growing season. Some managements, particularly continuous grazing by sheep, certainly restrict the growth of clover in that the proportion of clover increases far less than under cutting. But they do not reduce the rate of clover growth below the rate of grass growth — if they did, no increase in the *proportion* of clover would occur.

Where clover does appear, it is vulnerable outside the main growing season, over winter, when no defoliation may take place. Leaf growth and petiole extension in clover are reduced more by low temperatures than is leaf growth in grass. Not only is more new tissue produced by the grass but, at this time of year only, it may overtop the clover. Perhaps most important of all, a greater proportion of leaf is lost from clover, over winter, than is the case with grass. As a result, the clover content of the sward is generally lower each year, leaving the winter, than entering it. This annual setback to the growth of current clover varieties, relative to grass, inevitably erodes the advantage clover builds up over the main growing season in low N swards.

In *high N* swards, clover still does surprisingly well over the main growing season. It takes up and uses the applied N very effectively and, hence, ceases to rely on symbiotic N fixation, an energy expensive process requiring a constant supply of assimilates which otherwise go to increase the growth of the clover itself. As a result, clover plants supplied with fertilizer N can grow faster, other things being equal, than those relying on atmospheric N. However, the application of fertilizer N to mixed swards increases the growth of the grass far more than it does the growth of the clover. (Without an external supply of N the grass is grossly deficient, the clover is not.) As a result, in relative terms, fertilizer application favours the grass component of mixed swards although, the clover can just about hold its own over the main growing season.

Some important aspects of the effects of inorganic N on clover remain to be resolved. Nevertheless, without a concomitant advantage to clover during the summer, the disadvantage it suffers over the winter must tend, in the long term, to reduce its proportion in high N swards and eventually, perhaps, eliminate clover from them, as has often been observed in practice. Of course, applying high levels of N fertilizer to mixed swards nullifies one of the main advantages of including clover in the mixture in the first place, namely, its ability to fix atmospheric N and hence, reduce the need for expensive fertilizer N.

2.3.6   *Optimizing clover content on the farm*

The evidence, to date, strongly suggests that the physiological principles that govern the input of carbon to mixed swards, its output in respiration and tissue death and, hence, the net rate of tissue production, are fundamentally the same as for grass monocultures. Thus, the principles for optimizing herbage production based on maintaining a particular sward state (e.g. height), again apply. The problem is how to manage the sward to maintain an optimum clover content, consistent with maintaining a high level of production.

There is reasonable evidence that N fixation ha^{-1} increases, at least initially, with an increase in the proportion of legume in the mixture. Cutting trials suggest that herbage production, in the absence of applied N, increases as the proportion of clover increases, with a possible maximum at a clover content of around 40%. Growth rates of unweaned and weaned lambs also increase with an increase in the proportion of clover in the diet over the range 0 to 100% clover (Gibb & Treacher 1983, 1984). However, continuous stocking managements (section 2.2.3) that are designed to utilize the greatest proportion of what is grown, require that a grass/clover sward (like an all grass one) is grazed hard to maintain a small leaf area (low sward height) even though this reduces the clover content of the sward, and of the diet, to some 10–20% (Parsons *et al.* 1987). But under grazing (although not under cutting) much of the nitrogen fixed by the clover, and harvested by the animal, is returned to the sward in dung and urine. There, it supports the growth of the grass and may again be harvested and returned to the sward. Continuously grazed swards, containing as little as 10–20% of clover, by weight, can achieve levels of animal production equivalent to that of grass receiving some $200\,kg\,N\,ha^{-1}$ (Parsons *et al.* 1987), perhaps as a result of this rapid recycling of N between the animal and the sward, and the low losses of N from swards containing clover (see section 2.4.11).

Early grazing studies tended to focus on rotational, rather than continuous, grazing because evidence from cutting trials showed an increased clover content following infrequent (4–6 weeks) defoliation. Typically, the swards were grazed by ewes and lambs, with the lambs allowed to 'creep' through the fence to graze ahead of the ewes. This system achieved clover contents of close to 50% at the end of each regrowth period, and excellent lamb growth rates (Newton *et al.* 1985). But rotational grazing is not the only way to manage mixed swards successfully. Acceptable levels of clover can be maintained in continuously grazed swards providing both under and over-grazing are prevented. The way to achieve this is *not* to use a set number of animals on a set area of land (set-stocking), seasonal fluctuations in gross photosynthesis and gross tissue production will inevitably lead to periods of over and under grazing if the number of animals is constant. Instead, the desired sward state should be maintained by varying the area grazed (and hence varying the stocking rate on the grazed area). Detailed studies have provided management guidelines to achieve this in mixed swards which are, to date, very similar to those already described for grass (Parsons 1987, and see section 2.2.10).

2.4   Fertilizer and soil conditions

The main factors affecting grass growth are light, temperature, available water and nitrogen. Taking 6°C as the threshold soil temperature for grass growth, and correcting for altitude, maps have been constructed showing the mean length of the growing season in Britain. The coastal areas of Devon, Cornwall, south west Wales and Anglesey have a mean of above 300 growing days while large areas of lowland England have around 250 growing days decreasing to around 200 days in the more elevated areas of the Pennines, the Welsh hills and Scotland.

All green plants require water since nutrients are taken up, and physiological processes take place, in solution. Stomata remain open during daylight if there is adequate water within the leaf. They close, bringing photosynthesis to a halt, if a shortage of water occurs. As long as they remain open transpiration of water from the plant continues. The rate of transpiration is a function of the evaporative capacity of the environment and can be calculated from the duration of bright sunshine, mean air temperature, humidity and wind speed (MAFF 1954a), assuming a continuous cover of green vegetation with adequate soil moisture in the root zone. Transpiration so calculated is known as the *potential* evapo-transpiration. *Actual* transpiration can be reduced by low soil moisture conditions or an incomplete cover of green vegetation. Both are measured in terms of a depth of water. Maps of potential transpiration (MAFF 1954a, b) show average summer values ranging from 460 mm in Essex and Kent to 400 mm in northern England and Wales, whereas rainfall ranges from about 280 mm to over 380 mm for these areas, respectively. Water held in the soil in the root zone at the start of a drying cycle can meet about 75 mm of transpiration needs. Even so, irrigation would increase grass production 8 years out of 10 in areas south and east of a line from Dorset to the Wash, and 5 years out of 10 in a further area north and west to a line from Exeter to Scarborough.

Grassland farming involves a wide range of species, soils and climatic conditions and their interaction with management gives rise to a wide range of nutrient conditions and demands. All soils are inadequate sources of N for productive grass growth, but many provide the bulk of P and K demands, especially when these have been supplied as fertilizers in the past or when animal excreta have been returned to the sward. Tradition-ally, soil analysis has been used to indicate nutrient status and there will always be a need for soil analyses to identify marked deficiencies, but herbage analysis may be a more efficient indicator of nutrient require-ments for the healthy growth of both plants and animals. Requirements for nutrients will also depend upon whether swards are established or are being resown, whether they are cut for conservation (with the consequent removal of many nutrients) or grazed and, if the swards are cut, whether nutrients are being returned in animal excreta as applied slurries.

2.4.1 *Drainage*

Grassland may tolerate a degree of imperfect drainage which is not acceptable for arable crops. Nevertheless, poorly drained soils are lower in 'preferred' species (perennial ryegrass, cocksfoot, timothy, white clover) than better drained soils, and poor drainage is a factor contributing to the deterioration of sown swards (Hopkins & Green 1979). In badly drained situations, *Deschampsia caespitosa*, *Alopecuris geniculatus*, *Juncus spp.* and creeping buttercup (*Ranunculus repens*) are prevalent. Poor drainage limits the use of grassland in wet periods, and greatly increases soil compaction and poaching thereby accelerating sward deterioration. Rarely is all grassland on a farm poorly drained and much can be done through the use of better drained fields to carry the livestock during wet periods.

2.4.2 *Irrigation*

There is little differential response to irrigation between the commonly sown species, ryegrass, cocksfoot, timothy (Stiles 1965), but tall fescue is less susceptible to drought (Garwood & Sheldrick 1978). White clover is more susceptible than grasses, and responds better to irrigation. Lucerne shows little response to irrigation in summers with a soil water deficit of 150 mm, and it is unlikely that droughts of a severity to affect lucerne occur in the UK with sufficient regularity to warrant irrigation.

Growth is greatly restricted when soil water deficits exceed 40−50 mm, a quantity of water available in the top 300 mm of many soils. Grass roots can extract water from a further 300−600 mm depth (Garwood & Williams 1967a). The check on growth when water is obtained from the deeper soil horizons can be reversed if N is placed in those horizons (Garwood & Williams 1967b), but this is not possible in practice. It has, however, led to partial irrigation with the use of N fertilizer to enable some productive use of subsoil water (Garwood & Tyson 1973).

In ryegrass−white clover swards, the response to irrigation varies widely within the range $15-25\,kg\,DM\,mm^{-1}$ of water ha^{-1} in years with a potential water deficit greater that 100 mm. Irrigation generally increases yield by the same amount as an application of $300\,kg\,ha^{-1}$ of N. The benefits of irrigation are not only in increased productivity. The more uniform production of forage between years allows more accurate planning of stock carrying capacity and the area needed for conservation and, thus, permits a reduction in the safety margin allowed against the risk of drought. The cost of irrigation is high and it is seldom economical to install it for grassland alone.

2.4.3 Soil pH and liming

The pH of soils under grassland in Britain ranges from markedly acidic (pH < 4.0) to alkaline (pH > 7.0). Plant production is reduced at the extremes of this range through an excess of toxic ions (e.g. aluminium (Al), and manganese (Mn)) under acid conditions, and reduced nutrient availability (e.g. P) under alkaline conditions. The most productive species require a minimum pH of 5.5 and current recommendations are that grassland soils are limed to maintain pH 6.0, especially for swards in which white clover is an important component. On most non-calcareous soils periodic liming is needed to maintain an appropriate pH. Sensitive species such as lucerne and sainfoin require a pH of 6.5 and are generally grown only on calcareous soils. Where high rates of N application are used, acidity can build up rapidly at the top of the soil profile, especially in high rainfall areas. Because of the slow reactivity of liming agents, and their lack of mixing with the soil matrix, rates of change of pH down the soil profile are slow and regular liming is better than large infrequent doses.

2.4.4 Soil nutrient status

In England and Wales, the quantities of available nutrients are expressed as indices, ranging from 0 (deficient) to 9 (excess). At soil P and K index 2 or above, it is unlikely that economic responses of grassland to applied P and K would occur. Under these conditions the recommended applications are designed to maintain soil nutrient status. However, increasing rates of N application promote plant growth and the uptake of other nutrients. Recent work (Prins *et al.* 1986) suggests that, in relation to herbage N, P and K concentrations are often below the levels required for maximum grass production.

The return of nutrients in animal slurries helps maintain high herbage yields especially where that return is uniform. However, slurries often vary in composition, and knowledge of the availability of the nutrients and of the changes that occur after application is inadequate. In mixed swards, an adequate supply of P, K, S and, to some extent, calcium (Ca) and magnesium (Mg) is critical for the maintenance of vigorous clover growth, for efficient and adequate fixation of N, and to maintain an appropriate mineral balance for the ruminant in the herbage consumed.

2.4.5 *Phosphorus*

On grassland that has regularly received P, and where soil analysis reveals no deficiency, maintenance dressings of $14-18\,kg\,P$ $(32-41\,kg\,P_2O_5)$ $ha^{-1}y^{-1}$ should suffice. Phosphates are neither leached from soils to any great extent, nor taken up by grasses or legumes in excess of their needs. Thus, P may be applied every second or third year, in appropriately larger amounts, without fear of loss or luxury uptake. An additional input of $4\,kg\,P\,ha^{-1}$, t^{-1} herbage DM removed, should be adequate to maintain the soil P status, which must be checked by periodic soil analysis.

On old, neglected grasslands or upland pastures where little or no phosphate has been used, or where soil analysis shows a marked deficiency, dressings of $30-45\,kg\,P\,ha^{-1}$ are needed to achieve rapidly an improvement. Inputs during the next $3-4$ years could be reduced to the maintenance level. Fertilizer phosphate, even if water soluble, is rapidly converted into insoluble forms that do not move in the soil, although they continue to be available to the plant. Thus, heavy dressings, applied to correct initial deficiencies, must be cultivated into the soil.

2.4.6 *Potassium*

A maintenance plus replacement policy for K is not as satisfactory as for P for several reasons. Soil analysis indicates the amount of exchangeable (plant-available) K present, but soils may also contain large reserves of non-exchangeable K which replenish the exchangeable K as the latter is taken up by plants. Normal soil analyses do not reveal the rate at which K becomes available, and this varies greatly with soil type. Soils high in clay content release K at a rate sufficient to meet the needs of highly productive grass, whereas on light, sandy soils the supply of exchangeable K is inadequate. K can be taken up by grasses and legumes in excess of their requirements, i.e. luxury uptake. A K content of $20\,g\,kg^{-1}$ herbage DM is considered adequate to maintain maximum production, a lesser content implies deficiency, and a greater content that fertilizer is being wasted. Moreover, high K levels in herbage affect the availability of Mg to plants and may induce hypomagnesaemia in animals. Application of K to grassland should be closely related to current needs, and guided by soil and herbage analyses.

Soils deficient in K may require from 60 to $80\,kg\,K\,(72-96\,kg\,K_2O)$ ha^{-1} as an initial dressing. Subsequent dressings should aim to meet production requirements. Under grazing, virtually all the K is returned in the excreta, although its spatial distribution may be uneven, and dairy cows will deposit some away from the grazed area. From 15 to 40 kg K $ha^{-1}y^{-1}$ should meet the needs of grazed grassland, the higher amounts being applied to pastures receiving high quantities of N. For cut swards, about 20 kg K is needed t^{-1} DM harvested. Alternatively, the input of K on cut swards may be adjusted to the use of fertilizer N. Allowing for normal responses of grass swards to N, each 3 kg of N needs to be supported by 2 kg K, or by 1.5 kg K on soils known to be rich in K. If, after following the above programme, periodic sampling reveals levels of K in the herbage significantly in excess of 20 g kg^{-1} DM (Clement & Hopper 1968), rates of application should be reduced.

2.4.7 *Magnesium*

Applications of N fertilizer generally increase herbage Mg concentrations, although changes in the concentrations of both N and K may influence the absorption of the Mg by cattle. For example, at high K concentrations, Mg absorption may decrease and hypomagnesaemia result. In such cases, the most efficient means of increasing animal intake is by providing a Mg enriched diet.

2.4.8 *Sulphur*

Sulphur is essential for both plants and animals. Reduced industrial emissions of sulphur dioxide (and therefore decreased inputs to soils), coupled with the increased use at high rates of high analysis N fertilizers, containing little or no S, may result in widespread imbalances, especially in wet years. It is claimed that the N:S ratio (10:1 is about optimum) is much more critical than total S concentration so far as utilization by livestock is concerned.

2.4.9 *Minor and trace elements*

A deficiency of molybdenum (Mo) in white clover growing under acidic hill conditions has been reported: lime application cured this. In lowland Britain, there are no recorded trace element deficiencies that affect grass growth, although unrecognized deficiencies may possibly exist on some sites. Dramatic changes in productivity have followed the correction of such deficiencies in Australia and elsewhere.

Although few effects on plant growth have been recorded, contents of certain trace elements in herbage may be too low for animal requirements.

Low copper (Cu) contents have led to sub-clinical Cu deficiency in cattle, which is exacerbated by raised levels of Mo and S (see Chapter 3). Although selenium (Se) has not yet been found to be essential for plant growth, it is required by animals. Contents in herbages from a wide range of soils and environments may be inadequate for the healthy growth of ruminants, especially sheep. Vigilance is needed to ensure that imbalances of these and other elements (both essential and potentially toxic) are not promoted by particular management practices.

2.4.10 *Nitrogen*

When water and other minerals are non-limiting, grass yield responds markedly to N application. Fertilizer N has therefore been used in increasing amounts in intensively managed livestock systems to enhance profitability, either by increasing forage yield or reducing production costs. The general form of the response curve (Fig. 2.15) to fertilizer N is well established from trials throughout Europe (Van Burg *et al.* 1981), and is found when either herbage or animal production variables are recorded (Baker 1986b). After an initial linear phase, the response diminishes until a maximum yield is reached. The point at which the herbage

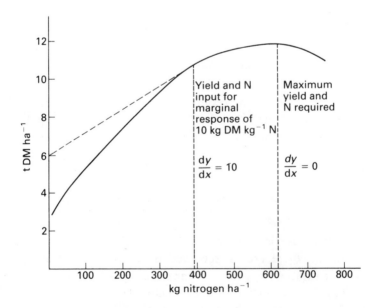

Fig. 2.15 Mean DM yields of grass and grass−clover swards in response to N fertilizer. Curve for grass sward (——); and curve for grass−white clover sward (−−−) (after Morrison *et al.* 1980).

response falls to $10 \, \text{kg} \, \text{DM} \, \text{kg}^{-1}$ N is usually defined as the optimum fertilizer rate. The slope of the response is strongly influenced by the supply of N from the soil (which in old grazed swards may be at least $100-150 \, \text{kg} \, \text{N} \, \text{ha}^{-1} \, \text{y}^{-1}$), available water, season, and the white clover content of the sward.

The inclusion of clover often results in yields double those of pure grass swards receiving no fertilizer N (Fig. 2.15) because of the ability of the clover to fix atmospheric N. With low fertilizer N, input from fixation is thought to be in the range of $100-200 \, \text{kg} \, \text{N} \, \text{ha}^{-1} \, \text{y}^{-1}$. Short-falls in yield that occur in early spring can be overcome by an application of up to about $50 \, \text{kg} \, \text{N} \, \text{ha}^{-1}$ without restricting the subsequent ability of the clover to fix N. Higher levels of fertilizer N ($150-200 \, \text{kg} \, \text{N} \, \text{ha}^{-1} \, \text{y}^{-1}$) drastically reduce N fixation and, eventually, the clover content of the sward.

Data from a major N trial carried out on uniformly managed grass monocultures, grown at 21 sites, and cut at monthly intervals (Morrison *et al.* 1980), support the general form of response noted in Fig. 2.15, but they also show great variation from site to site (Table 2.2). The mean maximum yield of $11.9 \, \text{t} \, \text{ha}^{-1}$ was achieved with an input of $624 \, \text{kg} \, \text{N} \, \text{ha}^{-1}$. In practice, maximum yield is of little interest because of the low DM returns for N applied as the maximum is approached. As N input was increased from low values, the DM : N ratio fell, reaching 10 : 1 at an input of $386 \, \text{kg} \, \text{N} \, \text{ha}^{-1}$ and a yield of $10.9 \, \text{t} \, \text{ha}^{-1}$. Going from this point to the maximum yield brought in only 1 t extra DM, but required an extra $238 \, \text{kg} \, \text{N}$ (Morrison *et al.* 1980). Extensive use is made of data from national trials such as this to predict herbage yields and thereby plan stocking rates (Corrall *et al.* 1982) (see Table 8.3). In the main, these predictions are for sown grass swards, and there is little information for either permanent pastures or grass/clover swards, although it is clear that the latter show a lower response to fertilizer N than grass monocultures (Baker 1986b).

Considerable interest has been expressed in the T-sum approach i.e.

Table 2.2. Mean annual yields and responses to fertilizer N (4-year averages).

	Mean	Range
Maximum DM yield ($\text{t} \, \text{ha}^{-1}$)	11.9	6.5–15.0
N required for maximum yield ($\text{kg} \, \text{ha}^{-1}$)	624	446–750
DM yield at 10:1, $\text{kg} \, \text{DM} : \text{kg} \, \text{N}$ ($\text{t} \, \text{ha}^{-1}$)	10.9	5.4–14.4
N required for 10:1 limit ($\text{kg} \, \text{ha}^{-1}$)	386	260–530
Response $\text{kg}^{-1} \, \text{N}$ at $300 \, \text{kg} \, \text{ha}^{-1}$ ($\text{kg} \, \text{DM}$)	23	14–29
DM yield with no N ($\text{t} \, \text{ha}^{-1}$)	2.6	0.6–5.7
% recovery of fertilizer N at $300 \, \text{kg} \, \text{ha}^{-1}$	70	51–87

applying fertilizer when the sum of the average daily temperatures above 0°C since January 1st reaches 200°C. Some investigations (Van Burg *et al.* 1981, Archer 1985) indicate that the system lacks reliability, and is little better than identifying a calendar date for a particular site from average temperature data. However, there is usually a 2–5 week period within which N application will produce yields within 90% of the maximum. On most farms, T-sum 200 will fall within this 2–5 week period and so is a reasonable guide to the timing of fertilizer application. Responses to fertilizer N are often better in early rather than mid season, and although the pattern of N application has little effect on total yield, especially at higher levels of N, it may influence the seasonal pattern.

Much research on N responses has been based on cut systems. Under grazing, responses may be much influenced by the returns of N in dung and urine. We would expect either higher yields at the same fertilizer N input, maximum responses at lower rates of addition, or higher concentrations of N in the herbage in grazed rather than in cut swards.

With sheep, response to fertilizer N up to $200 \, kg \, N \, ha^{-1}$ was enhanced by grazing compared to cutting (Shaw *et al.* 1966). Somewhat similar responses, measured through the animal, have been reported by Holmes (1968) and by Gordon (1974a) for dairy cows, and by Holmes (1974b) for beef cattle. These showed a linear response in grazing days up to $300 \, kg \, N \, ha^{-1}$ for cows and $500 \, kg \, N \, ha^{-1}$ for growing beef cattle, with declining responses above these levels, but with considerable variation around the response equations. In recent trials, although the results were again much more variable under continuous cattle grazing than under cutting, yields were greater under grazing than under cutting at a given level of fertilizer N (Baker 1986a).

Although, recycled and returned N (and other nutrients) might be expected to increase herbage yields under grazing, other factors, e.g. selection, treading damage and fouling of herbage by mud and faeces, might reduce it. Further, reservations must be expressed about some of the techniques used, in some of the studies, to estimate herbage yields under grazing.

2.4.11 *Nitrogen losses from grassland*

The use of fertilizer N is economically attractive and allows flexibility in grassland management, but, much of the applied N may be lost, and this loss represents a potential environmental risk as well as being inefficient. Whilst 65–90% of the applied fertilizer N can be recovered in herbage from well managed cut swards, poor conversion of the N in herbage (either grazed or conserved) by ruminants results in much of the ingested N being returned to pastures (either directly or in slurries) in forms which are easily lost.

Balance sheets of the type shown in Table 2.3 indicate the major forms of losses, their extent and the differences that result from different managements. The three major processes responsible for loss of inorganic N are: (1) denitrification, the conversion of nitrate to the gases N_2 and nitrous oxide by bacteria under anaerobic conditions; (2) volatilization of ammonia gas resulting from hydrolysis of urea in animal excreta or in fertilizers; and (3) leaching, the physical removal of excess nitrate in waters draining from the root zone into ground waters and rivers. From an environmental standpoint, leaching is probably of most concern.

The extent of the losses and the factors influencing them are the subject of much recent research (Jarvis *et al.* 1987). Some losses, especially those resulting from denitrification, can be avoided by using ammonium based and urea fertilizers, and by timing fertilizer application to avoid anaerobic soil conditions. However, the avoidance of losses from the mobile forms of N that may have accumulated at the end of the grazing season is more difficult. Although recent studies have indicated that N

Table 2.3. N balances for three contrasting swards on a freely drained soil at Hurley, with two of the swards grazed by beef cattle (Whitehead *et al.* 1985).

	$kg\,N\,ha^{-1}y^{-1}$		
	Cut ryegrass	Grazed ryegrass	Grazed ryegrass/ white clover
Inputs			
Fertilizer	420	420	0
N fixation by clover	0	0	160
Atmosphere	15	15	15
Total	435	435	175
Output			
Herbage or animal production	300	29	23
Ammonia volatilization	0	80	10
Denitrification	20	40	4
Leaching	29	160	23
Storage			
In soil organic matter	90	110	110
Total	439	419	170

losses from clover based pastures may be lower than those from heavily fertilized grass (Table 2.3), the behaviour of fixed N and its potential environmental impact must be considered in the same way as that of fertilizer N. Greater understanding and control of the various interacting processes within the nitrogen cycle, and of the impact of different management systems on these processes, are required to maximize the efficiency of N use and minimize environmental risk.

2.5   Species for sowing

Plant breeders select within grass and clover species, for types that possess desirable characteristics such as yield, seasonal productivity, persistency and environmental tolerance. Emphasis is currently on quality (digestibility, sugar content) and on improved compatability between grass and clover when grown in mixtures.

Mean heading date (ear emergence) is used to classify grass varieties (NIAB 1986). Within a species, early heading is usually associated with early spring growth and a less densely tillered more upright plant. Later heading varieties tend to tiller more, and to be prostrate and persistent. Red clover and lucerne varieties are classified according to time of flowering, and white clover according to leaf size.

2.5.1   *Grasses*

Perennial ryegrass

Perennial ryegrass (*Lolium perenne*) is the most widely sown grass in British agriculture. It is easy to establish and develops rapidly into a closed sward capable of withstanding grazing. It recovers well from defoliation and when utilized regularly under medium-high soil fertility, both the yield of DM and digestibility are usually greater than for most other species. Under infertile conditions it tends to produce stemmy growth, and swards may be invaded by 'less desirable' grasses. Production is reliable except under very dry conditions. A severe winter can cause damage depending on the variety. Currently, 34 varieties are recommended for use in England and Wales (NIAB 1987a) and a larger number in Scotland (The Scottish Agricultural Colleges 1986). The varieties are classified into three main groups (early, intermediate and late) based on heading date. In central England, heading dates range from about 7 May to 15 June, and in Scotland from 17 May to 28 June. Low temperatures during the 2 months prior to heading can delay it by up to a week particularly in early varieties. Judicious choice of varieties, grown pure and cut in sequence, can allow a period of 3 weeks for silage making from grass of high digestibility (NIAB 1987b). Similarly, the establishment of a single sward from a mixture of ryegrass varieties, may extend the grazing season somewhat. Perennial ryegrass swards predominate in intensive high N systems; combined with white clover, they may become increasingly important in moderate output/low N input systems.

Italian ryegrass

Italian ryegrass (*Lolium multiflorum*) is easy to establish from seed, which can be sown as late as October in milder areas. It develops rapidly to give a vigorous, high yielding but relatively short-lived (2–3 years) sward. It starts growth about 2 weeks earlier in the spring than perennial ryegrass, but heads about a week later. Early spring grazing can be followed by a leafy conservation cut. Mid season growth tends to be stemmy, can become unpalatable, and is best used for conservation. Autumn growth should be removed by grazing to improve winter hardiness. The species is best under intensive cropping with high levels of fertilizer N.

Hybrid ryegrasses

Hybrid ryegrasses (*Lolium perenne* × *multiflorum*) have been produced by breeders in an attempt to combine the vigorous growth of Italian ryegrass with the longevity of perennial ryegrass. They are increasingly included in short and medium term ryegrass swards, and now account for 6% of the grass seed sown. Most varieties are tetraploid and resemble the Italian parent. They combine early spring growth and a heavy conservation cut, with some of the leafier summer grazing and persistence of the perennial parent. Current breeding is placing emphasis on recovery growth and persistence.

Tetraploid varieties of perennial and Italian ryegrass

These tend to have slightly higher yields, higher sugar and water contents, and are more palatable than the normal diploid varieties. Seed size is almost double that of diploids and seed rates should be adjusted accordingly. Tillers are also larger but fewer in number, giving a more open type of sward which may be more compatible with white clover, but is liable to weed invasion. The improved persistence and tiller production of recent tetraploid perennial ryegrass varieties has led to their wider acceptance by farmers and advisers, although a higher water content and slower drying can make conservation of hay difficult in wetter regions.

Timothy

Timothy (*Phleum pratense*) is small-seeded and slow to establish. It is best combined with less vigorous species such as meadow fescue and white clover. It is winter hardy and well suited to growing on heavy wetter soils. It is late flowering and is traditionally regarded as a hay grass. Under a conservation management it is almost as productive as perennial ryegrass, but to obtain forage of high digestibility the crop must be harvested 2−3 weeks before head emergence (late May for early varieties). After the ryegrasses, timothy is the most widely sown grass.

Cocksfoot

Cocksfoot (*Dactylis glomerata*) is slow to establish, but then grows vigorously. Although it yields as much as perennial ryegrass, it has a lower feeding value and is less palatable. Its use has declined and it is now restricted to free draining soils in low rainfall areas. It shows good late summer and autumn growth which can be used to extend the grazing season for nonproductive stock.

Fescues

Meadow fescue (*Festuca pratensis*), tall fescue (*F. arundinacea*) and red fescue (*F. rubra*) have never been used extensively. They are slow to establish and do not compete well with other species during the seeding year. Meadow fescue is occasionally sown in mixture with timothy and white clover for moderate stocking systems. Tall fescue grows early in spring, is drought resistant and winter hardy, but low palatability has restricted its use to long-term swards for grass drying. Red fescue produces acceptable yields on infertile soils and can be used for hill re-seeding. Hybrids between ryegrasses and fescues have been produced with the object of combining the adaptability of the fescue with the establishment vigour and quality of the ryegrass. Preliminary trials have shown these new 'species' to have good potential.

Bromes

Prairie grass (*Bromus willdenowii*) has recently been tested under UK conditions and shows promise, outyielding the ryegrasses under an intensive conservation system. It is winter hardy and appears suited to drier regions of the country although its upright habit may make it liable to weed invasion.

2.5.2 *Legumes*

Legumes play a dual role: firstly they contribute to crop yield, and secondly they make N available for the benefit of companion grasses so increasing the protein content of the harvested crop. Compared with the grasses, they are more difficult to ensile. Their higher water content, buffering capacity and lower sugar content impair fermentation, although wilting and the use of suitable additives can overcome the problem. As in grasses, their D-value falls with maturity, although their voluntary intake and net energy content are higher than for grasses at the same D-value so that they can be harvested for conservation at a later stage of maturity (NIAB 1987b). Bloat can be a problem although progress in genetic manipulation suggests that bloat-free legumes may be possible. The importance of the different herbage legumes may be inferred from the relative amount of seed sold: white clover, red clover and lucerne account for 76, 15 and 3.5% by weight respectively. Other herbage legumes, sown in small quantities for specialized use, are Sainfoin (*Onobrychis viciifolia*), Trefoil (*Medicago lupulina*) and Alsike clover (*Trifolium hybridum*).

White clover

White clover (*Trifolium repens*) is a small-seeded perennial, with a creeping habit of growth, always grown in association with grass. It can be established on a wide range of soils, often without inoculation with rhizobium. It is best sown between April and mid August, on the soil surface (after drilling the grass), and lightly covered with soil. Classification of white clover is on leaf size, with varieties grouped into small, medium, large or very large. Small-leaved varieties, typified by Kent and S184, are productive and persistent under hard sheep grazing. Grasslands Huia and Menna are typical medium-leaved general purpose varieties. Large-leaved varieties such as Olwen, are suited to light grazing integrated with cutting and can withstand moderate levels of N. The main disease of white clover is clover rot (*Sclerotinia trifoliorum*); resistant varieties are available (NIAB 1987a). Slugs also cause damage particularly in wet years and in damp areas; again, varieties differ in their susceptibility.

Although mixed swards are usually grazed, the high digestibility of the clover leaves makes them valuable for silage. Moreover, the occasional cutting of grazed swards can help maintain clover content. Harvesting a light silage crop, from the first growth of older swards, in alternative years is recommended.

Red clover

Red clover (*Trifolium pratense*) is a short-lived (2 years) perennial, usually sown with grass and utilized for conservation. The seed is easy to establish without inoculation, on a large range of soils. Varieties are classified into either an early (Broad Red) or late group. The early group flower in early June, normally producing two conservation cuts, the first of which is particularly heavy, followed by autumn grazing. The later group start growth later in spring, flower in late June, and produce one conservation cut in mid June, followed by grazing; they are more persistent and suitable for medium term leys particularly in the uplands. Both groups contain recommended diploid and tetraploid varieties (NIAB 1987a). Choice of variety depends mainly on the resistance required to clover rot and stem eelworm (*Ditylenchus dipsaci*). Tetraploids offer good resistance to clover rot but are less resistant to stem eelworm and their seed is expensive. Some recent varieties, e.g. the diploid Meriot, combine resistance to both pathogens with high yield. Red clover is best conserved as silage; wilting and additives are recommended. It contains oestrogens and should not be grazed by ewes just before and during mating time. Bloat control measures should be used during cattle grazing.

Lucerne

Lucerne (*Medicago sativa*) is a deep rooted perennial, usually grown as a monoculture. It needs a well drained soil that is near alkaline at the surface and to depth. The crop is easy to establish from seed which must be fumigated, treated against seed borne pests and diseases, and inoculated with the appropriate strain of rhizobium to ensure effective nodulation. The young crop needs to be protected from weeds. The main disease and pest of lucerne are *Verticillium* wilt and stem eelworm respectively. Both are soil-borne and, if present, the use of resistant varieties (NIAB 1987a) is worthwhile, despite their slightly lower yield potential.

Lucerne is best harvested by cutting for conservation three or four times a year. Recommended varieties flower in mid June, but to obtain an acceptable D-value, the first growth should be harvested in late May (early flower-bud stage), with subsequent cuts at 6 week intervals. Grazing is not recommended; it weakens the plant and the animals are at risk from bloat. Lucerne, in contrast to the clovers, is best sown without a companion grass, thereby allowing the use of a suitable herbicide in late winter when the crop is still dormant.

2.5.3 *Seeds mixtures*

The majority of farmers sow seeds mixtures, rather than monocultures of a single cultivar. The reasons for combining grass with clover are clear and valid. The reasons for sowing a number of different grass species or cultivars together are less clear. They generally reflect a view that different genotypes may possess different but compatible characteristics, or exploit different natural resources, or respond differently to different managements, or perform better at different times of the year, or they may simply provide insurance against the failure of one or more components of the mixture. There is an element of truth in all of these, but their importance should not be exaggerated. As Snaydon (1979) points out, existing species and cultivars account for less than 5% of the variation in UK herbage production from field to field, farm to farm, and year to year; environment and management together account for 95% of the variation. Moreover, although the genetic composition of swards may be controlled briefly (1–4 years) by choice of mixture, thereafter, and many farmers intend leaving most of their grassland unploughed for 20 years or more (Forbes *et al.* 1978, Peel & Forbes 1978), it is controlled almost entirely by environment and management. The implication is that, while choosing a particular genotype or mix of genotypes, for a particular location and farming system will often be beneficial, it is more important to get the management right.

The current trend is for simpler mixtures. For cutting, time of heading is important because of its relation to yield and digestibility. Hence a single variety, or varieties with similar, usually early, heading dates are normally chosen. For grazing, varieties with a greater spread of heading date can be used. If grazing is intense, the denser tillering and leafier later flowering varieties are often preferred. They are also more persistent, although varieties with high persistence are now in all perennial ryegrass groups (NIAB 1987a). Varieties which combine early spring growth with high annual yield and good persistency, are most often found in the intermediate group (e.g. the tetraploid Merlinda). They are increasingly popular for inclusion in general purpose seed mixtures, particularly for grazing. Before choosing a seeds mixture, the characteristics of the component varieties should be compared, using Farmers leaflet No. 4, produced and updated annually, by the National Institute of Agricultural Botany, Cambridge (NIAB 1987a). In Table 2.4 some seeds mixtures are presented to illustrate the sort of approach that is normally adopted.

Mixture 1 is for a ley of 1−2 years duration, grown mainly for conservation in a high output system. It can be used for early bite or the first growth taken for silage. Regrowths can be harvested also for silage. A diploid or tetraploid Italian ryegrass variety can be used. If the latter, the seed rate must be increased by 10% to allow for the larger seed. Where the 'mixture' is to be established by undersowing, the seed rate should be reduced by a third. If some later summer grazing is required, the use of a hybrid ryegrass could be considered, but early spring growth and total yield may be slightly lower.

Mixture 2 is a clover dominant silage type. Red clover cannot compete successfully with modern Italian ryegrasses; perennial ryegrass is a better companion grass. The choice of an intermediate variety is intended to enhance the digestibility of the silage and increase production, particularly in the second year if the clover population declines.

Mixture 3 is for a medium duration ley of up to 5 years, for grazing and silage. The mixing of a tetraploid hybrid ryegrass with diploid perennial varieties of both intermediate and late heading dates, gives early spring

Table 2.4. Typical seed mixtures (kg seed ha^{-1}).

Species	Mixture number				
	1	2	3	4	5
Italian ryegrass	35				
Hybrid ryegrass		20	10		
Perennial ryegrass		5 I	10 I + L	20 I + L	15 I + L
Timothy				(5)	5
Cocksfoot					10
Red clover		15 E			
White clover			(5)	(5)	5

E = early; I = intermediate; L = late; ( ) alternative, see text.

growth, coupled with palatable, high quality summer and autumn production. Such a mixture has been recommended for a high output system for dairy or mixed cropping farms and for intensive beef production (MAFF 1986a). For a lower input system, white clover can be included, using medium and large leaved varieties. The clover seedrate should be $3.5-5\,kg\,ha^{-1}$, with that of the grass reduced to a total of $15\,kg\,ha^{-1}$. The tetraploid hybrid can aid clover establishment because of its lower tillering capacity and erect habit.

Mixture 4 can be used for a long-term ley of indefinite duration. It is based on perennial ryegrass, with or without white clover. For general use, the ryegrass component could contain intermediate and late heading varieties in the ratio of 1 : 2. Where heavy grazing is intended, timothy or one of the newer persistent tetraploid perennial ryegrass varieties (up to a third of the ryegrass component) could be included, or a single resistant late heading ryegrass variety could be used. If white clover is included, it should contain equal amounts of large and medium-leaved varieties (for general purpose use), or a 3 : 1 blend of medium and small leaved types (for grazing) with the grass seed rate reduced to $15\,kg\,ha^{-1}$. The mixture should be sown without a cover crop, and before mid August if white clover is included.

Mixture 5 is a special purpose mixture intended for long-term use on drier soils where production is often reduced by lack of soil moisture. It is useful for livestock rearing farms. The mixture is similar to, but simpler than, the traditional Cockle Park Mixture which is not often used today.

2.5.4 *Sward establishment*

Grassland is established by sowing seeds into a cultivated seedbed as part of a rotation involving other crops (reseeding) or following grass which needs replacement (direct reseeding). It can also be established or improved without resort to ploughing, when a chemical treatment is used to kill or control the existing vegetation prior to sowing the seed. Before embarking on any renovation programme, those factors which caused the sward to deteriorate (drainage, acidity, low fertility) must first be rectified.

Under UK conditions seeds will germinate in the field for much of the year, but low temperatures during the winter or dry soils in summer can restrict development. In wetter areas, sowing takes place from late April to mid August. In drier areas, sowing in late March to early April, as

soon as soil conditions allow the preparation of a fine tilth, is recommended. This allows maximum plant development before the onset of
summer drought. Mid summer months should be avoided. Grasses can be
sown in August and early September, depending on rainfall, but legumes
must be sown before mid August to maximize winter survival.

Optimum sowing depths range from 1 cm for small-seeded species
such as timothy and white clover, to about 2.5 cm for larger-seeded
grasses and legumes. A firm level seedbed allows seed to be placed evenly
at the correct depth. Consolidation after sowing aids rapid uptake of
water, maintains a constant environment for the seed, and reduces the
danger of pest damage. In higher rainfall areas, broadcasting the seed
followed by light harrowing gives good results. In lower rainfall areas,
where achieving a satisfactory depth of sowing is crucial, drilling in 10 cm
rows is more reliable, although it can place white clover and timothy seed
too deep. They should be broadcast on a ring rolled surface (after drilling
other species) lightly harrowed, and then ring or flat rolled.

Grass and clover seed sown alone (direct sowing) gives the best
establishment. However, to reduce the unproductive period between
crops, they are often sown with a cereal, or another short-term cover crop
(under-sowing). Whilst the cover crop provides shelter, it also competes
for water, nutrients and particularly light. A lodged cereal crop can cause
complete failure of the under-sown forage. Therefore: (1) sow the grass
and clover as soon as possible after sowing the cereal, delay cereal sowing
if necessary; (2) choose an early maturing spring cereal variety with a
short stiff straw; (3) reduce cereal seedrate and fertilizer application by
about a third of that for the cereal sown alone; and (4) if possible, harvest
the cover crop early for whole crop silage, when a later maturing cereal
can be used to improve the D-value. A mixed cereal crop which may
include forage peas or vetches, can also be used as a cover crop and
harvested for whole crop silage.

In high rainfall areas, a low seedrate of rape can be included in the
seeds mixture to act as a nurse crop. Similarly, in drier areas spring barley
can be included (at about 50 kg ha^{-1}) in spring sown swards. The nurse
crop and developing sward should be grazed 6—8 weeks after sowing and
then intermittently. Sheep may be preferable to cattle for the early
grazings particularly if the soil surface is wet. The developing seedlings
will benefit from soil consolidation, and defoliation will encourage tillering
in the grasses.

Longer term swards warrant every care during establishment and
should be sown direct. The loss of production can be reduced by sowing
in August after an early ripening cereal such as winter barley. After

harvest there is adequate time to establish grass and clover before winter. Similarly when direct reseeding, the second or third growth of the worn out sward can be treated with a suitable herbicide (such as glyphosate) and, after 5 days, the dying vegetation utilized for grazing, silage or hay. After the forage has been removed the area can be ploughed or cultivated immediately and sown to the new seeds mixture.

2.6   Permanent grassland

2.6.1   *Definition*

The term permanent grassland describes land maintained as grassland without the intervention of ploughing and reseeding. Unfortunately it is not separately recorded but is included in the category of grassland of 5 years old and over, of which there are about 5 million ha in the UK (Table 1.1). A survey of grassland in England and Wales indicated that of the 3.16 million ha of grassland of 5 years old and over, 23% was from 5 to 8 years old, 22% from 9 to 20 years and 55% was more than 20 years old (Green & Williams 1975). In 1987 these were 1.7 million ha under 5 years and 5.1 million ha over 5 years (Wilkins *et al.* 1987). Long-term grassland occupies a large proportion of the agricultural land in the higher rainfall areas. In all districts much of the old grassland occupies land with limitations to its cultivation, including ploughing, mowing, poor drainage, and excessive gradient or surface irregularities (Table 2.5). The most common limitation is poor drainage which also reduces the proportion of useful grasses, mainly perennial ryegrass (Green 1974).

Table 2.5. The proportion of grassland in different usability classes (%).

Usability (ease of management)	Age of grassland	
	> 20 years	< 20 years
No limitations to management	38	72
Moderate limitation to management	37	20
Severe limitation to management	25	8

2.6.2   *Grades of permanent grassland*

Permanent pastures have been classified according to their botanical composition particularly the abundance of perennial ryegrass or the dominance of bents, (*Agrostis* spp.) or red fescue (*Festuca rubra*). Field studies have shown that productivity measured by stock carrying capacity and performance was positively correlated with the abundance of perennial ryegrass, white clover, soil pH and P status (Neenan *et al*. 1959). For survey purposes (Stapledon *et al*. 1945) swards containing ryegrass were divided into three grades in which ryegrass contributed more than 30% (grade 1); from 15 to 30% (grade 2); and less than 15% (grade 3) to the ground cover. In these swards white clover is always present and rough meadow grass (*Poa trivialis*), is abundant. The other better grasses such as cocksfoot, timothy and meadow fescue, although frequently present, do not contribute in significant amounts to the herbage of permanent grassland. As the proportion of perennial ryegrass decreases, that of *Agrostis* increases and it is most frequently the dominant grass in third grade ryegrass pastures.

Agrostis swards in which ryegrass and other better grasses are absent or present in only insignificant amounts, are widespread and extensive. They are capable of subdivision according to soil conditions. Those on acid soils have a restricted flora and acid tolerant species are present such as Yorkshire fog (*Holcus lanatus*), sweet vernal (*Anthoxanthum odoratum*), sorrell (*Rumex acetosa, R. acetosella*) and others. On neutral and calcareous soils the dominance of *Agrostis* is less pronounced, and dicotyledonous weeds are more abundant including various calcicolous species.

These grades and types of permanent grassland are not discrete classes but subdivisions that cover a continuous range from one extreme to the other. No areas are exclusively occupied by any one grade of pasture. In any particular area one grade will be the most prevalent but better and poorer grades will also be present. Cartographic representation on this principle (Stapledon *et al*. 1945) showed a dominance of grade 1 ryegrass swards on two small localities in the Welland Valley in Leicestershire and Northamptonshire, and in Romney Marsh, Kent, whilst grade 2 pastures were the most plentiful type of sward over contiguous areas, with an additional area in Cheshire. These are areas of fertile soils mainly of heavy texture, but the most significant feature was the efficient utilization of the sward under a grazing management that ensured that grass was consumed at its highest nutritive value. Although these high quality swards were developed under a system of continuous grazing, stock numbers, particularly for fattening cattle and sheep, were carefully adjusted throughout the growing season to provide an adequate intake of grass of high nutritive value to maintain a high level of liveweight gain. Areas of predominantly grade 3 ryegrass or *Agrostis* ryegrass swards are widespread.

Changes in manuring and management and the adoption of reseeding have altered the quality of much of the permanent grassland. Thus in 1939 ryegrass was dominant on about 8%, whereas in 1971 it predominated over 25% of the old grassland (Green 1974). Nevertheless, *Agrostis* still dominates about half of the old grassland.

2.6.3 The management of permanent grassland

The management given to permanent grassland is highly variable both within and between localities. In England, Wales and Northern Ireland, about one-quarter is mown annually, usually once for hay or silage, but only half this proportion in Scotland. The overall average inputs (1986) of fertilizer at 104, 8 and 20 kg ha^{-1} of N, P and K respectively were approximately half those applied to leys. In any one year, about 4% of the area received lime and 21% an application of farmyard manure.

Permanent grassland occupies the largest proportion and area of land in the west and north of Britain; regions less suited to arable farming. The climate is favourable to the growth of herbage but is not the easiest in which to make hay or to use pasture without damaging the crop or soil structure by poaching. Nevertheless, this large area, including really old grass and also that which has been sown for more than ten years, represents a resource which is much underused. The most ready means of improving productivity is by correcting soil deficiencies of lime, phosphate and potash allied with good utilization through grazing and conservation. Under high rainfall conditions it is important to recognize the virtues of permanent swards including their resilience to poaching. An undisturbed soil under old grass develops a structure which improves permeability to water. With a continued and regular application of P and, where necessary, K fertilizer, sward productivity will be greatly increased, white clover will increase as will the proportion of the better grasses. The use of fertilizer N is not precluded but initially it should be used selectively to increase grass growth for grazing at specific times and for conservation. Hay is often the major form in which grass is conserved, but the quality of the swards themselves would improve if earlier, more nutritious but less heavy crops were taken and the wider adoption of ensilage would aid the better grasses and the maintenance of white clover. Recent studies show that permanent pastures gave similar yields to reseeded leys with low levels of N and over 90% of the yield from leys with high N (Wilkins *et al.* 1987).

2.6.4 Renovation of pasture

Improvement of permanent grassland by fertilizing and improved utilization management is possibly the most economical means of raising farm productivity in the higher rainfall areas on poorly drained soils. However, over a third of the old grassland is on soils with little impediment to cultivation, and ploughing and reseeding may be possible. The use of herbicides for partial or complete destruction of grass swards and direct drilling or broadcast sowing of seeds with a minimum of surface cultivation may be alternatives, Allen (1979), Haggar & Squires (1979). Nevertheless, the costs of renovation are high and the low productivity of grassland with dominance of poor grasses and low clover content is usually due to failure to manage grass as a crop. An adequate liming and fertilizer policy in conjunction with good grassland utilization is essential to improve existing grassland and to maintain the presence of sown grasses.

In the recent resurgence of interest in permanent grass, many studies have shown that with good management its yield may be comparable to that of leys and it incurs lower costs (Mudd & Meadowcroft 1964, Wilkins *et al.* 1987). Moreover, although the productivity of the 'weed' grasses is below that of preferred species, provided that soil deficiencies are corrected and nitrogenous fertilizers are applied, they can give useful yields and are often better adapted to the environment (Dibb & Haggar 1979, Frame 1983).

2.6.5   *Slot seeding of white clover*

Many grass swards are deficient in white clover. Slot or strip seeding offers the possibility of introducing clover without the necessity of a total reseed. Clover seed is sown in narrow slots on both sides of which a grass-suppressing herbicide (e.g. glyphosate) is band sprayed. Alternatively, seed can be sown into cultivated strips using a rotary seeder.

Any pH and phosphate deficiencies must be corrected before clover seed is sown and it is often worthwhile to inoculate the seed with rhizobia. Varieties of clover most suitable for this operation are the small leaved types. The sward must be grazed closely before seeding and rested thereafter, to permit the clover seedlings to colonize.

2.7   **Rough and hill grazings**

The rough and hill grazings occupy land above the limits of cultivation and enclosure which occurs at an altitude of from 250 to 300 m in England but at a lower elevation in Scotland. In addition, heath rough grazings occur on infertile soils at low elevation. Rough and hill grazings occupy nearly a half of the total agricultural area of Scotland, one-third of Wales, one-ninth of England and one-sixth of Northern Ireland, making a total of about 6 million ha.

The combination of soils and climate has a more decisive influence on the vegetation developed on the hill grazings than on that of permanent grassland at lower elevations (Table 2.6). Grazing mostly with sheep and a few cattle is far less intensive, and fertilizers are rarely used. With the exception of small areas on lime-bearing rocks, the upland soils are acidic and with the high rainfall a large proportion of the hill land is peat clad, frequently to a great depth.

Table 2.6. Summary of the main soil and vegetation types of the hill (HFRO 1979).

Soil	pH	Vegetation type	Principal species
Brown earth, freely drained	5.3−6.0	*Agrostis−Festuca* grassland high grade or spp. rich. Herbs abundant	*Agrostis tenuis* *Festuca rubra* *F. ovina* *Poa* spp. *Trifolium repens*
Gleys, poorly drained	5.3−6.0	As above with wet-land spp. *Carex, Juncus*	*Carex* spp. *Juncus* spp.
Brown earth, freely drained	4.5−5.2	*Festuca−Agrostis* grassland low grade or spp. poor	*Agrostis* spp. *Festuca ovina* *Pteridium aquilinum*
Gleys, poorly drained	4.5−5.2	As above with *Nardus* and wet-land spp. *Carex, Juncus*	*Nardus stricta* *Carex* spp. *Juncus* spp. *Deschampsia caespitosa*
Podsols, peaty podsols, freely drained	4.0−4.5	*Nardus* or *Deschampsia−Festuca* grass heath *or* *Calluna* shrub heath	*Nardus stricta* *Deschampsia flexuosa* *Calluna vulgaris* *Vaccinium* spp. *Erica* spp.
Peaty gleys, poorly drained	4.0−4.5	*Molinia* grass heath *or* *Calluna−Molinia* heath	*Molinia caerulea* *Festuca ovina* *Deschampsia flexuosa* *Calluna vulgaris*
Deep blanket peat, poorly drained	3.5−4.0	*Trichoporum−Eriophorum−Calluna* bog	*Trichoporum caespitosum* *Eriophorum* spp. *Calluna vulgaris* *Molinia caerulea* *Sphagnum* spp.

2.7.1   *The fescue pastures*

These form the link between the vegetation of the permanent grassland of the lowlands and that of the uplands. The downland fescue pastures were at one time extensive on the chalk and oolitic formations of southern England, but at present they are greatly reduced since many have been ploughed for cereal cropping. Those remaining are mainly on steep valley sides and escarpments. These floristically rich fescue pastures are threatened by the lack of sheep or rabbit grazing under which they were developed and maintained, and are being invaded by tor grass (*Brachypodium pinnatum*) and scrub.

The mountain fescue pastures are essentially pastures of hillsides, often steep, with thin well drained acid soils with some accumulation of undecayed root and tiller bases. On the more fertile patches, red fescue, *Festuca rubra* and bents *Agrostis* spp. are abundant constituents but elsewhere sheep's fescue, *F. ovina*, is dominant, and at higher elevations with thin peat development, mat grass, *Nardus stricta* occurs. Other grasses often present are heath grass (*Sieglingia decumbens*) and sweet vernal (*Anthoxanthum odoratum*).

The fescue pastures afford the best summer grazing on hill land and are dry and healthy. Where physical conditions of slope and access permit, they are capable of considerable improvement by liming, phosphate manuring, fencing and controlled grazing. However, with decreasing management large areas have been invaded by bracken (*Pteridium aquilinum*) and gorse (*Ulex* spp.) at the lower and *Nardus* at higher elevations.

2.7.2   *Moorland pastures*

Nardus moor

Nardus stricta occupies the drier hill slopes on very acidic soil with a development of a shallow layer of peat. This tussocky grass, commonly called mat grass or white bent, has a system of horizontal rhizomes and tough basal sheaths. Areas dominated by it are the least useful of the natural grazings. Sheep's fescue (*F. ovina*), in variable quantities, is almost always present, as are small areas of heath rush (*Juncus squarrosus*) which is sought after by sheep during the winter months. Other species usually present are *Deschampsia flexuosa*, *Galium hercynicum*, *Potentilla erecta* and stunted *Calluna* and *Vaccinium* spp.

Molinia moor

Extensive areas dominated by purple moor grass (*Molinia caerulea*) develop on wet peaty soils on moderate or slight gradients. Although growing under wet soil conditions *Molinia* does not thrive in stagnant water. Small quantities of other grasses typically present include fine bent (*Agrostis tenuis*) and brown bent (*A. canina*), *F. ovina* and *Nardus* and heath plants such as *Calluna vulgaris*, *Erica* spp. and *Juncus articulatus*.

Molinia starts growth at the end of May or early June, but this is rapid and luxuriant. Sheep are unable to keep pace with the growth but it affords good grazing for hill cattle from June to early September, which also maintains the grass in a better condition for sheep. With the onset of winter the leaves are shed and blow in the wind, hence its common name of flying bent. Burning at intervals of about 7 years helps to maintain *Molinia* moors in a good condition. *Molinia* is rapidly reduced by heavy grazing.

Molinia—Nardus moorland

Although Molinia and Nardus moorland occur extensively in Britain with dominance of one or other of the two species over appreciable areas, there are also extensive areas of the mixed *Molinia—Nardus* plant associations. The heterogeneity is associated with mixed topography, and springs and seepage of ground water give rise to mountain flush bogs.

Heather moor

Well developed heather moors occur on relatively shallow, but not excessively wet peat. Little real distinction can be made between lowland heaths dominated by heather and the upland heather moor. The most extensive heather moors occur on the drier eastern slopes of the Pennine hills in Yorkshire and Durham and similarly in Scotland. Local topography and soil variations in a heather moor give rise to small associations of and admixtures with *Nardus*, *Molinia*, *P. aquilinum*, *Vaccinium* spp., *Erica* spp. and *Empetrum nigrum*. Where the peat is poorly drained, cotton grass (*Eriophorum vaginatum*) and deer grass (*Trichophorum caespitosum*) will appear.

Heather moors provide pasturage for sheep, particularly valuable in the early part of the year when young shoots are available. In snow it may be the only accessible feed. Nevertheless access to grass moors in conjunction with heather moors is considered beneficial to the management of the sheep flock. Heather moors need to be appropriately managed to maintain the plant in young vigorous condition. This is achieved by regular burning at intervals of 5–10 years. Left unburnt it grows tall, grey or stick heather, which sheep find difficult to enter and provides less new growth. Heather when burnt after a suitable interval regenerates from the stools, but stick heather on burning is apt to be killed. Regeneration is then from seed, of which there is great abundance in the soil but seedlings are more sensitive to grazing than are regenerating stools and the return of heather is slow. If such burnt areas are small they may attract sheep in such intensity as to prevent regeneration of heather when reversion either to *Nardus*, or on the better areas to bracken, may be the consequence of burning. On wet peat, heather moor development can be assisted by open ditch draining to reduce cotton and deer grass. Heather moors apart from being valuable for hill and mountain sheep are essential for grouse. Fortunately the type of heather best suited for sheep is also that best for grouse.

On average, only 15% of the annual growth of heather is grazed by sheep. Work at the Hill Farming Research Organisation has shown that 40% of the annual growth may be grazed without affecting new shoot production. The heather was then maintained in a more juvenile condition and the intervals between burning could be extended (Grant *et al.* 1978).

Cotton and deer grass moors

Eriophorum vaginatum and *Trichophorum caespitosum* form the typical plant association of deep blanket peat under high rainfall conditions. In the most boggy areas *Eriophorum angustifolium* is present. These moors are the least valuable for sheep grazing although sheep seek the young basal sheaths of the developing inflorescence (draw moss) in early spring. Cotton grass moors occupy extensive areas of the highest ground in the Pennines and are distributed throughout Britain on deep, wet peat.

2.8   Competition between herbage species

When two or more species grow together in a community, they interact one with the other. Competition is for specific environmental factors that affect growth and development, e.g. water, plant nutrients and light. Its effects are expressed as dynamic changes in the relative growth of the individual species. The competitive characteristics of species may change at different stages of growth from the seedling to the vegetative and reproductive condition and also with environmental conditions of water supply, soil fertility, temperature and light. Utilization management may also change the relative competitive ability.

2.8.1   *Seedling competition*

Much of the early information on species competition was obtained from work on seed mixtures (Davies 1928). Seedling vigour is closely related to seed weight and while seedling competition may not occur at normal sowing densities, the sooner a seedling is established, the sooner it tillers and begins to exploit the environment. Species and varietal differences in seed weight and rate of tillering are thus of importance in determining competitive ranking. From mixed sowings the ranking in decreasing order of competitiveness is Italian ryegrass, perennial ryegrass, cocksfoot, timothy, meadow fescue and tall fescue. In the early development of sown seeds, clovers can establish well but suffer in competition as the ryegrasses begin to tiller rapidly. The degree of competition depends upon soil N, with lower N favouring clover.

Italian ryegrass, owing to its rapid growth, and extended autumn and early spring growth can become very aggressive to perennial ryegrass and red clover unless held in check by grazing or early cutting. On the other hand, broad red clover can dominate the developing sward, particularly in the autumn after sowing under a cereal nurse crop when a lush growth of red clover requires grazing to allow the development of the ryegrasses.

2.8.2   *Competition in established swards*

There has been little research directly related to competition between species in older associations of mixed swards either leys or permanent grass. However, many agronomic studies of response to fertilizers, grazing and cutting have noted changes in botanical composition resulting from the altered competitive conditions.

Rotational grazing, with judicious manuring, increases the proportion of perennial ryegrass and white clover with a reduction of *Agrostis* spp. rough meadow grass, Yorkshire fog and herbaceous weeds (Fenton 1931). With fertilizing and increased fertility, grazed swards tended to pass through the same phases of botanical change (Fenton 1934). The order of progression with increasing fertility and productivity was from *Festuca rubra* to *Agrostis* dominance followed by an increasing contribution of perennial ryegrass and white clover with rough meadow grass.

Similar species succession has been observed on hill pastures initially of low fertility consisting of either *Molinia* or *Festuca–Agrostis* swards.

With lime and complete fertilizer, *Molinia* and *F. ovina* soon disappeared to be replaced partly by *Agrostis*, white clover, rough and smooth meadow grass with the ultimate appearance of perennial ryegrass, cocksfoot and timothy. Successful improvement in a reasonable period of time was dependent on grazing; the taking of hay greatly reduced the rate of change (Milton & Davies 1947).

Controlled grazing experiments with swards containing perennial ryegrass, cocksfoot, *Agrostis* and white clover showed that the maintenance of perennial ryegrass required periodic grazing, with intensity of grazing adjusted to the seasonal production of the grass. Over-grazing in winter and spring with under-grazing in May and June at the time of maximum growth, increased *Agrostis* while cocksfoot increased with long rest periods from grazing in early autumn (Jones 1933a—d). More recent work is reviewed by Dibb & Haggar (1979) and by Hopkins (1979).

2.9   Weeds of grassland and their control

2.9.1   *The weeds of grassland*

Practically all grass swards, particularly those of long standing, contain grass species whose productive potential is less than that of better species which could exist in the prevailing conditions, although they are readily eaten by livestock. Such grasses, notably *Agrostis* spp. and the meadow grasses (*Poa* spp.) may and often do contribute more to the total production than do perennial ryegrass, cocksfoot or timothy although they may be considered as undesirable weeds. Nevertheless *Agrostis* would not be classed as a weed in a hill grazing composed largely of fine-leaved fescues and *Nardus*. Other grass species which are grazed only under duress, such as tussock grass (*Deschampsia caespitosa*), are easily defined as weeds. The concept of weed status amongst gramineous species that are edible to livestock is thus largely a matter of a ranking order within a given environment. The control of weed grasses involves cultural and management practices that prevent the initial establishment of the less desirable grass species or reduce their contribution to swards where they are already present. These practices favour the development of the more desirable species and are detrimental to the undesirable species. The development of herbicides that exhibit selectivity between grass species provides some opportunity for controlling the initial ingress of unsown grass species into sown swards and for regulating their presence in established swards, although much can be done by the traditional methods of grazing and fertilizing.

Broad-leaved weeds in grassland are frequently present in abundance. Many species may occur in impoverished grassland, as typified by ragwort (*Senecio jacobaea*), which is highly poisonous to livestock particularly in hay. Such weeds largely disappear with fertilization and improved management, however, some persist under fertile conditions to impede grazing and compete with better grasses. These include curled and broad-leaved docks (*Rumex crispus and R. obtusifolius*), nettles (*Urtica* spp.), common chickweed (*Stellaria media*) and, to a lesser extent, creeping and spear thistles (*Cirsium arvense* and *C. vulgare*). To these must be added the common rush (*Juncus effusus*) on poorly drained soils and bracken (*Pteridium aquilinum*) which is also harmful to cattle if eaten. All these may be controlled by herbicides and permanently reduced if accompanied by improved fertilization and management.

Some weeds are partial parasites of grasses, namely yellow rattle (*Rhinanthus crista-galli*), eyebright (*Euphrasia officinalis*), red bartsia (*Odontites verna*) and lousewort (*Pedicularis palustris*). These are rarely of agricultural consequence and are readily eliminated by fertilization and improved management. Broomrape (*Orabanche* spp.) is a root parasite of red clover and leguminous crops incapable of a separate existence. It is not uncommon in red clover on chalk soil.

While herbicides are not widely required on grass swards, many are now available which control weeds and undesirable species in grassland. The more commonly used herbicides are referred to in the following sections. For more information as to their use and efficacy, dose rates and other details the reader is referred to the *Weed Control Handbook* (Fryer & Makepeace 1978).

2.9.2 *Controlling broad-leaved weeds in established swards*

The majority of these weeds are controlled by a spray application of the hormone type of herbicide (MCPA or 2,4-D). It needs, however, to be supported by a state of fertility that ensures vigorous growth, efficient utilization of the pasture and attention to drainage, without which weeds would re-establish. Spraying is usually carried out when the weeds are actively growing. For buttercups, other than bulbous buttercup, spraying in late spring or early summer before flowering is most appropriate but it may be better to spray bulbous buttercup in the autumn when the new leaves appear. For the control of creeping thistle it is most appropriate to spray in the early flower bud stage, while a change of management to mowing, especially a silage cut, will increase the effectiveness of herbicides. Established docks in grassland are effectively controlled by spraying with mixtures of selective herbicides, including dicamba, mecoprop, triclopyr and asulam when the leaves are well expanded. If asulam is used, many grasses are temporarily checked but it may be safely used with ryegrass and clovers, although cocksfoot and Yorkshire fog are severely checked.

Although not strictly broad-leaved weeds, rushes may be controlled by MPCA or 2,4-D spraying when well grown, and are largely eliminated if treatment includes cutting, improved fertility and attention to drainage.

Asulam gives good control of bracken when sprayed at or near full frond expansion. In the year of treatment, yellowing and distortion of the fronds may occur and the bracken dies back normally but there is little or no regrowth the following year. It is essential that spraying is followed by a programme of fertilizer application, some cultivation and reseeding and adequate stock control to prevent re-incursion of bracken.

On established grassland where it is necessary to safeguard the contribution of white clover to the swards, MCPB, 2,4-DB asulam or benazolin herbicides should be used or mixtures with a smaller proportion of MCPA or 2,4-D. Alternatively, glyphosate can be selectively applied to tall growing weeds, using a weed wiping applicator.

2.9.3   *Control of grass weeds in established swards*

Differences exist between grass species in their response to herbicides although at present neither the range of herbicides nor the degree of selectivity is comparable to that available for the control of broad-leaved weeds. Thus a small dose of dalapon in June or July is much more toxic to creeping bent, Yorkshire fog and *Poa* spp. than to perennial ryegrass.

To be effective, swards must contain as much perennial ryegrass as susceptible grasses and little or no red fescue since this is not affected and may rapidly increase. Tussock grass is not affected but this species can be controlled by spot treatment with dalapon.

In established perennial ryegrass swards autumn application of ethofumesate or methabenz-thiazuron gives good control of *Poa* spp. and of seedling blackgrass (*A. myosuroides*).

2.9.4   *Grass control in established legume crops*

Grasses readily colonize legume stands and increase particularly after the first harvest year. They are especially troublesome in lucerne. Late winter application of paraquat, when the legumes are dormant, gives good control of *Poa* spp. and chickweed. Carbetamide will, in addition, give useful control of ryegrass and blackgrass, as will propyzamide, applied in late winter.

2.9.5 Weeds in newly sown swards

Erect annual weeds in newly sown swards without a cover crop may be controlled by mowing but this is ineffective with rosette type and prostrate weeds such as shepherds purse (*Capsella bursa-pastoris*) and knot-grass (*Polygonum aviculare*). In grass-only swards a wide range of herbicides may be used such as those based on MCPA, 2,4-D, mecoprop, dichlorprop and mixtures of these and other herbicides to deal with particular weed species. Grass seedlings are tolerant to these herbicides after the development of three leaves.

A few herbicides, for example methabenz-thiazuron and ethofumesate, can be used to control the seedlings of grasses such as *Poa* spp., blackgrass and Yorkshire fog in ryegrass swards.

Broad-leaved weeds in establishing grass–legume mixtures may be controlled by the use of MCPB and 2,4-DB or mixtures containing benazolin and bentazone. Legume seedlings are tolerant to these herbicides after the development of the first trifoliate leaf. However, 2,4-DB is slightly more toxic to red clover than MCPB, whilst MCPB is not recommended for use on lucerne.

2.9.6 Chemical sward destruction for reseeding

In many situations the chemical destruction of a sward as an alternative to ploughing will have attractions and advantages. In open swards free of plant debris, seed may be direct drilled without cultivation or a normal seedbed prepared by shallow cultivation. The presence of a thick mat requires more cultivation, rotovating being particularly suitable. Further destruction of the mat will take place if left over winter. Spraying is most effective when swards present a short cover of green growing herbage.

Paraquat gives a rapid desiccation of the turf and an effective kill of most grasses, but control of fine-leaved fescues, tussock grass and cocksfoot requires heavy doses. Split applications are more effective against resistant species. Deep rooted broad-leaved perennial weeds are best controlled by previous application of appropriate herbicides. Glyphosate is foliage-absorbed, rapidly translocated throughout the plant, and effective against all grasses. After paraquat, reseeding may be carried out preferably about 10 days after spraying, but glyphosate is slow acting and a 2–4 week interval is recommended.

Dalapon, although effective against grasses, gives poor control of broad-leaved weeds which must be dealt with by other herbicides. It is also slow acting, persists longer in the soil, and reseeding is not recommended earlier than 6 weeks after spraying. It is most frequently used in the autumn followed by sowing in the spring.

2.10   Diseases and pests of forage crops

Forage crops are hosts to many invertebrate pests and to diseases caused by fungi, bacteria, and viruses. Some are known to reduce yield, persistency or herbage quality, but the effects of many others are uncertain and difficult to assess. Those dealt with below are the most important in the UK (Jones & Jones 1964, O'Rourke 1976, Williams 1984, Lewis & Clements 1987).

2.10.1   *Fungal diseases of grasses*

Rust (*Puccinia* spp. and *Uromyces dactylidis*) attacks many herbage grasses. The most common, crown rust (*P. coronata*), is prevalent in ryegrasses in southern England, especially in warm dry autumns. The orange pustules on the leaves are distinctive. Crown rust is less severe under good conditions for growth, including high N and frequent defoliation. Severely infected herbage is unpalatable. Resistance ratings are given in the NIAB list of recommended varieties of perennial ryegrass. Fungicide treatment is possible, although the choice of chemicals is restricted.

Powdery mildew (*Erysiphe graminis*) infects most grasses and can reduce yield and quality. A greyish superficial fungal growth is apparent on the leaves. Infection is most severe in dense crops, where high levels of N are used, and following dry periods. Ratings for resistance are given in the NIAB list of recommended varieties of Italian ryegrass. Fungicide treatment is possible, although the choice of chemicals is restricted.

Drechslera leaf spot (*Drechslera spp.*) is common throughout the year in ryegrass and fescues. The brown spots vary in size and frequency depending on the species of host and fungus, and on environmental conditions. In ryegrass, loss of quality may occur even with low levels of infection (Lam 1985). Fungicide treatment is possible in seed crops, although the choice of chemicals is restricted.

Leaf blotch (*Rhynchosporium* spp.) causes large brown lesions with lighter coloured centres in ryegrasses and cocksfoot. Infection is most severe during cool, moist weather in spring and autumn, and where high levels of N are used. In Italian ryegrass, it can reduce herbage quality. Ratings for resistance are given in the NIAB list of recommended varieties of Italian ryegrass. Fungicide treatment is possible, although the choice of chemicals is restricted.

Leaf fleck (*Mastigosporium rubricosum*) causes elliptical purplish-brown lesions on several grasses but cocksfoot in particular can suffer loss of yield and quality (Carr 1962, O'Rourke 1967). Infection is most severe during cool moist weather in spring and autumn, and where high levels of N are used.

Blind-seed disease of ryegrass (*Gloeotinia temulenta*) causes low germination of perennial and, to a lesser extent, Italian ryegrass. Infection is most common in the wetter and cooler areas of Britain. Spores infect the developing ovules. Early infection destroys the embryo so that the seed does not form. Later infection results in 'blind' seeds which do not germinate when sown. Subsequently, spores produced from these buried seeds, infect plants at the flowering stage. The fungus can be destroyed by hot water treatment of infected seed.

Ergot (*Claviceps purpurea*) can infect most grasses at the flowering stage causing seed to be replaced by horn-shaped black sclerotia, or 'ergots'. These are most numerous in ears developed late in wet seasons, and in old pasture. Ergots in seed crops are removed in seed cleaning. If eaten in sufficient quantity by livestock, ergots are poisonous (Woods *et al*. 1966). Topping pastures late in the season avoids the problem. When highly infected pastures are reseeded, ploughing should be deep to bury ergots and prevent the release of spores.

Damping-off (species of *Fusarium*, *Pythium*, *Rhizoctonia*, etc.) causes death or loss of vigour in seedlings of all grasses. *F. culmorum* is particularly pathogenic to grass seedlings before emergence (Holmes 1983). The fungi are seed- and soil-borne and can be controlled by treating seed with fungicides (Holmes 1983, Lewis 1985).

2.10.2 *Fungal diseases of herbage legumes*

Clover rot (*Sclerotinia trifoliorum*) is a serious disease, prevalent in red clover crops in Britain (Lester & Large 1958) and reported in white clover crops at some trial sites in England (Aldrich 1970). Giant sainfoin and lucerne crops can be affected. Infection begins in the autumn as necrotic spots on the leaves and spreads within the stems into the crown, causing death. Sclerotia develop, fall onto the soil, and germinate to produce spores to continue the infection cycle. Sclerotia can survive in the soil for many years before germinating. Ratings for resistance to clover rot are given in the NIAB list of recommended varieties of red and white clover.

Verticillum wilt (*V. albo-atrum*) causes yellowing of leaves followed by wilting of stems and death of lucerne plants. Incidence increases with age of the crop and yield can be severely impaired. The fungus is retained in dead tissue, in soil and the seeds may carry spores. Ratings for resistance are given in the NIAB list of recommended varieties of lucerne.

Powdery mildew (*Erysiphe trifolii* and *E. pisi*) forms a white powdery growth on the upper surface of leaves of most herbage legumes and downy mildew (*Peronospora trifoliorum*) a greyish growth on the under surface. Scorch (*Kabatiella caulivora*), although uncommon, may severely infect red clover crops in wet seasons. Leaves of infected plants are blackened and hang down as if scorched by fire. Leaf spot (*Pseudopeziza* spp.) infects most herbage legumes, causing large brown lesions on the upper surface of leaves. Mature lesions produce yellowish glistening fruiting bodies in the centre. Other leaf-spotting fungi commonly found in white clover are black blotch (*Cymadothea trifolii*) and pepper spot (*Leptosphaerulina trifolii*).

2.10.3 *Pests of grasses*

Pest damage to grassland is most severe during the crucial establishment phase (Clements & Bentley 1985). Grass sown after grass is more prone to attack because of the carry over of pests from the old sward. Slugs, leatherjackets and various nematodes may all cause significant losses. The major problem, however, is caused by the larvae of the frit fly complex (e.g. *Oscinella* spp.).

Established grassland harbours large numbers of many invertebrate species, some of which may cause significant damage. Losses often go unnoticed because in farming practice there is no opportunity to compare the yield of an infected pasture with an uninfected one. In one series of experiments (Henderson & Clements 1977), insidious losses varied from 9 to 32% at eight of the ten sites studied. Visible damage is caused by leatherjackets, and other soil dwelling pests when their numbers exceed a threshold level. Chemical control of leatherjackets is probably justified on around 500 000 ha of grass in the UK during outbreaks, which occur about one year in five. A detailed account of pest damage and control is given in Williams (1984).

Frit fly larvae hatch from eggs laid on or near seedlings or mature grass plants. On a reseed, larvae may migrate from buried turf. The larvae mine within the base of grass plants and kill seedlings or greatly reduce their vigour. They may also reduce the vigour of mature plants and are implicated in the characteristic lack of persistence of Italian ryegrass (Clements & Henderson 1983). Control with a range of agrochemical sprays or seed-treatments is straightforward. Biological control methods are being developed.

Leatherjackets, the larvae of craneflies (*Tipula* spp.), damage the roots of most grasses, severing them just below soil surface. They are most active in the spring, causing the death of many plants in severe cases. They are most prevalent in wetter areas.

Wireworms, the larvae of click beetles (*Agriotes* and *Althous* spp.), are root-feeding pests, most abundant in old swards where their effect is rarely observable. They may cause seedling death in new sowings. Good cultivations and well consolidated seedbeds minimize damage.

Chafer grubs, the larvae of chafer beetles, cause damage similar to that of leatherjackets. Normally this occurs in rough pasture in small areas and rarely on well managed swards. The caterpillars of the Antler Moth occasionally damage upland pastures in the north of England.

Slugs (*Deroceras reticulatum* and other spp.) rasp away sections of leaves and may cause significant damage, particularly on clay soils.

Cocksfoot moth larvae (*Glyphipterix cramerella*) attack seed crops causing minute holes in seeds and stems and reduce seed yields. Although common, infestation is rarely serious and build-up of harmful populations is prevented by burning stubble and straw after harvest.

Grass seed midges attack the seed heads of most grasses, but only infrequently reduce seed yields (except in meadow foxtail).

Aphids of many species infest the cultivated grasses, but only assume importance in seed crops. If necessary, aphids may be controlled by organophosphorus insecticides.

Timothy flies (*Amaserosoma* spp.) attack the inflorescence, stripping parts of it bare of florets where the larvae have fed while the infloresence is still within the leaf sheath.

2.10.4 *Pests of herbage legumes*

Slugs cause extensive damage to seedlings and established plants of all herbage legumes, particularly during wet periods and on heavy soils. Leaf tissue is rasped away in strips between the veins. Ratings for resistance to slug damage are given in the NIAB lists of recommended varieties of white clover.

Stem eelworm (*Ditylenchus dipsaci*) causes stunting and swollen stem bases, nodes and petioles in most herbage legumes. Soil-borne infestation occurs in patches and is long-lived. Seed-borne infestation produces small scattered patches and can be avoided by fumigating seed with methyl-bromide. Ratings for resistance to stem eelworm are given in the NIAB list of recommended varieties of red clover and lucerne.

Sitona weevils (*Sitona* spp.) cause characteristic notching of leaf margins of clovers and lucerne. Newly sown crops can suffer severe damage which prompt treatment with insecticide can prevent. Weevil larvae feed on the root nodules but the impact of this on crop growth is unknown.

Clover seed weevils (*Apion* spp.) occasionally cause seed losses. Adults feed on the foliage before depositing eggs in the flower buds and the larvae devour the ovules. Seed crops should be isolated from hay crops to avoid cross-infestation. Defoliation of the first growth of red clover reduces the incidence. Insecticide treatment gives a further reduction when applied no later than 2 weeks after defoliating the first growth of early-flowering red clover, or immediately after the final defoliation of late red clover.

2.10.5 *Virus diseases of grasses and herbage legumes*

Virus infection is systemic and is not removed by defoliating the crop. Therefore viruses are likely to be more damaging than foliar fungal diseases. Numerous viruses have been reported in herbage legumes but there is little information on their effects on yield.

Barley yellow dwarf virus (BYDV) and ryegrass mosaic virus (RMV) are common in ryegrass crops in Britain. BYDV causes greater damage in perennial than in Italian ryegrass whereas the converse is true for RMV (Catherall 1987). Symptoms of RMV infection are light-green streaks in the leaves which may become necrotic; in severe cases the whole plant turns brown. RMV can severely reduce yield in Italian ryegrass (Holmes 1980) and ratings for resistance are given in the NIAB list of recommended varieties of Italian ryegrass. Sowing in autumn rather than spring delays the ingress of the mite vector of RMV. BYDV infection, spread by aphids, is mostly symptomless and the extent of yield losses in Britain has yet to be ascertained.

Cocksfoot mottle virus and cocksfoot streak virus can cause severe damage to cocksfoot crops. Mottle virus is lethal but some varieties, e.g. Cambria, have resistance.

Clover phyllody is caused by a mycoplasmic infection spread by leaf-hoppers and is common in white clover. The inflorescences of infected plants are transformed into leafy structures that set no seed. Small-leaved white clover varieties are less affected than larger-leaved ones.

2.10.6 *Ryegrass endophyte*

For many years cattle and sheep in New Zealand have suffered from a disorder known as 'ryegrass staggers'. Affected animals become unthrifty, lose co-ordination of their limbs and may fall over if startled or an attempt is made to move them. Cases of staggers are sporadic and until recently the cause was unknown. However, about 6 years ago it was noticed that pastures in which animals were affected, were free from most insect pests. But pastures where the disorder did not occur were often riddled with pests. A fungus (*Acremonium lolii*), is responsible for both the animal disorder and the resistance to insect pests. The fungus is endophytic, i.e. lives only within plant tissues and does not produce spores. It is only transmitted from plant to plant via infected seed. Substances produced by the fungus and called Lolitrems cause the animal disorder but a different substance, probably peramine, also produced by the fungus, bestows pest resistance. In the USA, a related fungus (*A. coenophialum*) in tall fescue causes animal disorders, promotes insect

resistance, and may increase plant DM yield, and enhance drought tolerance and winter hardiness. *A. lolii* is now known to be widespread at a
low level in old ryegrass pastures in the UK (Lewis & Clements 1986)
where it has caused a number of cases of staggers especially in Kent and
the Midlands. It should be possible to manipulate the fungus, so that it
promotes insect pest resistance, without causing animal disorders.

Further reading

Anslow R.C. (1962) A quantitative analysis of germination and early seedling growth in
    perennial ryegrass. *Journal of the British Grassland Society* **17**, 260–3.
Archer J. (1985) *Crop Nutrition and Fertilizer Use*. Farming Press Ltd, Ipswich.
Baker M.J. & Williams W.M. (eds) (1987) *White Clover*. Commonwealth Agricultural
    Bureaux International, Farnham.
Cooke G.W. (1982) *Fertilizing for Maximum Yield*, 3rd edn. Granada Publishing, London.
Davies W. (1960) *The Grass Crop*. Spon Ltd, London.
Harper J.L. (1977) *Population Biology of Plants*. Academic Press, London.
Hodgson J., Baker R.D., Davies A., Laidlaw A.S. & Leaver J.D. (eds) (1981) *Sward
    Measurement Handbook*. British Grassland Society, Hurley.
Hubbard C.E. (1968) *Grasses*. Penguin Books, Harmondsworth.
Jones F.G.W. & Jones M.G. (1984) *Pests of Field Crops*. Edward Arnold, London.
Jones M.B. & Lazenby A. (eds) (1988) *The Grass Crop*. Chapman & Hall, London.
Langer R.H.M. (1979) *How Grasses Grow*. Edward Arnold, London.
MAFF (Ministry of Agriculture, Fisheries and Food) (1986) *White Clover*. Report No.
    P3009. Agriculture Development and Advisory Service, Leeds.
O'Rourke C.J. (1976) *Diseases of Grasses and Forage Legumes in Ireland*. An Foras
    Taluntais, (Irish Agricultural Institute) Dublin.
Ryden J.C. (1984) The flow of nitrogen in grassland. *Proceedings of the Fertilizer Society*
    229.
The Scottish Agricultural Colleges (1983) *White Clover*. Publication No. 99. Edinburgh.
Sheldrick R., Thomson D. & Newman G. (1987) *Legumes for Milk and Meat*. Chalcombe
    Publications, Marlow.
Spedding C.R.W. (1971) *Grassland Ecology*. Clarendon Press, Oxford.
Spedding C.R.W. & Diekmahns E.C. (eds) (1972) *Grasses and Legumes in British Agricul-
    ture*. Bulletin 49, Commonwealth Bureau of Pastures and Field Crops, Commonwealth
    Agricultural Bureaux, Farnham.
Williams R.D. (1984) *Crop Protection Handbook — Grass and Clover Swards*. British Crop
    Protection Council, Croydon.

Chapter 3

The feeding value of grass and grass products

The capacity of a forage to promote animal production (its feeding value) depends on the composition of nutrients in the plant, the ability of the animal to utilize these nutrients and the amount of forage the animal will eat (its voluntary intake). The ruminant's ability to extract nutrients from forages is greatly enhanced by the presence in its forestomach of around 10^{10} bacteria per ml and 10^6 protozoa per ml, which can utilize the β-linked polysaccharides such as cellulose and hemicellulose which are abundant in most forages (Hungate 1966). The effects of this microbial fermentation in modifying the nutrients ingested by the ruminant and their subsequent metabolism by the tissues are included in this chapter, together with sections on the chemical composition and nutritive value of forages, the prediction of animal performance on forage based diets and the use of supplements to overcome nutrient limitations.

3.1   Chemical and physical characteristics of forage

The growth characteristics of grasses and legumes, with particular reference to the distinct phases of vegetative and reproductive development have been highlighted in Chapter 2, and the importance of forage species and variety, water, light and nutrient availability and environmental effects on forage growth have been considered. The factors which influence forage growth are dynamic, and change significantly with time. Consequently the chemical and physical characteristics of forages are influenced by the stage, and rate, of growth of the crop as well as the previous management of the sward. Because of this extensive variation, it is not possible to provide a complete assessment of forage composition, but some of the major features, changes and differences will be highlighted.

3.1.1   *Cell wall constituents*

The partition of feed stuffs into crude protein, crude fibre, ether extract, ash, and nitrogen extractives did not facilitate the assessment of feeding value. Attempts to provide a better chemical characterization of forages led to the concept of a division of forage DM into *cell contents* and *cell walls*, and on this basis, Van Soest & Wine (1967) established the neutral detergent fibre technique. In this fractionation, the cell walls are considered to consist of pectic substances, the structural polysaccharides, hemicellulose and cellulose, plus lignin. With advancing maturity, the concentration of cellulose, hemicellulose and lignin in grass all increase, but it is the increased lignin and in particular its spatial distribution which has the most significant negative effect on the rate and extent of digestion of the forage. In contrast, compared with grasses at comparable growth stages, legumes are characterized by reduced amounts of cell walls with markedly lower hemicellulose, but higher concentrations of pectic substances and lignin.

3.1.2 *Cell contents*

The cell contents are comprised primarily of the cell nucleus and cytoplasm and hence account for a major part of the proteins, peptides, nucleic acids, lipids, sugars and starches found in the whole plant.

In the early stages of growth, cell contents may account for at least two-thirds of forage DM, with protein being a major contributor. As grass matures, the proportion of total cell contents declines in response to a marked increase in cell wall constituents, accompanied by a pronounced decline in the percentage of protein due in part to the increase in stem : leaf ratio. At the same time, the concentration of sugars may increase although the sugar fraction (glucose, fructose, sucrose, fructans) of grasses and other forages is highly labile and the amounts present in the plant may vary considerably, especially in relation to the prevailing environmental conditions of light and temperature. Relative to grasses, legumes contain higher proportions of crude protein, organic acids and minerals but lower proportions of water soluble carbohydrates. In both grasses and legumes, the content of starch, or α-linked glucose polymer rarely exceeds 3–4% of the DM. A schematic representation of how the proportional contribution of the major chemical entities of grass may change during the various growth phases is illustrated in Fig. 3.1.

Through breeding programmes, some improvements in the percentage of crude protein in forage have been achieved, but of greater importance to the ruminant animal is the composition of the crude protein. In some instances, true protein may account for over 80% of the crude protein, but during periods of impaired growth, the non-protein nitrogen content of this fraction may increase markedly. In particular, autumn growth may

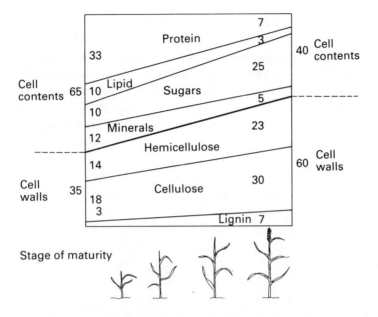

Fig. 3.1 Schematic representation of the changes in the chemical composition of grasses which accompany advancing maturity. As the grass plant matures, the proportion of cell walls and its constituent fractions increases and the cell content fraction decreases. The proportion of protein, lipid and mineral matter in the DM decreases as the plant matures, but the non-structural carbohydrates, mainly fructans, in the stem, stem base and inflorescence increase. The proportion of the crude protein that is true protein or amino acids varies from 70 to 90% and the composition of the total amino acid fraction is remarkably constant in both grasses and legumes at all stages of maturity.

contain significant amounts of nitrate N, with true protein comprising only about 50% of total crude protein. Equally, during periods of high light intensity and temperature, the synthesis of water soluble carbohydrates increases, but under such conditions the synthesis of cell walls, and in particular the degree of cell wall lignification, also increases. Increased nitrogen fertilization is known to increase the synthesis of crude protein, but when this is related to the increased yield of DM, the change in crude protein content is often minimal. Irrigation has been shown to have only marginal effects on chemical composition.

3.1.3 *Plant structure*

Clearly, whether the plant is in the vegetative or the reproductive phase affects the proportion of leaf to stem in the plant, and has a major effect on chemical composition. This is influenced by forage species, variety, environment and in particular, previous management of the sward. At all stages of growth, Italian ryegrass has a higher proportion of leaf to stem than other grass species, whilst timothy, meadow fescue and cocksfoot are characterized by higher cell wall contents. The prevailing environment also influences the rate of development of leaves and stems. It is generally found that regrowths tend to have higher proportions of leaf, although this will be influenced by the stage of growth when the primary growth is harvested and whether or not the inflorescence primordia have been removed.

Thus, whilst forage species and variety can affect the chemical and physical characteristics of the crop, many of the changes which occur are due to changes in the stem : leaf ratio of the crop as influenced by environment. Hence, management decisions regarding harvesting of the crop, either by grazing or cutting have a major bearing on the quality harvested and on the annual yield of digestible nutrients which can be obtained from grass and legume swards.

3.2   Nutritive value of forage

All animals require nutrients to maintain body weight. Additional nutrients are required by the growing animal to synthesize muscle, adipose tissue and bone, and by the lactating animal to synthesize fat, protein and lactose. While the major requirement is for nutrients which yield energy, there are also specific requirements for amino acids, glucose, fatty acids, minerals and vitamins which depend upon the stage of development, size, type and level of production of the animal.

The description of chemical composition of forages in section 3.1 characterized the constituents of a forage, but gave little information about their availability to the animal. Methods of characterizing the availability of nutrients for fermentation in the rumen, overall digestibility and efficiency of utilization of nutrients are considered in the following subsections.

3.2.1   *Degradability in the rumen*

When feed is ingested it passes into the rumen where the major portion of the organic matter is fermented. The digestion of a feed constituent, if it were to remain in the rumen for an indefinite period of time is referred to as the potential degradability (Dekker *et al.* 1972), while the fractional rate at which it is degraded is termed the degradation rate. These parameters have been estimated by placing small portions (~5 g DM) of the feed in polyester bags and incubating them in the rumen under standard conditions (Ørskov et al. 1980) for different lengths of time. The percentage disappearance of any feed fraction from the bag (P) is then plotted against time (t) and the potential degradability (a + b) calculated from the equation:

$$P = (a + b) (1 - e^{-ct}),$$

where a is the soluble fraction which disappears from the bag at time zero (t), b is the potentially digestible insoluble fraction and c is the rate of disappearance of the fraction as defined by Ørskov and McDonald (1979). In practice, however, feed does not remain in the rumen for an indefinite period, and some partially digested feed particles may leave the rumen. Values for the extent of degradation may be refined by taking into account the rate of passage of particles from the rumen. This is determined by marking a portion of the feed or a specific fraction of the feed (e.g. neutral detergent fibre, NDF) with an indigestible marker (e.g. chromium mordant or specific rare earth elements), dosing this into the rumen and measuring the decrease in marker concentration in the rumen (r) relative to time after dosing (t). This enables calculation of the fraction of the feed which leaves the rumen per unit of time (k) as follows:

$$r = e^{kt}.$$

This rate constant for passage (k) can then be used in the equation of Ørskov and McDonald (1979) as follows:

$$\text{Effective degradability} = a + \frac{(bc)}{c + k}.$$

Degradability values are most frequently used to estimate the amount of feed N available to the rumen micro-organisms (see section 3.7.2 for discussion of ARC protein system), although the method can be used to estimate the rate of fibre degradation in low quality feeds such as tropical forages, as an aid to predicting forage intake.

3.2.2. Digestibility in the whole digestive tract

The proportional amount of a particular nutrient extracted by an animal from the diet offered to it is defined as the digestibility coefficient, e.g. organic matter (OM) digestibility (OMD) is:

$$OMD = \frac{OM \text{ consumed} - OM \text{ in faeces}}{OM \text{ consumed}}.$$

This value can either be expressed as a proportion, e.g. 0.75, or when multiplied by 100, as a percentage, e.g. 75%.

Digestibility coefficients calculated in this manner are more accurately referred to as apparent digestibility coefficients, since the faeces contain not only the indigestible dietary intake, but also undigested microbes and endogenous secretions which do not arise directly from the feed. Equations exist to estimate the contribution of microbes and endogenous secretions to the faeces (e.g. Hogan & Weston 1970), and to correct apparent to true digestibilities. However, since these calculations are themselves approximations, the values most frequently quoted in the literature are apparent digestibilities.

Digestibility can be determined by conducting an experiment *in vivo* involving the total collection of faeces from animals eating a measured amount of feed (usually close to maintenance requirements) over a 7–10 day period (Cammell 1977). However, such procedures are laborious and costly; appropriate facilities for *in vivo* measurement are seldom available. Thus various *in vitro* laboratory methods have been developed to estimate digestibility although they must, at some stage, be calibrated against values determined *in vivo*. The most commonly used method is the two-stage digestion procedure developed by Tilley and Terry (1963) involving a 48 hour anaerobic incubation of dried forage, in buffered rumen liquor, followed by a further 48 hour incubation with acidified pepsin (to represent the protein digestion stage of the animal). Alternative methods based on cellulases have been developed (e.g. Hartley & Dhanoa 1981), but no standard method has yet been accepted.

Organic matter digestibility is a better estimate of nutritive value than DM digestibility since it discounts any possible effect of soil contamination of the forage and is thus more closely correlated with energy availability. However since intakes are normally given in terms of DM per day, a more useful parameter for rapid calculation of total DOM consumed is digestible organic matter in the DM, DOMD or D-value.

$$DOMD = \frac{OM \text{ consumed} - OM \text{ in faeces}}{DM \text{ consumed}} (\times 100).$$

This is represented diagrammatically in Fig. 3.2.

As discussed in section 3.7.1, since digestibility tends to decrease with advancing maturity as cell wall content increases, D-value can be predicted from a knowledge of stage of growth. However, a constant relationship between cell wall content and digestibility does not hold across species, since legumes tend to have a lower proportion of cell wall than do grasses of the same digestibility. Typical patterns of decline in D-value of primary

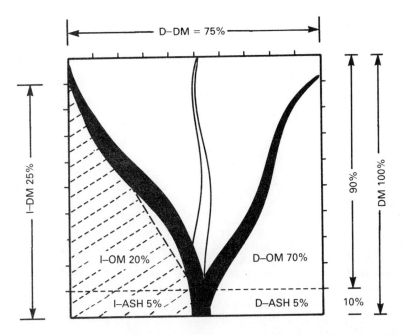

Fig. 3.2 The partitioning of plant DM between organic matter (90%) and ash (10%) contents and the further partitioning of these fractions into digestible (D) and indigestible (I) components. The plant used as an example has a DM digestibility of 75%.

$$\text{DM digestibility} = \frac{\text{Digestible DM}}{\text{Total DM}} \times 100 = \frac{75}{100} \times 100 = 75\%$$

$$\text{OM digestibility} = \frac{\text{Digestible OM}}{\text{Total OM}} \times 100 = \frac{70}{90} \times 100 = 77.7\%$$

$$\text{D-value} = \frac{\text{Digestible OM}}{\text{Total DM}} \times 100 = \frac{70}{100} \times 100 = 70\%$$

growth as the season progresses are 3–5 units D-value per week as shown in Fig. 3.3. The rate of decline of subsequent vegetative growth is lower, 1.5–2.0 units D-value per week.

Cocksfoot is characterized by a lower initial D-value than the other grass species, while Italian ryegrass and timothy show slower rates of decline, than meadow fescue, cocksfoot and perennial ryegrass. The D-value of white clover declines slowly at the rate of 0.8 units per week while D-values of red clover, sainfoin and lucerne decline at 2.5, 2.5 and 2.8 units per week respectively. In the Tropics, changes in D-value during the growing season are less marked but average digestibility of tropical forages is generally lower than for those grown in temperate regions,

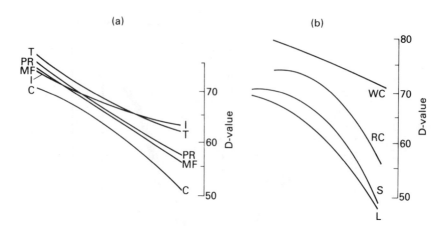

Fig. 3.3 Changes in the D-value of DOM $(t\,ha^{-1})$ of: (a) grass species; and (b) legume species, during primary growth. Italian ryegrass (I); timothy (T); perennial ryegrass (PR); meadow fescue (MF); cocksfoot (C); white clover (WC); red clover (RC); lucerne (L); sainfoin (S).

largely because tropical cell walls tend to have higher proportions of lignin.

3.2.3 *Metabolizability*

The digestibility measurements described in section 3.2.2. provide an estimate of the nutrients available for absorption. However, not all this energy is available to the tissues, since particularly in ruminants, energy is lost from the rumen as methane produced during microbial fermentations. The term metabolizable energy (ME) was proposed in the Agricultural Research Council's review No 2, *Ruminants* in 1965 (ARC 1965) and is now in common use in the UK as a parameter to describe the energy content of feeds (MAFF 1984). It is defined as the digestible energy content minus the loss of energy in methane and urine as depicted diagrammatically in Fig. 3.4.

In many situations the combined losses of energy as methane and urine vary little from 19% of the digestible energy content and ME is frequently assumed to equal $0.81 \times DE$. However, with the acquisition of more direct observations of ME contents, the validity of this assumption is being questioned.

The efficiency with which ME is utilized by the tissues depends on the process for which the energy is used. Separate values are given by ARC,

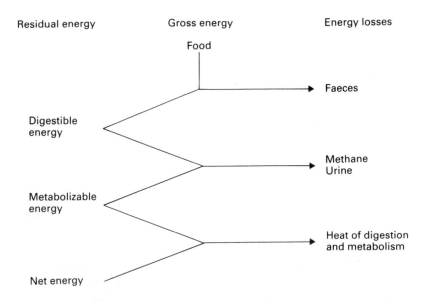

Fig. 3.4 The partition of food energy during digestion and metabolism by an animal.

(1980) for the efficiency of use of ME for maintenance (k_m), growth and fattening (k_f) and lactation (k_l). Values for the efficiency of growth and fattening (k_f) in particular depend on the diet and are lower on forage diets. This effect of diet is discussed in more detail in section 3.5.1.

3.3   Regulation of forage intake

The feeding value of a feed is related to the amount which the animal will consume voluntarily. The drive to eat in farm animals is generally related to the potential level of production, but few, if any, forages are eaten in sufficient quantity to meet in full the demands of high producing animals since intake appears to be limited by factors associated with the digestion and metabolism of the feed. With ruminants offered all-forage diets of medium to low digestibility, Conrad *et al.* (1966) suggested that physical distension of the rumen by the bulky forage is likely to be one of the major limiting factors, although other negative feedbacks such as high ruminal acetate concentrations may also be involved. General aspects of physical control of intake are discussed in section 3.3.1 whilst more specific problems related to intake by grazing animals and of silage are in sections 3.3.2 and 3.3.3. The final sub section (3.3.4) considers the effect of supplements on forage intake.

3.3.1   *Physical control of intake*

Where conserved forages are freely available to ruminants, their intake is controlled mainly by physical factors. The degree of physical distension of the rumen is monitored by both tension and epithelial receptors which respond to both stretch and mechanical stimulation of the rumen wall. Thus not only the volume of digesta in the rumen but also its fibrosity determines intake. The amount of time the ingested forage occupies space in, and thus distends, the rumen is dependent on both its rate of digestion and on the rate at which digesta flow out of the rumen. Factors affecting rate of digestion are considered in section 3.4, while factors affecting rate of outflow, or passage, are considered here. Since particles >1.2 mm are found in only low amounts in duodenal digesta of ruminants, it has been suggested that the probability with which particles larger than this can leave the rumen is low. This led to development of the hypothesis that the rate of physical breakdown of forages could restrict the rate of removal of digesta from the rumen and hence limit voluntary intake. Methods of determining the resistance of forages to breakdown have been developed. However, while the relationship between such measurements of resistance and intake appears to be reasonable in tropical forages (Laredo & Minson 1973), it is much less apparent in temperate grasses. Observations summarized by Ulyatt *et al.* (1986), show that the major proportion of material in the rumen at any one time is predominantly in the form of small particles, as illustrated for cattle offered hay or silage in Fig. 3.5. This implies that particle size reduction is not likely to be the rate-limiting step to removal of digesta from the rumen in animals offered temperate forages.

No single mechanism has been suggested to replace the earlier dominance of physical breakdown as a concept to explain the relatively slow rate of removal of digesta from the rumen. However, considerable interest is now placed on the function of the raft like structure which is frequently observed in the rumen of animals eating forage diets. This raft may act as a filter which retains small, rapidly digesting particles, within the rumen (Sutherland 1988). If this concept becomes generally accepted, it may have particular importance for considering differences between forages which stimulate the formation of a raft to different degrees. In summary, it appears that the long retention time of forage within the rumen makes a major contribution to the control of forage intake, but the reasons for long retention times are as yet not well understood.

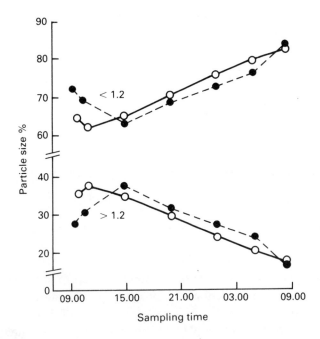

Fig. 3.5 Percentage of particles <1.2 mm and >1.2 mm in the rumen contents of young cattle eating hay (O——O) or silage (●– – –●). (L.R.S. Thiago, unpublished results.)

3.3.2 *Intake at grazing*

The same general principles of intake regulation apply to ruminants grazing on pasture, but additional factors related to the availability of forage and the ease of harvesting, may become dominant. Experiments conducted under different management conditions indicate that on rotational grazing, intake tends to increase with herbage allowance. This may be due to the greater opportunity for selection of material as the amount of pasture available per unit area increases (Penning *et al.* 1986). On continuously grazed swards, the relationship between intake by sheep and height of sward appears to be asymptotic with the critical height being between 3 and 6 cm.

Apart from availability of forage, the structure of the sward also influences intake by altering the amount of herbage which can be ingested per bite. Stobbs (1973a) with Jersey cows suggested that intake may be restricted when bite mass is less than 0.30 g organic matter, since there are limits to the extent to which the animal can compensate for decreased bite size by increasing either the biting rate or the time spent grazing. This is a particular problem with tropical pastures, owing to the erect

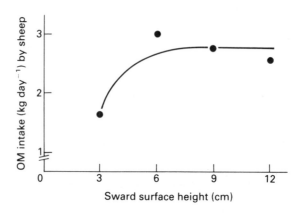

Fig. 3.6 The effects of sward surface height on intake (after Penning 1986).

nature of the sward. Stobbs (1973b) found bite size to decrease as tropical pasture matured and described the problem as 'starvation in the midst of plenty'.

Intake of fresh forage may be sensitive also to water content. In New Zealand, John and Ulyatt (1987) observed that voluntary consumption of feed DM was positively correlated with forage DM content at all stages of forage maturity for forage DMs ranging from 12 to 25%. Supporting data from the UK show that the rate of consumption of DM was significantly lower early in the morning (5 a.m.) when the DM of the herbage was only 12% (Penning & Hooper 1987). (See also section 3.7.3.)

3.3.3 *Specific problems of silage intake*

The intake of silage is generally less than the intake of hay or fresh forage of similar digestibility but the degree of difference is highly variable (1−64%) Demarquilly (1973). However, it is generally accepted that the physical effects of digestibility, which appear to exert a major control on hay intake, are modified by the presence of fermentation end products in silage. Thus, for example, short-term infusion of histamine or gamma amino butyric acid has been shown to reduce intake, as has the infusion of acetate and propionate. However, differences in fermentation end products between silages are unlikely to be related to one specific nutrient but research to consider the combined effects of changing more than one nutrient has proved difficult. For example, studies have shown that part of the negative response to acetate can be alleviated by the addition of citrate or the replacement of part of the acetate with propionate, whilst

the negative intake response to lactic acid addition to silage was removed
by the addition of fishmeal. Thus, the intake of a specific silage is likely to
be the combined response to a number of variables, of which the nature
of the fermentation end products is clearly important.

3.3.4   *The effect of supplements upon forage intake*

The effects of supplementation on production will be considered in more
detail in section 3.6, the discussion here relates solely to the effect on
voluntary intake. Very few energy supplements have a purely additive
effect on forage intake. Starch-based supplements tend to decrease rumen
pH and fibre digestion and, as a consequence, forage intake. The decrease
in forage DM intake per kg increase in concentrate DM intake (referred
to as the substitution rate) is dependent on the nature of both the forage
and the supplement.

As the digestibility and hence the cell contents of hay, increase,
addition of a starch based supplement has a greater depressive effect on
forage intake (Fig. 3.7). The response of supplements with silage is
different, since as with the intake of silage alone, the effect of digestibility
on substitution rate is modified by the fermentation acids. Hence Wilkins
(1974) proposed that substitution rates for silages are related to the intake
of the silage as the sole feed. This is illustrated schematically in Fig. 3.8.

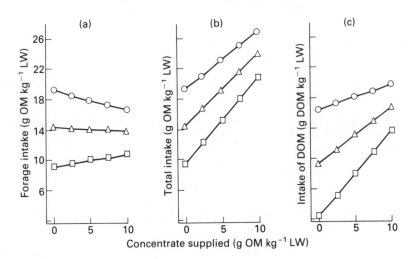

Fig. 3.7 Interaction between the level of concentrate consumption by cattle and the quality
of hay. Effects of level of concentrate consumption by finishing cattle on (a) forage OM
intake, (b) total OM intake, and (c) total digestible OM intake. High (○); medium (△);
and low (□) digestibility of hay (after Vadiveloo & Holmes 1979).

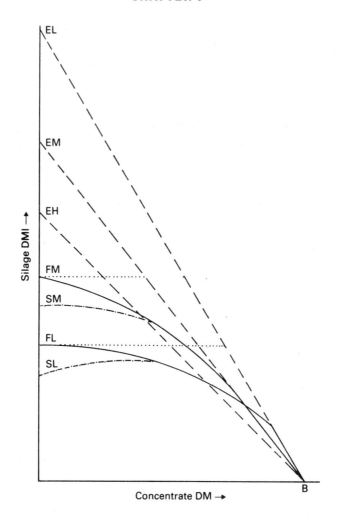

Fig. 3.8 Schematic representation of the relationship between silage intake and concentrate supplementation (Thomas 1987, after Osbourn 1980). Low (L), medium (M), and high (H) digestibility. Lines EL, EM and EH to B, represent the intakes of silage of low, medium and high digestibility respectively, assuming that the animal could eat to maintain constant energy intake. The solid curves FM and FL to B represent the effect of concentrate in depressing cellulolytic activity in the rumen and hence increasing rumen 'fill', while the dotted lines (FM and FL to B) predict the intake of M and L if the concentrate had no effect on fill. Finally, the broken lines SM and SL represent the control of intake by factors related to fermentation characteristics of the silage.

In general the intake of any forage on its own is a better indicator of likely substitution rate than is digestibility. Dulphy (1978) derived the following equation to predict substitution rate (SR) from experimental results obtained with dairy cows offered fresh forage, hay and ensiled grass and maize:

$$SR = -0.418 + 0.404x \qquad (r=0.88),$$

where x is the intake of the forage as the sole feed expressed as a percentage of liveweight.

The composition of the carbohydrate fraction (e.g. starch vs. fibre) of the concentrate may also affect substitution rate, through differing extents of depression of cellulolytic activity. However, the effect is not consistent. Thomas *et al.* (1986) and Sutton *et al.* (1987) reported higher forage intakes with fibre compared to starch based concentrates (Table 3.1), but Castle *et al.* (1981) found no difference and Mayne and Gordon (1984) reported higher forage intakes with barley.

In line with the relationship between substitution rate and digestibility of conserved forages, supplementation of animals grazing highly digestible pasture with high energy concentrates, has been associated with high substitution rates. Values of 0.79–0.84 were recorded for ewes by Milne *et al.* (1979) and of 0.87–0.95 for steers by Tayler and Wilkinson (1972).

High energy concentrates are not the only feeds which are used as supplements to forages. Some grasses, particularly those grown in the Tropics and sub Tropics, may be deficient in total N, whilst animal production on many temperate grasses, hays and silages is limited also by low protein supply. In contrast to energy, supplementation with nitrogen sources may increase forage intake. Thus, urea will increase the intake of low-N, high-fibre tropical grasses, and protein supplements may increase the intake of low-N temperate grass silages. However, as the N content of

Table 3.1. Influence of type of concentrate on substitution rate (SR) (after Thomas 1987).

			Intake (kg DM day^{-1})		
Source	Type	Level	Concentrate	Forage	SR
Thomas *et al.* (1986)	Starchy	Low	6.1	7.4	0.37
		High	10.7	5.7	
	Fibrous	Low	6.0	8.4	0.37
		High	11.1	6.5	
Sutton *et al.* (1987)	Starchy	Low	9.3	9.7	0.74
		High	12.0	7.7	
	Fibrous	Low	9.3	10.7	0.77
		High	12.0	8.6	

the silage increases, the intake response is likely to diminish, until with
high-N silages and high levels of inclusion, protein supplements may also
substitute for silage intake.

3.4   Digestion in the ruminant

3.4.1   *The ruminant digestive tract*

Ruminant animals are characterized by the development of a forestomach
comprising three diverticula or compartments anterior to the true stomach,
the abomasum (Moir 1968). Food eaten by the animal is subjected to
preliminary chewing which ruptures cell walls releasing considerable
quantities of the cell contents. Saliva is secreted into the mouth in large
amounts and mixed with the food to form a bolus which passes down the
oesophagus into the rumen, the first and largest of the forestomach's
compartments. Digesta pass freely between the first compartment, rumen
and the second compartment, the reticulum, in response to cyclic muscular
contractions.

Passage into the third stomach, the omasum, through the reticulo-
omasal orifice is restricted to fluids and small food particles in suspension.
The necessary reduction in particle size is achieved largely by the regurgitation of digesta from the rumen into the mouth where saliva is added
again and the digesta are subjected to prolonged chewing or rumination
prior to being reswallowed. The reflex mechanism of regurgitation which
initiates rumination is a response to the physical stimulus of coarse fibrous
food particles in the rumen. As rumination proceeds it reduces particle
size eventually removing the stimulus for regurgitation.

The reticulo-rumen serves as a large reservoir in which to store bulky
food consumed throughout the day. Within the reticulo-rumen the digesta
are maintained at a near constant temperature, in anaerobic conditions,
at a pH between 5·5 and 7·0. This and the flow of nutrients and water
through the organ combine to create a favourable and relatively constant
environment in which bacteria and protozoa develop. These micro-
organisms grow and multiply, degrading the protein, along with the
structural and non structural carbohydrates to supply the energy required
for the synthesis of the microbial biomass. The waste products of the
microbial metabolism are volatile fatty acids (VFA), which are absorbed
from the rumen to provide the major source of energy for the host
animal, ammonia, absorbed and converted into urea, and methane and
carbon dioxide largely eliminated from the rumen by eructation.

Undigested feed constituents, lipids, proteins and carbohydrates, together with a proportion of the micro-organisms synthesized in the rumen, pass via the omasum into the acidic conditions in the abomasum and the near neutral conditions in the small intestine where host enzyme secretions continue the process of digestion, reducing feed and microbial proteins to amino acids and α-linked polysaccharides to glucose. These, together with the long-chain fatty acids derived from dietary lipids, are absorbed from the small intestine. Any β-linked structural carbohydrates pass unchanged through the small intestine into the large intestine where they and any undigested residues of ruminal micro-organisms are subjected to a second anaerobic microbial fermentation largely in the caecum. This fermentation too produces VFA and ammonia which are absorbed, but any microbial biomass synthesized is excreted in the faeces together with undigested feed residues as there is no further host animal enzyme secretion in the colon and rectum.

3.4.2   *The rumen micro-organisms*

Bacteria comprise the largest proportion of the microbial population in the rumen and are actively involved in the fermentation of ingested carbohydrate and protein. The number and types of bacterial species present are affected by the nature of the diet, e.g. Theodorou *et al.* (1985) reported a more rapid (as measured in terms of numbers of viable bacteria) initiation of digestion in the rumen of cattle offered white clover compared to those offered grass. The occurrence of protozoa in the rumen has been known for many years and whilst present in lower numbers than bacteria (10^6 compared with 10^{10} ml^{-1}), their larger size means that they contribute significantly to overall rumen metabolism. Their ability to engulf bacteria and small particles is well established, as is the important metabolic role they assume on high grain and high legume containing diets. In contrast, several reports particularly with low-N roughages suggest benefits to the nutrition of the host animal following removal of some or all of the protozoa by defaunating agents (Bird *et al.* 1979).

Research over the last few years has demonstrated the presence of anaerobic fungi in the rumen contents of cattle and sheep (Bauchop 1979, Lowe *et al.* 1985). Life cycle studies of such organisms suggest that they may play a significant role in the ruminal degradation of fibre, especially in the primary stages of colonization and invasion prior to bacterial metabolism. However, the quantitative significance of their metabolism requires further elucidation.

3.4.3 *Microbial fermentation*

Following the onset of fermentation, the ingested carbohydrates are degraded to hexose units and may at this stage undergo further fermentation with the production of ATP, essential for the maintenance and growth of the microbial population. Alternatively some of the degraded hexose may be incorporated directly by the microbes in the synthesis of biomass. Associated with the fermentation of hexose, VFAs are produced and a concomitant decline in rumen pH is likely to occur. However, through the processes of continual salivation, and the animal's ability to secrete large quantities of bicarbonate into the rumen, the magnitude of this decline in pH will vary, although on diets containing a high proportion of cereals, where digestion and VFA production following a meal will be rapid, the animal's ability to maintain pH is often impaired and values below 6.0 may result. If this occurs the metabolic activity and contribution of the cellulolytic bacteria declines and fibre digestion will be impaired. This is a major contributory factor to the decrease in forage intake in response to energy-rich supplements (see section 3.3.4).

On most forages, between 80 and 90% of potentially digestible fibre and almost all of the water soluble carbohydrates and pectins are digested in the rumen. Since the main end products of this fermentation are VFA, the contribution of absorbed VFA to the total energy absorbed is high, accounting for some 75−85% of ruminally digested energy and between 450 and 600 kJ MJ^{-1} digestible energy. Correction to ME intake, by accounting for methane production raises these values to 490 and 660 kJ MJ^{-1} ME, confirming the importance of VFA as a major energy substrate for ruminants. In general on forage diets the molar proportion of acetate in the rumen fluid is enhanced while cereal based concentrate diets tend to promote high-propionate fermentations.

The proteins of fresh forages and most silage diets are extensively degraded in the rumen and the supply of nitrogenous substrates (e.g. amino acids and ammonia) for microbial protein synthesis often exceeds the desired balance of energy and N for microbial growth. Such processes are usually accompanied by a pronounced rise in rumen ammonia concentration some 2−3 hours after feed ingestion. Thus duodenal protein supply on fresh forages and silages (excluding formaldehyde treated silages) is often less than crude protein intake, suggesting a major loss of N from the rumen as ammonia and an associated inefficiency of N utilization. On high-N white clover diets, Beever *et al.* (1986) and Ulyatt *et al.* (1988) found duodenal NAN flows equivalent to only 60% of N intake and for a range of fresh forage diets of contrasting N contents Ulyatt *et al.* established the following relationship:

$$Y = 1.430 - 0.0169x \qquad (r = 0.72, \text{ RSD } 0.140),$$

where Y = NAN flow/N intake (g/g) and x = N content in crop (g kg^{-1} OM).

In contrast, on low-N diets the above equation shows that duodenal NAN flow may exceed N intake due to the inflow of endogenous N and an enhanced efficiency of capture of degraded N by the microbes. Research with a range of forage diets has established that the efficiency of microbial protein synthesis is highly variable (McAllan *et al.* 1988) and on many silage diets may be considerably less than the mean value proposed by ARC (1984) of 32 g microbial N kg^{-1} organic matter apparently digested in the rumen (OMADR). In Table 3.2, values range from 13 to 28 g kg^{-1} OMADR. Those values below 20 g kg^{-1} are particularly interesting and important but it is not possible, due to the variability in the nature of the crops, and ensiling conditions used in the different studies, to draw further conclusions from these data at this stage. In contrast, values for fresh forages are much higher (range 33–58 g kg^{-1}; Table 3.2), an effect which may be related to the enhanced ruminal energy supply, in the form

Table 3.2. Estimates of the efficiency of microbial N synthesis for ensiled and fresh forages fed to sheep or cattle.

	Animal species	g microbial N kg^{-1} OMADR
Ensiled forages (all grasses)		
Unwilted	S	28.1
Wilted	S	21.6
Formic, unwilted	S	19.1
Formic, wilted	S	21.6
Formic, unwilted	C	19.0
F+F, unwilted	S	13.1
F+F, unwilted	C	23.7
F+F, wilted	S	27.2
Fresh forages		
Perennial ryegrass	C	46.9
White clover	C	58.1
Lucerne	S	40.9
Subterranean clover	S	33.2
Perennial ryegrass	S	33.1

S = sheep; C = cattle; F+F = formic and formaldehyde containing additives.

of soluble carbohydrates usually found on such diets. The lipid components of forage undergo less extensive transformation within the rumen. Bacterial hydrolysis is known to occur with the production of long chain fatty acids and glycerol. The former then undergo extensive, although not necessarily complete, saturation due to the reducing conditions in the rumen, whilst the small amount of glycerol released is fermented with the production of VFA.

3.4.4   *Absorption of amino acids and lipids*

Duodenal protein comprises protein of microbial and undegraded feed origin, plus an endogenous contribution arising from gut secretions and gut wall sloughings. Apparent digestibility of duodenal protein is generally high and often exceeds $700 \, g \, kg^{-1}$. Thus, the contribution of absorbed protein to total ME supply will be significantly influenced by duodenal supply. On low-N diets or diets containing high quantities of readily degradable N, the amount of absorbed protein may be as low as $5.5 \, g \, MJ^{-1}$ ME intake, but on high N diets, including legumes or those containing quantities of undegradable protein this may rise to values in excess of $11.0 \, g \, MJ^{-1}$ ME (Beever 1980).

There is still surprisingly little information on the contribution of lipids to host animal nutrition. Virtually all studies conclude that duodenal long chain fatty acid supply exceeds dietary intake, reflecting microbial lipid synthesis within the rumen plus the non destructive transformation (i.e. hydrolysis and saturation) of ingested lipid. On a series of cocksfoot and red clover diets offered to sheep, Outen *et al.* (1974, 1975) concluded that long chain fatty acids absorbed from the small intestine accounted for some 7–10% of apparently digested energy. On lipid supplemented diets, this figure would rise, but is seldom likely to exceed 20% of DE intake.

3.4.5   *Digestion in the hindgut*

In most situations, digestion in the hindgut is insignificant amounting to less than $75 \, kJ \, MJ^{-1}$ DEI. An exception is when dried forages are fed in the ground and pelleted form, when passage of partially digested material from the rumen is accelerated. Beever *et al.* (1972) were able to account for 70% of the increased flow of duodenal OM as cellulose and hemicellulose, and extensive compensatory digestion in the hindgut was observed with as much as 25% of the digestible OMI being digested therein. However, as intake is increased on such diets, this compensation is not complete and overall digestibility falls.

3.5   Tissue utilization of forage energy and protein

The level of production achieved by ruminants, depends not only on the total amount of energy and protein reaching the tissues, but also on the efficiency with which these nutrients are used for growth or milk production. The concept of ME as the energy available to the tissues was introduced in section 3.2.3. Conversion of this ME to net energy, (the energy retained in the tissues), is achieved by using efficiency terms to correct for the losses associated with the oxidation of nutrients to provide energy to maintain the tissues (k_m); heat lost during the synthesis of fat and protein for growth (k_f) or fat, protein and lactose for milk (k_l). The efficiency of energy use for maintenance varies somewhat with diet, and is lower for forage only compared to mixed diets (Table 3.3). However, the efficiency of utilization for growth and fattening is more sensitive to diet as discussed below. During lactation, the dairy cow buffers dietary deficiencies by utilizing her own body reserves so that k_l appears to be relatively independent of diet. Both growth and milk production are also sensitive to protein supply. The utilization of energy and protein for these processes will be discussed, followed by consideration of the effect of forage diets on the composition of liveweight gain and milk.

Table 3.3. Variation in the efficiency of use of metabolizable energy (ME) with physiological function and type of diet (when metabolizability ME/GE = 0.50 or 0.60).

	Efficieny of use of ME					
	Maintenance, k_m		Growth, k_f		Lactation, k_l	
Metabolizability	0.50	0.60	0.50	0.60	0.50	0.60
Forages	0.66	0.68	0.34	0.47	0.60	0.63
Pelleted feeds	0.67	0.70	0.48	0.48	0.60	0.63
Mixed diets	0.73	0.75	0.47	0.51	0.60	0.63

Values from ARC (1980).

3.5.1   *The form of energy supplied in forage diets*

The efficiency values for growth (k_f) recommended by ARC (1980) are lower for forages than for pelleted feeds or mixed diets (Table 3.3). This lower efficiency for forages is well-known but poorly understood. Blaxter & Clapperton (1965) suggested that the inefficiency could be due to the higher proportion of acetate produced in the rumen on forage diets. Their evidence, from the effect of infusion of individual VFAs on heat production, indicated a higher heat production (lower efficiency) for acetate compared to propionate or butyrate. However, subsequent work has not always confirmed this observation (Hovell *et al.* 1976, Ørskov *et al.* 1979). These conflicting results may be explained by differences in the basal nutrients supplied, since Tyrrell *et al.* (1979) found that the efficiency of acetate utilization was greater when acetate was added to a diet of forage and concentrates than to a diet of forage alone. Armstrong (1965) had suggested that the rate of conversion of acetate to fatty acids may be limited by the low availability of the reduced co-factor NADPH, on high-fibre diets since NADPH is required for fatty acid synthesis, but its main precursor is glucose, the absorption of which is negligible on most forage diets. In ruminants the main precursors of glucose are propionate and amino acids and MacRae and Lobley (1982) suggested that the diets where efficiency of acetate utilization was high, would have supplied sufficient glucose precursors to ensure adequate NADPH supply. Black *et al.* (1987) examined this hypothesis using a mathematical model and suggested that with high protein diets additional acetate would be used to supply the energy required for increased protein synthesis. Hence it is probable that the ratio of individual nutrients supplied on forage diets may contribute to the low efficiency observed, but this is unlikely to be the sole explanation.

It has been suggested that the energy required to eat, ruminate and subsequently move fibrous digesta through the gut may be elevated on fibrous diets but experimental data suggest that the direct cost of this is small (Webster 1980). The possibility of an indirect cost on forage diets through the stimulation of increased metabolism within the gut was also examined by Webster, but the evidence is insufficient to draw any definite conclusions.

3.5.2 *Protein utilization by the tissues*

Since increased production can result from protein supplementation of both grazing animals and those offered silage it would appear that protein supply may limit production on some forages. Part of this limitation is due to the effect of low protein diets in limiting intake (see section 3.3.4), but even where protein supplementation has no effect on intake, a production response may still be observed (Gill *et al.* 1987). The effect of protein supplements on production will be considered in detail in section

3.6.2 and 3.6.4, the aim here is to consider differences in how absorbed protein is utilized.

The efficiency of utilization of absorbed amino acids is partly dependent on the ratio of amino acids absorbed relative to the requirements for specific amino acids, and the relative proportions in the proteins to be synthesized. When the ARC protein system was first introduced (ARC 1980) the efficiency of utilization was assumed to be 0.75 of amino acids apparently absorbed. The subsequent revision of the system (ARC 1984) considered truly absorbed amino acids and the efficiency value was increased to 0.80. However, there is increasing evidence to suggest that the overall utilization is much lower on forage diets. The reasons for this low efficiency are as yet unknown, but it may be due to the different ratio of non-protein containing nutrients absorbed from forage diets having a negative effect on the utilization of amino acids for protein synthesis.

3.5.3   *Effects of forage on composition of meat and milk*

Since the profile of nutrients absorbed from forage diets differs from those absorbed on concentrate or mixed diets, it is perhaps not surprising that the composition of both liveweight gain and milk tends to differ also. The well known effects of high fibre diets, in increasing the fat content of milk have been attributed to the higher contribution of acetate to the total absorbed energy (Fig. 3.9, after Broster *et al.* 1979). The protein and lactose contents in milk are much less sensitive to dietary manipulation. Similarly with liveweight gain, the percentages of water and protein in the fat free empty body are relatively constant, while the amount of fat associated with the fat free empty body tends to be higher on, for example, non-supplemented silage diets (Lonsdale 1976).

3.6   The use of supplements and nutritional manipulants

In systems of animal production which depend on forages, the provision of feed supplements will be based on one or more criteria. In the first instance, if the overall supply of metabolizable energy from forage is inadequate to meet the desired production targets, energy-rich feeds to increase the concentration of ME in the overall diet will be necessary. Secondly, specific feed supplements may lead to desirable changes in the composition of the final product (i.e. milk or meat). Finally, feed supplements are needed where nutritional deficiencies (e.g. minerals, vitamins) have been identified. As the use of supplements which fall into the first

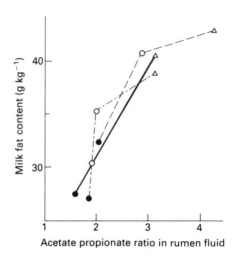

Fig. 3.9 Relationships between milk fat content and the ratio of acetic acid to propionic acid in the rumen. Ratio of concentrates : hay, 90 : 10 (●); 75 : 25 (○); 60 : 40 (△). Intake *ad libitum* (——); moderate intake (– – –); and high intake (–·–·–·) (after Broster *et al.* 1979).

two categories is easier with indoor feeding, energy and protein supplementation of conserved feeds is considered separately from grazing.

3.6.1 *Energy supplementation of conserved feeds*

It is common practice to feed a significant proportion (up to 70%) of the total diet of dairy cows as concentrates. These may be purchased compounds usually defined in terms of their fibre, oil and protein contents rather than in terms of their constituent feeds. Alternatively, the use of individual components (straights) is increasing in popularity and considerable quantities of barley, maize gluten, brewers grains, sugar beet pulp and some wheat and oats are used.

The overall effect of supplementation on the performance of the cow will be influenced by the amount and nature of the supplement used and the composition of the forage on offer. The effect of forage composition on the substitution rate of concentrate for forage intake has already been discussed (section 3.3.4). In addition to increasing total ME intake through the use of concentrate supplements, where an increased proportion of ME is derived from concentrates, improvements in the efficiency of utilization of ME for growth and fattening (k_f), may occur (Table 3.3). The origin of this effect probably lies at the tissue level, possibly associated with nutrition/hormonal interactions, but it is not yet well understood.

3.6.2   *Protein supplementation of conserved feeds*

Protein supplements have been used in forage-based diets, especially silages, for both dairy and beef cattle. The high-producing dairy cow and the young growing animal are known to have high protein requirements, and the discrepancy between supply (i.e. small intestinal absorption) and requirement is exacerbated on silage diets where, due to extensive proteolysis during harvesting and conservation, the supply of amino acids is often below expectations. Use of formaldehyde-containing silage additives and minimization of the wilt period can reduce this shortfall, but there is a need to improve the preservation of protein within the conservation process. In the meantime, the use of protein supplements of inherently low rumen degradability, e.g. fishmeal, at levels equivalent to or in excess of the recommendations established by ARC (1980, 1984) has led to sizeable responses in milk output and milk protein secretion in dairy cows Castle (1982), and in liveweight gain and the ratio of protein : fat in the carcass of growing cattle (Gill *et al.* 1987). However, with beef cattle receiving mixed diets of highly digestible silage plus concentrates, the response to fishmeal has been poor. Moreover in some instances, some or all of the apparent benefits in liveweight gain over the winter period have been lost over the subsequent grazing season.

3.6.3   *Energy supplementation at grazing*

As mentioned earlier (section 3.3.4) supplementation of highly digestible pasture with energy-rich supplements is associated with a high substitution rate. However, the substitution rate varies with herbage availability, increasing as the amount of herbage on offer increases (Meijs & Hoekstra 1984). Thus supplementation can have a beneficial effect when herbage availability is restricted (Le Du & Newberry 1982). Other forages can also be used as supplements when herbage availability is low, e.g. the cows may be yarded at night with silage or hay available.

Forages are also used to supplement tropical pastures during the dry season, although responses are not always reliable. Other economic possibilities include the use of crop byproducts such as molasses. However, their nutritive value is generally low and their use is largely governed by cost.

3.6.4   *Protein supplementation at grazing*

Protein supplementation of grazing lambs at pasture has been shown to increase rates of liveweight gain and the ratio of protein : fat in the resultant carcass (Black *et al.* 1979, Barry *et al.* 1982) but the problem is how to ensure consumption of the supplement. Urea-molasses blocks have been used to improve the intake of non-protein N, but uneven consumption of the blocks leads to poor utilization. The use of legumes (e.g. *Leucaena leucocephala*) has led to increased production on tropical pastures (Pound & Martinez-Cairo 1983), but while grazing of predominantly legume pastures may lead to higher production, it also increases the risk of bloat (see section 3.8.4).

3.6.5   *Mineral and vitamin supplementation*

When cattle are fed conserved feeds indoors it is relatively simple to supplement their diet with minerals, proprietary mixtures and blocks. Supplementation at pasture is more difficult. Deficiencies which may occur are discussed in sections 3.8.2 and 3.8.3.

3.7   **Prediction of animal performance**

Prediction of the level of animal performance by any particular forage requires estimation of both the nutritive value and voluntary intake. The main parameters used to define the energy and protein value of a feed, are DOMD, ME, crude protein and protein degradability (sections 3.2.1 and 3.2.2). The aim in this section is to discuss ways of predicting these values, and of predicting voluntary intake, concluding with a discussion on alternative methods of prediction which may become more important in the future.

3.7.1   *Energy value*

The energy value of a forage is closely related to the maturity of the crop and thus will change throughout the growth period. Each grass or legume variety has its own characteristic pattern of change in D-value during primary growth in the spring, which is related to stage of growth and calendar date, within broad bands of latitude (e.g. see Fig. 3.10). Charts to predict D-value, N content and moisture content for a range of varieties are available in the UK as NIAB Farmers Leaflets No. 16 (NIAB 1987a, b) and GRI Technical Bulletins Nos. 8 and 26, although these need to be modified to take account of unusually early or late, wet or dry seasons. These predictions are based on a particular management system during the previous autumn and further modification to take account of deviations from this are also necessary (Walters 1976).

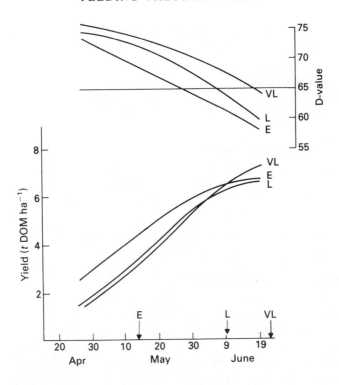

Fig. 3.10 Changes in the D-value and yield of DOM (t ha^{-1}) of early (E), late (L) and very late (VL) flowering varieties of perennial ryegrass during primary growth.

Prediction of D-value is particularly important for planning the winter feeding programme and estimating the level of performance which the amount of conserved feed will support. Thus, while approximate predictions can be made as to when to cut the crop for conservation to achieve a desired D-value, more accurate assessments necessary for rationing purposes, should be based on chemical analysis of the conserved crop rather than simply from date of harvest. In taking samples for analysis, care should be taken to ensure that the sample obtained is truly representative, with each batch of hay or silage sampled from at least 12 random points, the samples thoroughly mixed, and a representative sub sample taken for chemical analysis.

The method most commonly used for advisory purposes to assess fibre content determines the content of modified acid detergent fibre (MADF). Equations to estimate the digestible organic matter in the DM (DOMD) or ME from MADF (%) have been derived in the UK, by determining

digestibility and ME *in vivo* on a wide range of samples at the ADAS
Feed Evaluation Unit at Drayton.

For hay (MAFF 1987)
DOMD   = 102.3 − 1.20 MADF
ME (MJ/kg DM)   = 16.5 − 0.21 MADF

For grass silage (MAFF 1987)
DOMD (% TDM)   = 94.5 − 0.91 MADF (corrected)
ME (MJ/kg TDM) = 15.33 − 0.152 MADF (corrected
                              where TDM is ODM+ 1.9)

corrected MADF   = (MADF on ODM basis) × $\dfrac{ODM}{TDM}$

For fresh grass (Morgan 1973)
DOMD   = 99.4 − 1.17 MADF
ME (MJ kg^{-1} DM)   = 15.9 − 0.19 MADF
(TDM = toluene DM, ODM = oven DM)

The determination of ME is generally conducted with mature wether
sheep, offered the feed at a level sufficient to maintain body weight
(maintenance). Daily intake and faecal and urine excretion of energy are
measured for individual animals over a 10 day period, and the loss of
energy as methane after fermentation in the rumen is either determined
in calorimeters, or calculated from published equations (Blaxter &
Clapperton 1965). An alternative laboratory method for estimating
digestibility was developed by Jones and Hayward (1975), using a pepsin/
cellulase digestion. This method avoids the need to maintain fistulated
animals to provide the inoculum for the *in vitro* technique. However, a
comparison of these two 'digestion' methods with the summative equation
for fibre analysis (Van Soest 1967) carried out on tropical forages by
Thomas *et al.* (1980), showed that the *in vitro* method for estimating
digestibility was the most accurate.

3.7.2   *Prediction of protein supply*

Prediction of the protein supplied to the tissues requires estimation of the
degradation of feed protein and synthesis of microbial protein in the
rumen. Degradability of feed protein is usually determined by incubating
a small portion of the feed in polyester bags suspended in the rumen as

described in section 3.2.2. This value (Dg) can then be used in the ARC system (ARC 1984) to estimate the total protein supplied to the intestines as the sum of microbial (MP) and undegraded dietary protein (UDP) which leave the rumen, where:

MP   (g protein day $^{-1}$)
        = 8.4 × MEI (in MJ) for mixed diets, fresh or dried high-quality forages
        = 6.25 × MEI (in MJ) for grass silage diets
        = 8.75 × MEI (in MJ) for grass silage + concentrate diets

and UDP = protein intake (1 − effective degradability) (where the effective degradability is expressed as a fraction of the total protein in the feed; section 3.2.1)

The assumptions are then made that 80% of the microbial protein is present as amino acid N and only 85% of the protein entering the duodenum is truly absorbed. The efficiency of utilization of absorbed amino acids is assumed to be 0.80. Thus, the protein available to the tissues for protein synthesis is:

$$TP = (MP \times 0.8 + UDP) \times 0.85 \times 0.8.$$

While the assumptions of a constant digestibility of protein in the intestines and a constant efficiency of utilization by the tissues may be valid for concentrate diets, there is evidence (ARC 1984) (section 3.4.2.) that these values may not be the same for forages. Further, the digestibility of undegraded forage protein in the intestines may also be reduced when the protein is closely bound to the indigestible fibre (Wilson & Strachan 1981). Despite these criticisms, the concept, which requires consideration of both the requirements of the micro-organisms and the requirements of the tissues, is an improvement in our understanding of the protein requirements of the ruminant.

3.7.3 *Prediction of intake*

The prediction of intake is a necessary part of any rationing programme. Early equations for dairy cows tended to be general, i.e. to relate to more than one type of conserved feed, and to base their predictions solely on liveweight, milk yield and digestibility. More recently, separate equations have been derived for hay and silage, and some equations for silage (e.g. Lewis 1981) attempt to consider the fermentation quality of the silage, which, as discussed in section 3.3.3, can have a marked effect on intake. The prediction equations which are in use in practice, have been derived statistically from data sets where daily intakes and composition of the feed have been recorded. Thus, as the technology of silage making changes (e.g. acid based additives replaced by inoculants or other additives) extrapolation beyond the limits of the data set will occur, resulting in increased errors associated with the use of these equations. Neal *et al.* (1984) compared seven equations to predict silage intake in dairy cows, relative to an experimental data set for individually fed cows. They concluded that the error associated with all predictions was unacceptably high. The equation with the lowest error of prediction, was that reported by Vadiveloo and Holmes (1979b):

$$TDMI = 0.013\,LW + 0.14\,MY + 0.404\,C - 0.129\,WL + 4.12\log WL,$$

Where TDMI = total dry matter intake (kg), LW = live weight (kg), MY = milk yield (kg), C = concentrate DM intake (kg) and WL = week of lactation.

This equation has since been modified to avoid concentrate DM intakes on both sides of the equation, with forage DM intake (FDMI) predicted as:

$$FDMI = 0.013\,LW + 0.14\,MY - 0.596\,C - 0.129\,WL + 4.12\log WL.$$

A similar evaluation of prediction equations for silage intake by beef cattle was conducted by an AFRC working party on intake and from a comparison of two equations (Lewis 1981, ARC 1980) and the French Fill system (Jarrige *et al.* 1979), concluded that the equation suggested by ARC (1980) for coarse roughages gave the lowest prediction error. This equation is:

$$TDMI = 106.5\,q + 37.0\,C + 24.1,$$

where TDMI = total DM intake (g DMI per $kgW^{0.75}$), q = metabolizability (ME/GE), and C = proportion of concentrate in the diet represented as a decimal.

For fine roughages:

$$TDMI = 46.6\ q + 116.8.$$

Separate equations for the intake of coarse and fine roughages are also given by ARC (1980) for growing sheep.

Prediction of intake by grazing ruminants is likely to be less accurate than that of stall-fed animals, owing to the poor reliability of estimates of intake obtained at pasture. However, three new equations recently presented by Caird and Holmes (1986) illustrate the influence of sward related factors (see section 4.5.3). They also reported that the simple equation TDMI $= 0.1\,MY + 0.025\,LW$ (MAFF 1984) gave satisfactory overall predictions but underestimated intake in early lactation.

For rotationally grazed cows:

$$\text{Total OMI} = 0.323 + 0.177\,MY + 0.010\,LW + 1.636C - 1.008\,HM$$
$$+ 0.540\,HAL - 0.006\,HAL^2 - 0.048\,HAL \times C,$$

where MY = milk yield (kg d^{-1}), LW = liveweight (kg), C = concentrate intake (kgOM d^{-1}), HM = herbage mass (tOM ha^{-1}), and HAL = herbage allowance (kgOM $head^{-1}\,d^{-1}$).

For continuously grazed cows on sward of <5 cm:

$$\text{Total OMI} = 0.323\,MY - 0.006\,LW + 0.113\,WL + 3.142\,C + 3.613$$
$$SHT - 0.543\,C \times SHT + 0.019\,\text{week} - 9.791$$

where SHT = sward height (cm), week = week after 1 January.

3.7.4   *Future predictions*

The prediction equations described above are empirical, derived from data sets relating feed composition to ME content or intake. The protein system on the other hand incorporates known biological mechanisms and thus can be described as mechanistic. However, the criticisms presently levied at it reflect the current problem with such models, that of lack of appropriate biological data. Hence, while various mathematical models exist which attempt to predict for example intake, from a knowledge of the regulatory mechanisms (e.g. Forbes 1977), or duodenal protein supply based on nutrient input (France *et al.* 1982), these models operate successfully only within well defined boundaries. However, their use has highlighted areas wherein data are lacking, and are now currently being sought. Availability of these data in the future should result in the development of improved models with a wider applicability than the current empirical methods (see section 8.8).

3.8   **Nutritional disorders**

A nutritional disorder may result from either a deficiency of specific nutrients such as minerals and vitamins, the presence of a toxin in the diet, or the production of an abnormal state (e.g. bloat) by a particular diet. These three states are discussed separately in the following sub sections.

3.8.1 *Vitamins*

The vitamin content of herbage has little significance in the feeding of ruminants. Firstly, with the possible exception of vitamin E, fresh herbage contains ample fat soluble vitamins A, E and K to meet the requirements of ruminant animals. Secondly the intestinal bacteria of the ruminating animal normally synthesize adequate quantities of the B vitamins, and thirdly the animal itself synthesizes its requirements of vitamin C, and given adequate sunlight, vitamin D.

The suggested requirements for vitamin A, as β-carotene and retinol, and vitamin D proposed by the ARC in 1980 are given in Tables 3.4 and 3.5. Because of the complexity of the inter-relationship between vitamin E, selenium deficiency and the quantities of unsaturated fats in the diets of cattle, which interact to cause muscular dystrophy, no requirements for vitamin E are quoted. The effective prophylactic dose for calves would seem to be at least 20 mg α-tocopherol daily. Because of the toxicity of

Table 3.4. Requirements for vitamin A for cattle and sheep (ARC 1980).

	Daily requirement ($\mu g\, kg^{-1} LW$)	
	as retinol	as β-carotene
Cattle		
Maintenance and growth	20	120
Conception and pregnancy	30	180
Lactation (minimum)	25	150
Lactation with suckled calf	65	390
Sheep		
Maintenance and growth	10	60
Pregnancy	20	120
Lactation	15	90

$6\,\mu g$ β-carotene assumed to $= 1\,\mu g$ retinol or 3.33 iu in vitamin A.

Table 3.5. Requirements for vitamin D for cattle and sheep (ARC 1980).

	Daily requirement ($\mu g\, kg^{-1} LW$)
Cattle	
Calves	0.10
Growing cattle	0.10
Pregnant and lactating cows	0.25
Sheep	0.13

excess selenium, the use of vitamin E to treat muscular dystrophy is recommended.

The effects of conservation on vitamin contents are given in Table 3.6 from INRA (1980). It can be seen that β-carotene, the main precursor of vitamin A, is well preserved by dehydration but losses during haymaking and ensiling can be considerable. Vitamin D is not present in herbage and is formed only when either the ergosterol in plants or the dehydrocholesterol in the animal's skin is irradiated to give ergocalciferol, vitamin D_2, or cholecalciferol, vitamin D_3.

Table 3.6. The content ($mg\,kg^{-1}$) of fat-soluble vitamins in fresh and conserved feeds (after INRA 1980, see Table 5.6).

	Vitamin A as β-carotene	Vitamin D_2	Vitamin E as total tocopherols
Lucerne			
Fresh	30−60	—	114−280
Hay	15−8	400−2000	38
Dehydrated	200−>320	160−400	148−301
Grass			
Fresh	9−127	—	105−166
Hay	3.9−18	400−800	200
Silage	8−13	—	38−470

3.8.2 Minerals, major elements

The mineral elements essential for the normal functioning of both plants and animals are phosphorus, potassium, sodium, calcium, magnesium, sulphur, chlorine, iron, manganese, zinc, copper and cobalt. In addition, animals require iodine and selenium and possibly chromium, vanadium, nickel and tin, and may be harmed by excesses of molybdenum, fluorine, silica, selenium, lead and other heavy metals.

The mineral composition of grassland herbage summarized by Whitehead (1966) is given in Table 3.7, but is should be noted that the supply of minerals may be further augmented by the ingestion of soil, either indirectly through the contamination of crops harvested for conservation or directly through the grazing/overgrazing of pastures. The extent of soil ingestion by grazing animals will be influenced by the severity of defoliation and prevailing weather conditions, and under extreme conditions it has been estimated that up to 1.5 kg (cattle) and 0.3 kg

Table 3.7. The mineral content of pasture herbage (after Whitehead 1966).

Major elements	Mineral content $(\mathrm{g\,kg^{-1}\,DM})$
Calcium	2–10
Phosphorus	2–5
Sodium	0.5–10
Chlorine	1–20
Magnesium	1–4

(sheep) of soil may be ingested daily. However, knowing the quantities of minerals ingested is not sufficient to assess the ability of forages to supply an animal's mineral requirements, since the mineral elements are not all available to the animal. Apparent availabilities of 0.3 to 0.4 are commonly reported for the calcium, phosphorus and magnesium in herbage but true availabilities (accounting for endogenous losses) may be considerably higher. The effect of availability on requirement is considered in detail in ARC (1980). When animals are fed indoors it is a relatively simple task to supplement their diet with the required minerals, but grazing animals can and do suffer from a number of disorders arising from excesses, deficiencies or imbalances of mineral elements in the diet. Clinical signs of deficiency in the major elements are usually restricted to calcium, phosphorus and magnesium.

Hypocalcaemia results in 'milk fever' in cows and 'lambing sickness' in ewes. It generally occurs in cows in the winter and early spring months and is not directly attributable to a reduction in calcium availability in the diet. Rather it is the animal's inability to rapidly mobilize calcium from the skeleton in response to the increased demands of lactation which precipitate the symptoms, although the animal's previous nutritional history with respect to calcium and phosphorus intake may have some predisposing effect. Prevention, or minimization of the occurrence of the disease can be achieved by feeding low calcium diets prior to parturition, so stimulating calcium mobilization by the onset of lactation.

Phosphorus content in forages is influenced by the level of available phosphorus in the soil, and phosphorus deficiencies will reduce both forage yield and phosphorus content in the DM. Under such conditions, overall animal performance will decline, and if Ca : P ratio in the forage increases above 2, phosphorus availability to the animal will decline, often leading to impaired fertility in breeding stock.

Hypomagnesaemia or 'grass staggers' is attributable to low blood magnesium levels, and is generally found in early spring in animals under significant nutritional stress (e.g. milking cows, undernourished suckler cows). Excessive mobilization of body fat in post partum cows can induce hypomagnesaemia. During the most active period of grass growth which occurs in the spring, magnesium levels, and in particular the amount of available magnesium in grass falls. It is during such times that magnesium supplementation is needed either through magnesium enriched supplements (e.g. concentrates or blocks), by magnesium oxide dusting of pasture or addition of magnesium acetate to the drinking water. The use of ammonium and potassium fertilizers in early spring is another contributory cause to low forage magnesium levels (Paterson & Crichton 1960, 't Hart 1956). If cases of hypomagnesaemia are not observed and treated with some urgency with a subcutaneous injection of magnesium sulphate, then death will follow quite rapidly.

3.8.3 *Minerals, minor elements*

The content of minor elements in pasture is summarized in Table 3.8. Iodine deficiency is generally confined to particular areas of the country and to specific crops (e.g. brassicas), and may give rise to thyroid deficiency and goitre. The incidence of such diseases in the UK is, however, generally low with the use of iodized salt licks minimizing the effects in those areas known to be susceptible. In some countries (e.g. Australia) where iodine deficiency is known to occur, and the extensive grazing systems adopted minimize the effectiveness of mineral licks, slow release oral iodine capsules have been developed which are claimed to give linear release of iodine for up to 7 years after administration into the rumen.

Of the trace elements, copper related disorders are the most common. At copper concentrations of less than 5 ppm in the forage, frank copper deficiency will occur, resulting in general ill thrift of all affected animals. In sheep, the most common disease is swayback (neonatal ataxia) in

Table 3.8. The mineral content of pasture herbage (after Whitehead 1966).

Mineral elements	Mineral content $(\mu g\,kg^{-1}\,DM)$
Iodine	0.2−0.8
Iron	50−300
Cobalt	0.05−0.3
Copper	2−15
Manganese	25−1000
Zinc	15−60
Selenium	0.03−0.15

lambs whilst symptoms of impaired wool growth can be seen. In contrast, cattle manifest the deficiency as scouring, anaemia and impairment of bone development and coat pigmentation. Copper deficiency symptoms occur also on forages seemingly adequate in copper content but where high levels of molybdenum, alone or in combination with high levels of inorganic sulphate in the forage, markedly reduce copper utilization by the animal.

Pasture treatment with $CuSO_4$ every 3–4 years, or inclusion of Cu in salt licks can overcome most copper deficiencies, although in some regions routine administration of Cu to the animal by subcutaneous or intra-muscular injection is considered to be the most reliable procedure. The homeostatic mechanisms for controlling plasma copper levels appear to be less well developed in sheep than cattle. Consequently the liberal use of copper-containing salt licks for sheep should be avoided otherwise copper poisoning may result. Furthermore, housed sheep tend to accumu-late copper in the liver and other vital organs and there is a need in such situations to control (limit) copper levels in the diet. As an added compli-cation, recent studies have demonstrated that the susceptibility of sheep to high levels of copper, and hence the manifestation of copper poisoning varies between breeds.

Pine, is a nutritional disorder arising from cobalt insufficiency in the diet, related to the animal's inability to synthesize sufficient vitamin B_{12} in the rumen which manifests itself in inappetence and progressive emaci-ation. The incidence of the disease in Britain appears to be declining, maybe due in part to the provision of cobalt in salt licks or cobalt addition to fertilizer. In more extensive grazing situations, the use of slow release cobalt bullets has been actively promoted. Several trace mineral deficiencies are aggravated on calcareous soils, or after lime has been applied.

3.8.4 *Toxins*

The presence of oestrogens (e.g. formononetin) has been observed in some pasture legumes, especially red clover. Their concentration appears to be variable and related in some way to growing conditions of the plant. The effects may be observed in increased udder development in heifers, and the extension of teat length in both female and male sheep. The presence of oestrogens appears to have little effect on fertility in cattle, but in sheep it is advisable to remove all breeding stock from pastures which contain significant amounts of red clover at least 3 weeks prior to commencement of the breeding season. In growing animals, there may be beneficial effects of oestrogens on the deposition of carcass protein.

These may be worthy of exploitation at a time when the use of hormonal implants has been banned. However, the quantitative effect of naturally occurring oestrogens on growth has not been fully assessed.

White clover, unlike red clover, does not exhibit high oestrogen contents unless it is diseased. Much of the oestrogenic activity of legumes such as red clover is lost during the process of artificial dehydration using high temperatures.

The presence of thiaminases in a diet can reduce the absorption of thiamin producing a simple deficiency in horses and rather more complex disorders in sheep and cattle. Bracken *Pteridium aquilinum* and horsetails *Equisetum* spp. contain thiaminases. It has been suggested that cerebro-cortical necrosis which occurs sporadically in sheep and young cattle is caused by fungal infections of ryegrass which produce thiaminases.

The occurrence of toxins in tropical forages has been reviewed by Crowder and Chheda (1982) who point out that legumes generally contain a wider range of deleterious substances than grasses. For example, *Leucaena leucocephala* a leguminous shrub can induce toxicity due to high concentrations of the toxic amino acid mimosine. However, animals have adapted to mimosine in some areas of the world and new low-mimosine species of *Leucaena* have been bred.

3.8.5 *Bloat*

Ruminant bloat is the abnormal distension of the reticulo-rumen caused by excessive retention of fermentation gases within the ruminal cavity. Bloat can occur on stock grazing on grass pastures and brassica forage crops, but is most common on grazed pastures containing high proportions of legumes such as red clover, lucerne or particularly white clover. In frothy bloat, which is typical on such diets, the gas bubbles remain dispersed within the rumen contents, and it is this failure of the gas bubbles to coalesce which inhibits the removal of gases from the rumen by eructation.

With moderate stages of bloat, as measured by distension of the upper portion of the left flank immediately behind the ribs, it is advisable to monitor the affected animals but to take no further action unless the position deteriorates. If the severity of bloat does increase, the animal will suffer increased discomfort, followed by inappetance. In such cases, treatment is essential, otherwise in extreme cases death occurs. In New Zealand, where heavy reliance is placed on the use of legume-containing pastures, the annual death rate due to legume bloat has been estimated at between 0.3 and 1.2% of the dairy population.

Many reasons have been put forward to explain bloat, but the irregularity of its occurrence has hindered precise identification of the factors involved and made the prediction of bloat difficult. It is clearly related to the extensive ruminal fermentation which occurs immediately following the ingestion of a meal containing a significantly high proportion of legumes. In this regard, the animal's ability to deliberately select for legumes in a grass : legume sward exacerbates the situation, whilst dairy cows, which have to tolerate an interrupted grazing pattern due to twice daily milking are more susceptible than beef cattle which can be classed as continuous grazers within this context. Bloat in sheep occurs infrequently and generally sheep can be considered as bloat safe on most legume-containing diets.

There are several options available to reduce the risk of bloat. Minimizing the interruptions to grazing are recommended wherever feasible and limiting forage availability when animals are introduced onto legume-containing pastures is advisable. The provision of limited quantities of hay or straw may also reduce the incidence of bloat and cutting and partial wilting of the pasture prior to 'grazing' is an effective but expensive way of providing protection. Alternatively the use of proprietary anti-foaming agents and vegetable oils can be advocated, either by spraying onto the pasture or oral drenching. The practice of flank painting with vegetable oil is not recommended as a guaranteed way of minimizing the occurrence of bloat.

3.9   Potential for forages

The main limitations to animal production from forages described in the preceding sections are the relatively low DM intakes together with the poor efficiency with which the absorbed nutrients are utilized by the high producing ruminant. Forage intake is affected to a large extent by the potential digestibility of the diet, and if the rate and extent of digestion of the structural carbohydrates in particular are limited, especially within the rumen, then the level of nutrient intake will fail to reach expectations, and the need to use nutrient rich supplements to overcome such limitations will emerge. In systems which aim to exploit the low cost advantage of forages this option is counterproductive. Possible methods of fully utilizing the potential of forages are considered in this section.

3.9.1   *Introduction of legumes*

The introduction of legumes into pastures for grazing ruminants can confer major benefits in animal performance, provided the occurrence of bloat can be minimized or at least controlled. With grazed grass, daily DM intakes with cattle rarely exceed 2.4–2.6% of body weight, but with swards containing high proportions of white clover, intakes exceeding 3.0% of body weight can be achieved. Moreover, in a recent study Beever *et al.* (1986) compared spring, summer and autumn growths of both perennial ryegrass and white clover and found that on all occasions, the rate and extent of organic matter digestion in the rumen was significantly higher on the clover diet despite all crops having similar overall digestibilities. Further investigation of the cause of these differences should provide an impetus for grass breeders to reconsider the selection criteria currently in use.

One of the objectives of legume breeding is to decrease the potential for bloat. The trefoils *Medicago* spp., are known to be non bloating, and the same is true of sainfoin *Onobrychis viciifolia*. This is thought to be due to the presence of tannins in the crops which have been shown to control rumen proteolysis. There is a need to consider the feasibility of introducing tannins into bloating legumes such as red and white clover and lucerne through the techniques of genetic engineering.

3.9.2 *Chemical processing of low quality diets*

In animal production systems, the use of poorer quality forages is often unavoidable. With such diets chemical treatment (e.g. with ammonia or caustic soda) has increased forage digestibility and hence total nutrient intake. However, the economic implications of such processes should be fully considered before placing too much reliance upon them. Furthermore, ammoniation of poorer quality hays has led to animal health problems with some animals showing periods of unpredictable hyperactivity possibly related to the presence of 4-methyl imidiazole, thought to be produced during ammoniation when the treated forage contains significant quantities of residual sugars.

3.9.3 *Silage additives*

The voluntary DM intake of forage silage frequently fails to reach the level that would be obtained if the harvested crop were fed in the fresh non ensiled form and utilization of silage N is generally poor (Beever 1980). However, to date the major emphasis in the development of new silage additives has been to optimize the proportion of the harvested DM which is ultimately fed to the animals, with considerable emphasis being placed on silage stability, both during storage and feeding out. This does not necessarily result in improved nutritive value. Attempts have been made to improve the utilization of the N in the silage, e.g. through the use of formaldehyde-containing additives, but due to possible adverse effects with respect to human health, the potential exploitation of such methods appears to be limited. With a renewed interest in all aspects of the ensiling process, coupled with a greatly expanded range of silage additives, it should be possible to develop new ensiling techniques which pay greater attention to the nutritive value of the resulting silage, whilst not ignoring the importance of adequate silo management in its broadest sense. Clearly, the developments which have occurred over the last 10 years or so in this latter respect have improved the predictability of silage making, but considerable scope remains to improve the intake and nutritive value characteristics of silage when fed.

3.9.4 *The use of feed additives*

The use of feed additives such as the ionophores monensin and lasalocid has been shown to shift the production of VFA towards propionate with consequent beneficial effects on efficiencies of production. At the same time, such additives reduce the extent of methane production in the rumen which may in many situations account for up to 10% of digestible energy intake. However, when Beever *et al.* (1987) examined the effect of forage species (grass vs. white clover) and the use of two rumen manipulants (monensin supplement or formaldehyde treatment prior to feeding) on the digestion of N in fresh forages they found that both inclusion of clover and the use of formaldehyde-enhanced protein supply from 6.8 to $12.6 \, g \, MJ^{-1}$ ME. Thus, a better definition of the situations in which feed additives improve forage utilization is required.

3.9.5 *Protein supplementation*

With respect to the digestion of forages, two aspects have emerged from recent research. First due to the high solubility of dietary N in most silages and fresh forages, ruminal digestion of protein on such diets is extensive and high rates of ammonia absorption from the rumen lead to low supplies of duodenal protein, particularly with wilted grass silages (Siddons *et al.* 1979). Second, high forage diets tend to promote high acetate production rates in the rumen. Whilst this may be desirable for the production of milk fat by the lactating dairy cow, it may lead to high levels of fat deposition in the carcass of growing animals, which contrasts with current consumer preference. In both situations, protein supplements have been used to advantage (Castle 1982, Gill *et al.* 1987). Such supplements are required in small amounts and with low to medium quality forages their depressive effect on forage intake is less than that observed with energy-rich supplements. Thus protein supplements are generally more efficient in terms of optimizing forage utilization. However, further work is required to fully understand the long-term effects of periods of protein supplementation on whole-lactation yields of cows and the lifetime growth of beef cattle.

Further reading

Blaxter K.L. (1962) *The Energy Metabolism of Ruminants*. Hutchinson, London.
Forbes J.M. (1986) *The Voluntary Food Intake of Farm Animals*. Butterworths, London.
Frame J. (ed) (1988) *Efficient Beef Production from Grass*. British Grassland Society Occasional Symposium, No. 22. BGS, Hurley.
France J. & Thornley J.H.M. (1984) *Mathematical Models in Agriculture*. Butterworths, London.
Garnsworthy P.C. (ed) (1988) *Nutrition and Lactation in the Dairy Cow*. Butterworths, London.
Hungate R.E. (1966) *The Rumen and its Microbes*. Academic Press, New York.
MAFF (Ministry of Agriculture, Fisheries and Food) (1984) *Energy Allowances and Feeding Systems for Ruminants*. Reference Book No. 433. HMSO, London.
McDonald P., Edwards R.A. & Greenhalgh J.F.O. (1981) *Animal Nutrition*, 3rd edn. Longman, London.
Underwood E.J. (1966) *The Mineral Nutrition of Livestock*. Commonwealth Agricultural Bureaux, Farnham.
Underwood E.J. (1971) *Trace Elements in Human and Animal Nutrition*. Academic Press, New York.
Van Soest P.J. (1983) *Nutritional Ecology of the Ruminant*. O&B Books Inc., Corvallis, USA.

Chapter 4

Grazing management

4.1   Grazing management

Grazing management should aim to provide a supply of nutritious herbage over the growing season at low cost, avoid physical waste of herbage and inefficient utilization by the animal, and maintain the productive capacity of the sward. The needs of both the animal and the pasture must be considered, and severe adverse effects on either avoided. There is no universal system of grazing management and a wide range of systems can be found in practice (see section 4.10).

The principles and practices of grazing management are outlined in the following sections. Depending on the physical and economic circumstances, a range of optimal practices can be recommended. Throughout Britain and other temperate regions, for all but the most hardy stock, grazing is a major feed source for only a portion of the year, ranging from about 5 months in the extreme north of Scotland to about 9 months in south west England. Grazing cannot, therefore, be considered in isolation, and provision must be made also for feeding the stock in the winter. The conservation of grass is dealt with in Chapter 5.

4.2   Potential production from grazing

The production obtained from grazing depends on the quantity and quality of the herbage, on the numbers and potential productivity of the animals and on the efficiency of utilization of the pasture. Factors affecting the quantity of pasture are discussed in Chapter 2 and those affecting feeding value in Chapter 3. Some data are summarized in Table 4.1. The potential yield of DM ranges from about 2000 to 25 000 kg ha^{-1} and the quality in terms of metabolizable energy from 6 to 13 MJ kg^{-1} DM. The higher qualities also have high intake characteristics and as Table 4.1 indicates, milk yields of 30 kg and daily gains of 1.25 kg from cattle and 400 g from sheep are attainable on pastures.

Table 4.1. Approximate levels of performance attainable from grass diets of varying ME concentration. Based on ME requirements and assumptions on appetite of MAFF (1984).

	Energy concentration		
DOMD (%)*	62	68	75
MJ ME kg^{-1} DM	10	11	12
	Daily milk yield kg (no change in liveweight)		
Dairy cows			
Jersey	9	12	15
Ayrshire	17	21	24
Friesian	22	27	31
	Daily gain kg		
Beef cattle			
200 kg W	0.75	0.90	1.00
300 kg W	0.75	1.00	1.25
400 kg W	0.75	1.00	1.25
500 kg W	0.75	1.00	1.25
	Daily gain g		
Lambs			
20 kg W	200	250	300
40 kg W	300	350	400

* Approximate conversion from ME.

4.3   Grazing behaviour

This section refers both to the way in which the animal harvests grass from the sward and to the normal daily pattern of events when ruminants are grazing. Early work on grazing behaviour was reviewed by Waite (1963). Arnold and Dudzinski (1978) and Hodgson (1986) have summarized later studies.

Grazing may occupy from 6 to 11 hours per day, normally in two major periods, one before dusk and one after dawn, with additional shorter periods during the day, and at night, if the nights are long. In the tropics, animals may graze for longer times in the cooler hours of darkness. The provision of alternative feeds normally reduces the total grazing time.

During a grazing period cattle move slowly over the pasture and take successive bites by drawing grass into the mouth with the tongue and then, with the grass firmly held between the tongue and the lower incisors, pull or tear it from the sward, often with a jerking movement. Sheep follow a similar pattern but because of their smaller mouthparts they 'nibble' the grass, achieve a somewhat higher frequency of biting and may bite rather than tear the chosen grass by cutting it between the lower incisors and the dental pad of the upper jaw. This method may also be used by calves. The grazing animal moves only slowly through a uniform sward, whereas in a sparse or more variable sward it may take several steps between bites. The herbage grazed is swallowed and accumulates in the rumen. After a grazing period the animal rests and normally also ruminates, regurgitating the herbage, chewing it, mixing it with saliva and swallowing again. Rumination may occur while the animal is standing or lying. The time spent in ruminating depends on the fibrousness of the grass consumed, but normally ranges from 5 to 9 hours, the longer times with more fibrous material. Normally grazing time increases with the difficulty of harvesting the grass whether it is short, sparse or long but of low quality, while ruminating time increases as the quality of the grass eaten decreases. Bite size depends both on the size of the mouth and on the density of the sward. Hodgson (1986) records a range of 11 to 400 mg for sheep and 70 to 1610 mg for cattle.

Animals walking to and from pasture and seeking grazing may travel from 2 to 6 km per day. Faeces are deposited 8–14 times per day, with milk cows about half on the night pasture, 10–15% at or going to and from milking, and the remainder on day pasture. The animals normally urinate 4–12 times per day and drink water 2–4 times per day depending on the moisture content of the herbage (Marsh & Campling 1970).

Grazing animals select their food using the senses of touch, sight and smell (Arnold 1970). They tend to select the more leafy portion of a sward but may also choose immature seed heads partly because these are both more accessible. Sheep and calves with smaller mouthparts are more selective than larger ruminants. Grazing animals tend to avoid pasture fouled by, or near to, faeces of their own species. Whether they can do so depends on the abundance of pasture, and competition for feed.

The 'palatability' of pasture is difficult to assess and indeed is regarded as an unacceptable term by some research workers. However, green succulent material and material with a high content of sugars is usually preferred, while dead, mature or fungus infected material is usually rejected.

4.4   The measurement of herbage intake

The quantities of grass consumed by grazing cattle and sheep can be estimated by direct or indirect methods (Leaver 1982). For the direct method the mass of herbage per unit area is assessed before and after a grazing period by cutting or measuring a sufficient number of samples and the amount consumed is estimated by difference. If the grazing period exceeds 1 day, some allowance should be made for growth of grass. Recent work on this is summarized by Meijs, Walters and Keen (1982). Direct methods normally estimate the intake of groups of animals although they may be used with individual animals held in separate paddocks. Herbage consumption may be estimated also by recording the quantities of cut grass eaten by confined animals, or, in closely controlled conditions, by weighing animals before and after grazing.

There are two distinct indirect methods. One depends on the application of current feeding standards to the recorded animal performance (Baker 1982) (see Table 8.1.) The other, referred to as a faecal index method depends on assessing the daily output of faeces from each animal or group of animals, and estimating the digestibility of the feed consumed. Faeces can be collected from sheep fitted with suitable harnesses and collecting bags, although the possibility that grazing behaviour is affected cannot be discounted, but faeces collection is difficult with cattle. The alternative is to feed or dose the animal with known quantities of a nontoxic, indigestible, easily dispersible chemical (chromium sesquioxide, Cr_2O_3, is commonly used) for a period of 7 or more days so that it is uniformly distributed through the digestive tract, and then while continuing to administer Cr_2O_3, to collect representative samples of faeces from the dung pats or directly from the animals over a subsequent period of 4−6 days. From the quantity of marker supplied and its concentration in the faeces, the daily faecal output can be estimated.

Digestibility of the ingested feed and the consumption of digestible nutrients must then be estimated. Since the range of herbage digestibilities is now well known (e.g. MAFF 1984), an appropriate figure may be chosen. Alternatively, hand plucking may be attempted to simulate selection by the grazing animal, or in restricted conditions surgically modified animals with fistulae in the oesophagus may be used to select samples. These animals may, however, not be representative of the group nor may the sampling periods represent wholly the feed consumed. The *in vitro* digestibility of the samples is then estimated.

Other methods applicable to normal intact animals estimate digestibility from a constituent of the faeces. For this purpose it is desirable that a local relationship is calculated for the particular conditions and animals. These methods are described in detail by Mannetje L. 't (1978) and Le Du & Penning (1982). A simple example of a faecal index is:

$$OMD = 0.4 + 0.01 \text{ (g N kg}^{-1} \text{ faeces OM)},$$

e.g. if the N concentration in faeces organic matter is $30 \, g \, kg^{-1}$.

OMD $= 0.4 + 0.01 \, (30) = 0.7$ (or 70%).

The use of N as an indicator of digestibility has been criticized since a large proportion of faecal N is of microbial origin. The fibrous constituents of the feed, or naturally occurring chromogens have also been used as faecal indicators. The accurate estimation of intake by indirect methods remains difficult and subject to error. The coefficient of variation of a single estimate is usually 10–15% and there is also the possibility of bias (although several comparisons with cut herbage have shown close agreement). Comparisons within experiments are, therefore, more reliable than between experiments.

Even when animals receive feeds in addition to grazing, the total intake of nutrients can be estimated if the quantity of faeces attributable to the supplementary feed is calculated from its content of indigestible organic matter. The remaining digestible nutrients derived from grass can be estimated by one of the methods described. If a faecal index is used to estimate digestibility, it should be based on control animals which do not receive the supplement but graze on the same pasture. There is evidence that cereal based concentrates may depress the digestibility of forage and Kibon and Holmes (1987) showed that if this was not accounted for, total intakes of supplemented cows might be over estimated by about 10%. Milne and Mayes (1986) proposed a new intake method, based on the use of n-alkanes which exist in all herbages, which overcomes this problem.

4.5   The effect of the pasture on the animal

The pasture affects the animal as a source of major nutrients, minor nutrients including minerals and vitamins, and as a source of parasites.

4.5.1   *Factors affecting the intake of herbage*

The herbage intake of grazing animals is affected by the animal, the pasture and the management. The needs of the animal, the quality of the pasture and the ease with which herbage can be collected all affect the quantity of herbage consumed.

4.5.2   *Animal factors*

When herbage of adequate quality is available in adequate quantity the intake achieved is closely related to animal factors, the size of the animal and its potential productiveness in terms of yield and stage of lactation or stage of development.

Many simple equations have been recorded of the form:

Intake = a (metabolic weight) + b (milk yield) + c (liveweight change).

Curran and Holmes (1970) discussed the difficulties of interpreting such prediction equations.

4.5.3   *Pasture factors*

Pasture factors include dietary quality, quantity as affected by herbage mass, and sward structure.

Where there is no physical limitation, intake is almost linearly related to the organic matter digestibility of the herbage (Hodgson *et al.* 1977) over the range from 45 to 75 D-value. However in many practical situations other factors influence intake.

If there is free choice the grazing animal chooses a diet of higher digestibility than the total available but as stocking rate rises and herbage allowance falls, the quality and quantity of diet ingested are both reduced.

Relationships between herbage mass and herbage intake have now been described for sheep, dairy cattle and beef cattle and there are somewhat similar relationships for sward surface height and herbage intake. An example of these for sheep is in Fig. 4.1 and similar relationships have been recorded for dairy and beef cattle (Zoby & Holmes 1983, Wright 1986, Kibon & Holmes 1987). It is for this reason that there has been recent emphasis on sward height as a guide to grazing management.

Intake of herbage is proportional to grazing time and rate of grazing, which in turn depends on rate of biting and bite size. Changes in sward conditions affect grazing time, rate of biting and bite size as the animal attempts to maintain intake. Management therefore by influencing, by design or accident, the quality of pasture, the herbage mass available, the competition between animals and the time available to harvest herbage can profoundly affect herbage intake. While maximal intake will generally achieve maximal production, some reduction in intake and performance per animal may be acceptable to maximize performance ha^{-1}, as shown in section 4.7.

4.5.4   *The assessment of herbage available for grazing*

The quantity of herbage available can be assessed with reasonable accuracy where the crop is to be cut but poses additional problems on a grazed

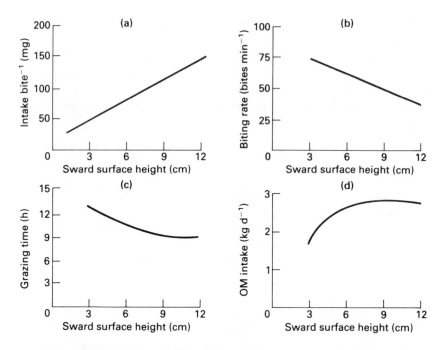

Fig. 4.1 The influence of sward height on the components of ingestive behaviour: (a) intake per bite; (b) biting rate; (c) grazing time; and (d) OM intake (after Penning 1986).

sward since it is affected by the quantity, the uniformity, the stage of development and the structure of the sward.

Herbage mass may be assessed by the clipping of samples but they should be cut to a height lower than that exerted by the animals grazing and in a variable sward large numbers of samples, preferably long and narrow, e.g. $1 \times 0.25\,\text{m}$ are required. This is a laborious operation undertaken only for research studies and even when herbage mass is recorded the nature of this herbage in terms of leafiness, and chemical composition affects its nutritive value and the ease with which it is prehended.

Many simpler methods of assessment have been investigated but none are of great accuracy. The sward height may be measured by rule, by a more sophisticated measuring device e.g. HFRO sward stick (HFRO 1986) or by a falling plate which exerts a pressure on the sward and enables the height of the compressed sward to be recorded, (Holmes 1974a, Castle 1976)

All these measures are highly variable within a grazed sward, with coefficients of variation of 20–50%, and although they may be correlated with concurrent estimates of herbage mass ($r = 0.8$), there is no constant relationship between height and mass over a season or between swards. A further approach has been visual assessment based on a collection of photographic standards.

The assessment of availability remains a subjective art and although guidelines are now available they must be combined with assessment of the needs and performance of the animals and account must be taken of the form of grazing adopted. A short dense sward which is acceptable with continuous stocking would provide insufficient grass if it were allotted daily by a system of rationed grazing.

In later sections reference to sward heights implies sward surface height as measured by a sward stick. Falling plate records are 1–2 cm lower.

4.5.5 The effort of grazing

Grazing animals expend energy, additional to their normal maintenance requirements, both in walking in search of food (and with milk cows to and from milking) and in the act of grazing.

The effort of walking on the level has been estimated at $2-2.5\,\mathrm{J\,kg^{-1}}$ $\mathrm{W\,m^{-1}}$ (ARC 1965) with an additional $28\,\mathrm{J\,kg^{-1}\,W\,m^{-1}}$ for climbing. A cow of 500 kg W would, therefore, require 1.0 MJ of $\mathrm{ME\,km^{-1}}$ travelled with additional $1.4\,\mathrm{kJ\,100\,m^{-1}}$ climbed, possibly $3-7\,\mathrm{MJ\,day^{-1}}$, a small proportion of the total requirement of $100-200\,\mathrm{MJ\,day^{-1}}$.

Graham (1964), with sheep in calorimeters, estimated that the maintenance requirement might be elevated by up to 50% in difficult grazing conditions. Langlands et al. (1963) estimated that for sheep the maintenance requirement on grazing was elevated on average by 25% and Van Es (1974) considered that with cows the overall increase in energy expenditure due to grazing was about 12%. It is probable that except in very difficult grazing conditions a 25% increase in maintenance allowance is appropriate for grazing effort. In estimating stocking rates (see Table 8.3), it has been assumed that the indoor standards which include an overall safety margin of 5% (MAFF 1984) apply, but some allowance has been made also for inefficiency of grazing which may compensate.

4.6 The effect of the animal on the pasture

The grazing animal can influence the botanical composition of the pasture directly by selection of plants, and indirectly by treading, poaching and distributing fertility.

4.6.1   *Botanical changes*

Frequency and severity of grazing can influence the botanical composition of the pasture. Frequent close grazing encourages prostrate species and on fertile soils in British conditions usually results in a dense sward of perennial ryegrass and white clover. In contrast, infrequent on lax grazing, or infrequent cutting, results in a less dense sward with less than 10000 tillers m^{-2} and encourages tall and stemmy plants such a cocksfoot.

With rotational grazing management, frequency of grazing is dictated largely by the length of the rotation cycle. On continuous stocking, frequency increases as herbage allowance declines, with individual tillers grazed at intervals of 10−20 days.

4.6.2   *Treading and poaching*

Grazing animals exert pressure on the sward estimated to be about 0.1 megapascals (MPa) (approximately 1 kg cm^{-2}) for sheep and 0.2−0.3 MPa for cows. These figures compare with 0.2 MPa for man and 0.1−0.2 for tractor tyres (Patto *et al.* 1978). Where this pressure is applied at normal stocking rates and in favourable conditions, treading occurs and the soil is gradually compacted until its bearing capacity equals the pressure exerted. Compaction is more severe when the soil is wet. The effect of treading depends on the stocking rate, the soil type and rainfall (Edmond 1970). Pasture species vary in resistance to treading. Perennial ryegrass is very resistant and Yorkshire fog less so. Treading may be beneficial by reducing the proportion of less desirable grasses e.g. *Holcus* spp., but in wet conditions, particularly on soils of high plasticity, treading may break the surface of the sward, allow invasion by weeds and weed grasses, cause poaching, impairment of the drainage and seriously reduce the production of the sward (Patto *et al.* 1978, Wilkins & Garwood 1986).

4.6.3   *Dung and urine*

The daily production of faeces from grazing stock varies with the quantity ingested and its digestibility, and ranges from about 2.5 to 3.5 kg DM for dairy cows, 1.2 to 2.0 kg for young cattle and 0.3 to 0.6 DM for sheep. Adult cattle faeces may cover 0.5−1.5 m^2 day^{-1} with proportionately smaller areas for smaller animals. For a similar weight of faeces, distribution is more widespread and uniform for smaller stock, particularly sheep, because the individual defaecations are smaller.

The total quantity of faeces deposited per year on pastures depends on the numbers of stock carried and may be as much as 3000 kg DM ha^{-1} (1 000 cow grazing days at 3 kg day^{-1}). The content of fertilizer nutrient in faeces is also variable depending on the composition of the diet and the type of animal. Typical values are from 20 to 40 g N, 5 to 11 g P and 4 to 14 g K kg^{-1} DM. These eventually contribute to the fertility of the soil but because of their uneven distribution and the low availability of the N (about 25% in the first year) Petersen *et al.* (1956) considered that dung was of little immediate fertilizer value.

Grazing which has provided 750 cow grazing days ha^{-1} would, at average values, receive some 67 kg N, 18 kg P and 20 kg K ha^{-1} from dung and urine. The rates of application on areas covered by faeces would be about 900, 240 and 270 kg ha^{-1} of N, P and K respectively. Grass surrounding dung pats is often rejected. Marsh and Campling (1970) concluded that the degree of rejection depended on stocking rate, and Yiakoumettis and Holmes (1972) in grazing trials with young beef cattle recorded that the area rejected was reduced from 42 to 29% as stocking rate was increased from 6.4 to 10.3 cattle ha^{-1}. Attempts to distribute faeces by mechanical treatment have not yielded worthwhile results. Harrowing tends to smear faeces over the grass and reduce acceptability.

The quantities of urine deposited on pastures and the composition of the urine are extremely variable. Individual urinations from cows may be from 1.5 to 3.5 l and from sheep about 150 ml in volume. Urine volumes therefore range from 14 to 30 l day^{-1} from cows and around 1 litre for sheep. Urine may contain 6−15 g N and 6−16 g K l^{-1} but P content is negligible. Areas covered by urine are larger than for dung. Those areas receiving urine may receive 300−600 Kg N and K ha^{-1} at one application and the total quantities deposited for an average of 750 cows grazing days would be about 100 kg each of N and K.

The plant nutrients from urine are readily available but recent work by Ryden (1984) and by Thomas *et al.* (1986) have shown that there are large losses of N on grazed swards. Ryden quoted 120 Kg N ha^{-1} on a fertile sward receiving 420 Kg fertilizer. N ha^{-1}. Thomas quotes less than 20% recovery of N on an upland grass sward.

Despite these losses urine contributes immediately to pasture growth and it does not cause rejection of pasture. The effect of urine patches on newly sown leys on infertile soils is dramatic. Sears (1950) and Wheeler (1958) showed that full return of sheep faeces and urine increased herbage yield by 20−40% compared with similar areas which were grazed by sheep but received neither dung nor urine. The major effect was attributable to urine. Occasionally in dry conditions or on heavily fertilized swards, urine 'burn' or scorching of the pasture by concentrated urine may occur, but it is seldom severe. Wolton (1979) reviewed the effects of excreta on pastures.

4.6.4   *The application of slurry to grazing*

In addition to the normal deposition of faeces and urine on pasture by grazing animals, slurries from housed cattle, pigs or poultry are often applied to grassland. Preferably they should be applied to arable land or to grass to be cut for conservation; if applied to pasture, at least 5 weeks should be allowed before grazing.

Slurries vary widely in composition and in uniformity of application. The range in composition is from 2 to $10\,g\,N\,l^{-1}$, 0.6 to $4\,g\,P\,l^{-1}$ and 0.6 to $7.0\,g\,K\,l^{-1}$, compared with N fertilizer the effectiveness was, for cattle slurries 26%, pig 38% and poultry 100%. Slurries applied at $30\,t\,ha^{-1}$ caused no difficulties but at higher rates of $60-90\,t\,ha^{-1}$ animal grazing was impaired for several weeks and there was considerable accumulation of K in the upper layers of the soil (Collins 1979).

4.7   Stocking rate and grazing pressure

Optimal production from pastures is gained only when the needs of the animal and the productive capacity of the pasture are in balance. Stocking rate which affects intake and animal performance has, therefore, a major influence on pasture utilization.

Stocking rate is normally expressed as number of animals ha^{-1} for a given time period. Since animals vary in size and in nutrient requirements a more precise measure is the weight, or for comparing animals of different sizes, the metabolic weight ($W^{0.75}$) ha^{-1}. With growing animals allowance should be made for growth over the season. However, at its crudest, stocking rate merely measures the robustness of the fences. It is common and preferable to express stocking rate as animals or animal weight ha^{-1}, although the reciprocal, ha per animal is used, especially in extensive hill or range conditions. *Stocking density* expresses stocking rate at a point of time.

Grazing pressure refers to the number of animals of a specified class (or to the weight, or metabolic weight, of animal) unit^{-1} mass of herbage. A more useful measure is the reciprocal, herbage allowance, the weight of herbage (DM or organic matter) present unit^{-1} of animal weight (or $W^{0.75}$). Herbage allowance is most precisely defined with daily allocations of pasture. Some examples of these measures are given in Table 4.2. As stocking rate increases, the grazing pressure rises accordingly, the herbage

Table 4.2. An illustration of terms relating to grazing management.
Example 1. Dairy cows on excellent pasture with $450 \, \text{kg N ha}^{-1}$.

Time periods	Herbage accumulation (kg ha⁻¹)	Average herbage mass d⁻¹ (kg)	Stocking rate (animals ha⁻¹)	Stocking density in 28 daily paddocks (animals ha⁻¹)	Herbage allowance (kg d⁻¹)	Grazing pressure (animals 100 kg⁻¹ DM)	Liveweight per animal (kg)	Liveweight (kg ha⁻¹)
Mid April– mid June	7060	118	8.3	232	14.2	7.1	520	3660
Mid June– mid August	4030	67	4.9	137	13.7	7.3	550	4015
Mid August– mid October	3310	55	4.2	118	13.1	7.6	580	4408
	14400		5.8					

Example 2. Beef cattle growing from 200–360 kg in 180 days on average pasture with clover.

Time periods	Herbage accumulation (kg ha⁻¹)	Average herbage mass d⁻¹ (kg)	Stocking rate (animals ha⁻¹)	Stocking density in 4 paddocks (animals ha⁻¹)	Herbage allowance (kg d⁻¹)	Grazing pressure (animals 100 kg⁻¹ DM)	Liveweight per animal (kg)	Liveweight (kg ha⁻¹)
April–May	3900	65	8	32	8.1	12.3	230	2829
June–July	2250	38	4.4	17.6	8.5	11.7	290	3393
Aug–Sept	1850	31	3.6	14.4	8.6	11.6	335	4118
	8000		5.3					

If mean herbage intakes were 13.5 for cows and 6.3 kg for beef cattle, average efficiency of grazing would be 85% and 75%.
If grazing pressures were expressed kg^{-1}, $W^{0.75}$ the value for mid April to mid June would be 7.05×108.8 (i.e. $520^{0.75}$) $= 767 \, \text{kg}^{0.75}$ and 12.3×59.1 $(230^{0.75}) = 727 \, \text{kg}^{0.75}$ for dairy cows and beef cattle respectively.

allowance falls in quantity and quality, competition between animals increases, the opportunity for the animals to select from the pasture is reduced, there is a reduction in intake and progressively the animal is prevented from satisfying its nutrient requirements. An inadequate herbage allowance is the most common reason for low production per animal from pasture.

The influence of herbage allowance in the short term and of stocking rate in the long term have been examined in many investigations. When herbage allowance is high, animal production is maximal and as the allowance declines production per animal declines. Over the normal range, production per animal declines linearly with increasing stocking rate. In consequence, production unit^{-1} area rises to a peak and then declines. Jones and Sandland (1974) in a review, showed that with beef cattle and sheep, liveweight gain ha^{-1} is maximal at a stocking rate half that which gives zero liveweight gain (Fig. 4.2). The situation is more complex with milk and wool production, when the animal may draw on the body reserves and continue to produce at a level higher than is justified by its current nutrition (Fig. 4.3). Journet and Demarquilly (1979) reported that on average, an increase of one cow ha^{-1} reduced milk yield per cow by 10% but increased yield ha^{-1} by 20%. Recorded data from a number of experiments are given in Table 4.3. The provision of supplementary feed in effect reduces the stocking rate. The major concern in intensive grazing

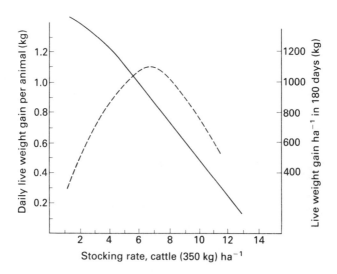

Fig. 4.2 Stocking rate and liveweight gain per animal and per ha (based on average conditions with 200 kg N per ha): per animal (———), per ha (– – – –).

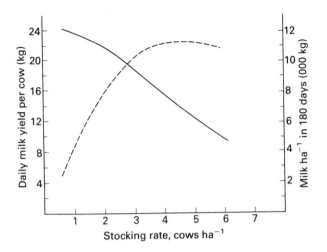

Fig. 4.3 Stocking rate and milk yield per animal and per ha (based on average conditions with 300 kg N per ha) : per animal (———), per ha (– – – –).

management is how to achieve the satisfactory combination of high production per animal with high production ha^{-1}.

4.8 Efficiency of grazing

Grazing efficiency measures the proportion of herbage grown which is consumed by animals. Direct comparisons with rotational methods of grazing are feasible, since the quantities of herbage present before and after grazing can be estimated, but comparisons with continuous methods of stocking are more difficult (Lantinga 1986, Parsons & Johnson 1986). For a single harvest the calculation of efficiency depends on the base line. An example is shown in Table 4.4. More important is the comparison over the whole season, since herbage inefficiently utilized at one grazing may be consumed later together with subsequent regrowths. The following relationship is based on Leaver (1976):

$$\frac{\text{Total utilization}}{\text{of herbage DM (\%)}} = \frac{\text{herbage consumed}}{\text{herbage accumulation}} \times 100$$

$$= \frac{I_1 + I_2 \ldots I_n}{A - B - C - D + G} \times \frac{100}{1},$$

where I_n = herbage DM intake in grazing number n, A = herbage mass at the beginning of the period, B = herbage mass at the end of the

Table 4.3. The effect of stocking rate on yield per animal and per hectare.

Reference	Animals (ha^{-1})			Production per animal (kg)			Production ha^{-1} (kg)			Comments
Dairy cows				*Milk*						
McMeekan & Walshe 1963	2.44	2.96		4282	3929		10352	11646		New Zealand 12 months, 2 years
Gordon 1973										
400 kg N ha^{-1}	4.94	7.41		2542	2139		12527	15815		N. Ireland 22 weeks, 3 years, 150 kg conc. per cow
700 kg N ha^{-1}	4.94	7.41		2455	2297		12099	16977		
Beef cattle				*Liveweight*						
Conway 1963	2.47	4.32	6.18	198	182	119	489	786	735	Ireland
Horton & Holmes 1974										
50 kg N ha^{-1}	5.0	6.7	—	154	132	—	771	885	—	England 24 weeks
504 kg N ha^{-1}	7.6	9.2	10.9	154	132	124	1171	1208	1348	
Sheep										
Conway 1962										
Ewes with twin lambs	7.5	15.0	22.5	23.3	18.9	14.7	350	567	662	Ireland
MacLeod 1975										
Ewes with lambs										
113 kg N ha^{-1}	11.1	13.3	15.6	52.2	52.7	53.0	580	701	829	England 12 months, 4 years
226 kg N ha^{-1}	13.3	15.6	17.8	54.4	52.7	50.2	724	822	894	

Note that the data refer to different periods of time.

Table 4.4. The efficiency of grazing for a single grazing.

	Herbage cut to ground level	Herbage cut to 5 cm above ground level
Herbage mass before grazing (kg DM ha^{-1})	2500	1800
Herbage mass after grazing (kg DM ha^{-1})	1000	300
Herbage consumed (kg DM ha^{-1})	1500	1500
Apparent efficiency (%)	60	83
$\left(\dfrac{c}{a} \times 100 \right)$		

period, C = herbage consumed by non-agricultural fauna, D = the sum of losses by decay in n grazings, and G = the sum of gross herbage accumulation in periods $1-n$.

The same principles apply to the utilization of continuously stocked pastures where herbage accumulation, consumption and decay occur also, although not at regular intervals on the pasture as a whole.

Efficiency of grazing ranges from under 50% to over 90%.

Another definition of efficiency of grazing is obtained from comparison of the utilized ME achieved with that expected from current standards (Thomas & Young 1982) (see Chapter 8). This assumes, however, that potential yields from different site classes can be predicted with accuracy.

4.9 Pastures and parasites

The helminth diseases: Parasitic worms cause a wide range of disease conditions described in detail by Soulsby (1965) and discussed in relation to grazing by Michel (1976) and Cawthorne (1986).

The parasitic worms all have complex life cycles. Generally eggs are passed into the alimentary tract and thence to the pastures and animal houses. With some parasites, another animal, the alternative host, is essential. Eventually an infective organism is ingested by an animal of the original host species. An example is the cycle for a trichostrongyloid infection outlined by Michel (1976) as follows:

Parasitic adult worms — eggs — larvated eggs — first stage larvae — second stage larvae — third stage larvae in faeces — third stage larvae on herbage — larvae ingested by the host — parasitic third stage larvae — early fourth stage larvae — late fourth stage larvae — immature fifth stage larvae — adult worms.

The numbers of eggs shed and larvae hatched are enormous, but their survival depends on climatic conditions, and desiccation in dry conditions or inactivation by low temperature may severely reduce numbers, although some species need a period of vernalization to initiate development. The life cycle in Fig. 4.4 shows many points where losses occur, so that only a small proportion of the organisms are likely to survive. However, so many ova are shed that the probability of some infection is very high.

An understanding of the biology of the parasites enables management and control methods to be applied. The likelihood of parasitic survival is reduced by hygiene in buildings, desiccation on pastures, removal of host animals, destruction within or outside the host by chemicals, and elimination or at least a reduction in the population of alternate hosts. The major parasites are referred to briefly below.

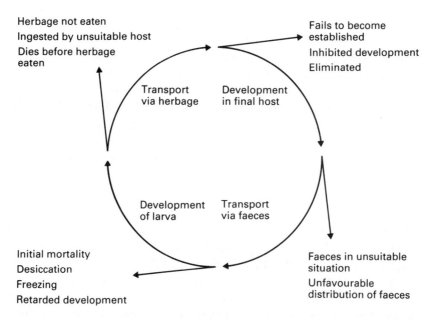

Fig. 4.4 A diagrammatic representation of the life cycle of *Dictyocaulus viviparus* (after Michel & Ollerenshaw 1963).

4.9.1   *Liver fluke — Fasciola hepatica*

This can cause ill-thrift and death in sheep and cattle and may also render sheep more susceptible to clostridial diseases. It can also infect rabbits which may become a source of infection for farm animals. The complicated life history of the fluke requires the snail *Limnaea truncatula* as an intermediate host. The snail in turn requires moist conditions and temperatures exceeding 10°C for its survival. The life cycle of the snail is weather-dependent and while it normally takes about 1 year, it can occur in a few weeks in favourable conditions. Control depends both on treatment of infected animals and on elimination of the snail. Rafoxanide may be administered to infected animals alone or with thiabendazole. In addition, control of conditions favourable to the fluke can be increased by draining or fencing off wet areas and applying molluscicides such as copper sulphate (at $30 \, kg \, ha^{-1}$). Elimination of the snail is almost impossible, but application of molluscicides in March or April to kill an overwintering infection, and in August, to reduce infection if the early summer has been wet have been recommended. Official warnings of fluke risk based on climatic conditions are now issued.

4.9.2 *Parasitic bronchitis — Dictyocaulus viviparus — husk*

This results in a distressing bronchitis normally in calves but occasionally in adult cattle. Infection is normally of 50–60 days duration. It may be fatal but if the animal survives it acquires an active immunity to the disease. This has led to the development of a vaccine containing a suspension of irradiated larvae. This can be given to calves, 6 weeks and 2 weeks before turnout to grass. Immunity may not be complete or permanent for all cattle in a group and the possibility of infection in adult cattle exposed to severe challenge remains. A particular risk to be avoided is the amalgamation of groups of calves. If an older group is turned out in spring and joined later in the season by younger cattle, the latter may be infected and suffer a severe attack. Similarly, calves which had grazed infected pastures in autumn could infect autumn and winter born calves if they were all turned out together in the following year. Complete elimination of the parasite is almost impossible. The use of clean pastures for calves and the avoidance of the practices referred to above should, however, reduce the risks.

4.9.3 *Parasitic gastroenteritis — gut worms*

Many organisms contribute to these diseases which result in scouring and impaired performance and may render the stock more susceptible to other infections. Infestation is seldom responsible for death but it can reduce growth rate and retard development of sheep and cattle. The main roundworms are *Haemonchus contortus* and several species of *Ostertagia* and *Trichostrongylus*. In addition, *Nematodirus battus* and *N. filicollis* cause nematodiarisis in lambs.

The life cycle of the round worms other than Nematodirus can be completed in a few weeks but may take as long as 6 months. Worm eggs in the faeces hatch, the larvae pass through several stages and become infective and, provided temperatures exceed 10°C, then move on the film of moisture on grass leaves. Larvae consumed infect the grazing animals and the cycle is repeated. With *Nematodirus* spp. there is an annual cycle and outbreaks normally occur between May and July.

Animals develop a tolerance to round worms with age. The presence of adult stock mixed with younger stock may be beneficial because the concentration of susceptible animals on the pasture is reduced and the adult stock may consume some of the infected herbage without suffering harm. Control is aided if susceptible animals can be turned on to clean pastures, but is commonly reinforced by the use of anthelminthics. These should be administered to ewes in the spring to combat the 'spring rise' of larvae embedded in the gut wall which may develop following the stress of lambing, to young cattle before turnout in spring and again in July after which they should move to clean pasture, and to lambs at weaning when they should move to clean pasture. Anthelminthic treatment of dairy cows at calving may be beneficial.

Confirmation of infection is usually based on worm egg counts but failure to detect worm eggs does not guarantee worm freedom. For all classes of stock and particularly for sheep where *Nematodirus* infection occurs, repeated grazing from year to year of the same field by the same class of stock should be avoided. Grazing by different classes of stock in successive years, the interpolation of cutting for conservation or, in extreme cases, ploughing and cropping the land may all be used to control severe worm infestations.

4.9.4   *Tapeworms*

Tapeworms of the genera *Moniezia*, *Multiceps*, *Echinococcus* and *Taenia* may all establish in grazing animals and impair production. These infections are generally of localized incidence. Clean grazing combined with specific dosing are the control measures.

4.9.5   *Protozoa*

Apart from worms, protozoans such as *Coccidia* may infect grazing animals. *Coccidia* are quite commonly found in faeces samples but when dense stocking coincides with favourable weather conditions, they may cause heavy losses in lambs and lowered production in milk and beef cattle. *Coccidia* are now responsible more frequently for ill thrift in lambs and young cattle.

4.9.6 *Ectoparasites*

Ticks and flies affect grazing animals. The most important tick, *Ixodes ricinus* occurs mainly on upland moors and hill pastures which provide a relatively moist environment for the free-living tick. The main incidence is in the spring months and again in late summer. The tick is more important as a vector of the virus diseases such as louping ill, tick-borne fever and pyaemia and of red water than because it sucks blood from its host. Regular dipping or spraying with an approved organophosphorus preparation is the method of control.

Fly pests include the sheep maggot fly *Lucillia sericata*, the sheep nostril fly *Oestrus ovis*, the warble fly *Hypoderma bovis* and the head fly *Hydrotaea irritans*. Maggots in sheep cause severe disturbance, pain and in neglected cases, death. Sheep should be sprayed or dipped to reduce the risk of fly strike, and daily inspection by the shepherd, especially in hot humid weather conditions is essential. The sheep nostril fly is of more limited incidence. It causes discomfort and disturbance and is difficult to control.

The warble fly disturbs cattle in hot summer weather when eggs are laid in the cattle. Larvae on hatching, penetrate the skin and migrate in the body. The hides of infected animals are seriously damaged by the breathing holes of the mature larvae which appear in the following spring. The warble fly is controlled by application of organophosphorus dressing to the back of the susceptible animal in November or by applications in spring. An eradication campaign to eliminate warble fly began in Britain in 1978, and it is now virtually eradicated. Head flies have been associated with the incidence of summer mastitis in cattle. Persistent insecticide sprays may reduce the incidence of all fly pests.

4.10 Grazing practices

Grazing practices vary widely in the degree of control which they provide, their requirements for capital and labour and their influence on animal performance and on pasture utilization.

Many of the experimental comparisons of grazing systems in recent years were reviewed by Journet and Demarquilly (1979) and Leaver (1985). There has recently been a return by the majority of farmers to simple grazing systems, but the development of more complex systems coupled with the increased use of nitrogenous fertilizer in the 1950s and 1960s are directly responsible for the current appreciation of the potential productivity of grassland. These studies of grazing systems have emphasized the over-riding importance of stocking rate and have indicated that the choice of grazing system should be affected more by ease of management than by any major differences in productivity between the systems. In comparing grazing practices, attention should be paid to simplicity and convenience of operation and to their effect in maintaining the productivity of the pastures.

The suitability of a grazing practice depends both on the pattern of pasture supply and on the needs of the animals. Ideally the supply of nutrients from grazing coincides with the nutrient requirements of the animals grazing on the pasture, but this is difficult to achieve since both the requirements of the stock and the production from the pasture are likely to vary over the season. Figure 4.5 compares the requirements of various grazing animals with the probable supply. Note that it is now considered that the supply of useful herbage is more uniformly distributed over the season with continuous stocking of pastures (Lantinga 1986, Parsons & Johnson 1986) than with rotational grazing.

A major distinction can be made between continuous and rotational methods which have different effects on the swards. Continuous stocking tends to encourage the development of a dense sward with over 20000 tillers m^{-1} and little bare ground and may encourage the maintenance of clover in the sward. In contrast, rotational methods, especially with long grazing cycles tend to develop a more open sward with less than 20000 tillers m^{-1} which may be as much or more productive, but may be more sensitive to damage from poaching. The main grazing systems are summarized in Fig. 4.6. Continuous systems result in only gradual changes in feed supply but with rotational grazing feed supply may fluctuate widely both within and between paddocks.

4.10.1 *Continuous stocking*

This occurs when a group of stock have access to one area of pasture for the whole grazing season. It exists in its pure form only in extensive conditions where the stocking rate in relation to pasture production is low. There are, therefore, periods when grass growth exceeds the needs of the animals, herbage becomes mature, dies and dilutes the available

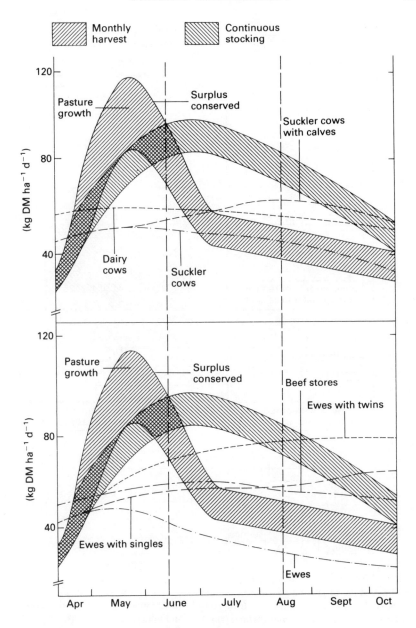

Fig. 4.5 Grazing requirements in relation to pasture growth.

feed. Conventional hill and range grazing systems may approach continuous stocking. If the overall herbage allowance is high, grassland is under-utilized, coarse grasses dominate, shrubs or trees may establish and the

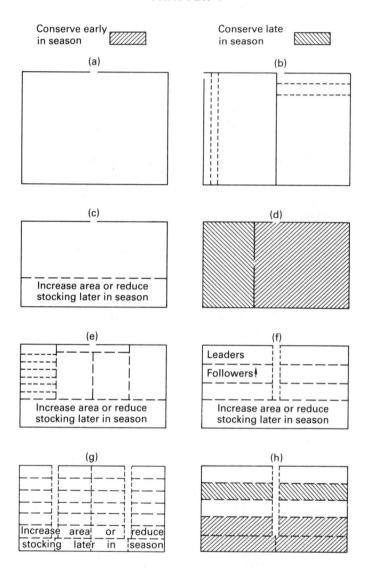

Fig. 4.6 Outline of grazing systems: (a) continuous stocking; (b) strip grazing (alternative methods); (c) intensive continuous stocking with buffer area; (d) integrated grazing and conservation; (e) rigid rotational grazing; (f) leader and follower rotational grazing; (g) daily rotational paddocks; and (h) flexible rotational paddocks. Permanent fence (——); temporary fence (— — — —); movable electric fence (----).

nutritive value of the pasture deteriorates. If the overall herbage allowance is low, pasture is severely grazed, poaching or erosion may occur and the stock are under nourished and may be heavily parasitized.

4.10.2 Intensive continuous stocking

The simplicity of continuous stocking, which makes few demands on fencing, water supplies or labour and allows the stock some choice in the selection of feed and shelter, coupled with the realization that stocking rate is the dominant factor affecting grazing output, has led to the widespread adoption of intensive continuous stocking both with sheep and with cattle. The stock are allowed access to an area of pasture for the early part of the season with numbers so adjusted that grass production and utilization are in balance. To allow for the lower rate of production of grass which normally occurs towards the end of the year, stock requirements are then reduced by the sale of fat stock, and the removal to other pastures of dry cows or ewes, or of weaned calves or lambs. Alternatively, the area available may be expanded by the inclusion of areas reserved as 'buffers', regrowths from areas previously cut for silage or hay, or pasture sown in the spring which becomes productive in mid season. The seasonal distribution of herbage over the season may be modified also by fertilizer practices. These intensive, continuous stocking methods are widely practised for cattle, cows and sheep.

4.10.3 Integrated grazing and conservation

This is also referred to as the '1, 2, 3' or 'full graze' system and combines some advantages of continuous stocking with some of rotational grazing. An area of pasture is allotted for a group of stock and subdivided in two in a ratio between 33 : 67 and 40 : 60 by the grouping of existing fields or by dividing one large field. At the beginning of the grazing season the larger area may be grazed for 1 to 2 weeks (see turnout of stock, section 4.11.1). During the period of maximal herbage growth (mid April to mid June) the smaller area is grazed and the larger area allowed to grow for 5−7 weeks and then cut for silage. During the middle of the growing season (mid June to mid August) the larger area is grazed while the smaller area, including any residues left when grazing ceased, is fertilized, allowed to grow for 5−7 weeks and then cut for silage. After mid August the stock are allowed access to the whole area. The area available increases in the ratio 1 : 2 : 3, hence the name. This method is simple to operate, requires few fences and few water supplies. It allows the stock considerable freedom of choice and if surplus grass accumulates it can be cut and conserved. It also allows each area of the pasture to grow vigorously and possibly build up root reserves before it is cut for conservation, and the fact that each area is free from stock for a period of 5−7 weeks helps to reduce the incidence of parasitic worms. This method is particularly suitable for young, growing cattle and can also be adopted for milking cows and suckler cows. It is less commonly used for sheep but the principle could be adapted, with the lambs weaned on to the regrowths.

4.10.4 *Management of continuous systems*

Continuous stocking methods allow the animal freedom of choice and are simple to operate. However, they are subject to variations in herbage growth associated with weather variations. If they are to be successful, it is essential that the stockman should regularly assess the state of the pasture and the progress of the animals both by inspection and by comparing the milk yields or growth rates with appropriate targets.

Fertilizer may be applied in continuous stocking systems. It is preferable to mark off three or four similar areas within each pasture and during the grazing phase to apply the appropriate fertilizer to each subdivision in sequence, at intervals of a week so that the whole area receives fertilizer once in 3–4 weeks. Applications to the whole area of one time increase risks of leaching and of damage to livestock.

4.10.5 *Rotational grazing*

In rotational grazing the pasture area is divided into a number of similar sized paddocks and the stock are moved in a regular sequence around the paddocks. Certain definitions apply:

Rotation or grazing cycle — the total number of days elapsing from the beginning of one grazing period in a particular area until the beginning of the next grazing period.

Grazing period — the average number of days within a cycle during which each paddock is occupied by grazing animals.

Rest period — the number of days within a cycle when there are no stock in the paddock.

Hence the rotation or grazing cycle = grazing period + rest period:

$$\text{Number of paddocks} = \frac{\text{Rotation cycle}}{\text{Grazing period}}, \qquad \text{e.g. } \frac{28}{4} = 7$$

or

$$= 1 + \left(\frac{\text{Rest period}}{\text{Grazing period}}\right), \qquad \text{e.g. } 1 + \left(\frac{24}{4}\right) = 7.$$

A greater degree of management control is provided by rotational methods of grazing and they may also facilitate greater grass production, although it is now accepted that the benefits in yield are small (McMeekan & Walshe 1963, Marsh 1975, Ernst, Le Du & Carlier 1980).

Many variations within the rotation grazing principle are possible. Experience has shown that in British conditions the grazing cycle should be within 20–30 days. Farmers may vary the length of the cycle and the rest period from time to time over the season, they may vary the number of paddocks, they may subdivide paddocks depending on grass growth, or they may even arrange that stock with varying nutrient demands occupy the paddocks in sequence. Rotational grazing systems may be classified as follows.

4.10.6 *Rigid rotational grazing*

Here the stock spend a similar time in each paddock of similar size and move according to a predetermined timetable, irrespective of the degree of defoliation of the sward. A degree of understocking may occur in the early part of the season, but the stocking rate is so chosen that overall utilization of the pasture will be high. A typical situation includes four paddocks each grazed for 1 week and rested for 3. For dairy cows it is preferable that each paddock is divided by a temporary electric fence to give a fresh allocation on each day of the week. The area allowed should be larger than one-seventh of the area on day 1 and less on day 7, to allow space for cow movement on day 1 and to avoid undergrazing on day 7. Similarly, seven paddocks may be occupied each for 4 days. Rigid rotational grazing is simple to operate and at appropriate stocking rates can achieve high performance with minimal management effort. To avoid excessive growth and deterioration of pasture quality the grazing sequence should be so arranged that the first cycle is completed before ear emergence. Subsequent tillering of leafy material then enhances the quality of any stemmy residue so that overall pasture quality is maintained. In seasons of unusual growth or on weedy pastures this system may produce unsightly pastures but normally they have been restored to good condition by grazing alone by the end of the third grazing cycle, if not, trimming is advisable. An additional area for grazing or a reduction of stock numbers is usually required later in the season.

4.10.7 *Flexible rotational grazing*

Adjustment for the variation in pasture growth rate is possible by varying the number of days within a paddock, depending on the quantity of grass present, and/or conserving some of the paddocks. This may be practised on inspection or it may be included in a basic plan, subject to modification according to the exigencies of the season. An example of the latter approach particularly suitable for milk cows is the allocation of eleven paddocks with the intention that four or five of these would be conserved in May. Each of the six or seven grazed paddocks would be occupied for 4 days in the first two cycles and thereafter paddocks which have been cut for conservation may be added, and others may be conserved to maintain grazing cycles with 22−23 days, with each grazing paddock occupied for 2−3 days. In such flexible systems it is most important that in the first half of the season the cycle remains within 21−28 days. Attempts to achieve apparently efficient utilization of the first paddocks grazed may result in the later paddocks reaching too advanced a stage of growth. It is also vital that conservation of surplus paddocks is so arranged that a continuous supply of fresh grass for grazing is maintained. While the provision of fresh regrowths following conservation cuts is beneficial, a comparison of rigid rotational grazing with the provision of a succession of regrowths revealed only a small and insignificant difference in yield per cow (Holmes *et al.* 1972). Unless the manager can exercise close control, rigid rotational systems or '1, 2, 3' systems are more effective than more flexible systems in maintaining stocking rate.

Daily paddock grazing provides a number of paddocks (21−30) where normally stock occupy each paddock for only one day.

Strip grazing describes the fresh allocation of pastures daily by moving an electric fence. It is best organized within a cycle of rotational paddocks, but may be employed in one field, for early bite, autumn saved pasture and in times of pasture scarcity. In these circumstances if the area is to be occupied for more than 4−7 days a back fence should be provided so that the regrowth is not regrazed too soon.

4.10.8 *Leader and follower rotational grazing*

Within the rotational pattern successive groups of stock of differing nutrient requirements may rotate. For ewes with lambs, two age groups of young beef cattle or of growing heifers the practice is useful. More than two groups complicate the operation and may restrict the recovery period. The animals which need the highest quality diet should be the leaders. With sheep and lambs forward creep grazing is the descriptive term. An eight paddock, 24−day cycle is preferred, lambs are encouraged to creep ahead through specially constructed gaps in the fences where they choose a high quality diet and are possibly less exposed to worm larvae. As the grass consumption of the lambs increases, the ewes receive a less digestible diet which coincides with their declining lactation. With dairy heifers, cycling the calves of 6–12 months age ahead of the 18–24 month old cattle gave better growth rates than grazing of the two groups together and reduced the incidence of worms (Leaver 1970). Leader-follower systems are complex to operate but are valuable with lambs and young cattle. The additional complication of leader-follower grazing of milk cows is probably not justified (Archibald *et al.* 1975, Mayne *et al.* 1986) except when it is convenient to subdivide a large herd for ease of management. In any leader-follower system, care should be taken that the followers are not penalized and the pasture is not overgrazed.

4.10.9 *The length of the rotation cycle*

Experiments with cut grass have shown that the yield of DOM is likely to increase with increasing length of rotation cycle over the range 21–42 days (Anslow 1967), but grazing studies on temperate pastures have failed to reveal any major effect of length of grazing cycle. With milk cows (Marsh *et al.* 1971) no difference was detected in performance between a 3 week and a 4 week cycle, and comparison of 15 and 30 day cycles (McFeely *et al.* 1975) also resulted in no significant differences. However, when Escuder *et al.* (1971) compared 2, 4 and 6 week cycles with beef cattle they found there was no significant difference between 4 and 6 week cycles but that the 2 week cycle, with 1 week grazed and 1 week rested, was harmful to the pasture and severely depressed output. The failure of any experiment to reveal any advantage from grazing cycles longer than 4 weeks is the basis of the current recommendation of 20–30 days. Voisin (1959) laid great stress on the importance of the rest period and on the avoidance of grazing of the regrowth within one occupation of a paddock. Ideally, rotational paddocks should not be occupied for more than 4 days at one grazing.

4.10.10 *Control of time of access*

Cattle normally graze from 6 to 11 hours of each day but the grazing pattern over the 24 hours can be affected by changing the time of providing fresh pasture from evening (which is preferred) to morning or by housing the cattle overnight. The efficiency of grazing might be increased, and waste from treading reduced by limiting the time for grazing, but since cattle indoors normally spend at least 5 hours eating it is unlikely that they can successfully gain a full diet from grazing in less than 6 hours. Restricted grazing times may be combined with buffer feeds.

4.10.11 *Rationed grazing*

When herbage is scarce, as may occur early or late in the season or in drought, rationing of grazing can be achieved with movable electric fences, preferably within a rotational paddock system.

4.10.12 *Buffer feeds*

Where alternative forage supplies are available, such as silage or a forage crop of maize, lucerne or grass at a more advanced stage of growth, a combination of grazing with indoor feeding may be suitable. Indeed a recent survey showed that over 40% of Dutch dairy farmers with more than 70 cows housed their cattle at night, offered them silage and severely rationed spring grazing. The storage of good quality silage in May for use as a buffer feed in dry periods in July–September facilitates the maintenance of higher stocking rates. It is also possible with restricted pasture supply to provide supplementary concentrated feed to maintain a normal level of animal production. Holmes & Curran (1967) reported that where pasture was restricted to half the normal allowance and cereal concentrates were provided at $0.3 \, kg \, kg^{-1}$, normal milk yield was maintained. Similar practices may be adopted for beef animals. They are not normally economic in the long term but they may be useful to overcome temporary shortages.

4.10.13 *Buffer grazing*

The systematic provision of an additional reserve of grazing (Fig 4.5c) has been designated buffer grazing and has been investigated recently (Illius *et al.* 1986). A portion (about 33%) of the grazing area is retained by electric fence in the early part of the season. If the occupied pasture falls below a defined height (6–7 cm for beef cattle) one third of the reserve is released for grazing and so on at weekly intervals if necessary. If the buffer area is not required early in the season it is important that it is cut with the earliest silage so that forage of high quality is available for grazing later in the season.

4.10.14 *Forage feeding (zero grazing or mechanical grazing)*

Because grazing is inefficient, the cutting and carrying of green herbage to stock has been claimed to increase output ha^{-1}. These claims are not well substantiated (Holmes & Allanson 1967) but forage feeding is useful with very large herds of cows on dissected farms where access is difficult, and with lucerne, maize or the large tropical forage grasses. Technical difficulties include the maintenance of herbage quality, the conflict between the ease of handling of long herbage and its lower nutritive value, and the daily provision of an adequate supply of herbage, without waste and reduction of choice by the animals. Other drawbacks include the initial cost of and maintenance of the machinery in working condition 7 days per week and the disposal of the slurry produced by the housed cattle. Provision must also be made to deal with surpluses at periods of maximal growth of the forages.

4.10.15 *Storage feeding*

In theory the ultimate method in grass and forage utilization is storage feeding where each parcel of herbage is cut and conserved at the optimal stage of growth, stored in silos and then used as required throughout the year. This is technically feasible but it makes heavy demands on agronomic skill and on capital for harvesting machinery, storage and feeding facilities although it avoids costs of fencing and water supplies. It is applicable only to large scale, intensive units in favourable economic conditions and is not widely practised in the UK, although there are some successful intensive grass silage beef units.

4.10.16 *Deferred grazing*

This term refers to range or upland pasture where in order to provide a reserve of 'standing hay', to restore the pasture, or allow stock to be concentrated on another area, an area of pasture is rested for several months. On tropical ranges a regular 2 year cycle might be operated in two grazing blocks with one of the blocks being rested for up to 6 months in each alternate wet season. The preservation of desirable species on conservation areas may be enhanced by deferring grazing until the preferred species have flowered and seeded (see Chapter 7).

4.11   Aspects of grazing management

4.11.1 *The transition to pasture*

Although there is little experimental evidence on this subject, when housed stock start grazing in spring it is preferable that the diet is changed gradually rather than abruptly. Ideally, animals should be turned out first to a well-drained, sheltered permanent pasture or one due to be ploughed, so that they can dissipate excitement without damaging the sward. Dairy cows might then be allowed strip grazing on forage rye, Italian ryegrass or other early ley. Dairy cows normally return to the shed at night for some time, with hay or silage, while concentrated feeds are reduced. Indeed this transition can take weeks, with advantage. Young cattle or in-wintered sheep are preferably turned on pasture 3—5 cm in height so that the grass 'grows to the stock'. Fodder should be offered in the field and concentrates may be discontinued or, for calves, gradually reduced and then eliminated within 2—3 weeks. The milk yield of dairy cows generally increases on turnout to pasture. If the increase exceeds 10%, they have been underfed. If milk yield declines, the herd has been fed too liberally in winter. Cattle usually lose body weight on turnout because of a reduction in gut contents (Balch & Line 1957).

The same principles apply to the return of stock to winter housing, in that a gradual change to the winter diet should be achieved by offering conserved forages and possibly concentrates in the field or the shed for some weeks before the stock are housed.

4.11.2 *Extending the grazing season*

Early bite

Early grazing can be obtained from autumn sown forage rye, Italian ryegrass or early cultivars of perennial ryegrass, grown on sheltered, well-drained sites. The pastures should be rested from January and receive fertilizer N about 4 weeks before grazing is expected to begin. They are usually strip grazed. The T-200 sum may indicate the optimum date for applying fertilizer (see section 2.4.10).

Autumn saved pasture, foggage, winter grazing

Fields with free draining soils and a sheltered aspect are also preferred for autumn grazing. A perennial ryegrass ley or permanent pasture may be used but pastures dominant in tall fescue (*Festuca elatior*) or cocksfoot (*Dactylis glomerata*) are particularly suitable. These should be rested from late August, fertilized and allowed to grow until November and then strip grazed. Cocksfoot has been grown in 50 cm drills to facilitate winter grazing but this is not now practised.

4.11.3 *Trimming, harrowing and rolling of pastures*

If pastures are weed infested or have been allowed to become stemmy due to understocking, it may be desirable to trim them mechanically to prevent the seeding of weeds and of grasses and, by eliminating apical dominance, to encourage the grasses to tiller. However, well-established and well-managed pastures, stocked at an appropriate rate should not become weed infested or stemmy. The need to trim pastures is an indication of understocking and is likely to result in loss of production since much of the trimmed material will decay, although the regrowth will be improved. Trimming if required should be to 5 cm from ground level to encourage tillering. Stock will eat some of the trimmings.

Harrowing is seldom beneficial in high quality pastures, but it may be necessary to spread mole hills and level poached areas. It is also practised in spring with spring tined harrows, on old matted pastures to aerate and open the sward.

Rolling is normally done in the spring on grassland which is to be cut for conservation in order to reduce damage to machinery and contamination of herbage with soil.

4.11.4 *Coping with shortages*

Summer rainfall is variable and unreliable. In the event of drought and a prolonged reduction in the rate of growth of pasture the following tactics may be adopted:

1 Give priority to the classes of stock which would suffer most and restrict the grazing of less important stock.

2 Reduce the number of stock by sale (seldom economic in practice).

3 Provide supplementary buffer feed as hay, silage, forage crops, brewers grains, treated straw or liquid feeds with straw, or an appropriate mixture of these.

Cows in early lactation, calves and lambs, and cattle in the later stages of finishing or in advanced pregnancy deserve the best nutrition. Ewes and heifers about to be mated also must be maintained in good body condition. Dairy cows in mid lactation, heifers in mid pregnancy, young cattle 6–15 months old and ewes at the end of lactation, can withstand a month of reduced feed availability. Growing stock will compensate when pasture growth resumes and milking stock will also recover milk yield. The quality of supplementary feeding should depend on the overall nutritional needs of the stock. If it can be provided from home-grown forage or by-products such as brewers grain, it will be more economical than from purchased compound feeds although concentrates are more convenient.

4.12   Fences

The separation of fields by walls, banks, hedges or fences is normal and their subdivision by temporary fences is common. Only where all the feed is carried to housed stock, where the stock are tethered or where a shepherd controls their movements is fencing unnecessary. Permanent divisions, provided they do not enclose areas too small for modern machinery, are valuable. Their maintenance in good repair is important (MAFF 1970). Permanent fences, of wooden post and rail, post and wire or post and wire netting, are commonly used as permanent field divisions and are described by MAFF (1969).

The advent of the electric fence in the 1940s greatly simplified the provision of fencing and reduced its cost. The electric fence provides, through a unit powered from mains electricity, batteries or by wind or solar generators, an electric pulse of high voltage. This is carried in the fence wire which may be plain wire 1.5−2 mm diameter, woven wire 1.5−2 mm diameter or stranded nylon including a metal strand. Stranded nylon netting is also available. The animal or man touching the wire completes the circuit to earth and receives a shock. These fences can provide field divisions and subdivisions for paddocks at low cost. Moreover with light post and strainers they provide an easily movable fence which may be used for 'strip' grazing. The electric fence is described in some detail in MAFF (1976).

It is essential that animals are trained to respect electric fences. When calves are turned out they should be in small enclosures not more than 0.5 ha. If a single electric wire is used, it should be made clearly visible by hanging string or other visible markers on the wire. Occasionally recalcitrant animals may need special treatment such as a light metal chain around the neck with a dangling end as an additional contact. In extreme cases they may need to be removed from the group.

4.13   Practical grazing management

In general, the more expensive the land or the more productive the stock the more intensive or controlled should be the grazing system. The extent to which fertilizer use is justifiable depends on the response to N, the efficiency of grazing and the type of livestock used as well as prices. It is likely to be more worthwhile with dairy cows or growing cattle than with beef sucklers or a sheep flock (Table 4.5). Different systems including extensive and intensive management, may be quite appropriate for different classes of stock on the same farm. Moreover some groups of stock at less critical stages of life may follow no clear cut system, and depending on the exigencies of the weather and the farming system, may move from one pasture to another over the grazing season. However, haphazard grazing management, like cropping without a rotational plan, increases the need for management decisions and the risk of poor performance, and should be avoided. (Appropriate stocking rates for each class of stock are given in Table 8.3.).

Table 4.5. Feed efficiency of dairy and beef cows (after Holmes 1980).

	Cow herd 6500 kg milk per cow. Replacements purchased	Suckler herd 95 calves per 100 cows reared to 250 kg
DM response per kg N	12	8
Efficiency of grass utilization	0.85	0.75
ME content of utilized grass, MJ per kg DM	11	9
Price per kg of product, as pence per kg milk solids or per kg carcass	90	150
MJ of ME required per kg of product (from Holmes 1977)	70	250
Value of product	140p	32.4p
If cost per kg N is then, benefit : cost is	30p 4.8	30p 1.1

4.14 Dairy cows

Dairy cows receiving from 500 to 1500 kg of concentrated feed per year are normally stocked at two to three cows ha^{-1} over the whole year, with grazing stocking rates of three to five over the grazing season and peak stocking rates of six to nine cows ha^{-1}. The grazing area is usually expanded later in the grazing season with silage regrowths, maiden seeds or specially grown forage crops. The preferred methods include continuous stocking, rotational paddock grazing and integrated grazing and conservation. Dairy cows are the most efficient of the grazing animals as feed converters and in economic terms they justify intensive pasture management and fertilizer application (see Table 4.5). Applications of 300–500 kg N ha^{-1} over the grazing season may be justifiable (Gordon 1974a) (Chapter 6 refers to input–output relationships). Routine application of 50–80 kg N ha^{-1} at 4 week intervals may be made or daily rates of application may be varied from 1.5 to 3 kg N ha^{-1} over the season. In rotational grazing, fertilizer should be applied to each paddock immediately after grazing since delay can reduce herbage yields. With continuous stocking fertilizer can be applied, preferably to successive blocks of pasture at weekly intervals (slurry may replace some fertilizer N applications). Applying fertilizer to the whole area at intervals of 4 weeks increases the risk of loss of fertilizer by leaching following heavy rain or by volatilization and might also, in wet conditions, produce a flush of grass too high in N content and temporarily unacceptable to stock. The need for mineral fertilizer must be considered but recycling of mineral nutrients occurs especially on intensively grazed dairy pastures. Potassium should not be applied in spring since this increases the risk of hypomagnesaemic tetany. Phosphorus should preferably be included in the seed bed but if more is required it may be applied at any suitable time over the season. Fertilizer application is simplified if parallel lines at intervals equal to the width of the fertilizer spreader are marked on the field by herbicide or a marker plant. If a rigid rotational system or a continuous stocking system is adopted, no decisions on movement of cows are required. With continuous stocking, however, it is now considered that if the average height of the sward measured by ruler falls below 7 cm, performance per cow will be impaired and in rotational paddock systems, pastures should not be grazed below 7.5–9.5 cm (Baker 1986a). Recommended heights increase over the season from 7 to 9 cm (ADAS 1987).

Ideally cattle should move to a fresh paddock in the afternoon. With strip grazing, a fresh strip should be allotted each day, preferably after the afternoon milking, since cows will eat the major proportion of their feed between turnout and dusk and the risk of bloat is slightly less since pasture is more likely to be dry. Moving the electric fence twice a day may not increase productivity and may increase bloat risk. Combined grazing systems are feasible. A convenient night paddock might be continuously stocked while more distant pastures are grazed in rotation during the day.

Herds of cows up to 100 in number may graze as a group. With larger herds stress and delay in milking will be reduced if the herd is divided into groups of up to 100 cows and each group is grazed and milked separately.

Access tracks and water supplies must be adequate for large numbers. Tracks should be not less than 6 m wide and water supplies should be capable of providing 50 litres per cow per day, much of it consumed at or after milking (Castle & Watkins 1979).

Attempts to deal mechanically with fouling of pastures by dung have failed and it is now accepted that occasional resting and cutting of the sward for conservation is the most practical method. As pastures become older, faeces and urine are more uniformly distributed, the population of natural fauna, of earthworms and insects increases, and these break down and distribute the animal faeces and the problem of fouling is reduced.

Some flexibility in grazing management should be retained. Particularly in rotational or strip grazed systems extreme conditions of rainfall or storm may result in poaching and severe damage to the pasture or exposure of the animals. The manager must be prepared to modify the system temporarily to avoid such difficulties without relaxing the overall stocking rate.

The feeding of concentrate supplements to cows on pasture is common although most surveys and experiments have shown that the practice is usually uneconomic (Arriaga-Jordan & Holmes 1986, Leaver et al. 1968). This is mainly because the net increase in nutrient intake from concentrates is small when grass of high digestibility is readily available (see Chapter 3). Supplements may be necessary to provide mineral supplements to each cow and they may increase the carrying capacity on small farms but the provision of additional protein and energy is seldom justified except as a buffer to temporary shortages. Even if it is judged desirable to supplement high yielding cows, care is needed to prevent waste of concentrates for other cows in the herd.

Application of the stocking rates suggested in Table 8.3 can support milk cows for 150–200 days per year, and result in milk yields ha^{-1} ranging from 6000 kg in poor conditions to 16000 kg in good conditions.

4.15   Suckler cows

Suckler cows graze over a wide range from good lowland pastures where overall stocking rates of one to two cows ha^{-1} and grazing stocking rates of two to four cows ha^{-1} are possible, to extensive hill or range conditions with overall stocking rates less than one cow ha^{-1}. In good conditions some grass conservation may be possible but less intensive methods of grazing management are usually adopted. Hence, although an integrated grazing and conservation method or rotational paddocks may be used, the majority of beef cattle are on continuous stocking. A grazing height of 8 cm is recommended.

Liberal fertilizer use is seldom justifiable and dependence on natural sources of fertility is normal.

Forward creep grazing can be practised but is rare. Autumn-born calves may be weaned at 7–9 months and placed on the better pasture, while the cows in mid pregnancy remain on the poorer pastures. It is important of course that the cows are well nourished in late pregnancy. Hypomagnesaemia is a common problem with suckler cows in the spring.

4.16   Calves

Calves deserve special attention. Suckled calves stay with their dams and learn to graze with them, otherwise calves in Britain are generally raised indoors until about 3 months of age and about 100 kg weight. Provided that parasitic problems have been avoided, or anticipated by the appropriate dosing or vaccination (section 4.9) calves then grow well on pasture. Pastures for calves should be clean and worm free, dense, 7–9 cm high and of high feeding value. They should preferably be recently sown or used previously for conservation or for sheep. Where, as is common for convenience, calves are grazed near the farm buildings, to reduce worm risks, these paddocks should be occupied if at all possible by calves only once in 2 years, and conserved followed by adult stock or sheep grazing in alternate years. Calves have a particularly selective habit of grazing and leave the pasture very patchy, so that an integrated cutting and conservation system where the residues are cut and removed is particularly suitable. A leader and follower system may be adopted where the calves precede older cattle, or indeed (but seldom in practice) dairy cows, in a rotational grazing cycle. Particular care is needed with calves as they change from indoor feeding to pasture and they should continue to receive hay and concentrate feed (0.5–1 kg per head per day) for the first few weeks.

4.17   Dairy heifers

Dairy heifers should be raised to the appropriate size and weight at target calving age, normally 2–2.5 years. Calving at 2 years demands fairly rapid growth throughout life and target liveweight gains on pasture are 0.7–0.8 kg day^{-1}. Where calving at 2.5 years is acceptable it is probable that similar overall liveweight gains will be expected in summer to compensate for slower winter growth. Intensive heifer rearing on a rotational grazing system with leaders and followers has been satisfactory. The younger heifers lead and the older in-calf heifers follow. Care must be taken that the growth rate of the latter is maintained. Heifers in calf should preferably be grazed on land which is free from steep banks which might cause injury, and should graze in airy sites, free from flies and less likely to result in summer mastitis infection. Intensive dairy farmers may find it worthwhile to transfer or 'agist' heifers to outlying rented pastures or hill grazings for the summer period although summer growth rates will then be lower.

Stocking rates and fertilizer rates on low land are similar to those suggested for beef cattle.

4.18   Beef cattle

The grazing of growing, finishing cattle has been studied intensively in recent years (MLC 1986). Overall stocking rates for the whole year may range from two to five cattle ha^{-1} depending on the size of the cattle, the natural conditions and the level of fertilizer applied. Peak stocking rates early in the season may reach 15 cattle of 200 kg W ha^{-1} or ten cattle of 350 kg W. It is difficult to provide conditions which favour continued growth of young beef cattle throughout the season and a reduction in stocking rate through sale of cattle or expansion of the area is essential. Even in favourable conditions it is unusual to maintain the high growth rates (1.25 kg per head per day) which can occur in the early part of the season and daily gains of 1.0 kg in mid season and 0.75 kg in late summer with an overall average of 0.9−1.0 kg are acceptable.

Rotational paddock systems or integrated grazing and conservation systems are preferred. With longer leys and large groups of cattle rotational paddock systems with a cycle of 24−32 days are convenient. Care should be taken, especially later in the season, that cattle are moved to a fresh paddock before intake is severely limited. Where the paddock layout permits, a leader−follower system with the finishing cattle leading may be adopted but this is not common.

On arable farms with short leys where the costs of fencing would be spread over 2−3 years, or for small groups of cattle, where paddock size would be too small for machinery to operate efficiently, the integrated system '1, 2, 3' is convenient and indeed it is preferred in many circumstances. The majority of beef pastures receive relatively little fertilizer but provided the stocking rates are adjusted in accordance with fertilizer level, responses to 450 kg N ha^{-1} have been recorded (Holmes 1974b, Marsh 1975). The targets shown in Table 8.3 should maintain cattle over a period of 180–200 days and yield from 500 to 1700 kg liveweight gain ha^{-1}.

Many beef cattle are purchased in the spring as stores and continuously stocked with a progressive reduction of stocking rate by the sale of finished cattle.

4.19   Sheep

Where sheep are grazed as a separate enterprise, overall stocking rates in the lowlands range from ten to 16 ewes ha^{-1} with higher rates in the summer months. It is much more common for sheep than cattle to graze all the year round and the need for conserved feed is less since even where sheep are housed this is seldom for more than 3 months.

Sheep normally graze on shorter pastures than cattle and are better adapted to do so. Continuous stocking methods are, therefore, preferred. (see Fig. 8.1) When intensive stocking is adopted it is convenient to wean the lambs and turn them on the regrowth from a conserved area to provide clean high quality pasture for the lambs, while the ewes can be dried off and then build up body reserves on the area which they grazed earlier in the season.

If a rotational forward creep grazing method is adopted, the sheep may be stocked at 12–18 ewes ha^{-1} depending on the level of fertility of the pasture area. Eight paddocks are usually preferred with a rotation cycle of 24 days. Fertilizer applications to sheep pastures seldom exceed 200 kg N ha^{-1}.

On mixed sheep and cattle farms it is common for the cattle to be housed during 4–6 months of the winter, and normal for the breeding flock of ewes to graze the cattle pastures in sequence during late autumn and winter until February. Not only does this provide clean sheep grazing but it is also valuable in closely grazing the cow pastures and reducing the risk of winter kill. Indeed to maintain pasture condition some dairy farmers buy store lambs to finish, or let winter grazing to sheep farmers. It is vital that sheep should be off the cow pastures by the end of February.

4.20   Mixed grazing

Sheep and cattle may graze together in the same field or in sequence. When they are grazed together it is claimed that the mixed grazing ensures better utilization of the pastures, reduces by dilution, the risk of parasitism and ensures that the nutrient requirements of the animals coincide more closely with grass growth. Sheep select a diet of higher quality than cattle on mixed grazing and lambs have grown better when grazed with cattle. A major benefit of mixed grazing in practice is due to the higher overall stocking rate which is commonly a result. The subject was reviewed by Nolan & Connolly (1977). Dixon, Frame & Waterhouse (1986) discussed mixed grazing but recorded similar yields from pastures grazed by cattle only and by cattle and sheep. They suggested that cattle would be beneficial in maintaining the pasture height at the optimum of 4.5−5 cm for sheep.

4.21 Hill and upland grazing

Hill and upland grazings account for about 8 million ha in the UK. On hill and upland grazing the same principles apply as on the lowland. Pasture growth depends on climatic conditions and natural fertility, and the animal's ability to select an adequate diet depends on the quality of the pasture and on the competition between animals. However, because of the greater extremes in weather on the hills and the tendency until recently to stock at a rate which would support animals throughout the winter with little supplementary feed, under-utilization of the summer growth was common and was responsible for the low productivity of many hill grazings. Under-utilization could establish an undesirable sequence of events. Because of understocking in June much of the hill pasture matures, decays and dilutes the remaining leafy growths so that the quality of the pasture is depressed. Sheep are therefore unable to attain good body condition at mating, ovulation and implantation are impaired, the ewes are undernourished through the winter, produce a weak lamb and cannot provide enough milk for it. In consequence many hill flocks wean 60−90 lambs per 100 ewes and the weight of the lambs at the autumn sales is low.

The Hill Farming Research Organisation (HFRO) (1979) identified these problems and has developed a programme to attain and maintain a higher pasture quality on the hills and provide better nutrition to the ewes and their lambs at the most critical points of their life.

The essentials of this programme are:

1 The improvement of selected areas of pasture which are accessible and well drained, by fencing, liming and possibly the sowing of white clover seed and fertilizer.

2 Identification of the critical periods in the annual cycle of the hill ewe, when a good plane of nutrition is particularly important. These include before and at mating, and before and after lambing.

3 Co-ordinating the use of the improved pasture with the critical periods in the ewe's life cycle so that the improved pasture contributes to the improved nutrition of the sheep, resulting in better conception rates, higher lambing percentages and better growth rate of lambs. This procedure is summarized in Fig. 4.7 and some results from a successful hill farm are given in Table 4.6.

These methods have permitted a gradual increase in stocking rate and an improvement in the overall utilization and quality of the hill pastures. Winter stocking rates have been improved by the introduction of supplementary feeding to augment the feed supply and improve the utilization of the low quality winter pasture. The accumulation of mature grass due to understocking in summer may be combated also by the adoption of

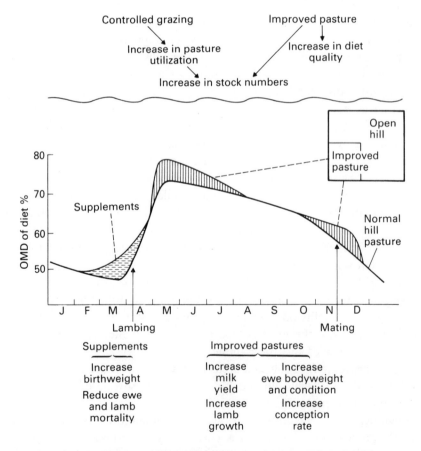

Fig. 4.7 Improved utilization of hill pasture (after Cunningham & Russel 1979).

Table 4.6. The increase in production following improvements on a hill grazing of 283 ha (HFRO Seventh Report 1977, Tables 1 and 12, pp. 74 and 92).

	1969	1972	1976
Total breeding sheep	398	582	620
Lambs weaned per 100 ewes	85	105	109
Weight of lamb weaned per ewe mated (kg)	19.6	26.6	28.9
Gross margin per ewe at 1975/76 prices (£)	9.24	13.42	15.88
Total gross margin (£)	3677	7810	9946

mixed grazing either with spring calving suckler cows or with young stock such as growing heifers agisted from the lowlands.

The recent interest in goats as sources of milk, meat and fibre has stimulated work on the goat by the HFRO (1986). This has shown that the goat preferentially grazes rushes (*Juncus* spp.) and may be useful for pasture improvement.

4.22   The utilization of heather grazing

Heather (*Calluna vulgaris*) is an important component of hill grazings which can contribute to the nutrition both of sheep and of grouse (*Lagopus L. scoticus*). Heather is a woody shrub but the young growing tips may attain 60% digestibility and the material then declines with maturity to about 45% digestibility.

Milne (1974) and Milne *et al.* (1979) examined the nutritive value of heather and have shown that on hill pastures an adequate diet for sheep can be provided with 40% from heather and 60% from indigenous grasses. On heather dominant moor the introduction of sown grasses and white clover in accessible patches to form 'mosaics' accounting for about 30% of the total area can improve the overall value of the hill grazing.

Heather becomes woody with age and must be maintained in youthful condition by regular controlled burning of woody material at 7–15 year intervals (see Chapter 7).

Further reading

Corrall A.J. (1982) *Efficient Grassland Farming*. British Grassland Society Occasional Symposium, No. 14. BGS, Hurley.

Cunningham J.M.M. & Russel A.J.F. (1979) The technical development of sheep production from hill land in Great Britain. *Livestock Production Science* **6**, 379–85.

Frame J. (ed) (1981) *The Effective Use of Forage and Animal Resources in the Hills and Uplands*. British Grassland Society Occasional Symposium, No. 12. BGS, Hurley.

Frame J. (ed) (1986) *Grazing*. British Grassland Society Occasional Symposium, No. 19. BGS, Hurley.

HFRO (Hill Farming Research Organisation) (1979) *Science and Hill Farming. HFRO 1954–1979*. HFRO, Edinburgh.

Holmes C.W. & Wilson G.F. (1984) *Milk Production from Grass*. Butterworth of New Zealand, Wellington.

Leaver, J.D. (ed) *Herbage Intake Handbook*. British Grassland Society, Hurley.

MAFF (Ministry of Agriculture, Fisheries and Food) (1984) *Energy Allowances and Feeding Systems for Ruminants*. Reference Book No. 433. HMSO, London.

Wilkinson J.M. (1984) *Milk and Meat from Grass*. Granada, London.

Whiteman P.C. (1980) *Tropical Pasture Science*. Oxford University Press, Oxford.

Chapter 5

The conservation of grass

5.1 Introduction

Production from cattle and sheep during winter is based largely on forage conserved from the grass crop. Grass conservation is not of course the only way of overcoming the winter feeding problem, and arable by-products, arable crops specifically grown for stock, homegrown grain and purchased compound feeds can also be used with advantage in many situations.

However, large quantities of hay and silage are made in the UK (MAFF 1986). There has been a consistent increase in the amount of silage made, this being most marked between 1970 and 1985, while the production of hay has tended to decrease, particularly in some areas. For example, on the basis of equal dry weights, in 1985 silage represented about 68% of the total herbage conserved as hay and silage in the UK, but about 80% for Northern Ireland. This difference reflects the difficulty of making hay in Northern Ireland, but the gap has narrowed which indicates a growing awareness that ensilage is the more efficient method of conservation.

Artificially dried forages form only a small proportion of the total conserved (in 1975 about 0.7%) and the amount is declining.

Table 5.1. Estimated production of silage and hay in the UK (thousand tonnes) (MAFF 1986).

Year	Grass silage	Hay	Artificially dried forage
1960	5580	6935	85
1965	6830	7313	84
1970	9010	7990	82
1975	16 780	6880	160
1980	27 600	6960	NA
1985	40 850	4650	NA

5.2   Principles of conservation

Foodstuffs can be preserved in several ways. The moisture content can be reduced to a level which will prevent the growth of bacteria and fungi as in haymaking and artificial dehydration. Substances can be added which inhibit bacterial growth, or an acid medium may be created which has a similar effect. These, in conjunction with airtight storage, form the basis of silage making. Finally, the product can be kept at a low temperature. Freezing has been used in preserving grass for experimental purposes and vegetables, but it is too costly for farm use.

The main objectives in conserving grass are to make a product which closely resembles the original herbage in feeding value, has suffered minimal losses and is acceptable to the animal. It is, unfortunately, true that much conserved forage is of poor quality, partly as a consequence of the original herbage having a low feeding value and also as a result of the use of inappropriate or inefficient methods (Unsworth 1981). Although low quality forage will suffice to feed stock of low productivity, for example suckler beef cows, this is no reason for accepting a badly made product. For milk production, beef cattle and sheep a product with a high feeding value is generally required.

It is also important that nutrient losses are controlled at all stages of the process including losses in the field, during storage and when the forage is being given to the animals. The relative importance of these sources of loss will depend on the conservation technique, but clearly nutrient losses represent a waste of resources and increased costs of production and it is desirable to conserve as much of the original material as possible.

5.3   The crop

5.3.1   Crop quality

The growth and management of the crop and the nutritive value of herbage is discussed in Chapters 2 and 3 and it is necessary only to relate this information to crop conservation because the technique employed can modify or limit herbage production and feeding value of the product.

The feeding value of any conserved product is largely dependent on that of the original herbage and a high digestibility product can only be obtained from a crop with a high digestibility. It follows that stage of maturity at time of cutting, the grass species or cultivar, the proportion of legumes present and the amount of N fertilizer applied to the crop will all influence the nutritive value of hay, silage and artificially dried forage.

5.3.2 *Method of conservation*

Artificially dried forage, barn-dried hay and silage can be produced efficiently from young, leafy herbage, However, immature herbage has a high moisture content and swaths formed by this type of herbage will tend to be too dense for normal hay making, impeding air flow and restricting the drying process. In addition, field-cured hay and, to a lesser extent, barn-dried hay, are dependent on weather conditions, which tend to be more favourable in early summer than late spring. For these reasons herbage for field curing is normally cut at a later stage of growth than other conserved products and, in consequence, is usually of lower feeding value.

The possibility of increasing herbage production by the use of N fertilizer is also limited with field-cured hay both because heavy crops are difficult to make into hay and because the interval between cuts is long so the optimum amount of N cannot be readily applied.

5.3.3 *Frequency of cutting*

The digestibility of the primary cut of grass crops falls as yield increases (Fig. 5.1). The difference in annual yield is, however, less when successive cuts are taken into consideration. The greatest increase in DM yield

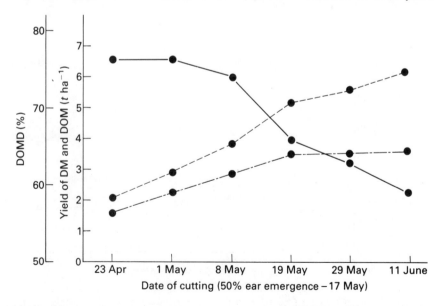

Fig. 5.1 The effect of date of cutting on the yield and digestibility of primary growth of grass. DOMD (———); DOM yield (—·—·—·—); DM yield (————). (After Minson *et al.* 1960.)

occurs with cutting frequencies more than 4 weeks but, as DM digestibility
is reduced as cutting interval increases, there is little difference in annual
yield of digestible DM with less frequent cutting (see Fig. 5.2).

When a forage is being offered *ad libitum*, as is common with silage, a
certain quantity is required to carry the animals through the winter
period. Animals will consume greater quantities of a high digestibility
material, but concentrate feeding can be reduced with a conserved product
of high digestibility. The problem, therefore, is to achieve the best com-
promise between yield and quality, except with artificially dried forage
where the main consideration is the production of a high quality feed.
Available information is conflicting, the best solution depends on the
circumstances of the particular farm and the ratio of feed costs to value of
animal product. However, an early first cut followed by cutting intervals
of about 6 weeks will produce grass silage of high digestibility, capable of
contributing significantly to the production of milk and beef and without a
marked reduction in herbage yield (Table 5.2). These results were obtained in Northern Ireland. It is possible that in areas subject to summer
drought a large first cut is more important, as herbage growth thereafter
might be affected by low soil moisture contents. Nevertheless, early

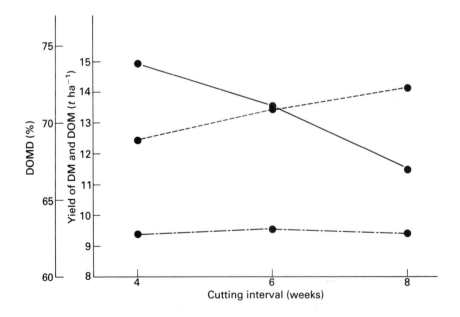

Fig. 5.2 The effect of cutting frequency on the yield and digestibility of grass. DOMD
(————); DOM yield (—·—·—·—); DM yield (————). (After Chestnutt *et al.* 1977.)

Table 5.2. The effect of frequency of cutting on the digestibility of silage and animal performance.

Cutting interval (weeks)	D-value (*in vivo*)	Silage and concentrates* Milk yield (kg d $^{-1}$)	Silage only† Liveweight gain (kg d $^{-1}$)
5	70–71	29.0	0.77
7	68	28.2	0.73
9	58–59	26.3	0.50

* Gordon (1983).
† McIlmoyle (1978).

harvesting of the primary cut maintains the vigour of the sward and allows application of N fertilizer at a time when soil moisture may be adequate to allow absorption and influence the succeeding growth.

5.3.4 *Height of cutting*

It is possible to vary the height of cutting but, in spite of arguments in favour of leaving a long stubble (Donald & Black 1958), yield of DM and digestible DM is not increased by cutting at heights greater than 2.5 cm above ground level in the UK (Table 5.3). Cutting very close to ground

Table 5.3. The effect of height of cutting on the annual yield of herbage (after Harrington & Binnie 1971).

Height of cutting (cm)	Yield of DM (kg ha $^{-1}$)	Yield of digestible DM (kg ha $^{-1}$)
2.5	11 530	8206
7.6	11 640	8043
12.7	11 040	7401

level can retard the recovery of the sward and can result in soil contamination of silage which can have an adverse effect on fermentation and on voluntary intake by animals. When the crop is to be partially or wholly dried in the field a cutting height about 5 cm above ground level will assist the drying process as there will be freer circulation of air through the swath.

5.3.5   *Sward composition*

Sward composition tends to deteriorate more rapidly under a cutting regime than under grazing. Infrequent defoliation, particularly in association with heavy applications of N, increases the proportion of bare ground (Bartholomew & Chestnutt 1977) and is likely to facilitate the ingress of less desirable species in the sward. Frequent defoliation is preferable if the maintenance of a sward is important. Recovery of a sward may also be retarded by wilting or drying herbage in a swath or by damage or soil compaction caused by harvesting equipment.

The crop may also influence the conservation technique. The soluble carbohydrate content of the herbage has an important bearing on the method of making silage. This can be affected adversely by either the use of N fertilizer or by choice of plant type, legumes having particularly low water-soluble carbohydrate contents.

5.4   Cutting the crop

A crop of silage or artificially dried forage may be cut direct with a forage harvester. However, for hay and for wilting before ensilage or artificial drying the crop is cut first and collected later. A pre-cut crop can be harvested more rapidly than with direct cutting.

Irrespective of the cutting system, ground preparation is vital. Stones and flints on the soil surface can damage cutter blades and forage harvesters and an uneven surface can lead to soil contamination. Heavy rolling when soil conditions are suitable can do much to reduce these difficulties.

The crop should be cut as rapidly as possible once it has reached the desired stage of growth. Machinery should be capable of a high rate of work, with a low maintenance requirement and with little risk of breakdown. Additionally, it should leave an open swath to allow aeration or one which is suitable for conditioning.

At the present time a high proportion of conserved forage, especially for silage, is cut with drum, disc or horizontal rotary mowers. These mowers have low maintenance requirements, are capable of a high work rate and are unlikely to block even in laid or very heavy crops. Reciprocating mowers, which were formerly used, had a lower power requirement but were difficult to maintain in good working order and were subject to frequent blocking except in relatively light, standing crops. The 'double-knife' form of this mower does not block to the same extent as the 'single-knife' type, but is even more difficult to maintain. Rotary mowers bruise the herbage to some extent as it is in contact with the blades more than once during cutting, but reciprocating-blade mowers do not have a similar action. However, for rapid drying some form of additional conditioning is necessary in both cases and, for the best results, this should take place at cutting or as soon as possible thereafter. The flail mower will both cut and condition the crop by bruising the herbage and this accelerates the rate of drying. This type of mower has a low maintenance requirement, but its disadvantages include a relatively high power requirement and a low rate of cutting. Unless it is operated carefully, it produces small herbage particles which are difficult to pick up, thus increasing field losses.

5.5 Silage

The changes taking place in silage result mainly from the action of plant enzymes, bacterial fermentation and, under aerobic conditions, from bacterial, fungal and yeast growth.

5.5.1 *Plant respiration*

Plant respiration can continue for some time after ensiling when oxygen is present in the mass and, even under anaerobic conditions, plant enzyme action can continue. More important, however, is aerobic respiration which involves the action of enzymes on the carbohydrate fraction of herbage and results in the production of water, carbon dioxide and heat. If sufficient oxygen is present, the result of gaseous movement rather than entrapped oxygen which is rapidly exhausted, two major effects ensue. The first is that carbohydrate supply is reduced and this may restrict the quantity of lactic acid formed in the silage. Secondly, the heat produced raises the temperature of the silage and, if this rises above 40°C, the digestibility of crude protein can be reduced markedly. It is essential, therefore, to control the gaseous exchange which leads to the presence of oxygen in the silage mass.

5.5.2 *Fermentation*

Coinciding with and following plant respiration, bacterial fermentation occurs and a major aim in silage making is to control this bacterial action. Silage which has undergone an undesirable fermentation is characterized by a relatively high butyric acid content and an extensive degree of proteolysis and has a reduced digestibility, low intake characteristics, and may increase the incidence of metabolic upsets in animals to which it is offered. Inhibition of the growth of clostridia, which are largely involved in an undesirable fermentation, is essential for the production of well-made silage. In many types of silage there is a negative correlation between lactic acid content and the contents of butyric acid and ammonia N, and a positive correlation between pH value and the latter two substances (Table 5.4). A notable exception is wilted silage where preservation appears to be the result of osmotic pressure rather than a reliance on acidity. Silage made from wilted herbage can have a relatively high pH value and a low content of lactic acid but contains little or no butyric acid and a small amount of ammonia N. In general, however, with unwilted silage a rapid increase in acidity is required to prevent an undesirable fermentation and a critical level of acidity must be attained to achieve this objective. However, the buffering capacity of herbage can vary widely, for example clover has twice the capacity of ryegrass, and it also increases markedly during ensilage. Wilting the herbage before ensiling reduces the buffering capacity (Playne & McDonald 1966).

The importance of the development of sufficient acidity has given rise to the concept of 'stable' and 'unstable' silages. A stable silage is sufficiently acid to prevent deterioration of the silage over a long period of time. On the other hand, an unstable silage will, in the initial stages, have had increased acidity (lactic acid will have been formed), but not sufficiently to control clostridial growth, and subsequently there will be a progressive deterioration in the fermentation quality of the silage. This deterioration occurs because clostridia utilize lactic acid as a substrate (Fig. 5.3).

If the silage is untreated, two essential requirements are a sufficient presence of lactobacilli, and an adequate supply of soluble carbohydrate (the substrate required for a lactic acid fermentation) in the plant tissue. There can be a considerable variation in the numbers and strains of lactobacilli present on the herbage and, in some cases, there may not be enough to ensure a rapid formation of lactic acid. To remedy this, an

Table 5.4. An example of acid and ammonia contents (as % of DM) of unwilted silage in relation to pH value.

pH	Lactic acid	Butyric acid	NH_3N
3.9	11.0	0	1.4
4.1	11.8	0	2.2
4.5	6.3	1.6	2.7
5.2	0.3	3.8	5.1
5.7	0.1	5.8	9.8

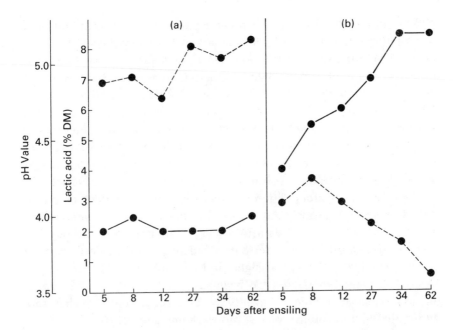

Fig. 5.3 Data illustrating the development of: (a) stable; and (b) unstable silages. pH (———); lactic acid (– – –) (after Langston *et al*. 1958).

inoculant, particularly one which contains an efficient strain of lactobacilli, could be added, but until recently, there was little evidence that inoculants were effective on a farm scale. However, data are now available which show that certain strains of lactobacilli can ensure a satisfactory fermentation in silage, even when carbohydrate contents in the herbage are relatively low, provided that large numbers of viable bacteria are applied.

Soluble carbohydrate content of the herbage is important in two respects. If the silage is untreated, the carbohydrate content must provide sufficient substrate for the production of enough lactic acid to preserve the silage. Alternatively, any deficiency should be known so that an appropriate treatment can be applied. Attempts are being made to provide an analytical service for this purpose, but information is already available on several factors which influence the soluble carbohydrate content of herbage.

The type of crop is a major consideration, some crops having an inherently low and others a high carbohydrate content. Maize and mature cereal crops always contain a sufficiently high carbohydrate content to ensure a desirable fermentation in silage. The grass crop may or may not have an adequate carbohydrate content depending on a number of factors. One of these is that there can be marked variations between grasses (Table 5.5), for example cocksfoot (*Dactylis* spp.) will usually have a lower carbohydrate content than ryegrass (*Lolium* spp.), but it has been demonstrated that this trait can be improved by breeding within a species. The legumes rarely, if ever, contain sufficient carbohydrate for a satisfactory fermentation although the difference in content between the legumes and grasses is not always as great as shown in Table 5.5. The non-structural carbohydrates of clover and lucerne also differ from those in grasses, as sucrose and starch rather than fructosan form the reserve material.

There is an apparent difference in carbohydrate content of grasses caused by stage of growth and season, but this may be confounded with the effect of climate. The data in Table 5.5 indicate that carbohydrate content increases until just after ear emergence and then declines. Generally, carbohydrate content is higher in May–June than later in the year (Aldrich & Dent 1963) and it has been suggested that this may be due to the low leaf : stem ratio following ear emergence and a higher ratio during the later vegetative phase, but the same general trend in content has been found for flowering and non-flowering ryegrass. The marked variations in carbohydrate content in monthly cuts suggest that climate has an effect (Aldrich & Dent 1963) and both light and temperature have

Table 5.5. The soluble carbohydrate content of primary growth of grasses and legumes (%) (after ap Griffiths 1963, Davies *et al.* 1966).

| | Date of cutting | | | |
	10 April	10 May	28 May	22 June
Grasses				
S.24 perennial ryegrass	18.1	25.4	28.5	22.6
S.48 timothy	18.4	19.0	24.0	15.9
S.215 meadow fescue	15.1	20.7	24.5	16.8
S.170 tall fescue	14.9	18.0	22.0	19.7
S.37 cocksfoot	10.5	15.9	22.1	17.4
	4 May	1 June	29 June	
Legumes				
White clover	8.1	10.7	13.1	
Red clover	8.5	9.8	10.3	
Lucerne	7.2	6.6	8.0	

been shown to influence carbohydrate content (Deinum 1966). Diurnal variations also occur, carbohydrate content of grasses increasing between 0600 and 1800 hours, but in lucerne increasing from 0600 to 1200 hours and levelling off thereafter (Holt & Hilst 1969).

Fertilizer N increases the N content of the herbage but decreases the carbohydrate content (Nowakowski 1962). Immature grass will also tend to have lower contents of carbohydrate than more mature grass, and herbage cut early in the day has a lower content. However, N is essential for high yields; leafy grass will produce silage with a high digestibility and in practice silage cannot be made only at selected periods of the day. Carbohydrate deficiency should therefore be remedied by an appropriate treatment rather than by attempting to modify management to increase carbohydrate content of the grass.

Plant respiration after ensiling reduces the amount of available carbohydrate and the extent of the enzymic action is indicated by a rise in temperature in the silage mass (McDonald et al. 1968). Respiration should therefore be controlled by efficient sealing of the silage overnight when the silage is being made and on completion to conserve the maximum amount of carbohydrate for fermentation and reduce nutrient losses. Chopping or lacerating the herbage before ensiling will make the carbohydrate content of cells more readily available as a substrate for bacteria and will promote rapid formation of the lactic acid (Murdoch et al. 1955). Neither of these techniques will guarantee a desirable fermentation, but they will be of some assistance.

5.5.3 *Nutrient losses*

Crop losses can occur during harvesting and filling the silo, but these can be minimized by good design and efficient operation of equipment. A further possible source of nutrient loss (arising from mechanical losses and continued plant respiration) occurs if the herbage is wilted before ensiling. Respiration losses are greater when the herbage has a low DM content and when ambient temperatures are high. They are also increased under poor weather conditions (Honig 1980). However, loss of DM appears to be negligible for wilting periods shorter than 24 hours (Nash 1959).

Losses during storage are caused by plant respiration and fermentation (gaseous losses), effluent and surface waste. An indication of the range of these losses is given in Table 5.6. Some gaseous losses are unavoidable, but they are increased when respiration is uncontrolled and when an undesirable fermentation occurs.

Table 5.6. The range of DM losses in silage (%).

Gaseous (respiration and fermentation)	5–10
Effluent	0–7
Waste	0–50
Secondary deterioration (after silo is opened)	0–15

Effluent losses, in terms of DM, are not large, but the DM is composed of soluble constituents which have a high feeding value. In addition, the effluent may contain a substantial proportion of some silage additives and can cause severe pollution of water courses. The amount of effluent produced is largely dependent on the DM content of the herbage ensiled, the pressure in the silo and some additives, notably some of the acid additives, may also affect the volume produced. Unless the herbage is wilted to a DM of over 25% before ensiling, some effluent losses must be accepted. However, silage effluent should not be regarded as a waste material as it can be used effectively as a food for cattle and pigs (Patterson & Steen 1982).

Surface waste is caused by aerobic conditions which allow the proliferation of putrefactive bacteria and fungi. The conditions are similar to those required for making compost and the results are similar with the formation of inedible waste or mouldy silage which will be rejected by animals. Waste can be eliminated by sealing the silage efficiently. However, with inefficient sealing, or in some cases no sealing, DM losses can be very high, the visible waste being only a fraction of the true loss.

Further loss may occur after the silo has been opened as a result of secondary deterioration of the silage caused by air entering the silage after it has been disturbed. Deterioration is accentuated by high ambient temperatures, high DM contents in the silage, poorly compacted silage or in a well-preserved silage with a relatively low lactic acid content. In grass silage secondary deterioration appears to be caused initially by the growth of yeast followed by bacterial action. It has been suggested that losses of DM in the order of 10–15% can take place in a 10 day period after exposure (Honig & Woolford 1980). Therefore, when the silo is being emptied by mechanical means the silage should be disturbed as little as possible and the silage face exposed for as short a time as is feasible. Block cutters are, therefore, preferred to fore-loader forks.

5.5.4   *Harvesting*

There are three main types of forage harvester, the flail, double-chop (combining flail cutting with a flywheel chopping mechanism) and precision-chop. The precision-chop harvester can cut direct or pick up herbage from a swath, the herbage being cut into short lengths by either a flywheel or a cylinder chopper. There is also the choice between trailed and self-propelled models. All harvesters chop the grass to some extent, but the variability in chop length is least with the precision-chop harvester and increases markedly with the double-chop and to an even greater extent with the flail harvester.

The choice of harvester is partly dependent on factors associated with particle size. Voluntary intake may be increased when silage has a smaller particle size, particularly with self-feeding where the animals have less difficulty in removing the silage, but the major advantages are in handling the herbage and the silage. Indeed, only silage harvested with a precision-chop harvester is suitable for tower silos and for self-unloading trailers or forage boxes. Herbage in short lengths packs better into trailers and by significantly increasing the amount carried in the trailers reduces transport time. Precision-chopped material is also more easily consolidated in the silo, an important asset when wilted herbage is being ensiled in a clamp silo. Precision-chop harvesters are relatively expensive. Harvesters with a chopping mechanism are more vulnerable to damage from metal objects or stones picked up with the herbage, but the risk can be reduced or eliminated by good ground preparation and some form of metal detector on the harvester. In contrast, flail harvesters are generally robust machines, have a low maintenance requirement, and are relatively cheap. However, the low maintenance needs may be deceptive as the flails may receive inadequate attention, becoming blunt and chipped with the result that cutting is uneven and less laceration takes place.

Although information is available on some parts of the silage-making process when different harvesters have been used, there are few data on the overall effect on animal production. However, results from one series of experiments have indicated that quantity of silage ensiled, cow feeding days and milk output ha^{-1} are higher when the herbage was harvested directly with a single or double-chop harvester than with a precision-chop harvester when the herbage has been pre-cut (Gordon 1986).

Although it is normal practice to use a forage harvester to make silage, a baler can be used, particularly to conserve surplus herbage. Conventional small bales are difficult to handle both in and out of the silo, but the 'big baler' provides a convenient method of storing batches of grass. The big bale can be stored either in a sealed plastic bag or in stretch film, the latter being the more efficient method as it limits any damage to the plastic by rodents or any other form of damage (Fenlon *et al.* 1987). However, the loss of nutrients is usually higher in big bale silage than in conventional silage making.

There are many possible combinations in harvesting systems, ranging from the one-man 'team' (one man harvesting, transporting and filling the silo) to the large four or five-man team (one cutting the crop, one harvesting, one filling the silo and the others transporting). Other things being equal, the larger the team the greater the amount of herbage ensiled in a given time. However, team size is clearly dependent on the availability of men and equipment and a small team may give an adequate output where distances from field to silo are small and the amount of silage to be made is limited. Distance from field to silo is usually the main determinant of team size as, with a given number of men, there is a marked reduction in output as distance increases (MAFF 1977b).

Speed of filling the crop into the silo is important. Herbage digestibility declines with time, particularly with the primary cut, and while harvesting the grass crop should begin on an appropriate date it is equally important that the period of harvesting should be as short as possible, otherwise there will be an inevitable decrease in feeding value. This problem, however, can be lessened by the use of a range of varieties with different dates of ear emergence (Chapters 2 and 3). Rapid filling of the silo reduces the risk of overheated silage and lack of uniformity which can create problems when self-feeding silage. Finally as with any farm oper-ation, the shorter the period devoted to silage making, the more time can be given to other important activities on the farm. It is essential, there-fore, that the preparation of machinery, to avoid delays due to break-downs and maintenance, and efficient organization of the harvesting system should be major considerations. Distance from field to silo is of importance and it is essential to keep the harvester in continual operation, bearing in mind that trailer changeover is where much time can be lost. Equally, the organization and technique of filling the silo can have a marked effect on output as this is often where bottlenecks occur.

The method of filling depends on the type of silo, a blower being required for the tower and bunker silo and usually some form of buckrake for the clamp silo. For the latter a front-mounted buckrake is preferable and some type of 'push-off' mechanism is an advantage in placing the loads.

Uniform filling of the silos is important particularly in a tower silo because there will be increased stress on the structure if herbage builds up on one side, and difficulties can also be encountered in mechanical unloading. With clamp silos uniform filling assists consolidation and sufficient herbage must be placed close to the silo walls, otherwise spoilage will occur.

All silos should be filled as rapidly as possible to reduce surface spoilage and variation in silage quality. Efficient consolidation of the silage by tractor rolling also reduces overheating and waste (Lancaster & McNaughton 1961). Spoilage can be controlled by an airtight seal or by the use of plastic sheeting on clamp silos. To be fully effective, this should be used at the end of each day and, for longer breaks in filling, put on immediately filling ceases (Henderson & McDonald 1975). It is essential that airtight conditions are obtained and considerable care should be taken to seal the edges effectively and to make sure that the sheet is not damaged.

Where the silo has a larger capacity than is required by a particular batch of silage, there is merit in a clamp silo in reducing the exposed surface as much as possible by filling the silo in a series of wedges rather than utilizing the whole floor space.

5.5.5 *Silos*

The type of silo will depend largely on the system adopted for feeding the stock and the choice of silo will influence methods of harvesting the crop, transporting the herbage and filling and emptying the silo. It is, therefore, part of an integrated system. The capacity of the silo, or silos, will be determined by the amount of forage required to feed the animals but, if possible, it is better to avoid the use of very large clamp silos as they can give rise to a variable product and may also increase the risk of secondary deterioration when a wide silage face is left exposed. Other considerations are effluent collection and disposal (when the herbage is ensiled unwilted), safe working conditions and cost.

Care must be taken in siting the silo. Generally, with forage harvester systems, the silo should be sited close to where the animals are housed. There should be easy access to the silo with a sufficiently large area of concrete for convenient and rapid unloading and filling operations. A concrete area is necessary to avoid soil contamination of herbage. The site should, if at all possible, allow for extension, but it is equally important that the area over which the animals move, as in self-feeding, should be restricted to a minimum to avoid the need for excessive cleaning.

There are several types of silo ranging from those which are basically heaps of silage in the shape of a clamp or stack to the sophisticated airtight tower silo. With unwalled silos it is difficult to control surface waste, and working conditions can be unsafe when they are being built. Wastage can be restricted, however, by the use of a plastic sheet covering. A variation of this is a complete enclosure of the silage with sheeting followed by evacuation of air, the 'vacuum silage' process (Lancaster 1968). This method can prevent waste and ensure low nutrient losses providing that the plastic sheet remains intact during the storage period but, as the silage is usually not as dense as when made by conventional methods, it is more subject to deterioration after opening.

In the UK the three main silo types are the walled clamp, the bunker and the tower silo, the most common being the clamp silo.

Normally the clamp silo will have three walls which should be airtight, and preferably sloping. They should also be sufficiently strong to sustain the lateral pressure from the silage and the weight of any tractor which is working on the silage. There is now a recommended safety standard (MAFF 1978). For safety and prevention of waste the walls should always be higher than the surface of the silage at the time of filling the silo, because unless the silage is packed tightly against airtight walls wastage will occur.

The preferred height of finished silage depends on the method of feeding the animals. For self-feeding with cattle the maximum height is about 2 m, but when the silo is emptied mechanically greater settled depths of silage can be used with a consequent better utilization of the silo.

Protection from rain is important, the acidity being reduced when rain enters silage. This can be accomplished with plastic sheeting, which also provides an airtight seal, or with a permanent roof over the silo. A roof will protect the silage at all times, as will plastic sheeting if the silo is covered when the silo is being filled and care is taken in stripping the sheet when the silo is being emptied, but if this is not done the silage is vulnerable during filling and emptying operations. Roofing a silo is a costly extra and, for new silos, may not be justifiable.

A bunker is rectangular with four walls and the finished height normally exceeds 2 m. It is intermediate in other characteristics between the clamp and the tower.

The tower silo is usually constructed of steel sheet or concrete staves. The steel silo can be airtight and losses due to aerobic spoilage can be eliminated. Even with the non-airtight types, control of surface waste is easier because of the relatively small surface which is exposed. The tower is the only type of silo which lends itself to complete automatic feeding, but this involves considerable cost in equipment. Also, because of filling and emptying requirements, pre-wilting of the herbage and the use of a precision-chop harvester are necessary.

Harvesting and feeding equipment costs may be higher with tower silos, but the silo cost is not much different from a roofed, walled clamp silo. Silage of equally good feeding value can be made in both types of silo. The other main consideration is the loss of nutrients. It is suggested that losses, particularly those associated with waste, are lower in the tower silo than in the clamp silo, because the less well the silage is protected from aerobic conditions the greater the losses. However, nutrient loss can be similar for a tower and clamp silo provided that the clamp silage has been sealed well with plastic sheeting (Table 5.7). The advantages of the tower silo lie in it being easier to attain a good seal and in simpler handling of the silage from the silo to the stock. The advent of mechanical unloaders for silage made in clamp silos has eroded the latter advantage.

Table 5.7. Sources of DM loss in tower and bunker silos (%) (after Gordon *et al.* 1959).

	Wilted silage (tower silo)	Unwilted silage (tower silo)	Unwilted silage (bunker silo)
DM (%)	30.2	26.4	23.7
Source of loss			
Spoilage	0	0	1.5
Effluent	1.6	7.4	2.8
Gaseous	8.8	10.2	8.1
Total loss	10.4	17.6	12.4

5.5.6 *Silage with a desirable fermentation*

When a crop has a high soluble carbohydrate content, a satisfactory fermentation will normally occur in silage without any treatment being given. However, some crops, such as legumes, will usually be deficient in carbohydrate, and grass crops, unless at a mature stage of growth, may or may not contain sufficient carbohydrate to ensure a good fermentation. When the carbohydrate content of grass is not known, an assessment can be made from the factors known to influence carbohydrate content. In some cases a treatment will be applied as an insurance against a poor fermentation, with no guarantee that the treatment was required. The inferiority of the product from a silage with a poor fermentation will, however, be so marked that it is a good policy where doubt exists to apply a treatment. An extreme example is shown in Table 5.8. Normally an additive improves intake by 8–12% and daily liveweight gain by 10–15%.

Table 5.8. Quality, intake and liveweight gain from silages made with and without an additive (after Collins *et al.* 1977).

	Untreated	With formic acid $(1.7 \mathrm{l\,t^{-1}})$
pH	4.8	4.2
DM digestibility (%)	70.7	73.5
Intake of silage DM (kg d^{-1})	6.3	8.7
Liveweight gain (kg d^{-1})	0.47	0.88

When the crop is deficient in carbohydrate, several approaches are possible. Additives applied at ensiling can supply soluble carbohydrate (e.g. molasses), partially acidify the mass (e.g. formic acid), inhibit bacterial growth (e.g. formaldehyde) or provide an inoculum containing large numbers of an efficient strain of lactobacilli. An alternative is to pre-wilt the herbage before it is ensiled.

The characteristics of wilted silage differ from those of unwilted silage. Wilted silage may have a relatively high pH value, usually has a low lactic acid content, but proteolysis is restricted and it has a high soluble carbohydrate content (Table 5.9.). This may be due to increased osmotic pressure in wilted silage (Wieringa 1960) or to the reduced buffering capacity of this type of silage (McDonald & Whittenbury 1967).

Table 5.9. The composition of wilted and unwilted silages (% of DM) (after McDonald *et al.* 1968).

	Unwilted	Wilted	Wilted	Wilted
DM (%)	15.9	28.4	34.1	47.6
Soluble carbohydrate	1.7	9.3	10.6	20.3
Non-protein N	2.0	1.9	1.2	1.1
pH	3.7	4.2	4.2	4.9
Lactic acid	12.1	5.5	5.5	0.9
Butyric acid	Nil	Nil	Nil	Nil

Additives

The choice of an additive depends on its effectiveness, availability, cost and ease of application. Application of the additive should not interfere with the speed of harvesting the crop and the method of application must be safe for the operator. It must also ensure a uniform mixing of herbage and additive, otherwise the effectiveness of the additive is considerably reduced. For this reason an additive is normally applied as a liquid by an applicator on a forage harvester, and is delivered in a steady stream to the incoming herbage. Further mixing occurs between this stage and filling the silo. It is also essential that the additive is applied at the correct rate; too low a rate may be ineffective and too highly wasteful.

About 80 silage additives commercially available in the UK have been listed. However, although this may appear to offer a vast choice they fall into five groups. The acid additives (about 36) are almost all based on formic and/or sulphuric acid with or without the addition of other organic acids or formaldehyde. A further large group (about 30) are inoculants all based on *Lactobacillus plantarum* with or without the addition of other organisms. The remainder are acid salts, sugars or enzymes.

At one time molasses was the main additive, but it suffered from severe disadvantages. Although some applicators were designed, the large quantity required ($5-20 l t^{-1}$) even of undiluted molasses interfered with harvesting operations.

At the recommended rate (about $2.5 l t^{-1}$) and concentration, formic and sulphuric acids only partially acidify the silage (to below pH 5.0) but, with the subsequent formation of lactic acid by bacteria, they normally will ensure a satisfactory fermentation in silage. There is now a large volume of information on formic acid, partly because it has been used as a control in additive comparisons, and there is no doubt that it is an effective additive. Fewer data are available for dilute sulphuric acid, but sufficient to show that it is also effective (Flynn & O'Kiely 1984). Both additives are in liquid form, and now that applicators are available, they can be uniformly distributed through the herbage. However, they are corrosive to machinery and dangerous for operatives, although with proper precautions they should be safe to handle.

Much interest has been shown in formaldehyde as an alternative to acids, following the observation that voluntary intake of silage with a high organic acid content may be low and that protein breakdown in the rumen is diminished when the silage is treated with formaldehyde (Wilkins *et al.* 1974). However, while silage with a low acid content can be produced with formaldehyde applied at high rates, rumen fermentation may be impaired and intake may also be reduced. Mixtures of formaldehyde and acid can be effective additives (Pike 1972).

Solid additives are also available in the form of acid salts and provided they are well mixed with the herbage some of these have been shown to be reasonably effective.

Earlier results from the use of inoculants were disappointing. In many cases they improved fermentation of silage under laboratory conditions, but did not reproduce this effect on the farm. However, there are now inoculants which have been tested widely under field conditions and have achieved satisfactory fermentation in silage, even at relatively low herbage carbohydrate contents, which was reflected in animal production (e.g. Gordon 1987, Henderson *et al.* 1987). Unlike acid additives, acid salts and inoculants are safe to handle and are non-corrosive.

Enzymes are also available commercially as silage additives. These break down cellulose into simpler forms of carbohydrate which could be a substrate for lactic acid producing bacteria. However, at the present time more information is needed to show that enzymes are effective under field conditions (Kennedy 1987).

The possibility of reducing the volume of effluent from silage has led to the marketing of absorbents. Some of these contain sugars, but others do not and the latter will not affect silage fermentation. A high rate of additive is required if absorbents are to be effective and this creates problems in application (Offer & Al Rividah 1987).

So far, consideration has been given only to additives which influence the fermentation of silage. Secondary deterioration of silage may take place after the silo had been opened and techniques which restrict bacterial growth tend to make silage more susceptible to deterioration. Propionic acid and other long chain fatty acids are effective in controlling secondary deterioration (Honig & Woolford 1980) but are expensive.

Wilted silage

Silage made from wilted herbage will be well preserved when the DM content of the silage is about 30% or greater, little or no effluent will be produced and losses during storage are low partly because of the reduced effluent loss (McDonald *et al.* 1968). The voluntary intake of wilted silage will normally be higher than that of unwilted silage from similar herbage (Moore *et al.* 1960). However, wilting herbage complicates harvesting, particularly in either excellent or poor weather conditions, there can be increased loss of nutrients in the field, physical damage being more important than wet weather or slow drying (Gordon *et al.* 1969), and it is more difficult to control heating in the silage and losses due to wastage both during and after storage. Under adverse conditions, regrowth of the sward may be restricted where wilting is practised and the importance of the increased voluntary intake of wilted silage is also being questioned as it may not be reflected in animal performance (see section 5.8.3). Wilting should not be confused with pre-cutting as, where facilities permit, this increases the speed of harvesting the crop.

It would seem, therefore, that wilting has the advantages only of reducing effluent production (and consequent losses) and eliminating the need to use an additive when a treatment is required. In the case of tower silos, high DM above 30% is essential to avoid the production of effluent, and for the operation of mechanical unloaders. Where weather conditions are favourable there may be good reasons for practising wilting, but in an adverse climate additives would be the preferred choice.

5.5.7   *Feeding methods*

Silage can be presented to animals on a self-feed basis or by mechanical methods.

For self-feeding, the silage depth should not exceed 2 m and it must be uniform, otherwise the animals will be selective. Access to the silage face must be controlled by an electrified or physical barrier to prevent waste. The length of face required depends on time of access. With 24-hour access about 15−18 cm per animal is sufficient, but with limited access when all animals feed at one time about 75 cm per animal is required. While self-feeding has a minimal labour requirement, silos and yards must be arranged so that the area between them is as small as possible to minimize time spent in cleaning.

Although self-feeding has low labour and equipment demands, mechanical removal of silage from clamp silos is being more widely practised, since suitable equipment is now available and because of the difficulty in planning a suitable self-feeding layout for large numbers of animals. Additionally, silage removed mechanically from the silo is usually eaten in greater quantities than with self-feeding or, alternatively, when necessary, restriction of the amount of silage on offer is more easily accomplished by mechanical methods. To minimize secondary deterioration of the silage, silos should be designed so that large areas of the face are not left exposed for long periods of time and there should be as little disturbance of the silage face as possible.

Tower silos are usually equipped with either top or bottom unloaders which may be controlled automatically. After unloading, the silage is either transported by conveyor or by a forage box (MAFF 1977b).

5.6   Hay

In haymaking the objective is to reduce the moisture content of the forage to 25% or less so that fungal and bacterial growth is suppressed. In extreme cases spontaneous combustion caused by the proliferation of thermophilic bacteria can occur when hay is stored with a high moisture content, especially in the loose form. Another risk is the production of mouldy and overheated hay which results in low intakes or possible rejection of the forage, increased nutrient losses, decreased feeding value and is a hazard to human health as the cause of 'farmer's lung' and allergies.

The overriding consideration is the weather at the time hay is being made. Under dry conditions with low humidity haymaking presents little problem, except possibly leaf shattering, because leaves dry more quickly that other parts of the plant. However, even in the most favoured areas of the UK the number of periods without rain is limited and the length of these periods restricted. There are on average 2.0−2.5 periods of 3 days or more of fine weather in May−August in the south of England and the mean length of these periods is 6−8 days (MAFF 1963). Conditions are less favourable in the north and west of the UK and also, even in the absence of rain, these regions will normally have a higher atmospheric humidity. These data indicate that there are limitations on the choice time when hay can be made and that the best use must be made of each occasion, with full use of weather forecasting services. With the possible exception of barn-dried hay this, associated with the fact that mature herbage is preferred, since it produces a swath with better ventilation characteristics, is the main reason why the feeding value of hay is normally lower than that of silage.

Crops at the haymaking stage may contain some 20−25 t water ha^{-1}, a quantity which can be removed by transpiration from plants in 1 day during the months May−July. However, in practice, at least 3 days are normally required to achieve this in haymaking under good weather conditions because of limitations in the loss of water from the cut herbage from the swath.

In cut herbage, water loss causes the closure of stomata, in some conditions as early as 1 hour after cutting, and thereafter moisture must pass through the cuticle which is less permeable. Damaging the cuticle, possibly by mechanical methods, increases the loss of moisture. The rate of drying diminishes as the drying process continues, the removal of water being more difficult at low moisture contents because of an increase in osmotic pressure in the plant cells. Leaves also dry at a more rapid rate than stem by a factor of 10–15 and about 30% of the water in stems is lost through the leaf.

Variations also occur in the rate of loss of moisture between different grasses and it may be possible to select for this trait in breeding programmes.

When herbage is cut for hay a swath of varying depth and density will be produced and drying is more rapid on the surface of the swath. Poor circulation of air through the swath is a further contributor, as humidity in the lower layers inhibits moisture loss, an effect which is more apparent in the early stages of the drying process. This is accentuated by the structure and depth of the swath, immature herbage producing a dense swath and a heavy crop a swath of greater depth. Immature herbage also has a higher moisture content and will, therefore, require a longer drying period.

In practice, therefore, the objective is to create swath conditions conducive to rapid drying of the herbage, thus reducing the nutrient losses caused by plant respiration and the risk of leaching of nutrients by rain. However, physical losses caused largely by leaf fragmentation can result from movement of the swath with a consequent marked reduction in feeding value of the product. These losses are accentuated by some forms of swath conditioning, by mechanical treatment in the later stages of drying and by increased swath movement following rain. The data in Table 5.10 illustrate effects of mechanical treatment and rain on nutrient losses, showing the marked effect on digestible crude protein losses caused by loss of leaf and the adverse effect of increased frequency of rainfall.

The conclusion is that severe mechanical treatment should be applied

Table 5.10 Losses of DM and digestible crude protein in haymaking (after Watson & Nash 1960).

	Loss of DM (%)	Loss of digestible crude protein (%)
No rain—no mechanical loss	8.7	16.5
No rain—mechanical losses	14.7	22.3
Rain	23.7	34.7
1–2 showers of rain (1–20 mm)	18.9	22.9
5–6 showers of rain (12–63 mm)	27.1	38.3

only before the leaf becomes brittle and that the period when the hay is exposed to the elements should be reduced as much as possible. For the latter, possibilities include accelerating the rate of drying and protecting the hay before drying is complete. With field-curing of hay the former is the only option, with the additional possibility of using a preservative if the hay is baled with a high moisture content.

In addition to an accelerated drying rate the field-curing phase can be curtailed by several methods. In the past curing was completed in small ricks in the field, this being modified subsequently by the use of tripods which enhanced ventilation. While drying on fences is still practised on the Continent, tripods are now seldom used in the British Isles largely because of labour requirements and handling problems. However, barn-drying of hay, involving artificial drying of hay with moisture contents of less than 55%, allows the production of highly digestible hay without incurring high nutrient losses.

Losses can occur during storage and the extent of these losses depends almost completely on the moisture content of the hay, nutrient losses increasing markedly as the moisture content increase. The adverse effect of high moisture content in the hay is increased by greater bale densities.

5.6.1 *Conditioning*

A major objective in haymaking is to reduce the period when the crop is at risk. Moreover, prolonged drying in the field will also reduce the yield of the regrowth. Only the flail mower or, to a much lesser extent, drum and rotary mowers will increase the drying rate and other methods, such as bruising the crop, turning or tedding, must also be used. Normally these techniques are complementary rather than exclusive, as severe treatment of the crop, such as crimping, can be practised only in the early stages of the drying process and must be followed by treatments of less severity.

An additional objective of any treatment is to produce hay which has dried uniformly. Moist patches in hay are subject to moulding and deterioration which may spread to adjacent areas, and a uniform product is desirable in all forms of haymaking including barn drying. It follows that all conditioning operations should not only be designed to increase the drying rate, but also to ensure uniform drying. Any technique which causes the swath to be uneven in thickness or 'ropes' the swath should be avoided, since this usually results in uneven drying and is difficult to remedy once it has occurred.

Before considering mechanical methods of increasing the DM content of the crop it should be noted that moisture content can be reduced by heat or steam treatment (Philipsen 1971), but the cost of the machines is high and they do not appear to be a viable proposition at the present time. Desiccants, such a formic acid and diquat, have also been used for this purpose (Klinner & Shepperson 1975), but results have been variable and they are less effective in poor weather conditions. Both forms of treatment suffer from the disadvantage that, at best, the crop is only partially dried and further drying in the swath is required to reach a sufficiently low moisture content for the hay to be stored safely.

Conditioning by machines usually results in increased nutrient losses. An example being the flail mower which, by reducing particle size, can give rise to high losses (Murdoch & Bare 1960), and to a varying extent all conditioning treatments tend to increase losses. Therefore, in good weather conditions the most gentle treatment of the swath is indicated, but weather is not predictable or guaranteed, and in the UK conditioning of the swath must be accepted to avoid the risk of even greater losses of nutrients than those incurred by conditioning.

Many conditioning machines are available and it is only possible to discuss the type of action without mentioning specific equipment. Some machines are designed to fulfil more than one function, for example cutting and conditioning or tedding and side-raking. In some cases the multipurpose machine may not be the most efficient at the individual operations.

Turning

This is the simplest and most widely used technique in haymaking both for making and wind-rowing hay. The objectives of turning are to invert the swath, increase aeration and transfer the hay to relatively dry ground. The reasons for this are that there is a drying gradient in the swath and inversion of the swath will expose relatively undried parts to the atmosphere, aeration of the swath will be increased by swath movement and a swath in contact with damp soil will inevitably have humid conditions underneath. While turning is useful in these respects and will normally be employed in conjunction with other techniques, it alone will not increase the drying rate to the same extent as other methods of conditioning.

Tedding

A swath of hay will become more dense as the herbage settles thus impeding air flow. For rapid drying it is essential that circulation of air should take place and tedding will assist in this, either as the sole treatment or as an adjunct to other forms of conditioning.

The effect of tedding on drying rate has been known for many years, with the results of Cashmore & Denham (1938) and others showing that there is a marked increase in drying rate when the swath is tedded and that frequent tedding is more effective than a single operation. Additionally, tedding can also improve the uniformity of drying provided that the operation of the machine does not create lumpiness in the swath.

Conditioners which bruise the herbage are normally used only in the early stages of the drying process and subsequent treatment is achieved by means of a tedder or turner. While tedding may be applied frequently and initially with some severity, it is essential that more gentle treatment is given when the leaves become brittle (at about 50% moisture content) otherwise loss of nutrients will occur. At this stage the turner or a 'back-action' tedder are the indicated equipment.

It is essential that the tedder is designed to deposit the hay gently, this usually being achieved by baffle plates on the machine, otherwise the objective of allowing maximum air circulation through the swath will not be achieved.

Bruising or laceration

The stems of herbage will dry more slowly than the leaves and bruising of the plants will reduce this differential drying and increase the drying rate. Bruising or laceration of the herbage results from the use of a flail mower, crimper, roller crusher or, more recently, with combined mower-conditioners involving the use of either metal or plastic mechanisms (Klinner & Hale 1980).

The drying rates which can be achieved by these techniques are substantially greater than those obtained by tedding, and a further improvement occurs when the hay is treated twice by certain machines (Table 5.11). The reduction in time required to reach the moisture

Table 5.11. The effect of some forms of conditioning on drying rate (after Murdoch & Bare 1963).

Conditioner	Experiment 1 Moisture content (%) 30 h after cutting	Experiment 2 Moisture content (%) 50 h after cutting
Tedder	34	44
Roller crusher × 1	25	36
Roller crusher × 2	21	32
Crimper × 1	—	33
Crimper × 2	—	27
Flail harvester	20	27

content required for safe storage will thus be reduced and the risk of the hay being damaged through poor weather conditions will be lessened. However, this form of conditioning will produce material which will absorb moisture from rain or dew to a greater extent than with less severe treatment, but nutrient losses do not appear to be increased when this occurs in the early stages of the drying process (Murdoch & Bare 1963). In spite of this the loss of nutrients is generally higher when the herbage is bruised as compared with hay which has only been tedded, particularly when a flail mower is used, although the adverse effect can be reduced by slowing rotor speed (Shepperson & Grundey 1962). These increased losses seem to result because the baler does not pick up the smaller particles of hay. This has led to the interest in mechanisms with less severe action (Klinner & Shepperson 1975).

Timing of conditioning

Conditioning is most effective in increasing drying rate when it takes place at, or close to, the time when the crop is cut (Murdoch & Bare 1963) and the number of operations can be reduced by combining mowing and conditioning. Conditioning at this time may, however, make the hay more vulnerable to damage by rain, but the advantage in rapid drying will normally outweigh this disadvantage. In addition, the hay will be less susceptible to mechanical damage in the early drying stages and it is preferable that any severe treatment should be applied at this time.

5.6.2 *Barn-drying*

Hay which has been barn-dried will normally have a higher feeding value than swath-cured hay. In one series of experiments the mean organic matter digestibilities were 69% and 64% respectively (Shepperson 1960), but the range extended from digestibility being about the same for the two types of hay to a 12 percentage unit difference in poor weather conditions. The difference in loss of DM is also dependent on weather conditions, but is normally higher with swath-cured than with barn-dried hay. For example, the mean DM losses for swath-cured and barn-dried hay were 28.3% and 15.0% respectively (Carter 1960). The difference is mainly due to the barn-dried hay being baled at moisture contents of up to 50%, which reduces the time the crop is at risk in the field and reduces leaf fragmentation, the difference being greater under adverse weather conditions. Although it has distinct advantages over field-curing, barn-drying of hay has not been widely accepted in the UK due to the additional capital required, the difficulty in conserving large quantities at any one time and, even with the use of bale-handling equipment, the requirement for hand-loading of the drier.

Several forms of radial drying are used in Europe, these being circular stacks of loose or chopped hay which are ventilated from a central duct. In the UK, however, the most common methods are tunnel, batch or storage drying of baled hay. Storage driers provide facilities for both drying and storing the hay, thus avoiding double-handling, but have the disadvantage that drying ducts are needed in each section of the barn. Batch drying refers to a suitably enclosed, roofed area which is used only for drying, the hay being stored elsewhere. Tunnel drying may be done either in the field or under a roof, the bales being built in the shape of a clamp around a portable plenum chamber—this again involves double-handling.

The moisture content at which the hay is baled depends on whether or not heat is used in the drying process. Where heat is used the hay may be baled at up to 55% moisture content, but without heat the maximum moisture content is about 35%. In all systems, it is essential that the air passes through the bales and this requires an adequate air flow, a suitable plenum chamber, bales of uniform density, and stacking of the bales so that they are bonded (Culpin 1962), to prevent air from flowing between the bales and the walls of the drier.

5.6.3   *Preservatives*

The techniques mentioned above have the objective of reducing the moisture content of hay to 25% or less, when it can be stored without any subsequent deterioration. If stored at higher moisture contents, there is progressive deterioration due to fungal and bacterial activity. The temperature in the bales will rise, nutrient losses will increase and the digestibility of the hay will decrease (Table 5.12). The higher temperatures will also reduce the digestibility of crude protein in the hay (Miller *et al.* 1967). Additionally, mouldy hay can give rise to mycotoxins and allergies which can create health problems in humans and animals (Nash & Easson 1972).

It may be difficult to achieve the desired safe moisture content in field-cured hay and this, along with the possibility of creating a system of storing hay at high moisture contents, has lead to an interest in the use of preservatives. A number of possible fungicides have been investigated and, of these, propionic acid or its salts, anhydrous ammonia and the hydroxides (ammonium or sodium) appear to have potential value. Propionic acid has been more widely tested than the other substances and it

Table 5.12. The effect of moisture content at storage on losses and digestibility of hay (after Nash & Easson 1977).

	Moisture content (%)		
	45	35	27
Maximum temperature (°C)	65	55	45
DM loss (%)	17.6	13.9	7.4
In vitro DOMD (%)	56.5	58.7	60.8

appears that rates of addition of 1–2.5% of the acid for hays ranging from 30 to 50% moisture content would be required (Nash & Easson 1978). At the appropriate rate of addition, temperature rise in the bales is controlled, losses of DM decreased and digestibility increased. Ammonium propionate appears to be the most effective of the salts, but is somewhat less so than propionic acid. A major difficulty in the use of these substances is method of application. It is important that the preservative is applied uniformly to the hay (partly due to differences in swath density) and adjusting the rate of application to cope with variations in moisture content of the hay is difficult.

Anhydrous ammonia is also an effective preservative except that there may be deterioration of the hay when it is exposed to the atmosphere for long periods. Apart from having to enclose the hay in plastic sheeting for application, ammonia has the advantage of being evenly distributed through the hay and also increasing its N content (Wylie 1982). Hydroxide treatment of hay has an additional advantage that, if preservation is adequate, there will also be some increase in the digestibility of the hay (Tetlow *et al.* 1978).

5.6.4 *Baling*

The standard bale (26 × 46 × 90 cm) weighing 15–20 kg has been the normal method of handling hay for many years. On the small farm it is a relatively convenient method of handling hay but, while bale-handling techniques are available, the conventional bale has to be manhandled into store and at feeding. For larger scale enterprises the 'big bale' has become popular because it can be fully mechanized.

Hay should have a moisture content of 20–25% when baled without the use of a preservative. At higher moisture contents, the bales should have a lower density, but precise rules are difficult to formulate. Weather conditions may allow baled hay to be left in the field to lose moisture; the type of crop, moisture content and setting of the baler will influence bale density. The only certain method of ensuring that hay is fit for storage is to bale at the correct moisture content.

Normally the standard bale is rectangular, but 'big bales' weighing up to 500 kg may be either rectangular or cylindrical ('round'). 'Round' bales are relatively impervious to rain and may be left outside with little deterioration occurring, but they do not allow moisture loss to the same extent as rectangular bales and moisture content at baling is more critical. On the other hand, large rectangular bales are susceptible to penetration by rain if unprotected and this results in high losses. 'Big bales' also present some difficulty in barn-drying. The only reliable way of barn-drying round bales is in a single layer, but rectangular bales can be dried satisfactorily provided that their moisture content does not exceed 30%.

5.7   Artificially dried forage

5.7.1   Green crop drying, or grass drying

Green crop drying was introduced into Britain in the 1930s and was practised fairly widely until about 1950. There followed a period of recession, but interest was renewed in the mid 1960s because of the introduction of more efficient driers and improved field equipment resulting in a reduction in labour and drying costs. However, the dramatic rise in the cost of oil has had an adverse effect on drying costs, and dehydration of forage for ruminant feed can only survive if there are marked economies in drying costs or an alternative, cheaper source of fuel is employed. To this end the moisture content of herbage can be reduced by wilting or mechanical de-watering and interest is again being shown in solid fuel.

There are two types of modern driers, conveyor driers which operate at relatively low temperatures (150–250°C), and high temperature (600–1000°C), rotary-drum driers. Both operate only with precision-chopped herbage. Low temperature driers have a low output caused largely by the time taken to dry the forage (a range of at least 30–60 minutes), while herbage is dried in only 2–3 minutes in a high temperature drier. Output of dried product is dependent largely on the initial moisture content of the crop and drier capacity, but can be $5-6 \, t \, h^{-1}$ or more, with about $25-30 \, t$ water h^{-1} being evaporated.

Dehydration is the most efficient conservation process, nutrient losses are low (in the order of 3–10% of DM) and, with efficient drying the product has a similar feeding value to that of the original herbage because the rapid removal of water from the herbage causes an immediate cessation of plant respiration. However, some loss of fine particles may occur after drying. As the moisture content of the dried product is controllable and low, there is little possibility of fungal or bacterial growth. Dehydration is a reliable process; a consistent product can be produced irrespective of weather conditions and immature grass or legumes can be conserved efficiently.

Dehydration has always been a relatively high cost method of conservation. The drier and field machinery are expensive and drying costs are high. It is, therefore, necessary to have a high output of dried forage over a long season to spread capital cost, and a high quality product is essential to justify the high production cost. This requires a high degree of management skill to ensure that a continuous supply of suitable herbage is available for drying.

Drying costs are highly correlated with the initial moisture content of the crop. Oil consumption decreases dramatically with decreasing moisture content (Table 5.13) thus reducing cost of production. These data indicate that dehydration will be more costly in the wetter regions of the country as the initial moisture content of the crop is normally higher than in drier areas, and wilting herbage before drying is also more difficult. They also show that costs may be lessened by reducing the moisture content of the herbage through wilting or de-watering.

Table 5.13. The effect of moisture content of herbage on oil consumption in crop drying (after Manby & Shepperson 1975).

Herbage moisture content (%)	Oil consumption ($1\,t^{-1}$ dried grass)
85	367
80	279
75	212
70	168

5.7.2 *Wilting*

Even a small degree of field drying will reduce oil consumption and increase output from the drier. With longer wilting periods, particularly when the crop has been conditioned, substantial economies can be obtained. However, nutrient losses may be incurred during wilting, which increase with the length of the wilting period. It is, moreover, more difficult to ensure a continuous flow of uniformly wilted herbage to the drier and marked variations in moisture content may lead to some of the product being overheated. Uniform drying in the swath is essential and treatment of the crop must have this objective in addition to obtaining rapid drying.

5.7.3   *Mechanical de-watering*

Interest in protein extraction from crops and the introduction of suitable presses have provided another method of reducing the moisture content of herbage. Jones (1976) suggested that there are three extraction stages. The first is de-watering where the objective is to remove the maximum amount of water with a minimum loss of DM to the juice. Wilting the crop reduces the proportion of protein which can be lost. The second is partial extraction, based on the argument that forages may contain protein in excess of requirements, the aim being to provide a more nutritionally balanced food rather than extracting the maximum amount of protein. Finally there is exhaustive extraction where the high protein juice is the primary product. Of these three, de-watering appears to be the appropriate method to be used in conjunction with green crop drying.

Some values for the change in feeding value are given in Table 5.14 for grass and lucerne before and after pressing when the objective was to limit protein extraction. It is suggested that fractionation reduced the crude protein content by about four percentage units, with a smaller reduction when the forage had a higher DM content, and that digestible organic matter in the DM may be reduced by up to five percentage units. Fractionation of the herbage results in fuel economy and a higher output from the drier, but this must be balanced against the cost of producing and

Table 5.14. The effect of de-watering (pressing) on the feeding value of herbage (after Connell & Houseman 1976).

	Grass		Lucerne	
	Before pressing	After pressing	Before pressing	After pressing
Moisture content (%)	83	74	80	72
Crude protein (% of DM)	18	15	20	16
In vitro DOMD (%)	68	66	58	56

utilizing the extracted juice, and the juice must be used effectively because of its valuable nutrient content.

5.7.4 Factors affecting feeding value

Potentially the product from artificial drying will suffer only a low nutrient loss and is not markedly different in feeding value from the original herbage, although the metabolizable energy content of dried grass may be 4% lower than that of the grass from which it was made (Ekern *et al.* 1965). However, several management factors may change this situation. A reduction in feeding value can result from wilting the crop. This depends on the length of the wilting period, weather conditions and the extent of physical losses.

It is also common practice for herbage to be kept for varying periods at the drier before being dried. Under these conditions plant respiration will continue and the temperature in the herbage will rise. Short storage periods are unlikely to have a marked effect on feeding value, but after 12 hours (or possibly less) digestible organic matter and digestible crude protein contents are depressed consistently (Marsh 1976).

If there is an excessive reduction of herbage moisture content in the drier, over-heating will occur. Particles which are dry should be removed from the drier, particularly with high temperature driers. Over-drying also reduces the efficiency of the drier. It will, also, have a marked effect on feeding value as shown by the effect of the related parameter, exit temperature of the drier (Table 5.15). There is a marked reduction in protein digestibility with overheating, although some denaturing of the protein may be acceptable because it reduces the loss of N as ammonia in the rumen.

The effect of processing on feeding value is discussed in section 5.8.4.

Table 5.15. The effect of drier exit temperature on the digestibility of dried grass (after Marsh 1976).

Exit temperature (°C)	OM digestibility (%)	Crude protein digestibility (%)
77	69.3	64.8
99	69.0	64.2
119	68.0	60.4
145	59.9	36.0
166	44.0	11.1

5.8   Conserved forages for animal feeding

5.8.1   *Evaluation*

Conserved forages vary in feeding value and it is necessary to have some method of assessment so that potential production can be estimated and the quantity of supplementary feed assessed. Assessment may be based on chemical analysis and advisory services are available to the farmer for this, the results usually being accompanied by recommendations on the level of supplementary feeding (see Chapter 3).

A cruder form of assessment is to judge the forage by sensory means and it has been shown that this method can give a useful estimate of feeding value (Troelson *et al.* 1968). Judgement is based on texture, smell and colour and, for silage, a squeeze test for DM content. The digestibility of the crop can be assessed by the proportion of leaf to stem present in the hay or silage. A bleached hay is one which has been badly weathered, a silage which has a dull, olive-green colour usually has undergone an undesirable fermentation and a brown colour in both products indicates over-heating. A stale smell is indicative of mouldy hay, and badly fermented silage has a characteristic, clinging odour. All these sensory evaluations show that the product has a reduced feeding value. Where an estimate of silage DM content is required a rough guide can be obtained by squeezing some silage by hand. When liquid is expressed easily the DM content is less than about 18% and no moisture can be expressed when the content is 25% or more. Further details are given in MAFF Bulletin No. 37 (MAFF 1977b).

5.8.2   *Hay*

Although it is possible to make hay of high quality, field-cured hay is a variable product, usually of relatively low feeding value, as a result of weathering and the late stage of growth at which the crop is cut. It is normally low in both energy and protein and as such can only be regarded as a maintenance feed, often being inadequate to achieve this modest objective.

On the other hand, barn-dried hay has the potential to maintain the animal and contribute substantially to production. This potential is largely dependent on the hay being made from a crop which has a high digestibility. It is expressed fully when the hay is offered *ad libitum* (Table 5.16.)

Normally hay is offered to animals in restricted quantities and, to a large extent, factors affecting voluntary food intake are unimportant.

Table 5.16. Intake and liveweight gain of cattle offered barn-dried hay or silage made from the same crop (after McCarrick 1966).

	DM intake ($kg\,d^{-1}$)	Liveweight gain ($kg\,d^{-1}$)
Early cut		
Barn-dried hay	7.69	0.77
Silage	6.50	0.75
Late cut		
Barn-dried hay	7.41	0.44
Silage	5.69	0.35

However, they are critical when hay is offered *ad libitum* or when given in large quantities. Intake of hay rises with increasing digestibility (Blaxter *et al.* 1961) and the effect of other factors may also be influenced by digestibility of the hay. Milling or grinding hay increases intake, but the response is greater with hays of low digestibility (Minson 1963). On the other hand chopping hay, even to fairly short lengths (2.5 cm), has no effect on intake (Murdoch 1965). Supplementing hay with concentrates reduces intake of the forage and this effect increases consistently with greater hay digestibility (Blaxter *et al.* 1961) (see Chapter 3)

The major disadvantage of hay is, however, its low digestibility caused by the poor quality of the original herbage and by the large nutrient losses which may take place in the field and during storage. Where the objective is to base animal production on grass products, the choice must lie between adopting another conservation method, usually ensilage, or using a technique which allows grass with a high digestibility to be made efficiently into hay. At the present time, and particularly in the wetter areas of the UK, the only method of haymaking which satisfies this requirement is barn-drying, which has not been widely adopted. Nevertheless, hay will continue to be made for sale, where convenience in handling is important, for example on hill farms, and when only small areas of herbage are available for conservation. In these circumstances it is likely that hay will continue to have a relatively low feeding value and that any improvement will be the result of better field methods and through the use of preservatives.

5.8.3 *Silage*

The chemical composition of silage is greatly different from that of the herbage from which it is made because of the various enzymic actions taking place during the ensilage process. The N content is mainly in the form of non-protein N, soluble carbohydrate content is low and the silage contains appreciable quantities of lactic and volatile fatty acids. However, many of these components are produced in the rumen and they can be utilized by the ruminant, but these changes in composition affect voluntary food intake and may also influence the utilization of nutrients by the animal. Nevertheless, silage can make a significant contribution to production. Substantial liveweight gains in beef cattle can be supported by unsupplemented silage (see Table 5.8) and a considerable part of the nutrient requirements for milk production can be obtained from silage (Table 5.17). Animal production from silage is, however, dependent on the digestibility of the original herbage, the efficiency of the ensilage process and intake of silage. Some indication of the effect of these factors is shown by the data in Tables 5.8 and 5.17. Silage is of value in the diet of ewes and lambs, but has to be of high quality for this purpose. It has been suggested that young animals do not grow well when given silage rather than hay. Some recent data, however, indicate that the liveweight gain of calves was similar when they were offered silage or hay as a basal forage, the lower intake of silage being compensated by its higher digestibility. The low DM intake of silage was particularly marked when the calves were less than 6 weeks of age, but this did not reduce the liveweight at 12 weeks of age compared with those receiving hay. While there was no marked production advantage in giving calves silage, the need to make or buy hay is obviated.

Table 5.17. The influence of silage quality and concentrate allowance on intake and milk yield (after Gordon & Murdoch 1978).

	Medium quality silage			High quality silage
DM digestibility of silage (%) (*in vivo*)	70.0			72.9
DM intake (kg d^{-1})				
Silage	9.2	9.6	10.0	11.5
Concentrate	6.4	4.9	3.3	3.3
Milk yield (kg d^{-1})	25.0	22.3	21.0	22.7

Supplementation

It is often necessary to supplement silage to obtain optimal animal production and both quantity and composition of concentrates affect silage intake. Intake is reduced progressively as the quantity of the supplement is increased (Campling & Murdoch 1966) and with decreasing protein content in the concentrate. Good quality silage normally has a relatively high crude protein content and feeding standards suggest that it is only necessary to use a low protein concentrate and, while protein supplementation would be expected to increase the intake of poor quality hay, a response with silage is unexpected. However, not only is silage intake increased, but milk production is usually increased by giving concentrates with a higher protein content, a response which is not wholly accounted for by the increased intake (Gordon & McMurray 1979). The response may be related to type of silage and may be greater with high digestibility, wilted silage. (See also section 3.3.4.)

While supplementation of silage is often necessary, the pursuit of maximum production may be self-defeating. As with all forages, silage intake is reduced by increasing supplementation with concentrates and, although replacement of silage DM by concentrates is seldom complete, the incremental value of concentrates is reduced. This is particularly important when residual, as well as direct effects, of supplementation are considered (Gordon 1983).

Voluntary intake

Silage is normally offered *ad libitum* to animals and factors affecting intake are, therefore, of importance. Voluntary intake usually increases with increasing silage digestibility, but other factors such as DM content of the silage may interfere with this relationship. However, intake of unwilted silage is always lower than with a dried forage of comparable digestibility (McCarrick 1966), thus limiting potential production. Several explanations have been suggested. Intake is reduced when the silage has undergone an unsatisfactory fermentation as indicated by a high ammonia N content and may also be limited by high acidity in the silage, the former having the greater adverse effect. In addition, retention time in the gut is greater for silage than for hay and this indicates that there is a possibility of physical restriction of intake.

For high silage intakes, the first essential is to produce silage which has been preserved satisfactorily and has a low ammonia N content. Further increases in intake may be obtained by several means and these include wilting the herbage prior to ensiling. Generally the intake of wilted silage is markedly higher than that of unwilted silage (Marsh 1979), but in the experiments reviewed there was some inconsistency in production response. This has been emphasized further by the lack of response in milk production (Unsworth & Gordon 1985) and carcase gain in beef cattle (Collins *et al.* 1977) to wilted silage, although intake was greater for this type of silage. It may be that the production response depends on whether wilted silage is compared with a well-preserved, unwilted silage or not. The value of wilted silage, therefore, rests on any saving from not using an additive, the elimination of effluent and advantages in harvesting the herbage.

The free acid content of silage can be partially neutralized, for example by applying sodium carbonate before the silage is given to the animals, or it may be reduced by the use of additives at a higher rate than normal. Formaldehyde has been used for this purpose and increases in intake have been obtained in a few cases, but high rates of application resulted in a severe depression of silage intake (Wilkins *et al.* 1974).

The possibility of physical restriction of intake has aroused interest in the effect of particle size. Intake is increased by short particle length (1−2 cm), the response being greater with sheep than with cattle. Length of chop may also influence silage fermentation, but it has been shown that chopping silage just prior to feeding also increases intake, although to a lesser extent. Response in production to increased intake is small but consistent (Marsh 1978).

Particle size also has an associated effect with feeding methods, production being higher when self-fed silage has a short chop length (Comerford & Flynn 1980). Intake is normally higher when silage is offered in troughs than with self-feeding. Physical restriction on intake may also be shown in the effect of time of access to silage. There is an increase in silage intake of up to 30% when access time is increased from 5 hours to 24 hours, although total feeding time is not increased to the same extent. Increasing time of access to hay being offered *ad libitum* has a much smaller effect than with silage.

If the objective is to achieve maximal production from silage, intake can be increased by ensuring satisfactory preservation of the silage, allowing 24 hour access, limiting supplementation to the minimum required level and reducing the chop length of silage, bearing in mind that the last mentioned will usually slow down harvesting operations.

5.8.4   *Artificially dried forage*

Dried forage is normally processed into small packages, as long material is difficult to handle without incurring physical losses. Wafers (about 55 mm diameter) and cobs (about 15 mm diameter) are formed from unmilled material, whereas pellets are made from the milled product, the choice of packaging depending on how the product will be used. Particle size in cobs is reduced to some extent by processing through a die and milling before pelleting produces uniformly small particles. As particle size is reduced there is a progressive reduction in digestibility, particularly that of crude fibre (Table 5.18). However, digestible organic matter intake is increased by reduction in particle size. In addition, while energy lost in faeces is greater with milled, dried forage, the energy lost in heat production and in methane formed in the rumen is lower than with unmilled material and the net energy value is similar for both products (Table 5.19). There is, therefore, little difference in animal production when the same quantity of milled and unmilled dried forage is given to animals. When offered *ad libitum*, production is normally higher with milled, pelleted forage as it is consumed in greater quantities than the unmilled product, the response increasing with decreasing forage digestibility (Minson 1963). It is important that some long fibrous feed, at least 0.5% of liveweight, be offered to maintain rumen function. The physical quality of the processed product also influences intake—unstable or high-density pellets reduce intake (Tayler 1970).

Table 5.18. The effect of processing of dried grass on digestibility and intake by sheep (after Marsh & Murdoch 1975).

	Chopped	Cobs	Milled and pelleted
OM digestibility (%)	64.2	57.2	51.1
Crude fibre digestibility (%)	63.8	51.3	38.4
Intake of DM (kg d^{-1})	0.92	1.22	1.56

Table 5.19. The effect of processing on energy losses and net energy of artificially dried grass (after Blaxter & Graham 1956).

	Chopped	Milled and pelleted
Energy loss in:		
Faeces (%)	26.8	34.8
Heat (%)	28.8	21.2
Methane (%)	7.6	5.9
Urine (%)	5.2	4.9
Digestible energy (MJ kg^{-1} DM)	16.1	12.0
Net energy (MJ kg^{-1} DM)	5.8	6.1

Production from artificially dried grass given alone can be high (McCarrick 1966), but on economic grounds it should be regarded as a concentrate supplement to grass or other conserved products as these supply basal nutrients at a lower unit cost. As such, dried forage must, therefore, be compared with cereals or compound concentrates.

It has been suggested that dried forage as a supplement may complement silage or grass better than conventional concentrates (Tayler & Aston 1973) and it appears that silage intake is greater when supplemented with dried grass than with barley (Castle & Watson 1975). However, when dried forage is compared with a concentrate of similar protein content the response in silage intake is less consistent, some results showing an increase and others not (McIlmoyle & Murdoch 1977a, b). When introduced as a proportion of the concentrate supplement, there is generally an increase in silage intake up to about 50% inclusion rate (Tayler & Aston 1973). Digestible organic matter content is normally lower for dried forage than for concentrates and higher total intake merely compensates for this, but higher milk yields have resulted when dried grass is compared with barley (Castle & Watson 1975), and similar results have been obtained when grass was supplemented with dried forage (Gordon 1975).

The quality of hay and, to a lesser extent, silage, is affected by season, but artificial dehydration is not affected except by variations in initial moisture content of the crop. Although there are marked differences in the crude protein and soluble carbohydrate content of dried grass made in spring and autumn, milk production was similar for both (Gordon 1974b).

Processed dried grass can contribute significantly to milk and meat production. It appears to be most suitable as a proportion of the concentrate diet or when it replaces barley as a supplement. When it is the only supplement or is a high proportion of the concentrate, production is normally lower than with normal concentrates.

Further reading

MAFF (Ministry of Agriculture, Fisheries and Food) (1977) *Silage*. Bulletin No. 37. HMSO, London.

McDonald P. (1981) *The Biochemistry of Silage*. John Wiley & Sons, Chichester.

Nash M.J. (1978) *Crop Conservation and Storage*. Pergamon Press, Oxford.

Raymond W.F., Shepperson G. & Waltham R. (1978) *Forage Conservation and Feeding*. Farming Press, Ipswich.

Rook J.A.F. & Thomas P.C. (1982) *Silage for Milk Production*. NIRD/HRI Technical Bulletin No. 2.

Spedding C.R.W. & Diekmahns E.C. (1972) *Grasses and Legumes in British Agriculture*. Commonwealth Agricultural Bureaux Bulletin No. 49. CAB, Farnham.

Thomas C. (ed) (1980) *Forage Conservation in the 80's.* British Grassland Society Occasional Symposium, No. 11. BGS, Hurley.
Watson S.J. & Nash M.J. (1960) *Conservation of Grass and Forage Crops.* Oliver & Boyd, Edinburgh.

Chapter 6

Economic aspects of grass production and utilization

6.1 The basic economic principles

Assuming it has already been decided to have the particular livestock enterprise on the farm, and how many to keep, there are two economic problems (Barnard & Nix 1979):

1 The optimal level of target yield, or performance, and thus the level of inputs;

2 The optimal feed mix, i.e. the least-cost combination of the different feeds, at any given level of target yield, or performance.

In practice, (1) is usually decided before (2), but in theory (2) should come before (1). Since the introduction of milk quotas in the UK, in 1984, the approach to question (1) has had to be re-assessed, as is explained in section 6.1.4, while question (2) has clearly gained in importance.

6.1.1 The optimal input/yield level

The two relevant principles here, where inputs and yields are both freely variable, are the *Law of diminishing returns* and the *Marginal principle* (marginal revenue (MR) = marginal costs (MC)), both of which are illustrated in Fig. 6.1. The former law states that when one or more variable inputs, e.g. a particular feed, or the optimal combination of feeds at each particular level of yield or performance, are added to one or more fixed inputs (such as a cow of a particular quality and yield potential), the extra production from each additional unit of input (i.e. the marginal product) will gradually decline. The marginal principle states that the most profitable level of yield will occur where the MC (i.e. the cost of the last unit input of feed) just equals the MR. Where the price of the product is constant (at a particular point in time), as with milk of a given quality, the MR equals the marginal product (i.e. extra milk obtained)

214

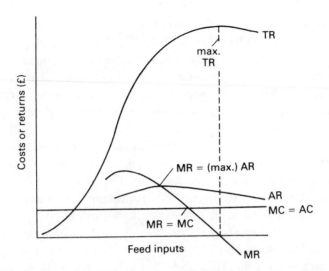

Fig. 6.1 Law of diminishing returns and optimal feed input (MR = MC). Total returns (TR); average returns (AR); marginal cost (MC); average cost (AC); marginal returns (MR).

multiplied by its price. While this principle is usually illustrated per animal, it is equally relevant per hectare.

Instead of *diminishing returns*, i.e. extra output from additional units of input, one may think in terms of *increasing costs*, i.e. extra input, e.g. feed, to obtain successive equal additions to output, e.g. milk yield.

6.1.2   The optimal feed mix

The main relevant economic principle here is the *principle of substitution*. This is applied to factor–factor relationships in order to find the optimum combination of variable resources, the 'least cost outlay', to produce a given output. The rate of substitution, i.e. the rate at which factor X substitutes for or replaces factor Y, is the amount of Y which is replaced by one additional unit of X without affecting performance. The marginal rate of substitution may be constant throughout the range of possible substitutions, but it often diminishes. The optimal combination is where the marginal rate of substitution equals the price ratio of the two factors (or feeds), i.e. where

$$\frac{\triangle \text{ quantity of feed } Y}{\triangle \text{ quantity of feed } X} = \frac{\text{Price per unit of feed } X}{\text{Price per unit of feed } Y}.$$

If within the appetite of the animal 1 unit of concentrate DM, X just substitutes for 1.5 units of silage DM, Y and the price of X is 15 p per kg DM and of Y 10 p per kg DM, this is the optimal point at the margin. The principle, and the optimum combination is illustrated for two feeds only, Fig. 6.2. For more complex mixtures, where many 'straight' feeds may be considered, linear programming can be employed to find the optimal (least-cost) feed mix (Taylor 1965).

This principle assumes that both, or all, factors under consideration are freely available in whatever amounts are required. If this is not so, the optimum use of a particular factor is determined by the *Law of equimarginal returns*, which states that the optimal utilization of a scarce factor is obtained when its marginal return from all alternative possible uses is the same, i.e. when nothing can be gained from transferring some of it from one use to another. This is allied to the concept of *opportunity cost*, which is the value forgone by not using a particular resource in the most profitable alternative way. This is particularly relevant when the optimal use of forage is being considered.

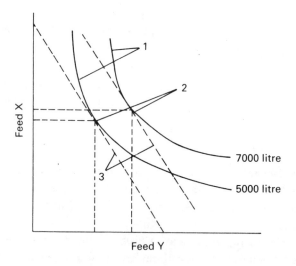

Fig. 6.2 Factor : factor relationships. 1, Product contours (isoquants) = combinations of the two feeds giving the same yield. 2, Optimal feed combinations. 3, Price lines = combinations of the two feeds available for the same total cost.

6.1.3   *Difficulties in implementing the theory*

If life were simple, optimal levels could be quickly determined, from the physical input substitutions and input−output relationships, the cost of each feed and the price of the product. In practice, however, there are many problems. Some of these are listed below. Those relating to grazing and conserved forage are amongst the most difficult to resolve.

With regard to the optimal input—yield level

1 Seasonality effects, i.e. variations in prices during the year and, for example, in growth rate or milk yield.
2 Compensatory and longer-term effects: for example with dairy cows, changes in the weight of the animal during the lactation and dry period.
3 The incidence of disease.

With regard to the optimal combination of feeds

1 Frequent, mainly unpredictable, variations in the prices of purchased feeds.
2 The considerable problems of costing grazing and home-grown conserved bulk fodder.
3 Limited available resources, particularly land, but also capital and seasonal labour, which require the application of opportunity costs instead of 'unit costs' and the former are far from easy to calculate.
4 Uncertainty concerning the marginal rates of substitution between alternative feeds, depending on variability in their digestibility and intake characteristics.
5 Variability of, and difficulty of predicting, the quality of the forages.

With regard both to the optimal yield/input level and the optimal combination of feeds

1 Variations between breeds and individual animals within the herd or flock.
2 Variations between years, owing primarily to the effect of variations in weather, on the timeliness of conservation and on the yields and quality of grazing and conserved fodder.
3 Variations in the operator's skill from farm to farm and on any one farm with changes in personnel or their skill.
4 Variations in managerial ability.

Despite these difficulties concerning their practical application, the basic economic principles provide a rational way of looking at problems and alternative approaches, although in practice there is considerable room for pragmatism and trial and error.

6.1.4   *The effect of quotas*

The application of the first principle referred to has been affected by the introduction of milk quotas. Indeed it has been said that the marginal principle no longer applies, since total herd yield cannot be increased beyond the quota level without the risk of a penalty. Thus, it is argued, what matters now is to produce the quota output at minimum cost per litre. However, this is an over simplification. The farmer still has the choice between producing at a lower yield per cow from the same number of cows, with savings in concentrate use and possibly other costs, and producing the same yield per cow as before, or more, with fewer cows. If the latter course is taken, the same stocking rate can be retained, thus releasing land for other enterprises (new ones introduced or existing ones expanded), or the stocking rate can be relaxed, thus saving fertilizer and possibly other costs, or more silage can be made, to substitute for part of the concentrate ration. There is yet another variable that at least some farmers will consider—whether to lease or buy extra quota. The marginal principle is highly relevant here.

All these possibilities raise problems and many permutations are possible and should be budgeted. This being the case, the best solution can be pursued only in relation to the circumstances of each particular herd, or farm.

6.2   Main economic factors affecting profitability

6.2.1   *Milk production*

It is obviously impossible to draw a clear line between economic and husbandry factors, and differences in the quality of animal and grassland husbandry explain many of the variations between farms in the level of the economic factors discussed below.

Many reports consider and compare the relative importance of the various economic factors. Those produced by the University Agricultural Economics Departments, the Milk Marketing Board (MMB) and ICI appear regularly, some each year. The latest available MMB results for the top and bottom 25% of herds on the basis of gross margin ha^{-1} are shown in Table 6.1. The large differences in stocking rate and yield per cow (in relation to use of concentrates) are apparent. Fixed costs are not considered in this comparison. The differences in fixed costs per cow between the top and bottom 25% when based on *profit* ha^{-1} was £225 per cow in 1986−7, including interest charges of £88.

Table 6.1. Milk production: comparison of top and bottom 25%, on the basis of gross margin ha^{-1} (1986−87) (after MMB 1987).

	Top 25%	Bottom 25%
Number of herds	187	187
Herd size	141	107
Yield per cow (litres)	5832	4987
Concentrate use per cow (kg)	1812	1508
Concentrate use per litre (kg)	0.31	0.30
Stocking rate (LSU ha^{-1})	2.62	1.50
N use ha^{-1} (kg)	334	196
Summer milk (%)	46.5	48.5
Dry cow (%)	15.4	15.6
Replacement rate (%)	24.9	26.2
	£ per cow	
Output		
Milk sales	932	784
Calf sales	80	70
Less herd depreciation	47	49
Total output	965	805
Variable costs		
Concentrates	230	205
Purchased bulk feed	19	15
Forage	70	71
Sundries	67	63
Total variable costs	386	354
Gross margin per cow (£)	579	451
Gross margin per forage ha (£)	1517	677
Margin over concentrates per cow (£)	702	579
Milk price received per litre (p)	15.90	15.70
Concentrate cost per tonne (£)	127	136

Data derived from a random sample may be subjected to detailed statistical analyses. Williams & Jones (1969), in one of the earliest rigorous statistical studies in the UK, refer to 'the overwhelming importance of stocking rate'. The other major factor positively correlated with profitability per cow, and usually per hectare, is yield per cow. Obviously the cost of obtaining a higher yield is vital; since the main variable is concentrate use per cow, the margin of milk value over concentrate costs is more useful and relevant than simply yield, especially as this measure also incorporates milk *price* and concentrate *cost* per tonne. The milk : concentrate price ratio and the beef : concentrate price ratio are major factors affecting the profitability and optimal yield levels for these two enterprises in any particular season.

All economic surveys show a strong correlation between both stocking rate and yield per cow with both gross and net margin ha^{-1}. This is illustrated in Table 6.2. However, the correlation with yield per cow often weakens at the higher yield levels, owing mainly to heavy increases in concentrate costs. Certain fixed costs are likely to rise as stocking rate increases, but to a much lesser extent as yield rises. The relationship between yield and fixed costs is considered in section 6.3.

Stressing the importance of stocking rate and yield per cow, together with concentrate use, does not of course imply that no other factors are important. For example, labour costs, net replacement cost (which combines the cost of replacements and the value of culls and calves), expenditure on buildings and fixed equipment, forage making and conservation costs, and fertilizer costs ha^{-1} are also important. Figure 6.3 shows a detailed analysis that can be used to trace reasons for differences in profitability between herds.

6.2.2   Beef systems: rearing and fattening

The results from many systems of beef production and the reasons for differences in profitability (or at least in gross margins) are published annually by the Meat and Livestock Commission (MLC). The vital economic factors, which vary according to the system, are summarized in Table 6.3. The number of asterisks (maximum four) indicates the relative importance of each factor, particularly as it affects differences in profitability ha^{-1} between farms. Some factors may be important, but may vary little from farm to farm, or season to season. As with milk production, stocking rate is a major factor in all systems involving grazing and conserved forage.

Yield is less easily defined in beef than in milk production; often it is 'fixed', i.e. the sale of a fattened animal will usually be defined within certain limits, in which case the time to achieve the required weight, or daily liveweight gain, is the measure of yield. Table 6.4 shows how energy requirement per kg of daily liveweight gain falls as the latter increases.

Where a continuous system of production is operating (e.g. grass silage beef where a finishing cattle shed is kept in continual use), liveweight gain per day will affect throughput. Although this tends to be of greater relative importance in a pig enterprise or in intensive beef systems

Table 6.2a. Association between milk yield per cow and profitability (£) 1985–86.

	Milk yield (litres per cow)								
	Under 4000	4000– 4499	4500– 4999	5000– 5249	5250– 5499	5500– 5749	5750– 5999	6000– 6499	6500 & over
GM per cow	336	427	459	505	535	571	603	589	632
GM per forage ha	534	693	799	974	966	1029	1079	1113	1337
NM per cow	−50	49	126	176	196	240	271	240	274
NM per forage ha	−79	79	217	338	356	436	484	453	583
NM per litre	−1.4	1.1	2.6	3.4	3.7	4.3	4.6	3.9	3.9

Table 6.2b. Association between stocking rate and profitability (£) 1985–86.

	Forage ha per cow*							
	Under 0.4	0.4– 0.49	0.5– 0.59	0.6– 0.69	0.7– 0.79	0.8– 0.89	0.9– 0.99	1.00 & over
GM per cow	502	527	519	505	440	519	443	373
GM per forage ha	1459	1166	956	803	603	613	478	345
NM per cow	188	199	182	149	37	96	69	−49
NM per forage ha	553	442	337	237	51	113	74	−45
NM per litre	3.3	3.7	3.5	2.9	0.8	2.0	1.4	−1.1

* Adjusted for purchased bulk fodder.
GM = gross margin; NM = net margin.
Source: University costings. Milk costs 1985–86 (working tables).

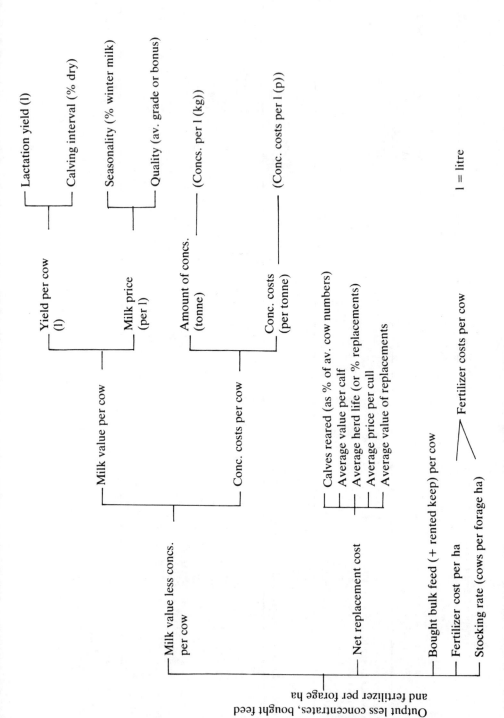

Fig. 6.3 Components of profitability of milk production (after Barnard & Nix 1979).

Table 6.3. Main profit factors in beef production.

	Stocking rate	No. calves sold per cow	Purchase price of calf/store	Sale price of animal	Conc. feed (per head)	LWG (day^{-1})
Single-suckling	****	*	—	***	**	**
Multiple-suckling	****	**	***	***	***	***
Bucket-rearing	—	—	***	***	***	***
Winter fattening	**	—	***	***	***	***
Summer fattening	****	—	***	***	*	***
Semi-intensive beef (18 m)	****	—	***	***	***	***
Intensive beef (12 m)	—	—	***	***	***	**

Table 6.4. Energy requirements of steers at three levels of daily liveweight gain (after MLC 1987a).

Gain day^{-1} (kg)	Metabolizable energy (ME) required day^{-1}	Energy (MJ) required kg^{-1} of gain*
0.5	47	93
1.0	61	60
1.5	80	53

* Average between 100 and 500 kg.

than in less intensive beef production from grass (Barnard & Nix 1979), it is nevertheless important to maintain good liveweight gains from grass.

In beef finishing systems, or in producing heavy stores for sale, a major profit determinant is the 'market margin', which depends on the price per kg at which the animal is bought and sold. It is illustrated in Table 6.5. In this example, selling at 20 p per kg less than the purchase price is worth £140 per head in market margin compared with the opposite. Although this may appear to be relevant only when store cattle are purchased, it also applies when they are reared on the same farm, since the farmer has the option of selling the cattle as stores instead of fattening them: the sale price that could be obtained is the opportunity cost.

6.2.3 *Sheep*

The two key factors affecting the difference in profitability between different flocks in any one year are stocking rate (ewes ha^{-1} all the year round) and lambing percentage (lambs reared per 100 ewes put to the ram). These two factors, together with the liveweight gain per lamb, determine the total weight of lamb sold ha^{-1}. The stocking rate depends

Table 6.5. Market margin (MM) and feeder's margin (FM) (£).

Sold	500 kg at 130p =	650	Sold	500 kg at 110p =	550
− Bought	350 kg at 110p =	385	− Bought	350 kg at 130p =	455
		265			95
MM =	350 kg at +20p = (+)70		MM =	350 kg at −20p = (−)70	
FM =	150 kg at 130p =	195	FM =	150 kg at 110p =	165
Total margin		265	Total margin		95

both on the quality of the land and on the skill of management. When different seasons are compared, lamb price per kg is another vital factor, especially in the hills. If the cost of replacement females is high, ewe depreciation also becomes important. Table 6.6 shows the relative importance of the above factors in lowland spring lambing flocks.

As with beef, the Meat and Livestock Commission's commercial recording schemes provide the main source of data (MLC 1987). Table 6.7 gives the average and top third results for lowland flocks selling lambs off grass. The top third have a gross margin ha^{-1} 50% above the overall average for the sample surveyed, which itself is above the national average, partly as a result of a 23% higher stocking rate.

Table 6.6. Factors in sheep profitability (lowland spring lambing flocks). Percentage contribution to the superiority of the top third flocks over the average (in terms of GM ha^{-1}) (after MLC 1987b).

	1985	1984	1983	1982	Average
Stocking rate	40	44	42	40	41.5
No. of lambs reared	25	19	8	17	17.5
Lamb sale price per head	9	14	14	11	12
Flock replacement cost	11	11	17	11	12.5
Feed and forage cost	8	8	15	7	9.5
Other factors	7	4	4	14	7

6.3   The importance of yield

Apart from the obvious fact that yield is one of the two major determinants, with price, of receipts, the main reason why yield is such an important determinant of profitability is that as yield increases fixed costs per head or per hectare are spread over a greater output, thus reducing fixed costs per unit of output. Fixed costs are a high proportion of total costs in most forms of production; they represent about two-thirds of costs in milk production. By 'fixed costs' in this context are meant all those costs which are necessarily incurred, and remain the same, once the herd or flock size has been determined, regardless of the yield obtained. They include all, or at least most of, the herd or flock depreciation, depreciation and interest on buildings, fixed and field equipment, rent or mortgage charges, regular labour, and several smaller cost items. By contrast the 'variable costs' change with yield. The main variable costs for most systems are the cost of concentrate feed and fertilizer, but there may be increases also in herd or flock depreciation, labour costs, forage

Table 6.7. Sheep production; lowland flocks selling lambs off grass (after MLC 1987).

	Average	Top third
Lambing %	150	157
Average value per lamb (£)	37.0	38.0
Stocking rate (ewes ha^{-1})		
Grass	13.2	15.8
Overall	12.3	15.1
Kg of N ha^{-1}	168	197
Output	£ per ewe to ram	
Lamb sales and valuations	55.5	59.6
Wool	2.9	3.0
Ewe premium	6.6	6.8
	65.0	69.4
Less flock replacements	9.7	8.1
Output per ewe	55.3	61.3
Variable costs		
Concentrate feed	9.5	9.1
Other purchased feed	0.8	0.6
Forage	6.9	6.3
Veterinary and medicine	3.6	3.2
Miscellaneous	1.3	1.4
Total variable costs per ewe	22.1	20.6
Gross margin per ewe	33.2	40.7
Gross margin ha^{-1}	409	614

conservation costs and veterinary and medicine expenses associated with an endeavour to raise yields. Figure 6.4 illustrates this point. No profit is made until point X_1 or X_2 and profits increase until point Y, beyond which the addition to variable costs (i.e. the marginal cost) exceeds the value of the additional output (i.e. the marginal revenue).

Figure 6.4 illustrates a further important point: that a higher level of fixed costs requires a greater output before a profit can be made. A higher level of fixed costs may in itself raise output given the same level of variable costs, but the important question is whether the added returns will cover the additional costs, e.g. of complete diet feeding, with feeder wagons instead of self-feed silage. There appears to be no evidence in dairying or beef production that extra capital spent, for example, on buildings or mechanized feeding systems will raise output per animal (Coward 1971), although they may reduce labour costs. When economic pressures are severe, systems with lower fixed costs are better able to survive.

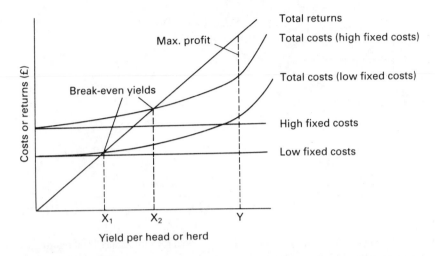

Fig. 6.4 Relationship between yield, returns and costs. Variable costs = total costs − fixed costs.

6.4   Yield per head and yield per hectare

As stocking rate is increased, at a given level of grassland production ha^{-1}, some reduction in yield per head must eventually be expected. It may be possible, up to a point, to maintain the yield per head by increased fertilizer use or supplementary feeding, but this means higher costs. Even if yield per head falls, or supplementary feeding costs are increased, the decline in yield or increased cost per animal will not necessarily be uneconomic, provided yield ha^{-1} continues to increase. Increased output ha^{-1} will further spread some fixed costs, but at the same time there will be an increase in other fixed costs per unit of production and in variable costs. The effect on items of fixed cost such as buildings and other whole-farm effects will depend on whether the increased stocking rate is achieved through keeping an increased number of stock on the same area or the same number on a smaller area, or some combination in between; this is discussed further in section 6.9.

Because of the additional costs incurred in raising yield ha^{-1}, maximum yield ha^{-1} is likely to be beyond the point of maximum profit ha^{-1}. The relationships involved are illustrated in Fig. 6.5. Furthermore, where capital is more limiting than land, it will pay to put more emphasis on profit per head than profit per hectare.

Evidence of declining yields per head as stocking rate is increased is not easy to find from farm survey data, since improved swards, higher

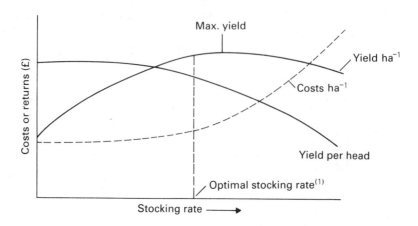

Fig. 6.5 Yield per head, and yield and profit per ha. Yield = returns. (1) Total returns ha^{-1} less total costs ha^{-1} at maximum.

fertilizer inputs and better management often accompany the higher density of stocking and offset any reduction in yield per head.

There has been a considerable amount of experimental work on this subject, referred to in Chapter 4 and, for example, by Morley (1978).

6.5   Timeliness and seasonality

Where production is not continuous, as with rearing beef cattle or finishing beef stores, there is often a choice of starting and finishing time. Even where it is continuous, as with beef from the dairy herd, it is still usually possible to vary the numbers produced seasonally. Yield, prices and costs may all be affected by decisions made about seasonality of production. Prices of beef cattle are normally higher in the spring and summer than in the autumn and winter. Costs are always higher in the winter than in the summer. Thus it is necessary to balance and calculate the net effect of differences in yields, prices and real costs in making decisions concerning seasonality.

6.5.1   *Milk production*

In dairy farming, costings have consistently shown that emphasis on winter milk production (i.e. predominantly autumn calving) has paid better than summer production (i.e. mainly spring calving): the higher milk yield and the higher price more than outweighed the higher costs.

This is illustrated in Table 6.8 (MMB 1985). Although the differences between 'the top 25%' of each type of producer usually reveal the same relative advantage in favour of winter milk production, it is frequently argued that this is because the summer milk producers contain a higher proportion of poorly managed herds. Thus one study (Amies 1978) showed that if herds were classified according to calving time, instead of according

Table 6.8. Analysis by seasonality of milk production, 1984−85.

Seasonality	<46%	46−60%	>60%
Number of herds	315	537	37
(% of sample)	(35)	(60)	(5)
Physical results			
Herd size	127	117	111
Yield (litres per cow)	5309	5126	4723
Milk price (p. litre^{-1})	14.59	14.42	14.25
Concentrate use			
(kg per cow)	1678	1550	1526
(kg litre^{-1})	0.32	0.30	0.32
Price (£ tonne^{-1})	153	153	147
Stocking rate (LSU ha^{-1})	2.14	2.13	2.03
N use (kg ha^{-1})	279	263	231
Summer milk (%)	41	51	63
Dry cow (%)	15	14	19
Replacement rate (%)	24	22	24
Financial results			
Output (£ per cow)			
Milk sales	775	739	673
Calf sales	66	66	64
Less herd depreciation	49	45	39
Gross output	792	760	698
Variable costs per cow (£)			
Concentrates	254	237	221
Purchased bulk feed	17	16	24
Forage	74	69	62
Sundries	57	54	44
Total variable costs	402	376	351
Gross margin			
Per cow (£)	390	384	347
Per forage ha (£)	835	818	704
Margin over concentrates per cow (£)	521	502	452

Seasonality % relates to milk production in April−September inclusive.
Source: MMB (1985).

Table 6.9. Autumn vs. spring calving herds (block calving)* (LCP costed herds, 1976—77) (after Amies 1978).

	Autumn calving	Spring calving
% summer milk	40	67
Yield per cow (litres)	5084	4684
Concentrates per cow (t)	2.01	1.45
Concentrates per litre (kg)	0.40	0.31
Stocking rate (LSU ha^{-1})	1.95	1.99
	£ per cow	
Milk sales	484	440
Concentrate costs	188	140
Margin of milk sales over concentrates	296	300
Gross margin per cow	216	245
Gross margin ha^{-1}	422	487

* Autumn calving: over 79% calving between August and December inclusive. Spring calving: over 75% calving between January and April inclusive.

to the proportion of milk sold in the six winter months, the spring calving herds gave higher profits than the autumn calving herds (Table 6.9). The importance of 'block calving' at the right time was far more important in the case of spring calving (January—April) than with autumn calving (August—December). Recent estimates by Holmes and Goss (1988) suggest that summer calving could pay best in certain circumstances.

6.5.2 *Beef*

With regard to beef, many examples occur, e.g. autumn versus spring born calves in semi-intensive (18 month) beef production, autumn/winter versus spring calving single-suckler herds. Table 6.10 contrasts winter and summer fattening of store cattle. Of major importance are the market margin (see p. 224), the level of concentrate feeding in winter finishing, which is largely dependent, given the target liveweight gain per day, on the quality of the bulk fodder, the amount and quality of arable by-products available, if any, and the rate of liveweight gain per day actually achieved. Of course more than one batch of cattle may be fattened, particularly in grass finishing. For example, two batches of early maturing crosses and heifers may be preferable to one late maturing batch to utilize fully all the grass grown during the summer, replacement cattle being introduced as those from the first batch are finished. The second batch

Table 6.10. Results from winter vs. summer finishing of beef suckler-bred stores, 1985–86.

	Winter finishing	Summer finishing*
Days feeding/grazing	165	125
Weight at start/turnout (kg)	345	282/366
Weight at finish (kg)	491	465
Daily liveweight gain (kg)	0.88	0.52/0.78[†]
Purchase price kg^{-1} (p)	109	99
Sale price kg^{-1} (p)	106	97
Stocking rate (no. ha^{-1})	9.64	3.85
Grazing liveweight gain ha^{-1} (kg)	—	581
	£ per head	
Sales	520	470
Cost of store (and mortality)	376	292
Concentrates	50	35[‡]
Feed, fertilizer, seed and other forage costs	26	28
Other variable costs	19	25
Gross margin per head	49	90
Gross margin ha^{-1}	472	332

* Over-wintering and grass finishing, average of heifers and steers.
[†] Over-winter at grass.
[‡] 30 kg over-winter, 5 kg at grass.
Source: MLC (1987a).

will have a lower stocking rate and daily gains, and probably require supplementary feeding, in contrast to the first batch. Table 6.11 compares results from two batches of earlier maturing Hereford crosses with a single batch of Charolais crosses.

To take another example, with silage of a given quality, alternative

Table 6.11. Grass finishing of beef stores of contrasting types (after MLC 1978).

	Hereford X		Charolais X
	First batch	Second batch	Single batch
Slaughter age (months)	17	18	19
Slaughter weight (kg)	430	430	520
Daily LWG on grass (kg)	0.8	0.7	0.8
Grazing period (d)	100	80	180
Stocking rate (cattle/ha^{-1})*	4.9	3.7	3.9
Concentrates per head (kg)	0	50	100
LWG ha^{-1} (kg)	390	205	560

* Assuming 300 kg N ha^{-1}.

feeding strategies may be employed, depending on the quantity available. Increasing the daily allowance of concentrates reduces the amount of silage eaten and increases the rate of gain. Higher daily gains mean a faster finish and a lighter slaughter weight. When the quantity of silage available is limited, therefore, the combined economic effect of these different factors has to be calculated. It may be more profitable to feed more concentrates to finish all the animals earlier, at lighter weights, than to sell a proportion of the cattle as stores and give the others more silage and finish them at heavier weights.

6.5.3   *Sheep, lowland lamb production*

Compared with lambing in mid season (March–April), early lambing results in a lower yield (lower lambing percentage and lower weight per lamb sold) and higher costs in feed and labour. On the other hand, price per kg of lamb and the stocking rate should be higher. The relative gross margin changes from year to year, according to various factors, but especially the severity of the winter and the price for early lambs in April and May. In recent years the average gross margin *per ewe* has been lower for early lambing than for mid season lambing but gross margin ha^{-1} has been higher, owing to the substantially higher stocking rate (Table 6.12). More skill and care is needed for successful early lambing. Hence most producers tend to opt for the easier life of mid season or late lambing. It has also to be remembered, when comparing the averages, that the average size of the early lambing flocks is only half that of those lambing later, and those farmers opting for early lambing are often

Table 6.12. Early vs. later lambing flocks (3-year average 1984–86) (after MLC 1987b).

	Early lambing	Later lambing
Lambing percentage	142	149
Price per lamb (£)	45.5	36.7
Stocking rate (ewes ha^{-1})	15.4	12.1
	£ per ewe to ram	
Lamb sales	64.6	54.5
Concentrate use (kg)		
Ewes	72	54
Lambs	71	8
Gross margin per ewe	30.4	31.9
Gross margin ha^{-1}	467	387

particularly dedicated producers and more likely to be farming in more favourable climatic conditions.

6.6   Fixed and working capital

One of the major reasons why many farmers in arable areas eschew livestock production despite the likely advantages of alternate husbandry, on many, if not all soil types, is the high capital cost. The additional skills, labour and management needed are of course further reasons. Capital is required for the livestock themselves, the buildings (unless outwintering is possible or adequate old buildings are available for winter fattening of beef, single suckling or sheep production), and working capital is also needed. The relative importance of each of these depends on the system. The initial capital cost of establishing a dairy herd is high, but thereafter little working capital is necessary to run it, whereas the working capital required for an intensively stocked 18-month beef enterprise is considerable. All these capital items, especially buildings, vary from farm to farm even for the same system. Table 6.13 gives some idea of capital costs per head and per hectare for selected systems.

Table 6.13. Capital costs in livestock production (approximate 1988 values) (£).

	System			
	Dairy cows	Single suckler cows (spring calving)	18-month beef	Lowland lamb
Animals (per head)	525	475	125	75
Buildings (per head)*	1000	†	400	†
Working (per head)†	25	125	275	25
Total (per head)	1550	600	800	100
Total ha^{-1}				
Average stocking rate	3000	1100	2650	1000
High stocking rate	4000	1350	3200	1300

* Capital cost after grant.
† Assuming outwintered.

6.7   The relative costs of grass and alternative feeds

All 'enterprise costing', which involves estimating the full cost of production of individual products, usually on a mixed farm, is fraught with difficulties. These include allocating joint costs, including, for example, tractors and general overhead expenses, and allowing for supplementary (i.e. use of 'surplus' resources) and complementary (i.e. beneficial effects on other enterprises) factors and opportunity costs. The evaluation of the product for grazing and conserved fodder raises still further problems, largely because of variations in quality within a single season and between seasons. The problems are so considerable and the value of the results so dubious, in fact, that most farm economists are loath to make the attempt.

One of the few published sources of relatively recent grass costings is from the National Investigation into the Economics of Milk Production 1985/86. The results are given in Table 6.14.

The hay : silage cost ratio (approximately 3.75 : 1 fresh weight) accords reasonably well with the usual approximation of their relative energy values, with the protein content favouring silage. In practice, the balance swings further in favour of silage in the wetter parts of the country, or where higher levels of N are used. These conditions produce heavier crops of grass which are more difficult to make into good quality hay. Although good results are obtained from barn-dried hay, the high cost of fuel (for carting and artificial drying) has shifted the balance towards traditional haymaking. On the individual farm, the labour available, the seasonal labour needs of other crops and the type and amount of storage available have also to be taken into account in deciding between hay and silage, kale and roots.

The importance of high quality forage may be illustrated from dairying

Table 6.14. The cost of growing and conserving grass 1985.

	Growing ha^{-1} (£)	Conserving hay		Conserving silage	
		ha^{-1} (£)	tonne^{-1} (£)	ha^{-1} (£)	tonne^{-1} (£)
Seed	2.80	—	—	—	—
Fertilizer	85.40	—	—	—	—
FYM and lime	17.40	—	—	—	—
Labour	7.85	41.95	6.20	31.35	1.05
Machinery	18.95	95.60	14.15	119.65	4.00
Field rent	75.75	—	—	—	—
Sundries	1.30	8.40	1.25	21.25	0.70
Share of growing costs	—	174.45	25.80	222.90	7.50
Total	209.45	320.40	47.40	395.15	13.25
Tonnes ha^{-1}		6.8		29.7	
Total cost tonne^{-1} (£)		78		20.5	

Source: MMB (University costings) 1986. Milk costs 1985–86 (working tables).

as follows. On the commonly used winter basis of feeding 0.4 kg concentrates per litre, the difference between a bulk fodder providing maintenance only and that giving maintenance + 5 litres, assuming concentrates average £140 a tonne in 1988, is £50 a year, assuming the cow is in milk over the whole of a 180 day winter. This amounts to £4 100 for a 100 cow herd, assuming all-the-year round calving and an average 18% dry, and gives an extra profit, at average stocking rates, of £78 ha^{-1}. This assumes no difference in the *amount* of bulk fodder fed (i.e. quality differences only) and no effect on yield per cow, although the higher quality might well improve yield.

However, the high quality fodder should not be obtained at too high a cost in terms of lower yield. The DOM yield *per hectare* is also important. For example, a high quality three-cut system of silage-making led to a lower DM yield per hectare and an increased silage DM intake per cow compared with a conventional two-cut system; the net result was a 35% increase in the forage area required per cow (Moisey & Leaver 1979). Similar conclusions from Grassland Research Institute and ADAS trials carried out between 1975 and 1977 were used to demonstrate the economic advantage of less frequent cutting systems (Brooke 1979), which also incur lower cutting costs.

One estimate of the equivalent values and comparative costs per unit of nutrient of different feeds is given in Table 6.15. Such data are

Table 6.15. Relative costs of grazing, conserved grass, etc. (1987).

	Yield DM tonnes ha^{-1}	Cost tonne^{-1} DM (£)	MJ kg^{-1} DM	Pence per MJ of ME
Grazed grass	11.1	38.6	11.8	0.33
Kale (direct drilled)	6.9	42.0	11.0	0.38
Forage turnips (direct drilled)	6.9	38.1	10.2	0.37
Grass silage	11.1	69.1	10.9	0.63
Big bale silage	11.1	74.1	10.9	0.68
Extra silage	2.5	37.0	10.9	0.34
Purchased hay*	—	76.5	8.8	0.87
Brewers' grains[†]	—	108.5	10.0	1.09
Concentrates[‡]	—	155.2	12.8	1.21

* At £65 tonne^{-1}.

[†] At £24 tonne^{-1}.

[‡] 14% CP, delivered in bulk, £133.50 tonne^{-1}.

Source: ICI, M. E. Hutchinson, Henley Manor Farm, unpublished data.

In interpreting the above comparative figures for use in planning feed use on the individual farm, it is important to remember two points: (a) that own land, labour and capital for equipment are required for home-produced fodder but not for purchased feed, and (b) the limitation on the consumption of bulk fodder by ruminant livestock — although this very much depends upon its quality/digestibility.

commonly provided to 'prove' how much more economic it is to feed bulk feeds rather than concentrates, within the limits of appetite. But this ignores the opportunity cost of the land needed to produce extra bulk feeds on the farm.

6.8   Grass, fertilizer and concentrates

Every detailed study of dairying reveals that the 'bulk feed' herds that make the highest profits are those that get the highest yields despite their greater dependence on bulk feeds, and that the 'high yielders' that fare best are those that achieve these yields with only a moderate use of concentrates litre^{-1}, in both cases combined with a good stocking rate. There is a continual range of 'systems', and an individual farm's circumstances largely determine its optimum 'system'. Although herds with a high dependence on concentrates would suffer most from a worsening of the milk price : concentrate cost ratio, this is true only if the price of concentrates rises more rapidly than the production costs of other feeds.

In several analyses of data from recorded farms, simple relationships have been established between economic performance and such factors as stocking rate, fertilizer use and concentrates fed. Linear relationships apply only to relatively small deviations from the means of the populations from which they were derived; curvilinear relationships must be expected when the inputs deviate widely from the mean. Moreover the samples are seldom randomly chosen and relationships shown are usually the result not only of direct effects of the inputs but also of correlated effects. Also, the type of model chosen for the relationship may influence the conclusions. However, with these qualifications, examples include:

1 An increase in stocking rate of 0.1 beef cattle ha^{-1} increased gross margin (at 1975–77 prices) by £13.1 (18-month beef), £21.6 (24-month beef), £14.9 (autumn calving suckler cows), £12.7 (spring calving suckler cows) (MLC 1978).

2 Each extra 100 kg N ha^{-1} increased cows ha^{-1} by 0.29, milk ha^{-1} by 1507 kg and gross margin ha^{-1} by £77 (MMB 1976).

3 More detailed interrelationships of concentrates, fertilizer N and stocking rate have been shown, e.g. Turkington and Townson (1978). Their results were as follows:

$$M = 2400 + 1697\ C + 2.446\ N$$
$$- 160.9\ C^2 - 0.8\ CN - 0.00038\ N^2$$
$$(\text{RSD} \pm 470)$$

$$D = 0.6655 + 0.00066\ C - 0.00059\ N - 0.0123\ C^2$$
$$+ 0.000032\ CN + 0.00000014\ N^2$$
$$(RSD \pm 0.086)$$

where M = litres per cow, C = concentrate tonnes per cow, N = N kg ha^{-1}, and D = hectares per cow.

Using such equations, ICI have calculated relationships between concentrates fed, N use, milk yields and stocking rate as shown in Table 6.16 (ICI 1988), which may be taken as guidelines for well-managed herds in British conditions.

4 With beef cattle, Holmes (1974b) showed that liveweight gain (LWG) ha^{-1} was closely associated with utilized ME ha^{-1} and could be predicted from the equation:

$$\text{LWG ha}^{-1} = 697 + 1.4\ N\ (\text{kg ha}^{-1}) - 0.00084\ N^2\ (RSD \pm 191).$$

These relationships can be used to describe the response curves referred to in section 6.1.1, although their variability must be remembered.

Table 6.16. Relationship between yield, stocking rate, concentrates and N use (after ICI 1988, unpublished data).

	(Assuming average grass growing conditions) N (kg ha^{-1})		
	250	345	440
Concentrates (t per cow)		Cows per forage ha	
0.9	1.55	1.90	2.25
1.4	1.90	2.25	2.65
1.9	2.25	2.75	3.30
		(assuming average yield per cow of 5500 litres)	
Milk yield per cow (litres)		Concentrates required t per cow	
4500	1.3	0.9	0.4
5500	1.9	1.4	0.9
6500	2.4	1.9	1.4
		(assuming stocking rate of 2.25 cows per forage ha)	

6.9   Whole farm aspects

6.9.1   *Effects on the whole farm*

Decisions on the optimal choice of feeds of different types, stocking rates
and purchases of winter fodder, normally as hay, should be based on the
expected effect on whole-farm profitability. This depends on many factors.
Increasing the gross margin ha^{-1} from a particular grazing livestock
enterprise does not necessarily result in an increase in total-farm profitability. If this were achieved through an increase in stocking rate, extra
fixed costs (e.g. depreciation and interest on additional housing, a new
milking parlour, extra labour, additional interest charges on the larger
number of stock) might outweigh the increase in gross margin even
ignoring the cost of acquiring extra quota. If the higher gross margin is
achieved by keeping the same number of stock on a smaller forage area,
much depends on the cost of intensification through extra fertilizer and/or
additional purchased feed and on the use to which the land saved is put.
The budgeted gross margin should be considered, together with any
increase in fixed costs resulting, for example, from increasing the area of
cereals. There are also possible rotational effects: a reduced area of ley
on a grass/cereals farm may reduce the area of winter wheat and will
certainly mean a longer run of cereals, with possibly decreasing yields
and/or higher fertilizer and spray costs.

6.9.2   *Purchase of fodder*

Buying in all, or most, of the winter fodder will almost certainly raise the
gross margin ha^{-1} from the dairy enterprise, but, again, it will not
necessarily increase total farm profitability. In addition to the points
made in the previous paragraph, further relevant factors include the price
of purchased fodder and its quality compared with home-grown fodder,
and the effect on seasonal labour and tractor requirements. Suppose the
gross margin per cow, with fodder conserved on the farm, is £600 per cow
and £1090 per forage hectare, with 0.3 ha grazing and 0.25 ha for conservation per cow. If the conserved fodder can be bought in as two tonnes of
hay per cow at £60 per tonne, the additional variable costs could be £90
per cow (£120 less £30 in variable costs saved on the 0.25 ha). The
'shadow' gross margin from the conserved area is £360 ha^{-1} (£90 ÷
0.25), and the gross margin from the grazing area £1700 ha^{-1} {(600−90)
÷ 0.3}. However, if the previously conserved area were then devoted to
sheep, with a gross margin of £300 ha^{-1}, or cereals, with a gross margin

less additional fixed costs at a similar level, farm profitability would be decreased. On the other hand, if, before quotas, the purchase of fodder allowed a larger herd to be maintained on a small farm, the financial benefit was often substantial.

Further reading

Barnard C.S. & Nix J.S. (1979) *Farm Planning and Control*, Part II, 2nd edn. Cambridge University Press, Cambridge.

MAFF (Ministry of Agriculture, Fisheries and Food) (1986) *Milk Production, 1985–86*. HMSO, London.

MLC (Meat and Livestock Commission) (1987a) *Beef Yearbook, 1987*. MLC, Milton Keynes.

MLC (Meat and Livestock Commission) (1987b) *Sheep Yearbook, 1987*. MLC, Milton Keynes.

MMB (Milk Marketing Board) (1987) *An Analysis of Farm Management Services Costed Farms, 1986–7*. (Specialist Dairy Sample.) MMB, Thames Ditton.

Nix J.S. (1988) *Farm Management Pocketbook*, 19th edn. Farm Business Unit, Wye College, University of London.

Norman L., Turner R. & Wilson K. (1985) *The Farm Business*, 2nd edn. Longman, London.

Chapter 7

Grassland management for wildlife conservation and amenity

7.1 The extent of amenity grassland

The protection of wildlife, landscape and the provision of access to the countryside are now important objectives in the management of a significant part of the UK land surface. Overlapping land designations make it difficult to estimate the total extent, but nearly half a million hectares are managed primarily, if not exclusively, for amenity purposes by Local Authorities, the Nature Conservancy Council, the National Trust, the Royal Society for the Protection of Birds and other conservation organizations as nature reserves, country parks, picnic sites and other public open spaces and statutory access areas. In addition there is a substantially larger area of land, mostly farmed, where amenity purposes are statutorily a secondary objective of land management. This applies to nearly 4000 Sites of Special Scientific Interest (SSSI) (1 438 404 ha) and to the ten National Parks of England and Wales (1 360 000 ha) where landowners, under the 1981 Wildlife and Countryside Act, must manage their land in consultation with the Nature Conservancy Council and National Park Authorities. There are also large areas of land where amenity objectives and normally, but not statutorily, integrated with the primary uses. These include commons (607 050 ha), Ministry of Defence lands (282 679 ha), road and rail verges and considerable areas on airfields, golf courses and marginal farmland.

Current changes in agricultural policy are increasing the area of land managed for amenity. The switching of some EEC financial support from production to environmental management is now considered desirable to meet the agricultural objectives of controlling surpluses and maintaining farm incomes, as well as protecting amenity and controlling pollution. In 1986 six Environmentally Sensitive Area (ESAs) covering 140 000 ha were designated in England and Wales, and others in Scotland and Northern Ireland, using new powers from the 1986 Agriculture Act and 1985 EEC Structures Regulation. A further six ESAs were designated in

240

1987. Within these areas farmers can opt to receive area based payments for practising environmentally benign types of husbandry. Further agricultural extensification and 'set-aside' measures were proposed by the EEC (1987) and will likely add to the extent of amenity lands, particularly to the extent of grassland. The South Downs ESA has two levels of compensation, the higher for the return of arable to grass. The introduction of measures to protect aquifers from nitrate pollution with protection zones, as considered by the Nitrate Coordination Group (DoE 1986) may extend this principle. Grassland already accounts for much of this protected land. In addition there is amenity grassland managed more intensively for organized sports such as cricket pitches, football fields, and for ornamental uses and lawns. It has been estimated that, including this, amenity grassland covers some 850 000 ha or 4% of the UK (Table 7.1).

7.2   Species composition

Whilst intensively managed lawn and sports turf is now largely planted from a limited range of species (Table 7.2) much was originally derived from extensively managed agricultural grassland in the agricultural categories of permanent grassland and rough grazings. Surviving extensively managed grasslands include species-rich downland and other limestone pastures over calcareous rendzina soils, species-poor heathlands over acidic podsols, and meadows over circumneutral waterlogged gleys. Gimingham (1972), Duffey et al. (1974) and Smith (1980) have described their ecology and Ratcliffe (1977) presents both a classification of grassland communities updated from Tansley's classic (1939) account and a description of the type localities considered most worthy of conservation.

In the UK virtually all amenity grasslands are semi-natural, plagioclimax ecosystems created and maintained by traditional forms of livestock husbandry. In the absence of grazing, mowing or burning they quickly revert to woodland, via a succession through rank grass and scrub communities. Although therefore they are not strictly natural, their component species were recruited from a variety of natural dune, cliff, marsh, fen and montane ecosystems and they have come to resemble natural climax ecosystems which occur in other parts of the world. Thus calcareous grasslands are analogous to the steppe and prairie grasslands of more arid continental climates; heathlands have some affinities in their structure and species composition with Mediterranean maquis and garrigue communities, and upland pastures and moorland with the tundra. Some typical bird species, for example the stone curlew (*Burhinus oedicnemus*), Dartford warbler (*Sylvia undata*) and snow bunting (*Plectrophenax*

Table 7.1. Amenity grass — categories, areas and costs of maintenance in 1973 (after Rorison 1980).

Categories	Area (km^2)	Cost (£m)
Intensively managed areas	c. 1100	57
School playing fields and lawns	490	
Armed services sports pitches and lawns	70	
Other football and hockey pitches	90	
Golf fairways	348	
Golf greens	17	
Golf tees	9	
Cricket grounds (privately owned)	62	
Bowling greens	5	
Horse race tracks	5	
Greyhound tracks	0.2	
Field sports stadia ⎫ No separate figures Tennis courts ⎭		
Trampled open spaces		
Man-made	c. 2700	66
Urban parks and open spaces	1345	
Domestic lawns	900	
Urban and suburban road verges	250	
Armed services sports outfields	190	
Semi-natural	c. 4070	12.5
Rural road verges	1010	
National Trust land	922	
Nature reserves	630	
'Common land'	526	
Golf 'rough'	497	
Miscellaneous County Council land	300	
Caravan and picnic sites, nature trails	70	
Waterway banks	49	
Country parks	60	
Untrampled open spaces	c. 630	1.5
Military airfields	259	
Railway embankments	202	
Civil airports	110	
Motorway embankments	56	
Dam faces	0.8	
	c. 8500	£137 m

* 1 km^2 = 247.106 acres = 100 ha.

nivalis), characteristic respectively of the European steppes, maquis and tundra are now rarities at the margins of their ranges on British downs, heaths and moors, but the stone curlew and Dartford warbler were once much more widespread.

Table 7.2. The relative merits and use of the main turfgrasses (after Shildrick 1980).

Turfgrass	Persistence under close mowing (5 = most persistent)	Low growth (5 = lowest growing)	Tolerance of heavy wear (5 = most tolerant)	UK seed use in year 1975–76 (tonnes)
Velvet bent (*Agrostis canina* ssp. *canina*)	5	4	2	⎫
Browntop bent European cultivars (*A. tenuis*)	5	4	2	⎬ 461
'Highland' (*A. castellana*)	5	3	2	
Creeping bent (*A. stolonifera*)	5	4	2	⎭
Fine-leaved sheep's fescue (*Festuca tenuifolia*) and sheep's fescue (*F. ovina*)	3	3	2	⎫ 14
Hard fescue (*F. longifolia*)	4	3	2	⎭
Red fescue (*F. rubra*) Chewings fescue spp. *commutata*)	4	3	2	1493
Slender creeping red fescue (ssp. *litoralis*, etc.)	4	3	2	⎫ 2284
Strong creeping red fescue (ssp. *rubra*)	3	2	1.5	⎭
Rough-stalked meadow-grass (*Poa trivialis*)	2	3	1	53
Annual meadow-grass (*Poa annua*)	3–5	4–5	3–5	0*
Smooth-stalked meadow-grass (*Poa pratensis*)	3	2–4	4	588
Crested dogstail (*Cynosurus cristatus*)	2	3	2	98
Small-leaved timothy (*Phleum bertolonii*)	3	3	4	⎫ 48†
Large-leaved timothy (*Phleum pratense*)	2	2–3	4	⎭
Perennial ryegrass (*Lolium perenne*)	1–2	1–2	5	4716†

* No official figures are published for this species: a very small amount of seed may be sold for use. In practice the species can readily be sown by spreading cuttings.
† Estimated.

7.3   The formation of grassland ecosystems

It is generally considered that most UK grassland originated from Neolithic and some earlier Mesolithic forest clearance (Godwin 1975, Dimbleby 1977). It is possible however that earlier in this interglacial period suitable climates for climax grassland may have prevailed and wild herbivores and wildfire have naturally maintained them free of succession to scrub and woodland. There is some evidence of this in peat deposits (Bush & Flenley 1987). Throughout most of the medieval period large tracts of the countryside were maintained as sheepwalks. In those parts of the country with outcrops of inherently infertile sandstone and calcareous formations, dung was as vital a commodity within the sheep and corn systems of husbandry as meat and wool. Sheep were folded on the arable land to provide the fertility necessary before the development of effective crop rotations or synthetic fertilizer. The outfield common grazings or 'waste' were thus systematically impoverished by huge sheep flocks in order to maintain the fertility of the arable land. On the Norfolk heaths, Kerridge (1967) quotes folding densities of 1000 sheep folding 40 ha per year, with sheep walk stocking at five sheep ha^{-1}. This gives a ratio of outfield : infield of 5 : 1; Gimingham & De Smidt (1983) give ratios of 3−11 : 1 in the Netherlands.

The agricultural revolution following the parliamentary enclosures led to great losses of common grazings. In 1696 an early land use survey showed that uncultivated rough grazings covered a quarter of the land surface of England and Wales; by 1901 their extent had more than halved (Best 1981). Some of their characteristic species, such as the great bustard (*Otis tarda*), became extinct in Britain and others such as the pasque flower (*Pulsatilla vulgaris*) very rare (Wells 1968). Since the war, modern technology coupled with high cereal prices has again led to loss of grassland at the expense of tillage (see Chapter 1). It has been estimated that between 1949 and 1984, 80% of limestone grasslands and 40% of lowland heaths were lost or substantially changed (NCC 1984). Their species have, as a result, declined further. In 1930 the snake's head fritillary (*Fritillaria meleagris*), a plant of wet meadows, occurred in 116 10 km squares in England. It now occurs in only 17 (Goode 1981).

7.4   Conservation and recreation

The loss, through enclosure, of the open access provided by commons led to the formation of the first conservation organization in Britain in 1865. This body, the Commons, Open Spaces and Footpaths Preservation Society still survives, now joined by numerous others. Their burgeoning membership (Table 7.3) reflects a rapidly growing participation in country-side recreation at the very time that the area of open country has been in decline. A recent national recreation survey showed that nearly one-third

Table 7.3. Membership of countryside recreation organizations (after Countryside Commission 1978).

	1950	1970	1975	1977	1984
County Nature Conservation Trusts	800	57 000	106 759	115 326	155 000
Royal Society for the Protection of Birds	6827	65 577	204 997	244 841	380 000
National Trust	23 403	226 200	539 285	613 128	1 300 000
Ramblers' Association	8778	22 178	31 953	29 541	44 000
National Federation of Anglers	—	354 901	—	446 136	—
Royal Yachting Association	1387	31 089	36 368	52 140	—
British Field Sports Society	27 269	20 965	43 000	55 000	—
Wildfowlers' Association of Gt Britain & Ireland	—	21 255	30 815	34 412	—
British Horse Society	4000	17 000	—	25 500	—
Pony Club	20 000	33 300	45 500	49 500	—

of the population in England and Wales visits the countryside on a typical summer Sunday (Countryside Commission 1985). Grasslands, especially downs, dunes and heaths are particularly attractive for informal recreational activities such as picnicking and rambling. They are open and dry, their short, springy, thyme-scented turf and their wildflowers are aesthetically pleasing and many are on hills and escarpments commanding fine views.

They are also of scientific importance as examples of ecosystem types and reservoirs of species now rare elsewhere. Some of these species, which include culinary herbs such as marjoram (*Origanum vulgare*), thyme (*Thymus* spp.), basil (*Clinopodium vulgare*) and ancestral varieties of forage crops and vegetables, such as sainfoin (*Onybrychis viciifolia*) and cabbage (*Brassica oleracea*), form important gene pools for breeding new varieties. These and other characteristic species of semi-natural grasslands are commonly components of species-rich communities which may contain as many as 50 or more species of vascular plant. This floristic diversity is usually reflected in a diversity of associated invertebrates, many of which have specific food plant requirements. An example is the dependence of both adonis and chalk hill blue butterflies (*Lysandra bellargus*, *L. coridon*) on the horseshoe vetch (*Hippocrepis comosa*).

The conservation of these species and of appropriate swards for recreation depends upon the maintenance of open conditions and the control of species composition. Both require an understanding of the causative ecological processes.

7.5   Control of species composition

The number of species in herbaceous swards is related to both pH and
fertility of the soil (Kruijne 1964) (Table 7.4). Below pH 5, heavy metals,
notably aluminium and manganese, come into solution in the soil and are
toxic to all but a restricted number of calcifuge species such as
Deschampsia flexuosa, *Agrostis setacea*, *Calluna vulgaris* and other ericoids
(Grime & Hodgson 1969, Rorison 1969). This is why heathlands are
normally so poor in species. The mechanisms employed to detoxify these
heavy metals may however preclude calcifuges taking up enough of
necessary heavy metals such as iron under conditions of higher pH, when
they are less available. Hence iron-induced chlorosis is exhibited by
calcifuges grown under calcareous conditions, and perhaps this explains
their absence from more calcareous soils. Other factors such as the form
of N and the presence of the bicarbonate ion may also influence the
distribution of species in relation to pH gradients.

Table 7.4. The number of species in herbaceous swards (after Kruijne 1964).

(a) Species number in relation to soil acidity and fertility.

	P, K status		
pH	Insufficient	Moderate	Sufficient
< 5.00	26*	28	26
5.05−5.50	41	31	27
5.55−6.00	44	36	29
6.05−7.00	45	37	28
> 7.00	40	39	26

(b) Effects of dominance on species number.

Degree of species dominance dryweight of sward	Impure <25%	Pure >25%	Very pure >50%
Lolium perenne	33*	28	24
Festuca pratensis	36	34	—
Poa trivialis	31	29	—
Agrostis stolonifera	36	30	26
Holcus lanatus	40	35	—
Festuca rubra	35	34	27
Molinia caerulea	—	34	28

* Numbers given in tables are numbers of species.

Fertilizer trials have long demonstrated the effects of the major nutrients, particularly N and phosphorus, on species diversity. Where the original conditions are very infertile, as for example on many Welsh hill pastures (Milton 1940), the addition of fertilizer increases species number in the sward. Where the original conditions are not quite so infertile, extra fertility brings about a loss of species. This is beautifully demonstrated in the Park Grass Trials at Rothamsted. Since these trials began in 1856, the control plot maintained without fertilizer has had over 60 species recorded. All fertilizer additions have caused loss of species; those most effective in increasing production have caused greatest loss. These changes in species composition have been recently analysed in detail by Silvertown (1980) and Tilman (1982). The species lost are those of small stature, including most of the herbs, which are unable to respond much to the increased fertility. Those which survive and assume dominance are a limited number of species, mostly grasses, which are able to respond to increased fertility by assuming a larger, fuller growth form with which they can monopolize space and light. The species-richness of swards is thus negatively related to both their fertility and to the extent to which a limited number of species assume dominance. This is also the case with natural grasslands (McNaughton 1968) (Fig. 7.1).

This differential response of grassland species has been demonstrated in agronomic experiment (Chapter 2) and laboratory culture, for example, by Bradshaw *et al.* (1960). Those species which come to dominate fertilized swards such as *Lolium perenne*, *Dactylis glomerata* and *Holcus lanatus* are indeed those which respond best to increased N and phosphorus availability (Fig. 7.2). Those species which respond poorly in culture, such as

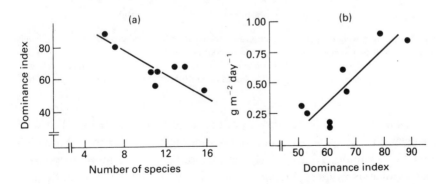

Fig. 7.1 (a) The relationship between dominance (% of peak standing crop contributed by the two most important species), and diversity. (b) The relationship between dominance and productivity of grasslands (after McNaughton 1968).

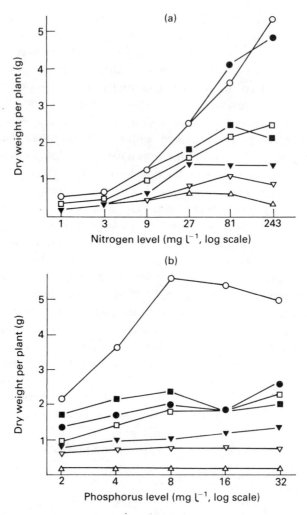

Fig. 7.2 (a) Dry weight yields of seven grass species after 8 weeks' growth at varying levels of nitrogen: *Lolium perenne* (○); *Agrostis stolonifera* (●); *Agrostis tenuis* (■); *Cynosurus cristatus* (□); *Agrostis canina* (▼); *Festuca ovina* (▽); *Nardus stricta* (△) (from Bradshaw *et al.* 1964). (b) as in (a), but with varying levels of phosphorus (from Bradshaw *et al.* 1960).

Festuca ovina and *Nardus stricta*, are the same species which are lost with fertilization. Competition experiments, both in the field and with divided pots, for example King (1971), demonstrate that the more responsive species such as *Lolium perenne* are able to competitively exclude the less responsive species such as *Festuca rubra* under fertile conditions by competing more effectively for light. Under less fertile conditions coexistence seems possible.

Grime (1974, 1979) collated the results of experimental studies of the autecology of individual species into a model relating the composition of herbaceous communities to the extent of competition, stress and disturbance to which they are subjected. By defining and measuring, or ranking, a number of attributes conferring competitive ability he has assigned competitive indices to species and demonstrated that maximum species-richness occurs in the middle ranges of environmental gradients. Here conditions are not too severe to exclude almost all species, nor too fertile to allow competitive exclusion of most others by a few strong competitors. Periodic disturbance, by grazing, mowing or fire can exert a similar effect to environmental stresses such as low fertility, or high toxicity, by constraining the growth of vigorous species to the benefit of others which they would otherwise competitively exclude. Thus moderate levels of grazing, or other disturbance factors can increase the botanical composition of swards, even at high soil fertilities. Heavy grazing, or other disturbance, can however eliminate all but a few tolerant species leading to species-poor communities. The species-richness of herbaceous swards can thus be related to their standing crop (Fig. 7.3).

This model provides a persuasive explanation of some of the factors controlling sward composition and is a useful basis for the practical management of swards both for amenity and production objectives. But it does not fully explain how so many species are able to coexist in species-rich grasslands, a phenomenon which seems to confound the principle of competitive exclusion that 'complete competitors cannot coexist'. Other species-rich ecosystems are easier to explain in terms of niche separation;

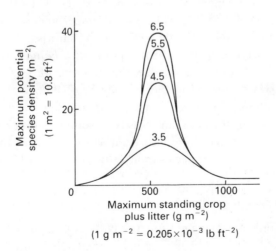

Fig. 7.3 A diagram summarizing the relationship between surface soil pH (values given on the curves), seasonal maximum biomass in standing crop plus litter and maximum potential species density in British herbaceous vegetation (after Grime 1979).

the complex structure of forest ecosystems, for example, clearly offers a variety of ways in which species can earn a living without coming into conflict with others. Grubb (1977) emphasized the importance of different regeneration requirements in generating grassland diversity. Tilman (1982) recently provided a convincing theoretical explanation backed up by some experimental evidence. He argues that species populations are controlled by a restricted number of key limiting factors and that where two or more limiting factors are involved, stable coexistence is possible within certain ranges of their availability.

7.6   Control of succession

In order to maintain desired ecosystem characteristics, a fine balance in grazing intensities is required. Unfortunately post-war agricultural policy has led to overgrazing of many hill grasslands of the north and west and undergrazing of those in the south. As a result many heather swards of moorlands have been pushed back along the sere to species-poor *Molinia/ Nardus* grasslands, whilst lowland heaths and downs have been colonized by rank grass and scrub (Welch & Rawes 1964, King *et al.* 1967, Anderson & Yalden 1981, Heil & Diemont 1983). Everywhere grassland has been agriculturally improved to more productive species-poor swards and grazed more intensively. Abandoned grasslands quickly become dominated by rank grasses, commonly *Bromus erectus*, *Brachypodium pinnatum* or *Festuca rubra* on dry limestone pastures. These species accumulate litter which suppresses most other species. They may stabilize with the equivalent of 2 or 3 years backlog of undecomposed litter in the system (Gay & Green 1984, Voight 1987) and be surprisingly resistant to shrub and tree invasion. Smith (1980) reports on a *Festuca rubra* sward which survived for 11 years and discusses the inhibition of N mineralization of which such swards seem capable. It may be that this is a factor in preventing the colonization of more nutrient-demanding species and constraining succession; just as the nutrients removed by traditional outfield/ infield grazing regimes may have also been as significant as the physical effects of grazing on woody species in arresting succession (Green 1972).

7.7   Management objectives

Amenity grasslands are managed for widely diverging purposes, varying from heavily used sports pitches to almost completely unused swards on nature reserves. There is however, no absolute distinction between even these uses at either end of the spectrum and many intermediates between them occur, for example in country parks. Grass on some airfields is managed specifically to discourage birds, but it can still be floristically rich (Mead & Carter 1973). Golf courses exhibit the whole spectrum of intensity of management from greens, through fairways, to the rough. There is now considerable interest in their value as wildlife habitats; some rare species such as the lizard orchid (*Himantoglossum hircinum*) and dune crocus (*Romulea columnae*) have their main populations on golf courses which also form important reservoirs for many commoner species in urban areas or in the intensively managed agricultural countryside (Green & Marshall 1987).

Factors such as wear tolerance, disease resistance and low maintenance tend to be over-riding objectives for sports turf (Shildrick 1980), whilst the preservation of desired ecosystem characteristics, especially plant species diversity, or the maintenance of particular, often rare plants or animals, or community types, are usually more important in more extensively managed amenity grassland. Sports turf management and related research has a much longer history than that of more natural grasslands. It developed from agronomic research; the renowned agronomist Sir George Stapledon was a keen golfer and early scientific adviser to the Sports Turf Research Institute. Agronomic principles still dictate sports turf management and some amenity grassland management. Geese for example, favour productive agricultural swards (Owen 1973). But the very different objectives of extensive amenity grassland management usually dictate very different methods on which this account focusses. Systems of management which follow or simulate traditional systems of livestock husbandry are usually favoured. Sheep grazing is most widely employed; in a survey of chalk grassland management on 55 nature reserves and farms in England (McLaren 1987), 63% were grazed with sheep, 12% with cattle, 13% mown and 4% burned. Mowing and burning were more characteristically a part of the traditional management of meadows and heaths respectively and this is still where they are mainly used. In some places herbicides have been used to control invasive species such as bracken, and sometimes to maintain swards.

7.8   Management techniques

7.8.1   *Grazing*

Sheep grazing tends to maximize botanical diversity (Bakker *et al.* 1983, Willems 1983) as the short, tight sward produced favours the dwarf perennial herbs of grasslands. Cattle leave longer grass, which, although depressing plant species diversity, does favour some insects, and the bare ground created by their trampling is also important to others, such as the Adonis Blue butterfly (Thomas 1983). Agricultural trials, designed with different objectives, nonetheless reveal valuable information on the effects of grazing on sward composition (Jones 1933a, Norman 1957, Kydd 1964). Rabbits maintained many amenity grasslands and were quite unappreciated, until myxomatosis in the late 1950s led to their population crash and invasion of scrub. Indeed a wide variety of grazing regimes using both domestic and feral stock have been successfully used to maintain amenity grasslands (Green 1973, Lowday & Wells 1977).

It is often possible to integrate amenity grassland management with livestock enterprises, though the needs of farmers and their stock may be very different from those of the amenity land managers concerned more with the state of the sward. Modern lowland breeds bred to exploit lush grass of high digestibility rarely make much impact on heather or the coarse rank grasses such as *Bromus erectus*, *Brachypodium pinnatum*, *Molinia caerulea*, *Nardus stricta* or *Agrostis setacea* which commonly dominate amenity grasslands. Tougher hill breeds of sheep such as Beulahs or Soay have thus been employed by some conservation organizations and managed primarily to maintain the sward (Large & King 1978, Lefeuvre 1980). Cattle and ponies are more effective in reclaiming rank swards than sheep, especially if there has been scrub or bracken invasion. A recent trial set up by the HFRO has shown cattle grazing to be very effective in controlling tussocky *Nardus stricta* swards, sheep much less so, with goats intermediate in their effectiveness (Hodgson *et al.* 1985a).

Information on stocking densities and grazing seasons employed in managing amenity grasslands is sparse. McLaren (1987) reports all year and autumn grazing seasons to be commonest in his survey of chalk grasslands, with stocking densities covering a wide range. There is some evidence that a spring grazing season can increase species diversity (Gibson *et al.* 1987). In country parks and other areas open to the public, winter grazing regimes are sometimes practised to avoid disturbance of stock from visitors and their dogs and to allow the flowering and seeding of herbs, and for birds and invertebrates to breed undisturbed. In the winter, however, it is rarely possible to get sufficient grazing pressure without threatening the wellbeing of the stock and any additional feed provides nutrients which may counter the fundamental objective of impoverishing the grassland. This is perhaps the greatest problem in managing amenity grasslands today for it is in direct conflict with productive systems of stock management. Most amenity grasslands cover relatively small areas and in such limited paddocks it is rarely possible to practise the folding systems of grazing which maintained them infertile in the past.

Replacement of heather by grass and species-rich swards with nutrient demanding weeds, results (Bakker *et al.* 1983). Fortunately most stock seem to dung in limited areas of their paddocks (Hilder 1966), so that the remainder is drained of nutrients. Prior to myxomatosis, rabbits did much the same, mostly dying and dunging in their warrens, which can still be identified as bright N-rich green patches of nettle, thistle, bramble, elder and other nutrient-demanding species in the more chlorotic yellowish downland turf.

7.8.2 *Mowing*

Traditionally managed hay meadows, the semi-rough of golf courses, airfields and other areas which are infrequently mown illustrate that swards rich in species can be thus maintained. Wells (1971) demonstrated the effectiveness of even one cut a year in controlling rank downland grasses such as *Bromus erectus* and increasing species' diversity. He emphasized the ability of cutting to favour, or penalize, species selectively according to their phenology and the time of year the cut is made. Similar results have been reported from other cutting trials, e.g. Green (1980), Parr & Way (1987). The latter, long term trial, run for 18 years, showed no significant differences between the effects of different types of mowing machine on the species composition of roadside grassland, nor increases in species-richness after more than two cuts a year. Species-richness was increased by removing the cut material. Soil analyses rather surprisingly showed little evidence of nutrient depletion, other than of potassium, and the changes in botanical composition of the sward instead were attributed to the smothering effect of litter and the germination sites opened up by raking it away. Unfortunately the cut material is rarely removed by local authority machines today, as it was in the past when it was often used for hay. The rank, lush, traffic-obscuring roadside swards of cow parsley (*Anthriscus sylvestris*), false oat grass (*Arrhenatherum elatius*) and nettles (*Urtica dioica*) are the direct result.

7.8.3 *Burning*

Amenity land managers are usually apprehensive about the use of fire to maintain grassland. Concern rightly centres on the difficulty of its control in small areas, often surrounded by flammable property, and on the loss of wildlife, especially invertebrates (Morris 1975), which can result. Burning however was a part of traditional grassland management to provide fresh bite for stock, is still practised in the hills and is a natural feature of steppe and Mediterranean ecosystems to which our semi-natural grasslands are closely allied. Lloyd (1968) has shown it to be effective in maintaining the botanical composition of limestone grasslands, though some of their characteristic species, notably *Festuca ovina*, were vulnerable to fire and replaced by other grasses. Management burns taking place in the statutory winter burning season between the beginning of October and the end of March, rarely do much damage to seeds, underground plant organs or over-wintering animals. Accidental summer fires can however be much more damaging (Maltby 1980). On heathlands the entire soil humus layer may be burnt off, leading not to the quick regeneration of heather that follows lighter burns, but to colonization by *Molinia caerulea*, *Pteridium aquilinum* and *Betula* spp. (Harrison 1974).

Much of the nutrient content of the standing crop is lost with firing. Chapman (1967) measured up to 95% of the N and 26% of the phosphorus for an area of 12-year-old lowland heath. Fire thus helps impoverish ecosystems as these nutrients can take up to 10−20 years to re-accumulate from rain. Small areas of amenity grassland which are too small to graze, and perhaps too steep to mow, are probably best maintained free of scrub colonization by burns at intervals of 3 or more years (Green 1980). Rotational small patch burning to restrict fuel accumulation is also probably the most effective means of avoiding disastrous accidental fires such as those of 1976 which devastated many amenity grasslands. Fire prior to grazing or mowing is also an effective means of restoring rank swards.

7.8.4 *Herbicides*

Herbicides have not been widely used to manage amenity grasslands because of fears of their side effects on non-target species, their cost and doubts about their long-term effectiveness. Brushwood killers are however commonly used to prevent regrowth from trees and shrubs cut to reclaim open grassland. Chemicals like dalapon, which have a degree of specificity for monocotyledons, and asulam, which is moderately, but not persistently, successful against bracken have been used to control these invasive species which otherwise become dominant to the detriment of less vigorous species (Haggar 1980). Growth retardants such as maleic hydrazide have also been successful in selectively penalizing the ranker undesirable species (Willis 1969).

7.8.5 *Rotational management*

There is abundant documentary evidence that in the past, extensive grasslands were commonly severely over-grazed and then abandoned to recover. The paring and 'burn baking' of turf for taking a crop harvest or two before letting the land tumble down back to grass, was also common on downs and heaths (Smith 1980). Rotational use, with heavy grazing, mowing, or burning, followed by 2 or 3 years without management is probably the most effective way of maintaining species diversity, especially of invertebrates (Morris 1973), but it is difficult to arrange. Electrified sheep netting greatly helps paddocking and has been used to great effect in this way at Winchester Hill, National Nature Reserve, where the rotational grazing has produced swards rich in both wildflowers and butterflies.

7.9   Creating wildflower swards

Some of the perennial herbs which make up the majority of the species found in grassland are long-lived; particularly the dwarf woody shrubs such as the rock rose (*Helianthemum chamaecistus*) which can survive to 100 years or more. But such species are often very slow colonists of new grassland (Cornish 1954). In a study of chalk grasslands of known age on Salisbury Plain, Wells *et al.* (1976) suggested that the slower colonists such as the rock rose, meadow oat (*Helictotrichon pratense*), spring sedge (*Carex caryophyllea*), squinancywort (*Asperula cynanchica*), dropwort (*Filipendula hexapetala*), milkwort (*Polygala vulgaris*) and burnet saxifrage (*Pimpinella saxifraga*) are good indicators of the older grasslands.

Grasslands rich in the commoner species can however be established readily from seed. This has been successfully achieved in experimental plots (Wells *et al.* 1981) and is now widely employed in establishing new grasslands on road verges, sports grounds, ornamental lawns and marginal farmland. Wildflower seed mixes suitable for a variety of soils are commercially available, but much can be achieved using existing soil seed banks or the natural recolonization of plants from adjacent areas. Spreading topsoil and its seed load retained from earth-moving operations can restore swards similar to the original vegetation (Wathern & Gilbert 1978, Putwain *et al.* 1982). The natural recolonization of quarries and industrial wastes shows how effective this can be (Lee & Greenwood 1976). Arable land can be restored to reasonably species-rich grassland in the remarkably short period of 5 years using suitable grazing regimes (Gibson *et al.* 1987).

The species composition of existing grasslands and heathlands can be diversified also by appropriately impoverishing management regimes; although some, such as sod removal, may seem rather drastic (Bakker 1978, Marrs 1985). Just as landscape architects are specifying wildflower swards increasingly for civic engineering schemes and inner city restoration, so are grounds managers experimenting with the diversification of existing swards. In golf there is a strong trend back towards courses and management more closely approaching that of the original conditions under which links golf evolved on sand dunes. There is no reason why much amenity grassland, including domestic lawns, should be rye grass monocultures. Their transformation to high diversity, low fertility, more herb-rich wildflower swards can be readily achieved. In doing so the objective of the amenity grassland manager will usually be to make one blade of grass grow where two grew before! Harper (1971) outlined some of the possibilities, holding out the prospect of creating swards for particular purposes, once our knowledge of species' ecological requirements are sufficiently known. The ecological needs of some species, for example butterflies, are now well known (NCC 1986); as are many effective techniques for amenity grassland management. What is lacking is knowledge of how to set up commercially viable systems of management.

7.10   The integration of agricultural and environmental objectives in grassland management

The conflicting objectives of the amenity land manager, usually desiring high species diversity and thus low fertility, and the farmer, usually aiming to maximize production and thus minimize sward diversity, has made their reconciliation difficult. The loss of species such as the snake's head fritillary referred to in section 7.4 is by no means due solely to this, or to conversion of permanent grassland to tillage or leys. The mechanization of haymaking and the widespread adoption of silage has also been significant. The earlier cutting of the crop does not give some plants time to set seed, nor ground nesting birds enough time to rear their broods. This is believed to be a cause in the decline of species such as the corncrake (*Crex crex*). Drainage of wet grasslands has also been an important factor in the decline of many plants and birds such as the redshank (*Tringa totanus*) and snipe (*Gallinago gallinago*). Some characteristic grassland birds, such as the skylark (*Alauda arvensis*) and lapwing (*Vanellus vanellus*), have however been less vulnerable to these changes. Flowering plants and invertebrates are perhaps more sensitive to changes in grassland management than birds. Even small amounts of fertilization can lead to loss of species as the Park Grass trials at Rothamsted clearly demonstrate (section 7.5). An unimproved grassland might easily contain 50 species of flowering plant and up to 20 species of butterfly. An improved ryegrass sward to maximize production should contain only the crop species of flowering plant and will therefore support no butterflies. Experiments show that grassland yield can also be substantially increased by the use of pesticides to eliminate soil invertebrates.

The move away from exclusively productionist objectives in agriculture now offers the opportunity for some compromises to be made to benefit wildlife. Nonetheless, whilst the switching of some state support from production to environmental objectives seems likely to be a successful means of maintaining farm livelihoods in schemes such as those operating in ESAs, there are few examples of amenity grassland management regimes which are economically viable in their own right. Most extensive amenity grassland management in nature reserves and parks is at a cost borne by the administering agency (Thiele-Wittig 1974). It is true that some such areas are grazed under licence by local farmers with some resultant rent income to the environmental agency. But such schemes nearly always involve compromises.

If extensive amenity grasslands are to be more widely and effectively created and managed in the future, they must become part of more commercially viable enterprises. There are some examples of this, such as the pony grazing in the New Forest for horsemeat, or sheep grazing of the Causse grasslands in the Cevennes National Park in France, where a low output, high value product — Roquefort cheese — helps sustain both farm livelihoods and the landscape. Current diversification of agriculture offers the opportunity to develop similar grassland management systems and this is the big challenge facing amenity grassland managers today.

Further reading

Duffey E., Morris M.G., Sheail J., Ward L.J., Wells D.A. & Wells T.C.E. (1974) *Grassland Ecology and Wildlife Management*. Chapman & Hall, London.
Gimingham C.H. (1972) *The Ecology of Heathlands*. Chapman & Hall, London.
Ratcliffe D.A. (ed) (1977) *A Nature Conservation Review*, 2 vols. Cambridge University Press, Cambridge.
Smith C.J. (1980) *The Ecology of the English Chalk*. Academic Press, London.
Tansley A.G. (1939) *The British Islands and their Vegetation*. Cambridge University Press, Cambridge.

Chapter 8

Application on the farm

8.1   The recording of grassland output

A record of the overall productivity of grassland is valuable on a well run grassland farm, and detailed records for individual fields may be required. Formerly this was calculated as utilized starch equivalent (USE) (Baker *et al*. 1964). It is now computed as utilized metabolizable energy (UME) (Baker 1982) (for normal conditions 2.1 GJ of UME ha^{-1} approximately equal 1 cwt of USE acre^{-1}.) Pasture productivity is expressed in terms of energy since intake of energy is normally the factor limiting animal production.

The calculation of UME is given in detail by Forbes *et al*. (1980) and by Baker (1982). It depends on assessing the ME requirements of the ruminant livestock from the numbers in various age classes (based on valuation numbers at the beginning and end of the year, or preferably, from monthly records) and the milk and weight of livestock sold. From this total is deducted the ME value of all additional feeds brought onto the farm. The remainder, divided by the area of grass and forage crops gives the ME utilized ha^{-1}. It is a crude measure and has been criticized since it gives full credit to purchased feed while all waste or inefficiency of feed use is debited to grass.

However, if values exceeding 90 GJ ha^{-1} are recorded in Britain the productivity of grass is satisfactory and if the values are below 40 GJ ha^{-1} the management should determine whether low grass productivity, poor utilization in grazing or conservation, excessive use of purchased feeds, or a combination of these are responsible.

If an estimate of the production from individual fields is required, a detailed record of type of stock, grazing days, quantities of feed conserved from the field, and of supplementary feed provided, may be maintained and converted to UME.

The more simple measures of *livestock units* or *livestock unit grazing days* have been adopted by several organizations. These are based more or less closely on the ME requirements.

Two sets of values are summarized in Appendices A and B together with the expected ME requirements for various classes of stock. The method is again crude and discrepancies can arise particularly when comparing data calculated by different systems.

An example of UME and LUGD measures is shown for a dairy cow in Table 8.1. Calculations for growing animals are more complex (because of differences in growth rate and duration of growth). Detailed calculations

Table 8.1. Calculation of utilized metabolizable energy (UME). If one cow of 550 kg weight is maintained for 1 year on the produce of 0.4 ha grassland and 1 tonne of purchased concentrated feed to yield 5500 kg milk containing 38 g kg^{-1} butterfat and 87 g kg^{-1} solids-not-fat, gains 50 kg in the year and calves again in 12 months, the total requirement of ME (in GJ) is given in the table (after MAFF 1984).

Maintenance 365 days × (8.3 + 0.091 W) MJ		= 21.3
Milk production 5500 litres × 5.10 MJ		= 28.0
Liveweight gain 80 kg × 34 MJ	= 2.72	
less *Liveweight loss in early lactation* 30 kg × 28 MJ	= 0.84	
Net liveweight change	= 1.88	= 1.9
Pregnancy allowance 120 days + 12.5 MJ		= 1.5
Total requirement for year		= 52.7
less concentrates 1000 kg at 12.5 MJ kg^{-1} DM		= 10.6
ME from grass		= 42.1
UME ha^{-1}	(42.1 ÷ 0.4)	= 105

If the cow grazed for 175 days on 0.2 ha of grass, the yield in LUGD would be:
175 × 1.0 ÷ 0.2 or 875 LUGD ha^{-1}.

If it produced 2500 kg milk in the grazing period it would yield 12500 kg milk ha^{-1} of grazing, before allowing for concentrates fed. If concentrates were fed at the average rate of 0.10 kg per kg milk over the summer period 250 kg would be used. Conventionally, concentrates are allowed for at 0.4 kg per kg milk. On this basis:

250 kg	= 625 kg milk
Milk per cow from grazing	= 2500 − 625 = 1875 kg
Adjusted milk ha^{-1} from grazing	= 1875/0.2 = 9375 kg

Alternatively, allowance may be made for concentrates in terms of the area to grow barley at say, 5000 kg grain ha^{-1}. Then 250 kg = 250/5000 ha = 0.05 ha and adjusted milk ha^{-1} of feed = 2500/(0.2 + 0.05) = 10000 kg.

are given by Baker (1982).

Even if records of grass utilization per farm or per field are not required, it is good practice to record where each group of livestock has grazed throughout the season so that frequency of grazing can be controlled, risks of parasitic infection avoided and 'clean fields' identified. These records may be made for each group of stock or for each pasture field.

8.2   Targets in relation to land potential and fertilizer use

The optimal stocking rate for the farm depends both on the productivity of the grassland and forage area and on additional feed purchases. The justifiable quantity of purchased feed depends on costs and prices, and on the overall size of the farm business. Some assessment of the potential grass productivity can be made from the soil and climatic conditions of the farm, or its individual fields, the level of fertilizer use and the expected range of weather conditions. The most important factors and the range of site classes (1−5) are shown in Table 8.2.

8.3   The estimation of appropriate stocking rates

The quantities of herbage DM which might be produced over the season can be estimated for each site class. Appropriate stocking rates can then

Table 8.2. The influence of summer rainfall and soil type on site quality for grassland production (after Corrall *et al.* 1982).

Soil texture	Average April−September rainfall		
	>400 mm (16 in)	300−400 mm (12−16 in)	<300 mm (12 in)
Clay loams and heavy soils	1	2	3
Loams, medium textured soils and deeper soils over chalk	2	3	4
Shallow soils over chalk or rock, gravelly and coarse sandy soils	3	4	5
Add 1 for: Northern areas, i.e. Scotland Over 300 m elevation			

Site classes: 1 = Very good; 5 = Very poor.

be calculated from the known ME requirement of the particular class of stock and the efficiency of grazing (E) which is expected.

The daily allowance per animal would thus be calculated from:

$$\text{Herbage allowance (kg DM)} = \frac{\text{Average daily ME required}}{\text{ME kg}^{-1}\text{DM in the herbage}} \times \frac{100}{E}.$$

For example a cow requiring 200 MJ per day on grass of ME 11.5 grazing with efficiency of 0.75 would require a daily allowance of:

$$\frac{200}{11.5} \times \frac{1.0}{0.75} = 23.3 \text{ (kg DM per day)}.$$

A beef animal requiring 68 MJ per day on pasture of 11 MJ/kg DM, grazing with efficiency of 0.70 would require:

$$\frac{68}{11} \times \frac{1.0}{0.7} = 8.8 \text{(kg DM)}.$$

Guidelines to appropriate stocking rates for the grazing season, calculated in this manner are in Table 8.3 .

8.4   Practical feeding

The practical feeding of stock is covered in MAFF (1984) and MAFF (1979c). Detailed calculations can be made based on the requirements and the expected appetite of the animals. It should be appreciated, however, that there are many assumptions inherent in all feeding systems and that direct assessment of performance by the stock in comparison with expectation is essential.

When stock are fed entirely on grazing or in the main on conserved products, they are in fact receiving complete feeds (provided care is taken to ensure that there is no deficiency of protein, minerals or vitamins). In these circumstances when the feed is readily available and offered *ad libitum*, the overall energy concentration of the diet has a major influence on intake and animal performance.

It can be calculated that for the most productive stock, cows in early lactation, calves and lambs in the early stages of ruminant growth and finishing cattle, a concentration of about $11-12$ MJ ME kg^{-1} DM is needed. Cows in mid lactation, growing cattle and suckler cows need diets in the

Table 8.3. Target stocking rates in relation to quality of site and level of N fertilizer for 180 day grazing period.

Site* quality	Fertilizer N (kg ha^{-1})	DM yield (t ha^{-1})	Dairy cows[a]	Suckler cows with calves[b]	Cattle from 200 kg[c]	Cattle from 350 kg[d]	Ewes with lambs
1 Excellent	150[†]	11.1	4.5	3.7	8.3	5.7	17
	300	12.9	5.2	4.4	9.7	6.6	20
	450	14.4	5.8	—	10.8	7.4	—
3 Average	150[†]	8.9	3.6	3.0	6.7	4.5	14
	300	10.3	4.2	3.5	7.7	5.3	16
	450	11.5	4.7	—	8.6	5.9	—
5 Poor	150[†]	6.7	2.7	2.2	5.0	3.4	10
	300	7.7	3.1	2.6	5.8	3.9	11
Approx. daily DM intake kg day^{-1}			13.0	14.0	5.9	8.7	3.0
Herbage allowance[‡] for 180 days (kg)			2463	2965	1327	1957	635

[a] Average Friesian cow receiving 0.1–0.2 kg concentrate kg^{-1} milk, 95% efficiency of grass utilization. Add 8% for autumn calvers, deduct 8% for spring calving herd.
[b] Suckler cow, 480 kg calving February and raising calf to 250 kg, 85% efficiency of grass utilization.
[c] Cattle 200 kg at turnout to gain 160 kg in 180 days, 80% efficiency of grass utilization.
[d] Cattle 350 kg at turnout to gain 180 kg in 180 days, 80% efficiency of grazing.
* For intermediate values for site grades 2 and 4 see Table 8.2.
[†] A good grass/clover sward can give yields similar to 150 kg N ha^{-1}.
[‡] This takes account of efficiency of grazing.

range 10–11 MJ kg^{-1} DM and the requirements of animals at low levels of performance are satisfied with diets in the range 8–9 MJ kg^{-1} DM. (MAFF 1984.)

In practice there is a wide range of forage feeding systems. On a grassland farm simple diets based on grazing or silage with a specialist compound concentrate formulated to balance the forage available in terms of protein and minerals, are practical and convenient. With more technical input and some saving in direct costs, the forage may be supplemented with straight feeds such as cereals or dried sugar beet pulp and maize gluten feed or fish meal, and minerals, to provide an adequately balanced diet.

Where arable by-products are available, even more diversity in stock feeding may be appropriate, with straight feeds, minerals, processed straw, stock feed potatoes and vegetable crops being incorporated with grass or maize silage in a complete mix by use of a mixer wagon. Additional protein is usually required when maize silage is a major portion of the mix. Feed mixes including a variety of sources of bulk feed may encourage increased appetite.

Apart from the design and calculation of the diet, the equipment and facilities should minimize waste of feed.

The allocation of feed to individual animals also requires attention. When they graze or have *ad libitum* access to silage, intake will vary broadly according to the animal's requirement, but if the forage quality is low, some additional more concentrated supplement may be required.

Most recent work with milk cows has indicated that flat rate feeding will achieve similar performance to individual allocation of concentrate provided the forage available is of high quality and freely available.

With young stock and sheep, the practical problem is to ensure reasonably uniform distribution of any concentrated feed between the individuals of the group.

Table 8.4 gives an indication of the range of appetites which will occur and shows the appropriate quantities of concentrate to provide a given percentage of the diet. These are intended as guidelines rather than precise recommendations. They do show how the use of concentrated feeds can supplement the lower grade forages to supply an adequate diet.

Table 8.4. Daily allowance of concentrates (86% DM) to provide various proportions of total DM intake (kg).

Class of stock	Total DM intake (kg)	Proportion of DM						
		0.20	0.30	0.40	0.50	0.60	0.70	0.80
Sheep (2)*	2	0.45	0.7	0.9	1.2	1.4	1.6	1.9
Calves (4)	4	0.9	1.4	1.9	2.3	2.8	3.2	3.7
Young	6	1.4	2.1	2.8	3.5	4.2	4.9	5.6
cattle (6–8)	8	1.9	2.8	3.7	4.6	5.6	6.5	7.4
Finishing cattle (8–12)	10	2.3	3.5	4.6	5.8	7.0	8.1	9.3
Low-yielding								
or suckler cows (10–14)	12	2.8	4.2	5.6	7.0	8.4	—	—
Average milk	14	3.2	4.9	6.5	8.1	9.8	—	—
cows (12–16)	16	3.7	5.6	7.4	9.3	11.2	—	—
High-yielding	18	4.2	6.3	8.4	10.5	12.5	—	—
milk cows (16–22)	20	4.6	7.0	9.3	11.6	13.9	—	—
	22	5.1	7.7	10.2	12.8	15.3	—	—

* Numbers in brackets refer to the total daily intake of DM (kg) by class of stock.

8.5   Feed budgeting

It is important both in the long and short-term to estimate feed requirements in relation to stock numbers.

8.5.1   *Assessing year round stocking rates*

The stocking rates from Table 8.3 provide an overall estimate of the
grazing stocking rate for the farm and of the quantity of forage available
for winter use. In straightforward dairy herd grassland systems, relationships have been estimated between forage area, fertilizer use and concentrated feed and these are given in Chapter 6. In more varied grazing
enterprises where dairy cows, dairy followers, beef and sheep are all
produced, the calculations are more complex. To simplify these it is
normal to standardize the numbers of animals by conversion to livestock
units (section 8.1). On good land with good management and normal
levels of concentrated feed use, an overall target for the year is 2.5
livestock units ha^{-1} of forage. Higher figures generally demand very
high pasture productivity, or appreciable quantities of purchased bulk
feed or of concentrates.

8.5.2   *Assessing short-term pasture supply*

Feed budgeting also refers to the assessment of pasture supply in the
short-term. Particularly with continuous stocking it is important to know
whether the feed supply is adequate, and with rotational paddock grazing
some method of forecasting stock-carrying capacity is also helpful.

Much effort has been expended in recent years to express this essentially subjective assessment on a more rigorous quantifiable basis. The
problem is to assess herbage mass and quality in a rapid but precise way.
Methods include the use of a falling plate meter which enables the height
of the grass sward compressed by a square or disc of standard dimensions
to be recorded (Holmes 1974a, Castle 1976). These proved rather
cumbersome to use in practice and a simpler sward stick which recorded
the surface height of grass in the sward was developed by HFRO (1986)
and was recently simplified by ADAS (1987). With both types of equipment, considerable variation occurs within grazed swards. Coefficients of
variation of 20–50% are normal, so that large numbers of observations
(30 or more) are needed for an accurate measure. Moreover, as has been
shown by Gibb *et al.* (1985) the distribution of pasture height within the

pasture varies as grazing continues and pastures may develop with some areas of short grazed grass and other areas of ungrazed long grass.

Several measures are now available, from grass meter plate to sward stick, to extended sward height, and simple conversion factors have also been suggested (Baker 1986a). These should all be treated with care, the correlation between one measure and another is not very high. Figures in Chapter 4 refer to sward surface height.

Guidelines have now been proposed which take account of the trend for grazing to become less uniform with a greater proportion of unused grass as the season progresses. One based on work at HFRO for sheep is shown in Fig. 8.1. A similar diagram for dairy cows ranges from 6 cm in spring to 8 cm in autumn.

An alternative approach is the development of photographic standards related to herbage mass and the visual assessment of pasture grade in the field.

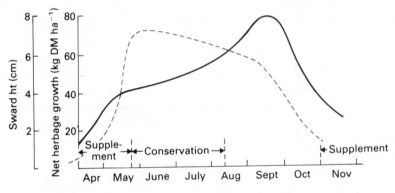

Fig. 8.1 Herbage height profile for sheep. Sward height (——); and net herbage growth (– – – –) (after HFRO 1986).

8.6 The allocation of grassland between different types of stock and between grazing and conservation

Practical matters of access, drainage and crop rotation normally influence how individual fields of grassland are used. Parasite control and uniformity of distribution of fertility should be considered also.

The control of parasites

The control of parasitic worms is improved, although seldom complete, if young stock graze on newly sown grass, grass that has been conserved throughout the previous year, or grass on which a different species has grazed in the previous year. Cawthorne (1986) describes several sequences which minimize the risk of infection: (1) cattle, (2) sheep, (3) conservation followed by grazing of lambs or calves which have been dosed with antihelminthic, is one possibility; (1) sheep, (2) cattle, (3) conservation, has also been proposed. Even a simple exchange of sheep and cattle in alternate years is beneficial. The essential principle is to ensure that young susceptible lambs or calves do not graze on land which has been recently grazed (and infected) by adults of the same species. These systems require stock-proof fencing for sheep and cattle in each field and easy access to each field for conservation, sheep handling, etc. Parasite control is also improved by resting and conservation of pasture within the season as in the integrated grazing and conservation '1, 2, 3' system. Earlier claims that rotational pasture management with a 20–30 day cycle might in itself control parasites, have not been realized, but leader–follower systems where the younger, more susceptible animals graze first on each cycle, reduce the risk of worm infestation (Leaver 1970).

Stabilization of fertility

Grazing recycles nutrients, while cutting for conservation removes N, P and K from the system. Alternating grazing and conservation from year to year or within the year reduces the risks of depletion of soil fertility by conservation cuts, or the accumulation of excessive levels of nutrients from repeated grazing. Repeated night grazing on some areas by dairy cows may accumulate fertility because of the higher proportion of the 24 hours spent there. Slurry applications on grazing may also raise the K content of the soil to dangerous levels.

Practical aspects

Topography or amenity often dictate grassland use. Steep banks are best used by sheep, parkland with trees by grazing cattle or sheep. The use of the same area for both grazing and conservation may be restricted by the shape of the farm and ease of access to the dairy, the presence of main roads through the farm, or the reliability of the fences. Here, especially for dairy cows, a two-sward system may be preferred, where the grassland accessible to the dairy herd is grazed with but few conservation cuts, and the less accessible areas provide forage for conservation and receive most of the slurry and farmyard manure. Fertilizer use should be adjusted accordingly.

The movement of stock from field to field is time wasting and grazing for the season should be planned to minimize stock movement. For dairy cows, whether rotational grazing or continuous stocking is practised, the access route to and from the dairy should be short and easily negotiated. With sheep and young cattle, appropriate size groups should be allotted to fields with the additional area for use later in the season nearby, as in the integrated '1, 2, 3' system.

8.7 Management control

The guidelines in the preceding sections should enable the formulation of reasonable targets for the season. It is vital that the management should monitor performance. Major variable expenditures are feed stuffs and fertilizers and the major influence on grass utilization is stocking rate. The concentrate requirements if any, for each month of the grazing season should be estimated for cows from predicted milk yields and calvings. The need for supplementary feeding of concentrates for grazing beef cattle at grass should be assessed. The quantities of feed consumed month by month should then be checked against these estimates. Similarly the fertilizer requirements over the season can be planned and actual consumption checked. Target areas for hay and ensilage must also be indicated. Failure to conserve silage or hay of sufficient quantity or quality can increase costs. A mid grazing season weighing enables cattle gains in the first and second half of the grazing season to be estimated. The gains in the second half of the season are a reflection of the success of the grassland management. MLC records consistently show that on average, gains in the second half of the grazing season are about 80% of those achieved in the first half.

A close degree of management control is necessary if high stocking rates are planned, and the provision of buffer grazing or of buffer feeds is of great benefit. With buffer grazing the condition of the grazed area must be assessed regularly so that an area of buffer grazing is released before production per animal is impaired. When a buffer feed, silage, or a mixed feed is available, careful assessment of the uptake of the buffer is important so that a correct balance of grazing and buffer feed is maintained. If the buffer is very palatable, grazing may be wasted.

8.8 Systems studies in grass utilization

Farmers realized long ago that grassland management, even more than other aspects of farming, is a complex activity, where factors affecting soil fertility, the growth of grass, and the nutrition of the animal, interact and culminate in the production of meat, milk or wool. With the development of a more quantitative approach to all aspects of agriculture and the availability of computers, the possibility of examining the interrelationships involved and of predicting the outcome of a range of possible procedures, has arisen. Spedding (1975) and Eadie & Maxwell (1975) have fostered these ideas in relation to grassland. The development and validation of a mathematical model of a sheep production system was described by Newton & Brockington (1975).

The systems approach establishes the important components of the system and indicates and quantifies their relationships one with the other. The components listed by Newton & Brockington are shown in Table 8.5. The interrelationships may be shown in a flow diagram or the circular diagram described by Spedding (1975, 1979). The initial procedure is valuable in itself in forcing the planner to consider all important components, and often draws attention to a lack of knowledge about some components of the system. If the relationships are not known, it may be necessary in the short-term to make best guesses at them and in the longer-term to initiate specific investigations to measure them. The information is then formulated in a mathematical model which allows the prediction of the probable outcome from various levels of input. Therefore it is important that the predictions are validated by comparison with independent data. Once the model is validated, the possible effects on production of a wide range of inputs can be examined in physical terms and, with the appropriate price information, economic predictions can be made. The possible effects of weather, of changes in animal performance, feed or fertilizer level or in price can then be predicted. The components

Table 8.5. Components of a sheep system.

1 Breed of ewe	11 Amount and form of conservation
2 Time of mating	12 Sheep movement between
3 Wool yield	paddocks
4 Herbage species	13 Weaning
5 Fertilizer application, quantity	14 Supplementation
and timing	15 Lamb disposal
6 Breed of ram	16 Ewe flushing
7 Pregnancy nutrition	17 Off-grazing
8 Stocking rate	18 Immunization policy
9 Grazing system	19 Parasite control
10 Lactation nutrition	20 Housing

of the system which have a major influence on production and those price changes which would seriously influence profitability can be identified by the systems approach. Recent examples include Doyle (1986) who modelled grassland management for dairy farming, and Holmes & Goss (1988) who considered the optimal levels of fertilizer and feed input on dairy farms to minimize cost and maximize profit per quota litre. Loewer *et al.* (1987) developed a model of selective grazing by beef cattle in response to environment, management practices and selective grazing. Parsh & Loewer (1987) applied this model to contrast continuous stocking with rotational grazing and concluded that although continuous stocking would give the highest net returns, in their conditions, risk might make rotational grazing preferable.

Modelling and the systems approach are powerful tools but they depend heavily on reliable data, and the unpredictability of weather remains a hazard.

8.9   Risk and uncertainty in grassland management

It is difficult to predict precisely the level of production from grass. The main uncontrollable factor is weather, and much of the variation in grassland yield is related to the summer rainfall and water-holding capacity of the soil. Because of the variability of climate and the high cost of replacing a shortage of grass, farmers often stock their land below the level needed to utilize fully its production. An integrated grazing and conservation system at modest stocking rates with the possibility of buffer feeding reduces the risks from drought while still ensuring efficient utilization of the grass. Weather imposes many other limitations; drought may impair the establishment of a pasture, a late spring may delay the grass growth, successful haymaking depends on good weather and good silage also requires reasonably good weather.

To avoid under-stocking the farmer should develop 'buffers' to combat yield variation, by reserving some paddocks to be grazed or cut depending on the season, building up stocks of conserved feed, investing in irrigation equipment, providing purchased feed to augment the pasture, or growing specific forage crops in anticipation of shortages. Where sufficient information is available, the systems method may help. For example on the basis of data accumulated over 9 years, Newton & Brockington (1975) compared the risk of low return likely from different stocking rates and Parsh & Loewer (1987) have also used the method to assess risk.

Further reading

Dent J.B. & Blackie M.J. (1979) *Systems Simulation in Agriculture*. Applied Science Publishers Ltd, London.
Spedding C.R.W. (1979) *An Introduction to Agricultural Systems*. Applied Science Publishers Ltd, London.

Appendix A Livestock unit values by type of stock (after MAFF 1980).

Type of stock	Specifications	Unit values
Dairy cows	Holstein, Friesian	1.0
	Ayrshire, Shorthorn	0.9
	Guernsey	0.8
	Jersey	0.75
Grazing cattle	Under 204 kg (0−11 months)	0.25
	204−340 kg (11−20 months)	0.5
	340−477 kg (21−30 months)	0.75
	Over 477 kg (over 30 months)	1.00
Suckler cows	Dry cow	1.0
	Spring calving cow with calf	1.2
	Autumn calving cow with calf	1.4
Weaned calves	Weaned calf, spring born	0.2
	Weaned, calf, autumn born	0.4
Breeding ewes (dry)	18−36 kg	0.08
	36−55 kg	0.1
	55−68 kg	0.13
	68−77 kg	0.15
	77−91 kg	0.17
	Over 91 kg	0.2
Weaned lambs	Light lambs (27−36 kg)	0.08
	Heavy lambs (36−54 kg)	0.1
Breeding ewes (lactating)	Add 0.01 per ewe to the dry ewe standard for each 25% lambing %	
1 tonne of silage = 20 LUGD		
1 tonne of hay = 70 LUGD		

Appendix B Livestock unit values (after MLC 1986).

Type of livestock	Liveweight (kg)	Age in months or as stated	Calculated recommended allowance of dietary ME (MJ)	LSU
Dairy cow (except Channel Island)	600	Mature animal for a complete year	48 000	1.0
Standard yield of 4500 litres ($36\,\text{g kg}^{-1}$ BF, $86\,\text{g kg}^{-1}$ SNF). Adjust for liveweight and milk yield 50 kg weight change ±.03 LSU 500 litres yield change ±.05 LSU				
Channel Island breeds	450	Mature animal for a complete year	41 689	0.87
Standard yield of 3600 litres ($48\,\text{g kg}^{-1}$ BF $90\,\text{g kg}^{-1}$ SNF). Adjust for liveweight and milk yield 50 kg weight change ±.03 LSU 500 litres yield change ±.06 LSU				
Beef cows (with calf)	550	Mature animal for a complete year	35 656	0.75
Standard yield of 2300 litres Adjust for liveweight and milk yield 50 kg weight change ±.03 LSU 100 litres yield change ±.01 LSU (assuming dairy and beef cows breeding regularly)				
Bulls (any breed)	750	Mature animal for a complete year	31 500	0.65
Dairy/beef replacements Birth to calving (approx. 2 years)	Birth–270 270–500	0–12 12–24	14 553 25 986	0.30 0.54

Appendix

The common temperate grasses and legumes

Grasses

Latin name	Common name	Agricultural importance
Agropyron repens	Couch grass	weed
Agrostis canina	Brown bent	major
Agrostis stolonifera	Creeping bent	minor
Agrostis tenuis	Fine bent	major
Alopecurus geniculatus	Floating foxtail	minor
Alopecurus pratensis	Meadow foxtail	minor
Alopecurus myosuroides	Black grass	weed
Anthoxanthum odoratum	Sweet vernal	minor
Arrhenatherum elatius	Tall or false oat grass	minor
Avena fatua	Spring or common wild oat	weed
Avena ludoviciana	Winter wild oat	weed
Brachypodium pinnatum	Tor grass	weed
Bromis inermis	Upright brome	weed
Bromis mollis	Soft brome	weed
Bromis sterilis	Sterile brome	weed
Bromus wildenowii	Prairie grass	minor
Cynosurus cristatus	Crested dogstail	minor
Dactylis glomerata	Cocksfoot	minor
Deschampsia caespitosa	Tussock grass	weed
Deschampsia flexuosa	Wavy hair grass	minor
Festuca arundinacea	Tall fescue	minor
Festuca ovina	Sheep's fescue	minor
Festuca pratensis	Meadow fescue	minor
Festuca rubra	Red fescue	major
Holcus lanatus	Yorkshire fog	major
Holcus mollis	Creeping soft grass	weed
Hordeum murinum	Wall barley	weed
Lolium italicum = L. multiflorum	Italian ryegrass	major
L. italicum var Westerwoldicum	Westernwold's grass	minor
Lolium perenne	Perennial ryegrass	major
Molina caerulea	Purple moor grass	minor
Nardus stricta	Mat grass	minor
Phleum bertolonii	Smaller cat's tail	minor
Phleum pratense	Timothy or Cats tail	major
Poa annua	Annual meadow grass	weed
Poa pratensis	Smooth meadow grass	minor
Poa trivialis	Rough meadow grass	major
Sieglingia decumbens	Heath grass	minor
Trisetum flavescens	Golden oat grass	minor

Leguminous plants

Latin name	Common name	Agricultural importance
Lotus corniculatus	Birdsfoot trefoil	minor
Medicago lupulina	Trefoil	minor
Medicago sativa	Lucerne	minor
Onobrichis viciifolia	Sainfoin	minor
Trifolium hybridum	Alsike clover	minor
Trifolium pratense	Red clover	minor
Trifolium repens	White clover	major

Further reading

Fitter R., Fitter A. & Farrer A. (1987) *Collins guide to the Grasses, Sedges, Rushes and Ferns of Britain and Northern Europe*. Collins, London.

Hubbard C.E. (1984) *Grasses. A Guide to their Structure, Identification, Uses and Distribution in the British Isles*, 3rd edn. (revised by Hubbard J.C.E.). Penguin, Harmondsworth.

References

Abbe E.C., Randolph L.F. & Einset J. (1941) The developmental relationship between shoot apex and growth pattern of leaf blade in diploid maize. *American Journal of Botany* **28**, 778–84.

ADAS (Agricultural Development and Advisory Service) (1987) *Grassland Management Calendar, Dairy Cows, Continuous Grazing.* HMSO, London.

Aitken F.C. & Hankin R.G. (1970) *Vitamins in Feeds for Livestock.* Technical Communication No. 25. Commonwealth Bureau of Animal Nutrition, Commonwealth Agricultural Bureaux, Farnham.

Alberda T. & Sibma L. (1968) Dry matter production and light interception of crop surfaces. III. Actual herbage production in different years as compared with potential values. *Journal of the British Grassland Society* **23**, 206–15.

Aldrich D.T.A. (1970) Clover rot (*Sclerotinia trifoliorum*) in white clover and its influence on varietal performance at different centres. *British Grassland Society Occasional Symposium, No. 6*, 143–6. BGS, Hurley.

Aldrich D.T.A. & Dent J.W. (1963) The interrelationships between heading date, yield, chemical composition and digestibility in varieties of perennial ryegrass, timothy, cocksfoot and meadow fescue. *Journal of the National Institute of Agricultural Botany* **9**, 261–81.

Allen H.P. (1979) Renewing pastures by direct drilling. In Charles A.H. & Haggar R.J. (eds) *Changes in Sward Composition and Productivity*, 217–22. British Grassland Society Occasional Symposium, No. 10. BGS, Hurley.

Amies S.J. (1978) The importance of block calving in relation to seasonality of production. *LCP Information Unit Report No. 15, MMB.* Milk Marketing Board, Thames Ditton.

Anderson P. & Yalden D.W. (1981) Increased sheep numbers and the loss of heather moorland in the Peak District, England. *Biological Conservation* **20**, 195–213.

Anslow R.C. (1962) A quantitative analysis of germination and early seedling growth in perennial ryegrass. *Journal of the British Grassland Society* **17**, 260–3.

Anslow R.C. (1967) Frequency of cutting and sward production. *Journal of Agricultural Science* **68**, 377–84.

Arber A. (1934) *The Gramineae. A Study of Cereal, Bamboo and Grass.* Cambridge University Press, London.

ARC (Agricultural Research Council) (1965) *The Nutrient Requirements of Farm Livestock. No. 2. Ruminants.* HMSO, London.

ARC (Agricultural Research Council) (1980) *The Nutrient Requirements of Ruminant Livestock.* Commonwealth Agricultural Bureaux, Farnham.

ARC (Agricultural Research Council) (1984) *Report on the Protein Group of the Agricultural Research Council Working Party on the Nutrient Requirements of Ruminants.* Supplementary report to Chapter 4, ARC 1980. Commonwealth Agricultural Bureaux, Farnham.

Archer J. (1985) *Crop Nutrition and Fertilizer Use.* Farming Press Ltd, Ipswich.

Archibald K.A.E., Campling R.C. & Holmes. W. (1975) Milk production and herbage intake of dairy cows kept on a leader and follower grazing system. *Animal Production* **21**, 147–56.

Armstrong D.G. (1965) Carbohydrate metabolism in ruminants and energy supply. In Dougherty R.W., Allen R.S., Burroughs W., Jacobson N.L. & McGilliard A.D. (eds) *Physiology of Digestion in the Ruminant*, 272–88. Butterworth, London.

Arnold G.W. (1970) Regulation of food intake in grazing ruminants. In Phillipson A.T. (ed) *Physiology of Digestion in the Ruminant*, 264–76. Oriel Press, Newcastle upon Tyne.

Arnold G.W. & Dudzinski M.L. (1978) *Ethology of Free-ranging Domestic Animals*. Elsevier North Holland Inc., Amsterdam.

Arriaga-Jordan C.A. & Holmes W. (1986) The effect of concentrate supplementation on high yielding cows under two systems of grazing. *Journal of Agricultural Science* **107**, 453–61.

Baker H.K., Baker R.D., Deakins R.M., Gould J.L., Hodges J. & Powell R.A. (1964) Grassland recording. V. Recommendations for recording the utilized output on dairy farms. *Journal of the British Grassland Society* **19**, 160–8.

Baker R.D. (1982) Estimating herbage intake from animal performance. In Leaver J.D. (ed) *Herbage Intake Handbook*, 77–93. British Grassland Society, Hurley.

Baker R.D. (1986a) Advances in dairy cow grazing systems. In Frame J. (ed) *Grazing*, 155–66. British Grassland Society Occasional Symposium, No. 19. BGS, Hurley.

Baker R.D. (1986b) Efficient use of nitrogen fertilizers. In Cooper J. P. & Raymond W.F. (eds) *Grassland Manuring*, 15–28. British Grassland Society, Hurley.

Bakker J.P. (1978). Some experiments on heathland conservation and regeneration. *Phytocenosis* **7**, 351–70.

Bakker J.P., De Bie S., Dallinga J.H., Tjaden P. & de Vries Y. (1983) Sheep grazing as a management tool for heathland conservation and regeneration in the Netherlands. *Journal of Applied Ecology* **20**, 541–60.

Balch C.C. & Campling R.C. (1969) Voluntary intake of food. In Lenkeit W., Brierem K. & Craseman E. (eds) *Handbuch der Tierernahrung* Vol. 1. Verlag Paul Parey, Hamburg and Berlin.

Balch C.C. & Line C. (1957) Gut fill changes in cows. *Journal of Dairy Research* **24**, 11–19.

Barnard C.S. & Nix J.S. (1979) *Farm Planning and Control*. 2nd edn. Cambridge University Press, Cambridge.

Barry T.N., Manley T.R., Davis S.R., & Redekopp C. (1982) Protein metabolism and response to abomasal infusion of casein + methionine in growing lambs fed fresh primary growth ryegrass/clover pasture, *ad libitum*. In Thomson D.J., Beever D.E. & Gunn R.G. (eds) *Forage Protein in Animal Production*. B.S.A.P. Occasional Publication, No. 6. 146–8.

Bartholomew P.W. & Chestnutt D.M.B. (1977) The effect of fertilizer nitrogen and defoliation intervals on dry matter production, seasonal response and chemical composition of perennial ryegrass. *Journal of Agricultural Science* **88**, 711–21.

Barthram G.T. & Grant S.A. (1984) Defoliation of ryegrass dominated swards by sheep. *Grass & Forage Science* **39**, 211–19.

Bauchop T. (1979) Rumen anaerobic fungi of cattle and sheep. *Applied and Environmental Microbiology* **38**, 148–58.

Beever D.E. (1980) The utilization of protein in conserved forage. In Thomas C. (ed) *Forage Conservation in the 80s*, 131–43. British Grassland Society Occasional Symposium, No. 11. BGS, Hurley.

Beever D.E., Coehlo da Silva J.F., Prescott J.H.D. & Armstrong D.G. (1972) The effect in sheep of physical form and stage of growth on the sites of digestion of a dried grass. 1. Sites of digestion of organic matter, energy and carbohydrate. *British Journal of Nutrition* **28**, 347–56.

Beever D.E., Losada H.R., Cammell S.B., Evans R.T. & Haines M.J. (1986) Effect of forage species and season on nutrient digestion and supply in grazing cattle. *British Journal of Nutrition* **56**, 209–25.

Beever D.E., Dhanoa M.S., Losada H.R., Evans R.T., Cammell S.B. & France J. (1987). The effect of forage species and stage of harvest on the processes of digestion occurring in the rumen of cattle. *British Journal of Nutrition* **56**, 439–54.

Best R.H. (1981) *Land Use and Living Space*. Methuen, London.

Bircham J.S. & Hodgson J. (1983) The influence of sward condition on rates of herbage growth and senescence in mixed swards under continuous stocking management. *Grass and Forage Science* **38**, 323–31.

Bird S.H., Hill M.K. & Leng R.A. (1979) The effects of defaunation of the rumen on the growth of lambs on low-protein-high-energy diets. *British Journal of Nutrition* **42**, 81–7.

Black J.L., Dawes S.T., Colebrook W.F. & James K.J. (1979) Protein deficiency in young lambs grazing irrigated summer pasture. *Proceedings of the Nutrition Society of Australia* **4**, 126.

Black J.L., Gill M., Beever D.E., Thornley J.H.M. & Oldham J.D. (1987) Simulation of the metabolism of absorbed energy-yielding nutrients in young sheep: efficiency of utilization of acetate. *Journal of Nutrition* **117**, 105–15.'

Blaxter K.L. & Clapperton J.L. (1965) Prediction of the amount of methane produced by ruminants. *British Journal of Nutrition* **19**, 511–22.

Blaxter K.L. & Graham N. McC. (1956) The effect of the grinding and cubing process on the utilization of the energy of dried grass. *Journal of Agricultural Science* **47**, 207–17.

Blaxter K.L., Wainman F.W. & Wilson R.S. (1961) The regulation of food intake by sheep. *Animal Production* **3** 51–61.

Bradshaw A.D., Chadwick M.J., Jowett D., Lodge R.W. & Snaydon R.W. (1960) Experimental investigations into the mineral nutrition of several grass species. III Phosphate level. *Journal of Ecology* **48**, 621–37.

Bradshaw A.D., Chadwick M.J., Jowett D. & Snaydon R.W. (1964) Experimental investigations into the mineral nutrition of several grass species. IV Nitrogen level. *Journal of Ecology* **52**, 665–76.

Brooke D. (1979) Silage: quantity or quality? *Farm Management* **3**, 520–9.

Broster W.H., Sutton J.D. & Bines J.A. (1979) Concentrate: forage ratios for high yielding dairy cows. In Haresign W. (ed) *Recent Developments in Animal Nutrition – 1978*, 99–126. Butterworths, London.

Brougham R.W. (1956) Effects of intensity of defoliation on regrowth of pasture. *Australian Journal of Agricultural Research* **7**, 377.

Brougham R.W. (1970) Frequency and intensity of grazing and their effects on pasture production. *Proceedings of the New Zealand Grassland Association* **32**, 137–44.

Brown R.H. & Blaser R.E. (1968) Leaf area index in pasture growth. *Herbage Abstracts* **38**, 1–9.

Brown W.V. (1960) The morphology of the grass embryo. *Phytomorphology* **10**, 215–23.

Bush M.B. & Flenley J.R. (1987) The age of British chalk grassland. *Nature* **329**, 434–6.

Caird L. & Holmes W. (1986) The prediction of voluntary intake of grazing dairy cows. *Journal of Agricultural Science* **107**, 43–54.

Cammell S.B. (1977) *Equipment and Techniques used for Research into the Intake and Digestion of Forages by Sheep*. Technical Report, No. 24. Grassland Research Institute, Hurley.

Campling R.C. & Murdoch J.C. (1966) The effect of concentrates on the voluntary intake of roughages by cows. *Journal of Dairy Research* **33**, 1–11.

Carlson G.E. (1966) Growth of clover leaves — developmental morphology and parameters at ten stages. *Crop Science* **6**, 293–4.

Carr A.J.H. (1962) *Plant Pathology.* Report of the Welsh Plant Breeding Station, 1961, 102.

Carter W.R.B. (1960) A review of nutrient losses and efficiency of conserving herbage on silage, barn-dried hay and field-cured hay. *Journal of the British Grassland Society* **15**, 220–30.

Cashmore W.H. & Denham H.J. (1938) The drying of hay in the swath and windrow. *Journal of the Ministry of Agriculture* **45**, 211–20.

Castle M.E. (1976) A simple disc instrument for estimating herbage yield. *Journal of the British Grassland Society* **31**, 37–40.

Castle M.E. (1982) Making high quality silage. In Rook J.A.F. & Thomas P.C. (eds) *Silage for Milk Production*, 127–50. Technical Bulletin, No. 2, Hannah Research Institute.

Castle M.E., Gill M.S. & Watson J.N. (1981) Silage and milk production: a comparison between barley and dried sugar-beet pulp as silage supplements. *Grass & Forage Science* **36**, 319–24.

Castle M.E. & Watkins P. (1979) *Modern Milk Production.* Faber & Faber, London.

Castle M.E. & Watson J.N. (1975) A comparison between barley and dried grass as supplements to silage of high digestibility. *Journal of the British Grassland Society* **30**, 217–22.

Catherall P.L. (1987) Effects of barley yellow dwarf and ryegrass mosaic viruses alone and in combination on the productivity of perennial and Italian ryegrasses. *Plant Pathology* **36**, 73–8.

Cawthorne R.J.G. (1986) Management for the control of parasites. In Frame J. (ed) *Grazing*, 89–97. British Grassland Society Occasional Symposium, No. 19. BGS, Hurley.

Chapman S.B. (1967) Nutrient budgets for a dry heath ecosystem in the south of England. *Journal of Ecology* **55**, 677–89.

Clement C.R. & Hopper M.J. (1968) The supply of potassium for high yielding cut grass. *National Agricultural Advisory Service, Quarterly Review* **79**, 101–9.

Clements R.O. & Bentley B.R. (1985) *Incidence, Impact and Control of Insect Pests in Newly-sown Grassland in the UK.* British Grassland Society Occasional Symposium, No. 18. BGS, Hurley.

Clements R.O. & Henderson I.F. (1983) Improvement of yield and persistence of Italian ryegrass through pest control. In Allan Smith J. & Hays V.W. (eds) *Proceedings of the 14th International Grassland Congress, Lexington 1981*, 581–4. Westview Press, Boulder, Colorado.

Collins D.P. (1979) *The Use of Animal Manures on Pasture.* Mimeo Publication, An Foras Taluntais.

Collins D.P., Drennan M.J. & Flynn A.V. (1977) Potential of Irish grassland for beef production. *Proceedings of the International Meeting on Animal Production from Temperate Grassland, Dublin*, 12–19.

Comerford P. (1980) The effects of chop length and laceration of grass silage on weight gain of beef cattle. In Thomas C. & Flynn A.V. (eds) Forage Conservation in the 80s, 388–96. *Occasional Symposium No. 11.* BGS, Hurley.

Connel J. & Houseman R.J. (1976) In Wilkins R.J. (ed) *Green Crop Fractionation.* British Grassland Society Occasional Symposium, No. 9, 57–64. BGS, Hurley.

Conrad H.R., Pratt A.D. & Hibbs J.W. (1966) Regulation of feed intake in dairy cows. I. Change in importance of physical and physiological factors with increasing digestibility. *Journal of Dairy Science* **47**, 54–62.

Conway A. (1962) *An Foras Taluntais Research Report*, Animal Production Division, 15–16. An Foras Taluntais.

Conway A. (1963) Effect of grazing management on beef production. II. Comparison of three stocking rates under two systems of grazing *Irish Journal of Agricultural Research* **2**, 243–58.

Cooper J.P. (1951) Studies on growth and development in *Lolium*. II. Pattern of bud development of the shoot apex and its ecological significance. *Journal of Ecology* **39**, 228–70.

Cooper J.P. (1958) The effect of temperature and photoperiod on inflorescence development in strains of timothy (*Phleum* spp.). *Journal of the British Grassland Society* **13**, 81–91.

Cooper J.P. (1964) Climatic variation in forage grasses. I. Leaf development in climatic rates of *Lolium* and *Dactylis*. *Journal of Applied Ecology* **1**, 45–61.

Cooper J.P. (1970) Potential production and energy conversion in temperate and tropical grasses. *Herbage Abstracts* **40**, 1–15.

Cornish M.W. (1954) The origin and structure of the grassland types of the central North Downs. *Journal of Ecology* **42**, 359–74.

Corrall A.J. & Fenlon J.S. (1978) A comparative method for describing the seasonal distribution of production from grasses. *Journal of Agricultural Science* **91**, 61–67.

Corrall A.J., Morrison J. & Young J.W.O. (1982) Grass production. In Thomas C. & Young J.W.O. (eds) *Milk from Grass*, 1–19. Grassland Research Institute, Hurley and ICI, Billingham.

Countryside Commission (1985) *National Countryside Recreation Survey*: Countryside Commission Publication No. 201, Cheltenham.

Coward N. (1971) Finance for dairy farm buildings. *Journal of the University of Newcastle Agriculture Society* **24**, 4–10.

Crowder L.V. & Chheda H.R. (1982) *Tropical Grassland Husbandry*. Longman, London.

Culpin C. (1962) Developments in methods of barn hay drying. *Journal of the British Grassland Society* **17**, 150–6.

Cunningham J.M.M. & Russel A.J.F. (1979) The technical development of sheep production from hill land in Great Britain. *Livestock Production Science* **6**, 379–85.

Curran M.K. & Holmes W. (1970) Prediction of the voluntary intake of food by dairy cows. *Animal Production* **12**, 213–24.

Davidson I.A. & Robson M.J. (1985) Effect of nitrogen supply on the grass and clover components of simulated mixed swards grown under favourable environmental conditions. I. Carbon assimilation and utilization. *Annals of Botany* **55**, 685–95.

Davidson I.A., Robson M.J. & Drennan D.S.H. (1986) Effect of temperature and nitrogen supply on the growth of Perennial Ryegrass and White Clover. I. Carbon and nitrogen economies of mixed swards at low temperature. *Annals of Botany* **57**, 697–708.

Davies W. (1928) The factor of competition between one species and another in seeds mixtures. *Bulletin H8 Welsh Plant Breeding Station, Aberystwyth* 82–149.

Davies W.E., ap Griffiths G. & Ellington A. (1966) The assessment of herbage legume varieties. II: *In vitro* digestibility water-soluble carbohydrate crude protein and mineral content of primary growth of clover and lucerne *Journal of Agricultural Science* **66**, 351.

Deinum B. (1966) Influence of some climatological factors on the chemical composition and feeding value of herbage. *Proceedings of the 10th International Grassland Congress*, Helsinski, 415–18.

Dekker R.F.H, Richards G.N., & Playne M.J. (1972) Digestion of polysaccharide constituents of tropical pasture herbage in the bovine rumen. I. Townsville stylo (*Stylosanthes humilus*). *Carbohydrate Research* **22**, 173–77.

Demarquilly C. (1973) Chemical composition, fermentation characteristics, digestibility and voluntary intake of forage silages: changes compared to the initial green forage *Annales de Zootechnie* **22**, 1–35.

Dennis W.D. & Woledge J. (1985) The effect of nitrogenous fertilizer on the photosynthesis and growth of white clover/perennial ryegrass swards. *Annals of Botany* **55**, 171–78.

Dibb G. & Haggar R.J. (1979) Evidence of sward changes on yield. In Charles A.H. & Haggar R.J. (eds) *Changes in Sward Composition and Productivity*, 11–20. British Grassland Society Occasional Symposium, No. 10. BGS, Hurley.

Dimbleby G.W. (1977) Climate, soil and man. In Clark J.G.C. & Hutchinson J. (eds) *The Early History of Agriculture*. Oxford University Press, Oxford.

Dixon I.A., Frame J. & Waterhouse A. (1986) The potential for mixed grazing systems. In Frame J. (ed) *Grazing*, 189–98. British Grassland Society Occasional Symposium, No. 19. BGS, Hurley.

DoE (Department of the Environment) (1986) *Nitrate in Water. A Report by the Nitrate Co-ordination Group*. Pollution Paper, No. 26. HMSO, London.

Donald C.M. (1961) Competition for light in crops and pastures. In Milthorpe F.L. (ed) *Mechanisms in Biological Competition*, 283–313. Cambridge University Press Cambridge.

Donald C.M. (1963) Competition among crop and pasture plants. *Advances in Agronomy* **15**, 1–118.

Donald C.M. & Black J.N. (1958) The significance of leaf area in pasture growth. *Herbage Abstracts* **28**, 1–6.

Doyle C.J. (1986) A model for evaluating grassland management decisions on dairy farms in the UK. *Agricultural Systems* **21** 243–66.

Duffey E., Morris M.G., Sheail J., Ward L.J., Wells D.A. & Wells T.C.E. (1974) *Grassland Ecology and Wildlife Management*. Chapman & Hall, London.

Dulphy J.P. (1978) Quantites ingerees et phenomenes de substitution — consequences pour le rationnement. In Journet M. & Hoden A. (eds) *La Vache Laitière*. Institut National de la Recherche Agronomique, Versailles.

Dutta M.J. (1988) *Bud Viability in White Clover*. MSc. Thesis. University of Wales.

Eadie J. & Maxwell T.J. (1975) Systems research in hill sheep farming. In Dalton G.E. (ed) *Study of Agricultural Systems*, 395–413. Applied Science Publishers, London.

Edmond D.B. (1970) Effects of treading on pastures using different animals and soils. *Proceedings of the 11th International Grassland Congress, Surfers Paradise, Australia*, 604–11.

EEC (European Economic Community) (1987) *Proposal for a Council Regulation Establishing a Community Scheme to Encourage the Cessation of Farming*. Com (87) 166 final Brussels.

Ekern A., Blaxter K.L. & Sawers D. (1965) The effect of artificial drying on the energy value of grass *British Journal of Nutrition* **19**, 417–34.

Ernst P., Le Du Y.L.P. & Carlier L. (1980) Animal and sward production under rotational and continuous grazing management — a critical review. In Prins W.H. & Arnold G.H. (eds) *Proceedings of the International Symposium on the role of Nitrogen in Intensive Grassland Production, Pudoc, Wageningen.* 119–26.

Escuder J.C., Andrews R.P. & Holmes W. (1971) The effect of nitrogen, stocking rate and frequency of grazing by beef cattle on the output of pasture. *Journal of the British Grassland Society* **26**, 74–84.

Evans L.T., Wardlaw, I.F. & Williams C.N. (1964) Environmental control of growth. In Barnard C. (ed) *Grasses and Grasslands*, 102–25. Macmillan,. London.

Fenlon D.R., Wilson J. & Weddell J.R. (1987) A comparison of bagged and wrapped big-bale silage-storage losses and animal performance. *Proceedings of the 8th Silage Conference, Hurley*, 115–16.

Fenton E.W. (1931) The influence of seasonal grazing and manuring on the flora of grassland. *Journal of Ecology* **19**, 75–97.

Fenton E.W. (1934) Grassland retrogression in Devonshire permanent pastures. *Journal of Ecology* **22**, 279–88.

Flynn A.V. & O'Kiely P. (1984) The use of sulphuric acid as a silage preservative. *Proceedings of the 7th Silage Conference, Belfast*, 15–16.

Forbes J.M. (1977) Models for the prediction of food intake and energy balance in dairy cows. *Animal Production* **24**, 203–14.

Forbes T.J., Dibb C., Green J.O. & Fenlon K.A. (1978) *Permanent Grassland Studies. 1.*

The Permanent Pasture Project Objectives and Methods. GRI-ADAS Joint Permanent Pasture Group, Hurley.

Forbes T.J., Dibb C., Green J.O., Hopkins A. & Peel S. (1980) *Factors Affecting the Productivity of Permanent Grassland.* Joint Permanent Pasture Group, Hurley.

France J., Thornley J.H.M. & Beever D.E. (1982) A mathematical model of the rumen. *Journal of Agricultural Science* **99**, 343–53.

Fryer J.D. & Makepeace R.J. (eds) (1978) *Weed Control Handbook, Vol. II Recommendations*, 8th edn. Blackwell Scientific Publications, Oxford.

Garwood E.A. & Sheldrick R.D. (1978) Dry matter production by tall fescue under dry conditions. *Journal of the British Grassland Society* **33**, 67–8.

Garwood E.A. & Tyson K.C. (1973) The response of S.24 perennial ryegrass swards to irrigation. I. Effects of partial irrigation on DM yield and on the utilization of applied nitrogen. *Journal of the British Grassland Society* **28**, 223–33.

Garwood E.A. & Williams T.E. (1967a) Soil water use and growth of a grass sward. *Journal of Agricultural Science* **68**, 281–92.

Garwood E.A. & Williams T.E. (1967b) Growth, water use and nutrient uptake from the subsoil by grass swards. *Journal of Agricultural Science* **69**, 125–30.

Gay P.A. & Green B.H. (1984) Grassland deterioration found stable. *Restoration and Management Notes* **2**, 26–7. Nature Conservancy.

Gibb M.J. & Treacher T.T. (1983) The performance of lactating ewes offered diets containing different proportions of fresh perennial ryegrass and white clover. *Animal Production* **37**, 433–40.

Gibb M.J. & Treacher T.T. (1984) The performance of weaned lambs offered diets containing different proportions of fresh perennial ryegrass and white clover. *Animal Production* **39**, 413–20.

Gibb M.J., Ridout M.S., Orr R.J., Penning P.D., Baker R.D. & Treacher T.T. (1985) Observations on the distribution of height measurements in swards stocked continuously with cattle or sheep. *Animal Production* **40**, 531.

Gibson C.W.D., Watt T.A. & Brown V.K. (1987) The use of sheep grazing to recreate species-rich grassland from abandoned arable land. *Biological Conservation* **42**, 165–83.

Gill M., Beever D.E., Buttery P.J., England P., Gibb M.J. & Baker R.D. (1987) The effect of oestradiol-17β implantation on the response in voluntary intake, live-weight gain and body composition, to fishmeal supplementation of silage offered to growing calves. *Journal of Agricultural Science* **108**, 9–16.

Gimingham C.H. (1972) *The Ecology of Heathlands.* Chapman & Hall, London.

Gimingham C.H. & De Smidt J.T. (1983) Heaths as natural and semi-natural vegetation. In Holzner W., Werger M.J.A. & Ikosuria I. (eds) *Man's Impact upon Vegetation.* Junk, The Hague.

Godwin H. (1975) *The History of the British Flora*, 2nd edn, Cambridge University Press, Cambridge.

Goode D.A. (1981) The threat to wildlife habitats. *New Scientist* **89**, 219–23.

Gordon A.J., Ryle G.J.A. & Powell C.E. (1977) The strategy of carbon utilization in uniculm barley. I. The chemical fate of photosynthetically assimilated ^{14}C. *Journal of Experimental Botany* **28**, 1258–69.

Gordon C.H., Kane E.A., Derbyshire J.C., Jacobson W.C., Melin C.G. & McCalmont J.R. (1959) Nutrient losses, quality and feeding values of wilted and direct-cut orchard grass stored in bunker and tower silos. *Journal of Dairy Science* **42**, 1703–11.

Gordon C.H., Holdren R.D. & Derbyshire J.C. (1969) Field losses in harvesting wilted forage. *Agronomy Journal* **61**, 924–7.

Gordon F.J. (1973) The effect of high nitrogen levels and stocking rates on milk output from pasture. *Journal of the British Grassland Society* **28**, 193–201.

Gordon F.J. (1974a) The use of nitrogen fertilizer on grassland for milk production. In *The Role of Nitrogen in Grassland Productivity. Proceedings No. 142*, 14–27. The Fertilizer Society, London.

Gordon F.J. (1974b) A comparison of spring and autumn produced dried grass for milk production. *Journal of the British Grassland Society* **29**, 113–16.

Gordon F.J. (1975) The effect of including dried grass in the supplement given to lactating cows at pasture. *Journal of the British Grassland Society* **30**, 79–83.

Gordon F.J. (1980) The effect of interval between harvests and wilting of herbage for silage on milk production. In Thomas C. (ed) *Forage Conservation in the 80s*. British Grassland Society Occasional Symposium, No. 11, 379–82. BGS, Hurley.

Gordon F.J. (1983) Concentrates for the autumn-calving cow. *56th Annual Report of the Agriculture Research Institute of Northern Ireland*, 12–22. Hillsborough.

Gordon F.J. (1986) The influence of system of harvesting grass for silage on milk output. *59th Annual Report of the Agriculture Research Institute of Northern Ireland*, 13–22. Hillsborough.

Gordon F.J. (1987) An evaluation of an inoculant as an additive for grass silage being offered to dairy cattle. *Proceedings of the 8th Silage Conference, Hurley*, 19–20.

Gordon F.J. & McMurray C.H. (1979) The optimum level of protein in the supplement for dairy cows with access to grass silage. *Animal Production* **29**, 283–91.

Gordon F.J. & Murdoch J.C. (1978) An evaluation of a high-quality grass silage for milk production. *Journal of the British Grassland Society* **33**, 5–11.

Graham N. McC. (1964) Energy costs of feeding activities and energy expenditure of grazing sheep. *Australian Journal of Agricultural Research* **15**, 969–73.

Grant, S.A., Barthram G.T., Lamb W.I.C. & Milne J.A. (1978) Effect of season and level of grazing on the utilization of heather by sheep. I. Responses of the sward. *Journal of the British Grassland Society* **33**, 289–300.

Grant S.A., Barthram G.T., Torvill L., King J. & Smith H.K. (1983) Sward management, lamina turnover and tiller population density in continuously stocked *Lolium perenne*-dominated swards. *Grass and Forage Science* **38**, 333–44.

Green B.H. (1972) The relevance of seral eutrophication and plant competition to the management of successional communities. *Biological Conservation* **4**, 378–84.

Green B.H. (1973) Practical aspects of chalk grassland management in the Nature Conservancy's south-east region. In Jermy A.C. & Stott P.A. (eds) *Chalk Grassland*. Kent Trust for Nature Conservation, Maidstone.

Green B.H. (1980) Management of extensive amenity grasslands by mowing. In Hunt R. & Rorison I.H. (eds) *Amenity Grassland: an Ecological Perspective*. John Wiley, Chichester.

Green B.H. & Marshall I.C. (1987) An assessment of the role of golf courses in Kent, England, in protecting wildlife and landscapes. *Landscape and Urban Planning* **14**, 143–154.

Green J.O. (1974) *Preliminary Report on a Sample Survey of Grassland in England and Wales 1970/72*. Internal Report, No. 310, Grassland Research Institute, Hurley.

Green J.O., Corrall A.J. & Terry R.A. (1971) *Grass Species and Varieties: Relationships between Stage of Growth, Yield and Forage Quality*. Technical Report, No. 8, Grassland Research Institute, Hurley.

Green J.O. & Williams T.E. (1975) *National Grassland and Forage Resources*. Paper read at Winter Meeting, British Grassland Society, December 1974.

ap Griffiths G. (1963) Effect of flowering on water soluble carbohydrate content. *Report of the Welsh Plant Breeding Station, Aberystwyth 1962*, 87.

Grime J.P. (1974) Vegetation classification by reference to strategies. *Nature* **250**, 26–31.

Grime J.P. (1979) *Plant Strategies and Vegetation Processes*. Wiley. Chichester.

Grime J.P. & Hodgson J.G. (1969) An investigation into the ecological significance of lime chlorosis by means of large-scale comparative experiments. In Rorison I.H. (ed) *Ecological Aspects of the Mineral Nutrition of Plants*, 67–99. Blackwell Scientific Publications, Oxford.

Grubb P.J. (1977) The Importance of species-richness in plant communities: the importance of the regeneration niche. *Biological Review* **52**, 107–45.

Haggar R.J. (1980) Weed control and vegetation management by herbicides. In Rorison I.H. & Hunt R. (eds) *Amenity Grassland: an Ecological Perspective*, 163–73. Wiley, Chichester.

Haggar R.J. & Squires N.R.W. (1979) The scientific manipulation of sward constituents in grassland by herbicides and one pass seeding. In Charles A.H. & Haggar R.J. (eds) *Changes in Sward Composition and Productivity*. British Grassland Society Occasional Symposium, No. 10, 223–34. BGS, Hurley.

Harper J.L. (1971) Grazing, fertilizers and pesticides in the management of grasslands. In Duffey E. & Watts A.S. (eds) *The Scientific Management of Animal and Plant Communities for Conservation*, 15–31. Blackwell Scientific Publications, Oxford.

Harrington F.J. & Binnie R.C. (1971) The effect of height and frequency of cutting on grass production. *44th Annual Report of the Agricultural Research Institute of Northern Ireland*, 17–24.

Harris W. (1978) Defoliation as a determinant of the growth, persistence and composition of pasture. In Wilson J.R. (ed) *Plant Relations in Pastures*, 67–85. CSIRO, Australia.

Harrison C.M. (1974) The ecology and conservation of British lowland heaths. In Warren A. & Goldsmith F.B. (eds) *Conservation in Practice*, 117–29. Wiley, London.

Harrod T.R. (1979) Soil suitability for grassland. In Jarvis M.G. & Mackney D. (eds) *Soil Survey Applications No. 13*. Harpenden.

't Hart M.L. (1956) In Neale G.J. (ed) Some problems of intensive grassland farming in The Netherlands. *Proceedings of the 7th Interational Grassland Congress, Palmerston North, New Zealand*, 70–9.

Hartley R.D. & Dhanoa M.S. (1981) Rates of degradation of plant cell walls measured with a commercial cellulase preparation. *Journal of the Science of Food and Agriculture* 32, 849–56.

Heil G.W. & Diemont W.H. (1983) Raised nutrient levels change heath into grassland. *Vegetatio* 53, 113–20.

Helsper H.P.G., Glenn-Lewin D. & Werger M.J.A. (1983) Early regeneration of Calluna heathland under various fertilizer treatments. *Oecologia* 58, 208–14.

Henderson A.R., Anderson D.H. & Neilson D.R. (1987) The effect of a commercial inoculant on the chemical characteristics and utilization of ryegrass silages over two years. *Proceedings of the 8th Silage Conference,' Hurley*, 13–14.

Henderson A.R. & McDonald P. (1975) The effect of delayed sealing on fermentation and losses during ensilage. *Journal of the Science of Food and Agriculture* 26, 653–67.

Henderson I.F. & Clements R.O. (1977) Grass growth in different parts of England in relation to invertebrate numbers and pesticide treatment. *Journal of the British Grassland Society* 32, 89–98.

Henderson I.F. & Clements R.O. (1979) Differential susceptibility to pest damage in agricultural grasses. *Journal of Agricultural Science* 73, 465–72.

HFRO (Hill Farming Research Organization) (1979) Soils and vegetation of the hills and their limitations. In *Science and Hill Farming, HFRO, 1954–1979*, 9–21. HFRO, Edinburgh.

HFRO (Hill Farming Research Organization) (1986) The HFRO sward stick. HFRO *Biennial Report 1984–85*, 29. HFRO, Edinburgh.

Hilder E.J. (1966) Distribution of excreta by sheep at pasture. *Proceedings of the 10th International Grassland Congress, Helsinki*, 977–81.

Hodgson J. (1985) The significance of sward characteristics in the management of temperate sown pastures. *Proceedings of the 15th International Grassland Congress, Kyoto, 1985*, 31–4.

Hodgson J. (1986) Grazing behaviour and herbage intake. In Frame J. (ed) *Grazing*, 51–64. British Grassland Society Occasional Symposium, No. 19. BGS, Hurley.

Hodgson J., Grant S.A., & Armstrong R.H. (1985a) Grazing ecology and the management of hill vegetation. *HFRO Biennial Report 1984–5*, 101–8. HFRO, Edinburgh.

Hodgson J., Mackie C.K. & Parker J.W.G. (1985b) Sward surface heights for efficient grazing. *Grass Farmer* **24**, 5–10.

Hodgson J., Rodriguez Capriles J.M. & Fenlon J.S. (1977) The influence of sward characteristics on the herbage intake of grazing calves. *Journal of Agricultural Science* **89**, 743–50.

Hogan J.P. & Weston R.F. (1970) Quantitative aspects of microbial protein synthesis in the rumen. In Phillipson A.T. (ed) *Physiology of Digestion and Metabolism in the Ruminant*, 474–85 Oriel Press, Newcastle upon Tyne.

Holmes C.W. (1974a) The Massey grass meter. In *Dairy Farming Annual*, 26–30. Ruakura, New Zealand.

Holmes S.J.I. (1980) Field studies on the effects of ryegrass mosaic virus on the yield of Italian ryegrass cv. S22. *Annals of Applied Biology* **96**, 209–17.

Holmes S.J.I. (1983) The susceptibility of agricultural grasses to pre-emergence damage caused by *Fusarium culmorum* and its control by fungicidal seed treatment. *Grass and Forage Science* **38**, 209–14.

Holmes W. (1968) The use of nitrogen in the management of pasture for cattle. *Herbage Abstracts* **38**, 265–77.

Holmes W. (1974b) The role of nitrogen fertilizer in the production of beef from grass. In *The Role of Nitrogen in Grassland Productivity*, 57–69. Proceedings, No. 142. The Fertilizer Society, London.

Holmes W. (1977) Choosing between animals. *Philosophical Transactions of the Royal Society, London* **B281**, 121–37.

Holmes W. (1980) Secondary production from land. In Blaxter K.L. (ed) *Food Chains and Human Nutrition*, 129. Applied Science Publishers Ltd, London.

Holmes W. & Allanson G. (1967) Grassland systems. *Journal of the British Grassland Society.* **22**, 77–84.

Holmes W., Campling R.C. & Joshi N.D. (1972) A comparison between a rigid rotational grazing system for dairy cows and a system in which grazing alternated with cutting. *Animal Production* **14**, 283–94.

Holmes W. & Curran M.K. (1967) Feed intake of grazing cattle. V.A further study of the influence of pasture restriction combined with supplementary feeding on production per animal and per acre. *Animal Production* **9**, 313–24.

Holmes W. & Goss S. (1988) Low cost systems of milk production. In Garnsworthy J. (ed) *Nutrition and Lactation in the Dairy Cow*, 395–410. Butterworths, Guildford.

Holt D.A. & Hilst A.R. (1969) Daily variation in carbohydrate content of selected forage crops. *Agronomy Journal* **61**, 239–42.

Honig H. (1980) Mechanical and respiration losses during pre-wilting of grass. In Thomas C. (ed) *Forage Conservation in the 80s*. British Grassland Society Occasional Symposium, No. 11, 201–4. BGS, Hurley.

Honig H. & Woolford M.K. (1980) Changes in silage on exposure to air. In Thomas C. (ed) *Forage Conservation in the 80s*. British Grassland Society Occasional Symposium. No. 11, 16–87. BGS, Hurley.

Hopkins A. (1979) Botanical composition of grasslands in England and Wales. *Journal of the Royal Agricultural Society of England* **140**, 140–50.

Hopkins A. & Green J.O. (1979) The effect of soil fertility and drainage on sward changes. In Charles A.H. & Haggar R.J. (eds) *Changes in Sward Composition and Productivity*, 115–29. British Grassland Society Occasional Symposium, No. 10, BGS Hurley.

Horton G.M.J. & Holmes W. (1974) The effect of nitrogen, stocking rate and grazing method on the output of pasture grazed by beef cattle. *Journal of the British Grassland Society* **29**, 93–9.

Hovell F.D. De B., Greenhalgh J.F.D. & Wainman F.W. (1976) The utilization of diets containing acetate salts by growing lambs as measured by comparative slaughter and respiration calorimetry together with rumen fermentation. *British Journal of Nutrition* **35**, 343–63.

284 REFERENCES

Hungate R.E. (1966) *The Rumen and its Microbes*. Academic Press, New York.

Hunt L.A. & Brougham R.W. (1967) Some changes in the structure of a perennial ryegrass sward frequently but leniently defoliated during the summer. *New Zealand Journal of Agricultural Research* **10**, 397–404.

Illius A.W., Lowman B.G. & Hunter E.A. (1986) The use of buffer grazing to maintain sward quality and increase late season cattle performance. In Frame J. (ed) *Grazing*, 119–28. British Grassland Society Occasional Symposium, No. 19. BGS, Hurley.

INRA (Institut National de Reserche Agronomique) (1980) *Alimentation des Ruminants*, 2nd edn. INRA Publication, (Route de St Cyr) 7800 Versailles.

Jarrige R., Demarquilly C., Dulphy J.P., Hoden A., Journet M., Beranger C., Geay Y., Malterre C., Micol D., Petit M. & Robelin J. (1979) The system of bulk units for cattle. *Bull. Techn. CRZV Theix, INRA* **38**, 57–9.

Jarvis S.C., Sheerwood M. & Steenvoorden J.H.A.M. (1987) Nitrogen losses from animal manures: from grazed pastures and from applied slurry. In Van Der Meer H.G. *et al.* (eds) *Animal Manure on Grassland and Fodder Crops*, 195–212. Martin Nijhoff, Dordrecht.

John A. & Ulyatt M.J. (1987) Importance of dry matter content to voluntary intake of fresh grass forages. *Proceedings of the New Zealand Society of Animal Production*. Hamilton, New Zealand.

Johnson I.R. & Parsons A.J. (1985a) A theoretical analysis of grass growth under grazing. *Journal of Theoretical Biology* **112**, 345–67.

Johnson I.R. & Parsons A.J. (1985b) Use of a model to analyse the effects of continuous grazing managements on seasonal patterns of grass production. *Grass and Forage Science* **40**, 449–58.

Johnson I.R. & Thornley J.H.M. (1983) Vegetative crop growth model incorporating leaf area expansion and senescence, applied to grass. *Plant, Cell and Environment* **6**, 721–99.

Jones A.S. (1976) The principles of greencrop fractionation. *British Grassland Society/British Society of Animal Production Occasional Symposium, No. 9*, 1–7.

Jones D.I.H & Hayward, M.V. (1975) The effect of pepsin pretreatment of herbage on the prediction of dry matter digestibility from solubility in fungal cellulase solution. *Journal of the Science of Food and Agriculture* **26**, 711–18.

Jones F.G.W. & Jones M.G. (1964) *Pests of Field Crops*. Edward Arnold Ltd, London.

Jones L. (1971) The development and morphology of seedling grasses Part 2. *Annual Report Grassland Research Institute, Hurley, 1970*, 151–7.

Jones M.B., Collettt B. & Brown S. (1982) Sward growth under cutting and continuous stocking managements: sward structure, tiller density and leaf turnover. *Grass and Forage Science* **37**, 67–73.

Jones Martin G. (1933a) Grassland management and its influence on the sward. I. Factors influencing the growth of pasture plants. *Empire Journal of Experimental Agriculture* **1**, 43–57.

Jones Martin G. (1933b) Grassland management and its influence on the sward. II. The management of a clover sward and its effects. *Empire Journal of Experimental Agriculture* **1**, 122–8.

Jones Martin G. (1933c) Grassland management and its influence on the sward. III. The management of a grassy sward and its effects. *Empire Journal of Experimental Agriculture* **1**, 223–34.

Jones Martin G. (1933d) Grassland management and its influence on the sward. IV. The management of poor pastures. V. Edaphic and biotic influences on pastures. *Empire Journal of Experimental Agriculture* **1**, 361–7.

Jones R.J. & Sandland R.L. (1974) The relation between animal gain and stocking rate. Derivation of the relation from the results of grazing trials. *Journal of Agricultural Science* **83**, 335–42.

Journet M. & Demarquilly C. (1979) Grazing. In Broster W.H. & Swan H. (eds) *Feeding Strategy for the High Yielding Cow*, 295–321. Granada Publishing Co, St. Albans.

Kays S. & Harper J.L. (1974) The regulation of plant and tiller density in a grass sward. *Journal of Applied Ecology* **62**, 97–105.

Kennedy S.J. (1987) The effect of an enzyme additive on the preservation and nutritive value of grass silage fed to beef cattle, 25–6. *Proceedings of the 8th Silage Conference, Hurley.*

Kerridge E. (1967) *The Agricultural Revolution.* Allen & Unwin, London.

Kibon A. & Holmes W. (1987) The effect of height of pasture and concentrate composition on dairy cows grazed on continuously stocked pastures. *Journal of Agricultural Science* **109**, 293–301.

King J. (1971) Competition between established and newly sown grass species. *Journal of the British Grassland Society* **26**, 221.

King J., Grant S.A. & Roger J.A. (1967) Hill pastures. *Hill Farming Research Organization 4th Report 1964–1967*, 22–32. HFRO, Edinburgh.

Klinner W.E. & Hale O.D. (1980) Engineering developments in the field treatment of green crops. In Thomas C. (ed) *Forage Conservation in the 80s.* British Grassland Society Occasional Symposium. No. 11, 224–8. BGS, Hurley.

Klinner W.E. & Shepperson G. (1975) The state of haymaking technology *Journal of the British Grassland Society* **30**, 259–66.

Korte C.J., Watkins B.R. & Harris W. (1982) Use of residual leaf area index and light interception as criteria for spring-grazing management of a ryegrass-dominant pasture. *New Zealand Journal of Agricultural Research* **25**, 309–19.

Kruijne A.A. (1964) The number of species in grassland. *Jaarboek IBS Wageningen* 167–75.

Kydd D.D. (1964) The effect of different systems of cattle grazing on the botanical composition of permanent downland pasture. *Journal of Ecology* **52**, 139–49.

Lam A. (1985) Effect of fungal pathogens on digestibility and chemical composition of Italian ryegrass (*Lolium multiforum*) and tall fescue (*Festuca arundinacea*). *Plant Pathology* **34**, 190–9.

Lancaster R.J. (1968) Quality and storage losses of silages made in bunkers, stacks and by vacuum compression. *New Zealand Journal of Agricultural Research* **11**, 63–70.

Lancaster R.J. & McNaughton M. (1961) Effects of initial consolidation on silage. *New Zealand Journal of Agricultural Research* **4**, 504–15.

Langer R.H.M. (1956) Growth and nutrition of timothy (*Phleum pratense*). I. The life history of individual tillers. *Annals of Applied Biology* **44**, 166–87.

Langer R.H.M. & Ryle G.J.A. (1958) Vegetative proliferation in herbage grasses. *Journal of the British Grassland Society* **13**, 29–33.

Langlands J.P., Corbett J.L., McDonald I. & Reid G.W. (1963) Estimates of the energy required for maintenance by adult sheep. *Animal Production* **5**, 11–16.

Langston C.W. Irvin H., Gordon C.H., Bouma J., Wiseman H.G., Melin C.G., Moore L.A. & McCalmont J.R. (1958) Microbiology and chemistry of grass silage. *US Department of Agriculture, Technical Bulletin*, No. 1187.

Lantinga E.A. (1986) Seasonal pattern of grass assimilation and net herbage production under continuous stocking. In Frame J. (ed) *Grazing*, 32–8. British Grassland Society Occasional Symposium, No. 19. British Grassland Society, Hurley.

Laredo M.A. & Minson D.J. (1973) The voluntary intake, digestibility and retention time by sheep of leaf and stem fractions of five grasses. *Australian Journal of Agricultural Research* **24**, 875–88.

Large R.V. & King N. (1978) *The Integrated Use of Land for Agricultural and Amenity Purposes: Lamb Production from Soay Sheep Used to Control Scrub and Improve the Grass Cover of Chalk Downland.* Grassland Research Institute, Hurley.

Lazenby A. (1981) British grasslands, past, present and future. *Grass and Forage Science* **36**, 243–66.

Leafe E.L., Stiles W. & Dickinson S. (1974) Physiological processes influencing the pattern of productivity of the intensively managed grass sward. *Proceedings of the 12th International Grassland Congress, Moscow, 1,* 442–57.

Leaver J.D. (1970) A comparison of grazing systems for dairy herd replacements. *Journal of Agricultural Science* **75,** 265–72.

Leaver J.D. (1976) Utilisation of grassland by dairy cows. In Swan H. & Broster W.H. (eds), *Principles of Cattle Production,* 307–27. Butterworths, London.

Leaver J.D. (ed) (1982) *Herbage Intake Handbook.* British Grassland Society, Hurley.

Leaver J.D. (1985) Milk production from grazed temperate grassland. *Journal of Dairy Research* **52,** 313–44.

Leaver J.D., Campling R.C. & Holmes W. (1968) Use of supplementary feeds for grazing dairy cattle. *Dairy Science Abstracts* **30,** 355–61.

Le Du Y.L.P. & Penning P.D. (1982) Animal based techniques for estimating herbage intake. In Leaver J.D. *Herbage Intake Handbook,* 37–75. British Grassland Society, Hurley.

Le Du Y.L.P. & Newberry R.D. (1982) Supplementing the grazing dairy cow during periods of pasture restriction. *Grass and Forage Science* **37,** 173–74.

Lee J.A. & Greenwood B. (1976) The colonization by plants of calcareous wastes from the salt and alkali industry in Cheshire, England. *Biological Conservation* **10,** 131–49.

Lefeuvre J.C. (1980) Possibilité d'élevage de moutons de race rustique dans les landes des Monts d'Arrée. I Considerations générales. *Bulletin d'Ecologie* **11,** 765–73.

Lester E. & Large E.C. (1958) Surveys of clover rot with incidental observations on eelworm in clover: England and Wales, 1953–55. *Plant Pathology* **7,** 115–24.

Lewis G.C. (1985) Effect of soil-borne pathogens on ryegrass and white clover seedlings and their control. *British Grassland Society Occasional Symposium, No. 18/British Crop Protection Council, Monograph No. 29,* 82–9.

Lewis G.C. & Clements R.O. (1986) A survey of ryegrass endophyte (*Acremonium loliae*) in the UK and its apparent ineffectuality on a seedling pest. *Journal of Agricultural Science* **107,** 633–8.

Lewis G.C. & Clements R.O. (1987) Pests and diseases of grass and fodder crops. In Scopes N.E.A. & Ledieu M. (eds) *Pest and Disease Control Handbook.* British Crop Protection Council, Croydon.

Lewis M. (1981) Equations for predicting silage intake by beef and dairy cattle. *Proceedings of the 6th Silage Conference, Edinburgh,* 35–6.

Lloyd P.S. (1968) The ecological significance of fire in limestone grassland communities of the Derbyshire Dales. *Journal of Ecology* **56,** 811–26.

Loewer O.J., Taul K.L., Turner L.W., Gay N. & Muntiferung R. (1987) Graze, a model of selective grazing by beef animals. *Agricultural Systems* **25,** 297–309.

Lonsdale C.R. (1976) *The effect of season of harvest on the utilization by young cattle of dried grass given alone or as a supplement to grass silage.* Ph.D. Thesis, University of Reading.

Lowday J.E. & Wells T.C.E. (1977) *The Management of Grasslands and Heathlands in Country Parks.* Countryside Commission, Cheltenham.

Lowe S.E., Theodorou M.K., Trinci A.P.J. & Hespell R.B. (1985) Growth of anaerobic rumen fungi on defined and semi-defined media lacking rumen fluid. *Journal of General Microbiology* **131,** 2225–29.

Macrae J.C. & Lobley G.E. (1982) Some factors which influence thermal energy losses during the metabolism by ruminants. *Livestock Production Science* **9,** 447–56.

Maeda S. & Tonetani T. (1978) Optimum cutting stage of forage plants. II. Seasonal changes in CGR and average productivity in Italian ryegrass population. *Journal of the Japanese Society of Grassland Science* **24,** 10–16.

MAFF (Ministry of Agriculture, Fisheries and Food) (1954a) *The Calculation of Irrigation Needs.* Technical Bulletin No. 4. HMSO, London.

MAFF (Ministry of Agriculture, Fisheries and Food) (1954b) *Irrigation*. Bulletin No. 138. HMSO, London.

MAFF (Ministry of Agriculture, Fisheries and Food) (1963). *Quick Haymaking*. Bulletin No. 188. HMSO, London.

MAFF (Ministry of Agriculture, Fisheries and Food) (1968) *Grass and Clover Crops for Seed*. Bulletin 204. HMSO, London.

MAFF (Ministry of Agriculture, Fisheries and Food (1969) *Fixed Equipment on the farm. No. 6. Permanent Farm Fences*. HMSO, London.

MAFF (Ministry of Agriculture, Fisheries and Foods) (1970) *Fixed Equipment on the farm No. 11. Farm and Estate Hedges*. HMSO, London.

MAFF (Ministry of Agriculture, Fisheries and Food) (1976) *Electric Fencing*. Technical Bulletin No. 147. HMSO, London.

MAFF (Ministry of Agriculture, Fisheries and Food) (1977a) *Sampling of Farm Crops, Feedingstuffs, Milk and Water for Analysis*. Agricultural Development and Advisory Service, Advisory paper No. 20. HMSO, LONDON

MAFF (Ministry of Agriculture, Fisheries and Food (1977b) *Silage*. Bulletin No. 37. HMSO, London.

MAFF (Ministry of Agriculture, Fisheries and Food) (1978) *Minimum Requirements for the Structural Design of Bunker Silos for Forage*. Farm Buildings Group, Agriculture Development and Advisory Service, Leeds.

MAFF (Ministry of Agriculture, Fisheries and Food) (1979a). *The Drying of Grass Seed*. GFS 22. Grassland Practice No. 6. HMSO, London.

MAFF (Ministry of Agriculture, Fisheries and Food) (1979b). *Harvesting Grass Seed*. Booklet 2048, Grassland Practice No. 8. HMSO, London.

MAFF (Ministry of Agriculture, Fisheries and Food) (1979) *Nutrient Allowances and Composition of Feedingstuffs for Ruminants*. LGR 21. HMSO, London.

MAFF (Ministry of Agriculture, Fisheries and Food) (1980)) *Livestock Units Handbook*. Booklet 2267. Pinner, Middlesex.

MAFF (Ministry of Agriculture, Fisheries and Food) (1984) *Energy Allowances and Feeding Systems for Ruminants*. Reference Book No. 433. HMSO, London.

MAFF (Ministry of Agriculture, Fisheries and Food) (1986) *Grass Seed Mixtures*, Booklet 2041. Agriculture Development and Advisory Service, Leeds.

MAFF (Ministry of Agriculture, Fisheries and Food) (1986) *Output and Utilization of Farm Produce in the UK*. HMSO, London.

MAFF (Ministry of Agriculture, Fisheries and Food) (1987) *Feed Evaluation Unit*, Technical Bulletin.

Maltby E. (1980) The impact of severe fire on *Calluna* moorland in the North York moors. *Bulletin d'Ecologie* **11**, 683−708.

Manby T.C.D. & Shepperson G. (1975) Increasing the efficiency of grass conservation. *Agricultural Engineer* **30**, 77−85.

't Mannetje L. (1978) Measurement of grassland vegetation and animal production. *Commonwealth Bureau of Pastures and Field Crops, Bulletin No. 52*. Commonwealth Agricultural Bureaux, Farnham.

Marsh R. (1975) Systems of grazing management for beef cattle. In Hodgson J. & Jackson D.K. (eds) *Pasture Utilization by the Grazing Animal*, 119−128. Occasional Symposium No. 8, British Grassland Society, Hurley.

Marsh R. (1976) Effect of rotary-drum-drier exit temperature and length of pre-drying storage time on digestibility of dried grass cobs. *Journal of the British Grassland Society* **31**, 53−8.

Marsh R. (1978) The effects of mechanical treatment of forages on fermentation in the silo and on the feeding value of the silages. *New Zealand Journal of Experimental Agriculture* **6**, 271−8.

Marsh R. (1979) The effects of wilting on fermentation in the silo and on the nutritive value of silage. *Journal of the British Grassland Society* **34**, 1−9.

Marsh R. & Campling R.C. (1970) Fouling of pastures by dung. *Herbage Abstracts* **40**, 123−30.

Marsh R., Campling R.C. & Holmes W. (1971) A further study of a rigid grazing management system for dairy cows. *Animal Production* **13**, 441−8.

Marsh R. & Murdoch J.C. (1975) Effect of some green-crop-drying processes on the digestibility and voluntary intake of herbage by sheep. *Journal of the British Grassland Society* **30**, 9−15.

Marrs R.H. (1985) Techniques for reducing soil fertility for nature conservation purposes: a review in relation to research at Roper's Heath, Suffolk, England. *Biological Conservation* **34**, 307−32.

Mayne C.S. & Gordon F.J. (1984) The effect of type of concentrate and level of concentrate feeding on milk production. *Animal Production* **39**, 65−76.

Mayne C.S., Woodcock S.C.F., Clements A.J. & Newberry R.D. (1986) The effects on milk production of grazing management systems involving preferential treatment of high yielding cows, In Frame J. (ed) *Grazing*, 114–18. Occasional Symposium, No. 19. British Grassland Society, Hurley.

McAllan A.B., Siddons R.C. & Beever D.E. (1988) The efficiency of conversion of degraded nitrogen to microbial nitrogen in the rumen of sheep and cattle. In Jarrige R. & Alderman G. (eds) *Feed Evaluation and Protein Requirement Systems for Ruminants.* Commission of the European Community Luxembourg.

McCarrick R.B. (1966) Effect of method of grass conservation and herbage maturity on performance and body composition of beef cattle. *Proceedings of the 10th International Grassland Congress, Helsinki*, 575−80.

McCree K.J. (1970) An equation for the rate of respiration of white clover plants grown under controlled conditions. In Malek I. (ed) *Prediction and Measurement of Photosynthetic Productivity*, 221−9. Pudoc, Wageningen.

McDonald P., Henderson A.R. & McGregor A.W. (1968) Chemical changes and losses during the ensilage of wilted grass. *Journal of the Science of Food and Agriculture* **19**, 125−32.

McDonald P. & Whittenbury R. (1967) Losses during ensilage. *British Grassland Society Occasional Symposium, No. 3*. 76−84. BGS, Hurley.

McDougall I. & Jackson N. (1977) Chemical composition and nutritional value of hay made in Northern Ireland during the period 1966−75. *Record of Agricultural Research in Northern Ireland.* **25**, 63−9.

McFeely P.C., Browne D. & Carty O. (1975) Effect of grazing interval and stocking rate on milk production and pasture yield. *Irish Journal of Agricultural Research* **14**, 309−19.

McIlmoyle W.A. & Murdoch J.C. (1977a) The effect of dried grass and cereal-based concentrate on the voluntary intake of unwilted grass silage. *Animal Production* **24**, 227−35.

McIlmoyle W.A. & Murdoch J.C. (1977b) The effect of concentrate, barley and dried grass on the voluntary intake of different silages. *Animal Production* **24**, 393−400.

McLaren D.P. (1987) *Chalk grassland: a review of management experience.* M.Sc. Dissertation, Wye College, London.

McMeekan C.P. & Walshe M.J. (1963) The inter-relationships of grazing method and stocking rate on the efficiency of pasture utilization by dairy cattle. *Journal of Agricultural Science* **61**, 147−66.

McNaughton S.J. (1968) Structure and function in California grasslands. *Ecology* **49**, 962−72.

Mead H. & Carter A.W. (1973) The management of long grass as a bird repellent on airfields *Journal of the British Grassland Society* **28**, 219−21.

Meijs J.A.C. & Hoekstra J.A. (1984) Concentrate supplementation of grazing dairy cows. I. Effect of concentrate intake and herbage allowance on herbage intake. *Grass and Forage Science* **39**, 59−66.

Meijs J.A.C., Walters R.J.K. & Keen A. (1982) Sward methods. In Leaver J.D. (ed) *Herbage Intake Handbook*, 11–36. British Grassland Society, Hurley.

Michel J.F. (1976) The epidemiology and control of some nematode infections in grazing animals. *Advances in Parasitology* **14**, 355–97.

Michel J.F. & Ollerenshaw C.B. (1963) Helminth diseases of grazing animals. In Worden A.N., Sellers K.C. & Tribe D.E. (eds) *Animal Health, Production and Pasture*, 445–57. Longman, London.

Miller I.L. (1973) Evaluation of feeds as sources of nitrogen and amino acids. *Proceedings of the Nutrition Society* **32**, 79.

Miller L.G., Clanton D.C., Nelson L.F. & Hoehue O.E. (1967) Nutritive value of hay baled at various contents. *Journal of Animal Science* **26**, 1369–73.

Milne J.A. (1974) The effects of season and age of stand on the nutritive value of heather (*Calluna vulgaris L* Hull) to sheep. *Journal of Agricultural Science* **83**, 281–8.

Milne J.A., Christie A. & Russel A.J.F. (1979) The effects of nitrogen and energy supplementation on the voluntary intake and digestion of heather by sheep. *Journal of Agricultural Science* **92**, 635–43.

Milne J.A., Maxwell T.J. & Souter W. (1979) Effect of level of concentrate feeding and amount of herbage on the intake and performance of ewes with twin lambs at pasture in early lactation. *Proceedings of the British Society for Animal Production* **28** 452, Abstract 91.

Milne J.A. & Mayes R.W. (1986) Supplementary feeding and herbage intake. In *HFRO, Biennial Report 1984–85*, 115–19. Penicuik, Scotland.

Milton W.E.J. (1940) The effect of manuring, grazing and liming on the yield, botanical and chemical composition of natural hill pastures. *Journal of Ecology* **28**, 326–56.

Minson D.J. (1963) The effect of pelleting and wafering on the feeding value of roughage. *Journal of the British Grassland Society* **18**, 39–44.

Mitchell K.J. (1935a) Influence of light and temperature on the growth of ryegrass (*Lolium* spp). I. Pattern of vegetative development. *Physiologia Plantarum* **6**, 21–46.

Mitchell K.J. (1953b) Influence of light and temperature on the growth of ryegrass (*Lolium* spp). II. The control of lateral bud development. *Physiologia Plantarum* **6**, 425–43.

MLC (Meat and Livestock Commission) (1978) *Grazing Management*. Beef Production Handbook, No. 4. MLC, Milton Keynes.

MLC (Meat and Livestock Commission) (1986) *Beef Yearbook*. MLC, Milton Keynes.

MLC (Meat and Livestock Commission) (1987) *Beef Yearbook*. MLC, Milton Keynes.

MMB (Milk Marketing Board) (1976) *Report of the Breeding and Production Organization. No. 26 1975–76*, 35. MMB, Thames Ditton.

MMB (Milk Marketing Board) (1985) *An Analysis of Farm Management Services Costed Farms*. MMB, Thames Ditton.

MMB (Milk Marketing Board) (1986) *Milk Costs, 1985–86* (working tables). MMB, Thames Ditton.

MMB (Milk Marketing Board) (1987) *Milk Minder Annual Report 1986–87*. MMB, Thames Ditton.

Moir R.J. (1968) Ruminant Digestion and Evolution. In Code C.F. (ed) *Handbook of Physiology*, Vol. 5, 2673–94. Waverley Press, Baltimore.

Moisey F.R. & Leaver J.D. (1979) A comparison of a three-cut with a two-cut silage system for dairy cattle. *Animal Production* **28**, 422 (Abstract).

Monteith J.L. (1977) Climate and the efficiency of crop production in Britain. *Philosophical Transactions of the Royal Society, London* B **281**, 277–94.

Moore L.A., Thomas J.W. & Sykes J.F. (1960) The acceptability of grass/legume silage by dairy cattle. *Proceedings of the 8th International Grassland Congress, Reading*, 701–4.

Morgan D.E. (1973) *Agricultural Development and Advisory Service Annual Report 1972*. ADAS, Leeds.

Morley F.H.W. (1966) Stability and productivity of pastures. *Proceedings of the New Zealand Society of Animal Production* **26**, 8–21.

Morley F.H.W. (1978) Animal production studies of grassland. In Mannetje L.t' (ed) *The Measurement of Grassland, Vegetation and Animal Production*. Bulletin 52, Commonwealth Agricultural Bureaux, Farnham.

Morris M.G. (1973) The effects of seasonal grazing on the *Heteroptera* and *Auchenorhyncha (Hemiptera)* of chalk grassland. *Journal of Applied Ecology* 10, 761–80.

Morris M.G. (1975) Preliminary observations on the effects of burning on the *Hemiptera (Heteroptera* and *Auchenorhyncha)* of limestone grassland. *Biological Conservation* 7, 311–19.

Morrison J., Jackson M.V. & Sparrow P.E. (1980) The response of perennial ryegrass to fertilizer nitrogen in relation to climate and soil. *Technical Report No. 27.* Grassland Research Institute, Hurley.

Mott G.O. (1960) Grazing pressure and the measurement of pasture production. *Proceedings of the 8th International Grassland Congress, Reading,* 606–11.

Mudd C.H. & Meadowcroft S.C. (1964) Comparison between the improvement of pastures by the use of fertilizers and by reseeding. *Experimental Husbandry* 10, 66–84.

Murdoch J.C. (1965) The effect of length of silage on its voluntary intake by cattle. *Journal of the British Grassland Society* 20, 54–8.

Murdoch J.C., Balch D.A., Holdsworth M.C. & Wood M. (1955) The effect of chopping, lacerating and wilting of herbage on the chemical composition of silage. *Journal of the British Grassland Society* 10, 181–8.

Murdoch J.C. & Bare D.I. (1960) The effect of mechanical treatment on the rate of drying and loss of nutrients in hay. *Journal of the British Grassland Society* 15, 94–9.

Murdoch J.C. & Bare D.I. (1963) The effect of conditioning on the rate of drying and loss of nutrients in hay. *Journal of the British Grassland Society* 18, 334–8.

Nash M.J. (1959) Partial wilting of grass crop for silage. *Journal of the British Grassland Society* 14, 65–73.

Nash M.J. & Easson D.L. (1972) Farmer's lung—an agricultural assessment of recent findings. *Scottish Agriculture* 51, 1–7.

Nash M.J. & Easson D.J. (1977) Preservation of moist hay with propionic acid. *Journal of Stored Products Research* 13, 65–75.

Nash M.J. & Easson D.L. (1978) Preservation of moist hay in miniature bales treated with propionic acid. *Journal of Stored Products Research* 14, 25–33.

NCC (Nature Conservancy Council) (1984) *Nature Conservation in Great Britain.* NCC, Peterborough.

NCC (Nature Conservancy Council) (1986) The management of chalk grassland for butterflies. *Focus on Nature Conservation, No. 17.* NCC, Peterborough.

Neal H.D. St C., Thomas C. & Cobby J.M. (1984) Comparison of equations for predicting voluntary intakes by dairy cows. *Journal of Agricultural Science,* 103, 1–10.

NEDO (National Economic Development Office) (1974) *Grass and Grass Products.* NEDO, London.

Neenan M., Conway M. & Murphy W.E. (1959) The output of Irish pastures. *Journal of the British Grassland Society* 14, 78–87.

Newton J.E. & Brockington N.R. (1975) A logical approach to the study of grazing systems. In Hodgson J. & Jackson D.K. (eds) *Pasture Utilization by the Grazing Animal,* 29–38. British Grassland Society Occasional Symposium, No. 8. BGS, Hurley.

Newton J.E., Wilde R. & Betts J.E. (1985) Lamb production from perennial ryegrass and perennial ryegrass-white clover swards using set-stocking or rotational grazing. *Research and Development in Agriculture* 2, 1–6.

NIAB (National Institute of Agricultural Botany) (1979) *Recommended Varieties of Herbage Legumes 1979/80.* Farmers leaflet, No. 4. NIAB, Cambridge.

NIAB (National Institute of Agricultural Botany) (1986) *Classified List of Herbage Varieties, England and Wales, 1986/87.* NIAB, Cambridge.

NIAB (National Institute of Agricultural Botany) (1987a) *Recommended Varieties of Grasses and Herbage Legumes 1987/88.* Farmers Leaflet, No. 4. NIAB, Cambridge.

NIAB (National Institute of Agricultural Botany) (1987b) *Grasses and Legumes for Conservation 1987/88.* Technical leaflet No. 2. NIAB, Cambridge.

Nolan T. & Connolly J. (1977) Mixed stocking by sheep and steers — a review. *Herbage Abstracts* **47**, 367–74.

Norman M.J.T. (1957) The influence of various grazing treatments upon the botanical composition of a downland permanent pasture. *Journal of the British Grassland Society* **12**, 246–56.

Nowakowski T.Z. (1962) Effects of nitrogen fertilisers on total nitrogen, soluble nitrogen and soluble carbohydrate contents of grass. *Journal of Agricultural Science* **59**, 387–92.

Noy-Meir I. (1975) Stability in grazing systems: an application of predator-prey graphs. *Journal of Ecology* **63**, 459–81.

Offer N.W. & Al Ravidah M.N. (1987) Some consequences of ensiling grass with absorbent materials. *Proceedings of the 8th Silage Conference, Hurley*, 139–40.

O'Rourke C.J. (1967) Effect of foliar pathogens on grass yield. *Research Report, Plant Science and Crop Husbandry. An Foras Taluntais 1966*, 81.

O'Rourke C.J. (1976) *Diseases of Grasses and Forage Legumes in Ireland.* An Foras Taluntais, Dublin.

Orr R., Parsons A.J., Treacher T.T. & Penning P.D. (1988) Seasonal patterns of grass production under cutting or continuous stocking managements. *Grass and Forage Science*, **43**, 199–207.

Ørskov E.R., Grubb D.A., Smith J.S., Webster A.J.F. & Corrigall W. (1979) Efficiency of utilization of volatile fatty acids for maintenance and energy retention by sheep. *British Journal of Nutrition*, **41**, 541–55.

Ørskov E.R., Hovell F.D., De B & Mould F. (1980) The use of the nylon bag technique for the evaluation of feedstuffs. *Tropical Animal Production* **5**, 195–213.

Ørskov E.R. & McDonald I. (1979) The estimation of protein degradability in the rumen from incubation measurements weighted according to rate of passage. *Journal of Agricultural Science* **92**, 499–504.

Osbourn D.F. (1980) The Feeding value of grass and grass products. In Holmes W. (ed) *Grass: Its Production and Utilization*, Chap 3. Blackwell Scientific Publications, Oxford.

Outen G.E., Beever D.E., Osbourn D.F. & Thomson D.J. (1974) The digestion and absorption of lipids by sheep fed chopped and ground dried grass. *Journal of the Science of Food and Agriculture* **25**, 981–87.

Outen G.E., Beever D.E., Osbourn D.F. & Thomson D.J. (1975) The digestion of the lipids of processed red clover herbage by sheep. *Journal of the Science of Food and Agriculture* **26**, 1381–9.

Owen J.B. & Ridgman W.J. (1968) The design and interpretation of experiments to study animal production from grazed pasture. *Journal of Agricultural Science* **71**, 327–35.

Owen M. (1973) The management of grassland areas for wintering geese. *Wildfowl* **24**, 123–30.

Parr T.W. & Way J.M. (1987) The management of roadside vegetation: the long term effects of cutting. *Journal of Applied Ecology* in press

Parsh L.D. & Loewer O.J. (1987) Economics of simulated beef forage rotational grazing under weather uncertainty. *Agricultural Systems* **25**, 279–95.

Parsons A.J. (1984) Guidelines for management of continuously grazed swards. *Grass Farmer*, No. 17, 5–9. British Grassland Society, Hurley.

Parsons A.J. (1987) The management of grass/clover swards for sheep. *Grass Farmer*, No. 26, 26–31. British Grassland Society, Hurley.

Parsons A.J., Collett B. & Lewis J. (1984) Changes in the structure and physiology of a perennial ryegrass sward when released from a continuous stocking management:

Implications for the use of exclusion cages in continuously stocked swards. *Grass and Forage Science* **39**, 1–9.

Parsons A.J. & Johnson I.R. (1986) The physiology of grass growth under grazing. In Frame J. (ed) *Grazing*, 3–13. British Grassland Society Occasional Symposium, No. 19. BGS, Hurley.

Parsons A.J., Johnson I.R. & Harvey A. (1988) The use of a model to optimize the interaction between the frequency and severity of intermittent defoliation and to provide a fundamental comparison of the continuous and intermittent defoliation of grass. *Grass and Forage Science* **43**, 49–59.

Parsons A.J., Leafe E.L., Collett B. & Stiles W. (1983a) The physiology of grass production under grazing. I. Characteristics of leaf and canopy photosynthesis of continuously grazed swards. *Journal of Applied Ecology* **20**, 117–26.

Parsons A.J., Leafe E.L., Collett B., Penning P.D. & Lewis J. (1983b) The physiology of grass production under grazing. II. Photosynthesis, crop growth and animal intake of continuously grazed swards. *Journal of Applied Ecology* **20**, 127–39.

Parsons A.J., Penning P., Orr R. & Jarvis S. (1987) Are grass-clover swards the answer to nitrogen pollution? In Hardcastle J.E.Y. (ed) *Science Agriculture and the Environment*, 10–11. Agriculture and Food Research Council, London.

Parsons A.J. & Penning P.D. (1988) The effect of the duration of regrowth on photosynthesis, leaf death and the average rate of growth in a rotationally grazed sward. *Grass and Forage Science* **43**, 15–27.

Parsons A.J. & Robson M.J. (1980) Seasonal changes in the physiology of S24 perennial ryegrass (*Lolium perenne* L.). I. Response of leaf extension to temperature during the transition from vegetative to reproductive growth. *Annals of Botany* **46**, 435–44.

Parsons A.J. & Robson M.J. (1981a) Seasonal changes in the physiology of S24 perennial ryegrass (*Lolium perenne*. L.). II. Potential leaf and canopy photosynthesis during the transition from vegetative to reproductive growth. *Annals of Botany* **47**, 249–58.

Parsons A.J. & Robson M.J. (1981b) Seasonal changes in the physiology of S24 perennial ryegrass (*Lolium perenne* L.). III. Partition of assimilates between root and shoot during the transition from vegetative to reproductive growth. *Annals of Botany* **48**, 733–44.

Parsons A.J. & Robson M.J. (1982) Seasonal changes in the physiology of S24 perennial ryegrass (*Lolium perenne* L.). IV. Comparison of the carbon balance of the reproductive crop in spring and the vegetative crop in autumn. *Annals of Botany* **50**, 167–77.

Paterson R. & Crichton C. (1960) Grass staggers in large scale dairying on grass. *Journal of the British Grassland Society* **15**, 100–5.

Patterson D.C. & Steen R.W.J. (1982) Studies on the composition of effluent from grass silage and its feeding value for pigs and beef cattle. *55th Annual Report of the Agricultural Research Institute of Northern Ireland*, 23–32. Hillsborough.

Patto P.M., Clement C.R. & Forbes T.J. (1978) *Permanent Pasture Studies. II. Grassland Poaching in England and Wales.* GRI/ADAS Joint Permanent Pasture Group, Hurley.

Peacock J.M. (1975a) Temperature and leaf growth in Lolium perenne. I. The thermal microclimate, its measurement and relation to crop growth. *Journal of Applied Ecology* **12**, 99–114.

Peacock J.M. (1975b) Temperature and leaf growth in *Lolium perenne*. II. The site of temperature perception. *Journal of Applied Ecology* **12**, 115–23.

Peacock J.M. (1975c) Temperature and leaf growth in *Lolium perenne*. III. Factors affecting seasonal differences. *Journal of Applied Ecology* **12**, 685–97.

Peacock J.M. (1976) Temperature and leaf growth in four grass species. *Journal of Applied Ecology* **13**, 225–32.

Peel S. & Forbes T.J. (1978) *Permanent Grassland Studies III. A Study of Permanent Grassland Farms with Beef Suckler Herds.* Permanent Pasture Group, Hurley.

Penning P.D. (1986) Some effects of sward conditions on grazing behaviour and intake by sheep. In Gudmundsson O. (ed) *Grazing Research in Northern Latitudes, NATO Iceland*, 219–26. Plenum Publishing Co., London.

Penning P.D. & Hooper G.E. (1987) Further developments in the use of short-term weight changes in grazing sheep for estimating intake. In *Proceedings of the 6th European Grazing Workshop, Rome*.

Penning P.D., Hooper G.E. & Treacher T.T. (1986) The effect of herbage allowances on intake and performance of ewes suckling twin lambs. *Grass and Forage Science* **41**, 199–208.

Penning de Vries F.W.T. (1972) Respiration and Growth. In Rees A.R., Cockshull K.E., Hand D.W. & Hurd R.G. (eds) *Crop Processes in Controlled Environments*, 327–47. Academic Press, London & New York.

Petersen R.G., Lucas H.L. & Woodhouse W.W. (1956) The distribution of excreta by freely grazing cattle and its effect on pasture fertility. II. Effect of returned excreta on the residual concentration of some fertilizer elements. *Agronomy Journal* **48**, 444–9.

Philipsen P.J.J. (1971) Heat treatment of the standing crop. *Power Farming* **47**, 22–4.

Pike I.H. (1972) Nutritional evaluation of silage made from grass treated with a formalin/sulphuric acid mixture. *Journal of the British Grassland Society* **27**, 195 (abstract).

Playne M.J. & McDonald P. (1966) The buffering constituents of herbage and of silage. *Journal of the Science of Food and Agriculture*, **17**, 264–8.

Pollock C.J. & Jones T. (1979) Seasonal patterns of fructosan metabolism in forage grasses. *New Phytologist* **83**, 9–15.

Pound B. & Martinez-Cairo L. (1983) *Leucaena: Its Cultivation and Uses*. Overseas Development Administration, London.

Prins W.H., De Boer D.J. & Van Burg P.F.J. (1986) Requirements for phosphorus, potassium and other nutrients for grassland in relation to nitrogen usage. In Cooper J.P. & Raymond W.F. (eds) *Grassland Manuring*, 28–45. British Grassland Society, Hurley.

Prioul J.L. (1971) Reaction des feuilles de *Lolium multiflorum* a l'eclairement pendant la croissance et variation des resistance aux exchange gazeux photosynthetiques. *Photosynthetica* **5**, 364–75.

Putwain P.D., Gillham D.A. & Holliday R.J. (1982) Restoration of heather moorland and lowland heathland, with special reference to pipelines. *Environmental Conservation* **9**, 225–35.

Ratcliffe D.A. (ed) (1977) *A Nature Conservation Review*, 2 Vols. Cambridge University Press, Cambridge.

Rattray P.V. (1978) Pasture constraints to sheep production. *Proceedings of the Agronomy Society of New Zealand* **8**, 103–8.

Reid D. (1966) Studies on cutting managements of grass clover swards. IV. The effect of close and lax cutting on the yield of herbage from swards cut at different frequencies. *Journal of Agricultural Science*, **66**, 101–6.

Robson M.J. (1968) The changing tiller population of spaced plants of S170 tall fescue (*Festuca arundinacea*). *Journal of Applied Ecology* **5**, 575–90.

Robson M.J. (1972) The effect of temperature on the growth of S170 tall fescue (*Festuca arundinacea*). I. Constant temperature. *Journal of Applied Ecology* **9**, 647–57.

Robson M.J. (1973a) The growth and development of simulated swards of perennial ryegrass. I. Leaf growth and dry weight change as related to the ceiling yield of a seedling sward. *Annals of Botany* **37**, 487–500.

Robson M.J. (1973b) The growth and development of simulated swards of perennial ryegrass. II. Carbon assimilation and respiration in a seedling sward. *Annals of Botany* **37**, 501–18.

Robson M.J. (1973c) The effect of temperature on the growth of S170 tall fescue (*Festuca arundinacea*). II. Independent variation of day and night temperature. *Journal of Applied Ecology* **10**, 93–105.

Robson M.J. (1974) The effect of temperature on the growth of S170 tall fescue (*Festuca arundinacea*). III. Leaf growth and tiller production as affected by transfer between contrasting regimes: *Journal of Applied Ecology* **11**, 265–79.

Robson M.J. (1981) Potential production — what is it and can we increase it? In Wright C.E. (ed) *Plant Physiology and Herbage Production*, 5–18. British Grassland Society, Hurley.

Robson M.J. (1982a) The growth and carbon economy of selection lines of *Lolium perenne* cv.S23 with 'fast' and 'slow' rates of dark respiration. I. Grown as simulated swards during a regrowth period. *Annals of Botany* **49**, 321–9.

Robson M.J. (1982b) The growth and carbon economy of selection lines of *Lolium perenne* cv. S23 with 'fast' and 'slow' rates of dark respiration. II. Grown as young plants from seed. *Annals of Botany* **49**, 331–9.

Robson M.J., Ryle G.J.A. & Woledge J. (1988) The grass plant — its form and function. In Jones M.B. & Lazenby A. (eds) *The Grass Crop*, 25–83. Chapman & Hall, London.

Rorison I.H. (1969) Ecological inferences from laboratory experiments on mineral nutrition. In Rorison I.H. (ed) *Ecological Aspects of the Mineral Nutrition of Plants*. Blackwell Scientific Publications, Oxford.

Roy M.G. & Peacock J.M. (1972) Seasonal forecasting of the spring growth and flowering of grass crops in the British Isles. In Taylor J.A. (ed) *Weather Forecasting for Agriculture and Industry*, 99–114. David & Charles, Newton Abbott.

Ryden J.C. (1984) The flow of nitrogen in grassland. *Proceedings of the Fertiliser Society*, No. 229, 3–44. London.

Ryle G.J.A. (1964) A comparison of leaf and tiller growth in seven perennial grasses as influenced by nitrogen and temperature. *Journal of the British Grassland Society* **19**, 281–90.

Ryle G.J.A. & Langer R.H.M. (1963) Studies on the physiology of flowering of timothy. I. Influence of day length and temperature on initiation and differentiation of the inflorescence. *Annals of Botany* **27**, 213–31.

The Scottish Agricultural Colleges (1986) *Classification of Grass and Clover Varieties for Scotland, 1986/87*. Publication No. 166. Scottish Agricultural Colleges, Edinburgh.

Sears P.D. (1950) Soil fertility and pasture growth. *Journal of the British Grassland Society* **5**, 267–80.

Shaw P.G., Brockman J.S. & Wolton K.M. (1966) The effect of cutting and grazing on the response of grass/white clover swards to fertilizer nitrogen. *Proceedings of the 10th International Grassland Congress, Helsinki*, 240–4.

Shepperson G. (1960) Effect of time of cutting and method of making on the feed value of hay. *Proceedings of the 8th International Grassland Congress, Reading*, 704–8.

Shepperson G. & Grundey J.K. (1962) Recent developments in quick haymaking techniques. *Journal of the British Grassland Society* **17**, 141–9.

Shildrick J.P. (1980) Species and cultivar selection. In Rorison I.H. and Hunt R. (eds) *Amenity Grassland: an Ecological Perspective*. Wiley, Chichester.

Siddons R.C., Evans R.T. & Beever D.E. (1979) The effect of formaldehyde treatment before ensiling on the digestion of wilted grass silage by sheep. *British Journal of Nutrition* **42**, 535–45.

Silvertown J.W. (1980) The dynamics of a grassland system: botanical equilibrium in the Park Grass Experiment. *Journal of Applied Ecology* **17**, 491–504.

Smetham M.L. (1975) The influence of herbage utilization on pasture production and animal performance. *Proceedings of the New Zealand Grassland Association 1975*, 95–103.

Smith C.J. (1980) *The Ecology of the English Chalk*. Academic Press, London.

Snaydon R.W. (1979) Selecting the most suitable species and cultivars. In Charles A.H. & Haggar R.J. (eds) *Changes in Sward Composition and Productivity*, 179–89. British Grassland Society Occasional Symposium, No. 10. BGS, Hurley.

Soulsby E.J.L. (1965) *Textbook of Veterinary Clinical Parasitology. Vol 1. Helminths.* Blackwell Scientific Publications, Oxford.

Spedding C.R.W. (1975) *The Biology of Agricultural Systems.* Academic Press, London.

Spedding C.R.W. (1979) *An Introduction to Agricultural Systems.* Applied Science Publishers, London.

Spedding C.R.W. & Diekmahns E.C. (eds) (1972) *Grasses and Legumes in British Agriculture* Bulletin 49, Commonwealth Bureau of Pastures & Field Crops. Commonwealth Agricultural Bureaux, Farnham.

Stapledon R.G. & Davies W. (1942) *Ley Farming.* Penguin Books, Harmondsworth.

Stapledon R.G., Davies W., Williams T.E., Hughes G.P. & Davis A.G. (1945) *Map, Vegetation: Grassland of England and Wales.* Ordnance Survey, Southampton.

Stiles W. (1965) Ten years of irrigation experiments. *Annual Report 1965,* 57–66. Grassland Research Institute, Hurley.

Stobbs T.H. (1973a) The effect of plant structure on the intake of tropical pastures. I. Variation in the bite size of grazing cattle. *Australian Journal of Agricultural Research* 24, 809–19.

Stobbs T.H. (1973b) The effect of plant structure on the intake of tropical pasture. II. Differences in sward structure, nutritive value and bite size of animals grazing *Setaria anceps* and *Chloris gayana* at various stages of growth and nutrition. *Australian Journal of Agricultural Research* 24, 821–9.

Sutherland T.M. (1988) Particle separation in the forestomachs of sheep. In Dobson A. & Dobson M.J. (eds) *Aspects of Physiology of Digestion in Ruminants.* 43–73. Cornell University.

Sutton J.D., Bines J.A., Morant S.V., Napper D.J. & Givenes D.I. (1987) A comparison of starchy and fibrous concentrates for milk production, energy utilization and hay intake by Friesian cows. *Journal of Agricultural Science,* 109, 375–86.

Tainton N.M. (1974) Effect of different grazing rotations on pasture production. *Journal of the British Grassland Society* 29, 191–202.

Tansley A.G. (1939) *The British Islands and their Vegetation.* Cambridge University Press, Cambridge.

Tayler J.C. (1970) Dried forages and beef production. *Journal of the British Grassland Society* 25, 180–90.

Tayler J.C. & Aston K. (1973) Dried grass *v* barley as a concentrate for milk production. *Journal of the Association of Green Crop Driers* 6, 3–8.

Tayler J.C. & Wilkinson J.M. (1972) The influence of level of concentrate feeding on the voluntary intake of grass and on liveweight gain by cattle. *Animal Production* 14, 85–96.

Taylor N.W. (1965) The use of linear programming in least-cost feed compounding. *Agricultural Economics Research Unit, Lincoln College, N.Z.* Publication No. 20.

Tetlow R.M., Wilkinson J.M., Cammell S.B. & Spooner M.C. (1978) Physical and chemical treatment of low quality grass to improve nutritive value. *Annual Report of Grassland Research Institute,* 46–7. Hurley.

Theodorou M.K., Austin A.R. & Hitching S. (1985) A comparison of steers fed on grass and on clover in relation to some microbiological aspects of bloat. In Thomson D.J. (ed) *Forage Legumes.* British Grassland Society Occasional Symposium, No. 16, 104–8.

Thiele-Wittig H.C. (1974) Maintenance of previously cultivated land not now used for agriculture. *Agriculture and Environment* 1, 129–37.

Thomas C. (1987) Factors affecting substitution rates in dairy cows on silage based rations. In Haresign W. & Cole D.J.A. (eds) *Recent Advances in Animal Nutrition,* 1987 Butterworths, London.

Thomas C., Aston K., Daley S.R. & Bass J. (1986) Milk production from silage. IV. The effect of the composition of the supplement. *Animal Production* 42, 315–25.

Thomas C., Njoroge P.F. & Fenlon J.S. (1980) Prediction of digestibility in three tropical grasses. *Tropical Agriculture (Trinidad)* 57, 75–81.

Thomas C. & Young J.W.O. (eds) (1982) *Milk from Grass*. ICI, Billingham and the Grassland Research Institute, Hurley.

Thomas J.A. (1983) The ecology and conservation of *Lysandra bellargus (Lepidoptera: Lycaenidae)* in Britain. *Journal of Applied Ecology* **20**, 59–83.

Thomas R.G. (1987a) The structure of the mature plant In Baker M.J. & Williams W.M. (eds) *White Clover*, 1–29. C.A.B. International, Farnham.

Thomas R.G. (1987b) Vegetative growth and development. In Baker M.J. & Williams W.M. (eds) *White Clover*, 31–62. C.A.B. International, Farnham.

Thomas R.J., Logan K.A.B., Ironside A.D. & Milne J.A. (1986) Fate of sheep urine-N applied to an upland grass sward. *Plant and Soil* **91**, 425–7.

Thomson D.J. (ed) (1984) *Forage Legumes* British Grassland Society Occasional Symposium, No. 16. BGS, Hurley.

Tilley J.M.A. & Terry R.A. (1963) A two stage technique for *in vitro* digestion of forage crops. *Journal of the British Grassland Society* **18**, 104–11.

Tilman D. (1982) *Resources, Competition and Community Structure*. Princeton University Press, Princeton.

Troelson J.E., Myhr P.I., Lodge R.W. & Kilcher M. (1968) Sensory evaluation of the feeding value of hay. *Canadian Journal of Animal Science* **48**, 373–81.

Turkington D.J. & Townson W.S. (1978) Statistical analysis of ICI 'dairymaid' results. *Grass and Forage Science* **33**, 69–70.

Tyrrell H.F., Reynolds P.J. & Moe P.W. (1979) Effect of diet on partial efficiency of acetate use for body tissue synthesis by mature cattle. *Journal of Animal Science* **48**, 598–606.

Unsworth E.F. (1981) The composition and quality of grass silage made in Northern Ireland—an analysis of seven years results. *Record of Agricultural Research* **29**, 91–97.

Unsworth E.F. & Gordon F.J. (1985) The energy utilization of wilted and unwilted silages by lactating cows. *58th Annual Report of the Agricultural Research Institute of Northern Ireland*, 13–20.

Ulyatt M.J., Dellow D.W., John A., Reid C.S.W. & Waghorn G.C. (1986) Contribution of chewing during eating and rumination to the clearance of digesta from the rumino-reticulum. In Milligan L.P., Grovsin W.L. & Dobson A. (eds) *Control of Digestion and Metabolism in Ruminants*, 498–515. Prentice-Hall, Hemel Hempstead.

Ulyatt M.J., Thomson D.J., Beever D.E., Evans R.T. & Haines M.J. (1988) The digestion of perennial ryegrass and white clover by grazing cattle. *British Journal of Nutrition.* **60**, 137–49.

Vadiveloo J. & Holmes W. (1979a) The effects of forage digestibility and concentrate supplementation on the nutritive value of the diet and performance of finishing cattle. *Animal Production* **29**, 121–30.

Vadiveloo J. & Holmes W. (1979b) The prediction of the voluntary feed intake of dairy cows. *Journal of Agricultural Science* **93**, 553–62.

Van Burg P.F.J., Prins W.H., Den Boer D.J. & Sluiman W.J. (1981) Nitrogen and intensification of livestock farming in EEC countries. *Proceedings of the Fertiliser Society*, London. No. 199, 78.

Van Es A.J.H. (1974) Energy intake and requirement of cows during the whole year. *Livestock Production Science* **1**, 21–32.

Van Soest P.J. (1967) Development of a comprehensive system of feed analyses and its application to forages. *Journal of Animal Science* **26**, 119–28.

Van Soest P.J. & Wine R.H. (1967) Use of detergents in the analysis of fibrous feeds. IV. Determination of plant cell wall constituents *Journal of the Association of Official Analytical Chemists* **50**, 50–6.

Voight J. (1987) Burning — always necessary, always best? *Restoration and Management Notes* **5**, 45.

Voisin A. (1959) *Grass Productivity*. Crosby Lockwood, London.

Waite R. (1963) Grazing behaviour. In Worden A.N., Sellers K.C. & Tribe D.E. (eds) *Animal Health, Production and Pasture*. Longman, London.

Walters R.J.K. (1976) The field assessment of digestibility of grass for conservation *Agricultural Development and Advisory Service Quarterly Review* **23**, 323–8.

Watanabe K. & Takahashi Y. (1979) Effects of fertilization level on the regrowth of orchard grass. I. Changes in yield and growth with time. *Journal of the Japanese Society of Grassland Science* **25**, 195–202.

Wathern P. & Gilbert O.L. (1978) Artificial diversification of grassland with native herbs. *Journal of Environmental Management* **7**, 29–42.

Watson S.J. & Nash M.J. (1960) *Conservation of Grass and Forage Crops*. Oliver & Boyd, Edinburgh.

Webster A.J.F. (1980) Energy costs of digestion and metabolism in the gut. In Ruckebusch Y. & Thivend, P. (eds) *Digestive Physiology and Metabolism in Ruminants* 468–84. MTP Press, Lancaster.

Welch D. & Rawes M. (1964) The early effects of excluding sheep from high-level grasslands in the North Pennines. *Journal of Applied Ecology* **1**, 281–300.

Wells T.C.E. (1968) Land use changes affecting *Pulsatilla vulgaris* in England and Wales. *Biological Conservation* **1**, 37–44.

Wells T.C.E. (1971) A comparison of the effects of sheep grazing and mechanical cutting on the structure and botanical composition of chalk grassland. In Duffey E. & Watt A.S. (eds) *The Scientific Management of Animal and Plant Communities for Conservation*, 497–515. Blackwell Scientific Publications, Oxford.

Wells T.C.E., Bell S. & Frost A. (1981) *Creating Attractive Grasslands Using Native Plant Species*. Nature Conservancy Council, London.

Wells T.C.E., Sheail J., Ball D.F. & Ward L.K. (1976) Ecological studies on the Porton Ranges: relationships between vegetation, soils and land use history. *Journal of Ecology* **64**, 589–626.

Welsh Plant Breeding Station (1978) *Principles of Herbage Seed Production*, 2nd edn. Welsh Plant Breeding Station, Aberystwyth.

Wheeler J.L. (1958) The effect of sheep excreta and nitrogen fertilizer on the botanical composition and production of a ley. *Journal of the British Grassland Society* **13**, 196–202.

Whitehead D.C. (1966) *Nutrient Minerals in Grassland Herbage*. Review Series 1/1966. Commonwealth Bureau of Pastures and Field Crops, Farnham.

Whitehead D.C., Garwood E.A. & Ryden J.C. (1985) The efficiency of nitrogen use in relation to grassland productivity. *Animal and Grassland Research Institute, Annual Report, 1985*, 86–9. Hurley.

Wilkins R.J. (1974) The nutritive value of silages. In Swan H. & Lewis D. *University of Nottingham Nutrition Conference for Feed Manufacturers*.

Wilkins R.J., Wilson R.J. & Cook J.E. (1974) Restriction of fermentation during ensilage: the nutritive value of silages made with the addition of formaldehyde. *Proceedings of the 12th International Grassland Congress, Moscow*. 674–90.

Wilkins R.J. & Garwood E.A. (1986) Effects of treading, poaching and fouling on grassland production and utilization. In Frame J. (ed) *Grazing*, 19–31. British Grassland Society Occasional Symposium, No. 19. BGS, Hurley.

Wilkins R.J., Hopkins A., & Dibb C. (1987) *Reseeding. British Grassland Society, Winter Meeting*, 1.1–1.10. BGS, Hurley.

Williams R.D. (1984) *Crop Protection Handbook—Grass and Clover Swards*. British Crop Protection Council, Croydon.

Williams R.E. & Jones M.T. (1969) Economic relationships in milk production. *Journal of Agricultural Economics* **20**, 81–109.

Wilman D., Ojuederie B.M. & Asare E.O. (1976) Nitrogen and Italian ryegrass. III. Growth up to 14 weeks: yields, preparations, digestibilities and nitrogen contents of crop fractions and tiller populations. *Journal of the British Grassland Society* **31**, 73−80.

Wilson D. (1975) Variation in leaf respiration in relation to growth and photosynthesis of *Lolium*. *Annals of Applied Biology* **80**, 323−38.

Wilson D. (1981) The role of physiology in breeding herbage cultivars adapted to their environment. In Wright C.E. (ed) *Plant Physiology and Herbage Production*, 95−108. British Grassland Society, Hurley.

Wilson D. & Jones J.G. (1982) Effects of selection for dark respiration rate of mature leaves on crop yields of *Lolium perenne* cv.S23. *Annals of Botany* **49**, 313−20.

Wilson D. & Robson M.J. (1981) Varietal improvement by selection for dark respiration rate in perennial ryegrass. In Wright C.E. (ed) *Plant Physiology and Herbage Production*, 209−11. British Grassland Society, Hurley.

Wilson P.N. & Strachan P.J. (1981) The contribution of undergraded protein to the protein requirements of dairy cows. In Haresign W. & Cole D.J.A. (eds) *Recent Developments in Ruminant Nutrition*, 228−47. Butterworth, London.

Willems J.H. (1983) Composition and above ground phytomass in chalk grassland with different management. *Vegetation* **52**, 171−80.

Willis A.J. (1969) Road verges — experiments on the chemical control of grass and weeds. In Way J.M. (ed) *Road Verges, Their Function and Management*, 52−60. Nature Conservancy, Monks Wood.

Woledge J. (1971) The effect of light intensity during growth on the subsequent rate of photosynthesis of leaves of tall fescue (*Festuca arundinacea* Schreb.) *Annals of Botany* **35**, 311−22.

Woledge J. (1972) The effect of shading on the photosynthetic rate and longevity of grass leaves. *Annals of Botany* **36**, 551−61.

Woledge J. (1973) The photosynthesis of ryegrass leaves grown in a simulated sward. *Annals of Applied Biology* **73**, 229−37.

Woledge J. (1988) Competition between grass and clover in spring as affected by nitrogen fertilizer. *Annals of Applied Biology* **112**, 175−86.

Woledge J. & Dennis W.D. (1982) The effect of temperature on photosynthesis of ryegrass and white clover leaves. *Annals of Botany* **50**, 25−35.

Woledge J. & Jewiss O.R. (1969) The effect of temperature during growth on the subsequent rate of photosynthesis in leaves of tall fescue (*Festuca arundinacea* Schreb.) *Annals of Botany* **33**, 897−913.

Woledge J., & Leafe E.L. (1976) Single leaf and canopy photosynthesis in a ryegrass sward. *Annals of Botany* **40**, 773−83.

Woledge J., & Parsons A.J. (1986) Temperate Grassland. In Baker N.R. & Long S.P. (eds) *Photosynthesis in Contrasting Environments*, 173−97. Elsevier Science Publishers B.V. Amsterdam.

Woledge J. & Pearse P.J. (1985) The effect of nitrogenous fertilizer on photosynthesis of leaves in a ryegrass sward. *Grass and Forage Science* **40**, 305−9.

Wolton K.M. (1979) Dung and urine as agents of change. In Charles A.H. & Haggar R.J. (eds) *Changes in Sward Composition and Productivity*. British Grassland Society Occasional Symposium, No. 10., BGS, Hurley.

Woods A.J., Bradley Jones J. & Mantle P.G. (1966) An outbreak of gangrenous ergotism in cattle. *Veterinary Record* **78**, 742−9.

Wright I.A. (1986) Grazing management for beef cows and calves. In *HFRO Biennial Report 1984−85*, 129−133.

Wright N.C. (1940) Britain's supplies of feeding stuffs. *Empire Journal of Experimental Agriculture* **8**, 231−48.

Wylie A.R.G. (1982) A greater potential for low-quality conserved forage. *55th Annual Report of the Agricultural Research Institute of Northern Ireland*, 13−22. Hillsborough.

Yiakoumettis I. & Holmes W. (1972) The effect of nitrogen and stocking rate on the output of pasture grazed by beef cattle. *Journal of the British Grassland Society* **27**, 183–91.

Zoby J.L.F. & Holmes W. (1983) The influence of size of animal and stocking rate on the herbage intake and grazing behaviour of cattle. *Journal of Agricultural Science* **100**, 139–48.

Index